Learning to Play

Aske Plaat

Learning to Play

Reinforcement Learning and Games

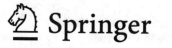 Springer

Aske Plaat
Leiden Institute of Advanced Computer Science
Leiden University
Leiden, The Netherlands

ISBN 978-3-030-59240-0   ISBN 978-3-030-59238-7   (eBook)
https://doi.org/10.1007/978-3-030-59238-7

This Springer imprint is published by the registered company Springer Nature Switzerland AG
The registered company address is: Gewerbestrasse 11, 6330 Cham, Switzerland

To my students

Contents

Preface

Amazing breakthroughs in reinforcement learning have taken place. Computers teach themselves to play Chess and Go and beat world champions. There is talk about expanding application areas towards general artificial intelligence (AI). The breakthroughs in Backgammon, Checkers, Chess, Atari, Go, Poker, and StarCraft have shown that we can build machines that exhibit intelligent game playing of the highest level. These successes have been widely publicized in the media, and inspire AI entrepreneurs and scientists alike. Reinforcement learning in games has become a mainstream AI research topic. It is a broad topic, and the successes build on a range of diverse techniques, from exact planning algorithms, to adaptive sampling, deep function approximation, and ingenious self-play methods.

Perhaps because of the breadth of these technologies, or because of the recency of the breakthroughs, there are few books that explain these methods in depth. This book covers all methods in one comprehensive volume, explaining the latest research, bringing you as close as possible to working implementations, with many references to the original research papers.

The programming examples in this book are in Python, the language in which most current reinforcement learning research is conducted. We help you to get started with machine learning frameworks such as Gym, TensorFlow, and Keras, and provide exercises to help understand how AI is learning to play.

This is not a typical reinforcement learning textbook. Most books on reinforcement learning take the single-agent perspective, of path finding and robot planning. We take as inspiration the breakthroughs in game playing, and use two-agent games to explain the full power of deep reinforcement learning.

Board games have always been associated with reasoning and intelligence. Our games perspective allows us to make connections with artificial intelligence and general intelligence, giving a philosophical flavor to an otherwise technical field.

Artificial Intelligence

Ever since my early days as a student I have been captivated by artificial intelligence, by machines that behave in seemingly intelligent ways. Initially I had been taught that, because computers were deterministic machines, they could never do something new. Yet in AI these machines do complicated things such as recognize patterns, and play Chess games. Actions emerged from these machines, behavior that appeared not to have been programmed into them. The actions seemed new, and even creative, at times.

For my thesis I got to work on game playing programs for combinatorial games such as Chess, Checkers, and Othello. The paradox became even more apparent. These game playing programs all followed an elegant architecture, consisting of a search function and an evaluation function.[1] These two functions together could find good moves all by themselves. Could intelligence be so simple?

The search-evaluation architecture has been around since the earliest days of computer Chess. Together with minimax, it was proposed in a 1952 paper by Alan Turing, mathematician, code-breaking war hero, and one of the fathers of computer science and artificial intelligence. The search-evaluation architecture is also used in Deep Blue, the Chess program that beat World Champion Garry Kasparov in 1997 in New York.

After that historic moment, the attention of the AI community shifted to a new game with which to further develop ideas for intelligent game play. It was the East Asian game of Go that emerged as the new grand test of intelligence. Simple, elegant, and mind-bogglingly complex.

This new game spawned the creation of important new algorithms, and not one, but two, paradigm shifts. The first algorithm to upset the worldview of games researchers was Monte Carlo Tree Search, in 2006. Since the 1950s generations of game playing researchers, myself included, were brought up with minimax. The essence of minimax is to look ahead as far as you can, to then choose the best move, and to make sure that all moves are tried (since behind seemingly harmless moves deep attacks may hide that you can only uncover if you search all moves). And now Monte Carlo Tree Search introduced randomness into the search, and sampling, deliberately missing moves. Yet it worked in Go, and much better than minimax.

Monte Carlo Tree Search caused a strong increase in playing strength, although not yet enough to beat world champions. For that, we had to wait another ten years.

In 2013 our worldview was in for a new shock, because again a new paradigm shook up the conventional wisdom. Neural networks were widely viewed to be too slow and too inaccurate to be useful in games. Many Master's theses of stubborn students had sadly confirmed this to be the case. Yet in 2013 GPU power allowed the use of a simple neural net to learn to play Atari video games just from looking at the video pixels, using a method called deep reinforcement learning. Two years and much hard work later, deep reinforcement learning was combined with Monte Carlo

---

[1] The search function simulates the kind of look-ahead that many human game players do in their head, and the evaluation function assigns a numeric score to a board position indicating how good the position is.

Tree Search in the program AlphaGo. The level of play was improved so much that a year later finally world champions in Go were beaten, many years before experts had expected that this would happen. And in other games, such as StarCraft and Poker, self-play reinforcement learning also caused breakthroughs.

The AlphaGo wins were widely publicized. They have had a large impact, on science, on the public perception of AI, and on society. AI researchers everywhere were invited to give lectures. Audiences wanted to know what had happened, whether computers finally had become intelligent, what more could be expected from AI, and what all this would mean for the future of the human race. Many start-ups were created, and existing technology companies started researching what AI could do for them.

The modern history of computer games spans some 70 years. There has been much excitement. Many ideas were tried, some with success. Games research in reinforcement learning has witnessed multiple paradigm shifts, going from heuristic planning, to adaptive sampling, to deep learning, to self-play. The achievements are large, and so is the range of techniques that are used. We are now at a point where the techniques have matured somewhat, and achievements can be documented and put into perspective.

In explaining the technologies, I will tell the story of how one kind of intelligence works, the intelligence needed to play two-person games of tactics and strategy. (As to knowing the future of the human race, surely more is needed than an understanding of heuristics, deep reinforcement learning, and game playing programs.) It will be a story involving many scientists, programmers, and game enthusiasts, all fascinated by the same goal: creating artificial intelligence. Come and join this fascinating ride.

Acknowledgments

This book would not have been possible without the help of many friends. First of all, I want to thank everybody at LIACS, for creating such a wonderful and vibrant CS & AI department to work in. So many people make this place such a joy to do research; I love you all!

Many people have read and commented on drafts of this book. Thank you Vedran Dunjko, Mike Huisman, Walter Kosters, Wojtek Kowalczyk, Alfons Laarman, Thomas Moerland, and Mike Preuß for your very sharp eyes and criticism. Thank you to Andrius Bernatavicius, Hui Wang, Zhao Yang, Michael Emmerich, Wojtek Kowalczyk, Mike Preuß, Thomas Moerland, Xuhan Lu, Joost Broekens, Matthias Müller-Brockhausen, my friends and fellow conspirators in the reinforcement learning group. In addition, thank you to Lise Stork and Wojtek Kowalczyk for discussions on deep learning and zero-shot learning. Thanks to Michael Emmerich for curriculum learning. Thank you to Walter Kosters, Frank Takes, Jan van Rijn, and Jonathan Vis for discussions on teaching, MCTS, and combinatorial games. Thanks to Mike Preuß for countless discussions and for running the games research at Leiden. Thanks to Max van Duijn for inspiring discussions on theory of mind and creativity. Thank you Walter Kosters for a shared love of combinatorics and a sense of humor. A very special thank you to Thomas Bäck, with whom I have had so many discussions on science, the universe, and everything. Without you, this book would not have been possible.

I thank all students of the reinforcement learning course in Leiden, past, present, and future, for their wonderful enthusiasm, sharp questions, and many suggestions.

Finally, I thank Saskia, Isabel, Rosalin, and little Lily, for being who they are, for knowing no limits, for playing games, for enduring me, and for their boundless love.

Leiden,
April 2020

Aske Plaat

Chapter 1
Introduction

1.1 Tuesday March 15, 2016

Tuesday March 15, 2016, is an important day in the history of artificial intelligence, and not just in the history of artificial intelligence, but in the history of intelligence, period. That day was the final day of a five-game match in which a computer challenged one of the strongest human Go players. Go is an ancient game of strategy, played by millions around the world, originating in East Asia. Playing the game well requires years of training and a considerable amount of intelligence. Dedicated Go schools exist in China, Korea, and Japan, and professional Go players enjoy star status in their countries and can live well from their prize money. Go is considered to be a hallmark of human intelligence and creativity, and the game was thought to be safe from machine intelligence for at least another decade.

Yet on March 15, 2016, at the luxurious Four Seasons Hotel in Seoul, the computer program AlphaGo beat top Go professional Lee Sedol (Fig. 1.1). AlphaGo had been developed by a team of scientists of the AI company DeepMind. The prize money, 1 million dollars, was donated to charities. Lee Sedol received 170,000 dollars for his efforts. The match consisted of 5 games, and the human champion was beaten 4–1. A subsequent match in 2017 in China against champion Ke Jie was also won by the computer. Commentators described AlphaGo's level of play as very strong, and the style of play as refreshing, with a few highly surprising moves, that some described as beautiful and creative. AlphaGo was awarded a 9 dan professional rank, the highest rank possible, by the Chinese Weiqi association, and the journal *Science* chose the event as one of the *breakthrough of the year* runners up. Today, human Go players are taking inspiration from the games played by AlphaGo, trying to learn from its deep insights and unusual moves [778].

The breakthrough performance of AlphaGo came as a surprise to the world and to the research community. The level of play of computer Go programs had been stagnant around the strong amateur level for years. Experts in computer games had expected grandmaster level play to be at least ten years away, let alone beating the world's strongest players.

© Springer Nature Switzerland AG 2020
A. Plaat, *Learning to Play*, https://doi.org/10.1007/978-3-030-59238-7_1

Fig. 1.1 AlphaGo versus Lee Sedol

The techniques used in AlphaGo are the result of many years of research, and cover a surprisingly wide range of topics. It is a culmination of decades of research by many researchers. A main motivation for writing this book is to provide a comprehensive overview of the technologies that led to the creation of AlphaGo.

This brings us to the problem statement of this book, to describe the core of what this book is about.

Problem Statement

The main question that we are concerned with in this book is the following:

> *What are the machine learning methods that are used in Chess and Go to achieve a level of play stronger than the strongest humans?*

Among the technologies used are (1) heuristic planning methods, (2) adaptive sampling, (3) deep reinforcement learning, and (4) self-play. We provide an in-depth introduction to all four technologies, each in their own chapter. We will explain how they work with example code. We use the formalism of reinforcement learning as the common language to describe all the technologies that are covered in this book, both for planning and learning. We describe the algorithms and architectures.

Our style is hands-on, providing the intuition behind the algorithms to apply them in practice. References to the literature are provided to find more details and the relevant mathematics behind the methods.

1.2 Intended Audience

Now that we know what this book is about, we can see who this book is for.

This book is intended for you if you are excited about finding out how computers play games, and which techniques are used to achieve such amazing displays of intelligent behavior. We aim to be comprehensive, to provide all necessary details. Basic introductions to Markov decision processes, reinforcement learning, and deep learning are provided. We also aim to make these details more accessible than the scientific papers on which the content is based, translating formulas in research papers into intuitive concepts. The level of difficulty of this book is targeted at a graduate-level university course in AI. We explain the algorithms, and we provide opportunity for practice.

Our approach to artificial intelligence is hands-on. After each new method is described, we will show how the concepts can be implemented in examples, exercises, and small programs. After basic methods are explained, move advanced enhancements are discussed, enhancements that are necessary to achieve high performance in practice.

Games AI is an open field. Researchers have released their algorithms and code allowing replication of results. This is a sharing-oriented research field. We point you to code bases at GitHub throughout the book. Even when you do not have access to Google-scale compute power, at the end of this book, you should be able to create a fully functioning self-learning program, and you can join the active community of reinforcement learning researchers. For that purpose, Appendix A contains pointers to software environments and open-source code frameworks for machine learning, deep reinforcement learning, and games.

As you may have noticed, there is great excitement about reinforcement learning, excitement that also prompted the writing of this book. The algorithms and the pointers to code also serve this purpose: to make it easy for you to join the excitement and to stimulate you to join the people already active in the field.

Graduate Course

This book is designed for a graduate course in Reinforcement Learning with Games. The material is organized in chapters that roughly correspond to a full semester course. The availability of source code provides for practical assignments where you can get your hands dirty and immerse yourself in this fascinating topic. Pieces of working code can be extended to your liking for further study and research.

Each chapter starts with an introduction in which the core problems and core solution concepts of the chapter are summarized. Chapters end with questions to refresh your memory of the material that was covered, and with larger programming exercises. Chapters are concluded with a summary and with more pointers to the literature.

Figure 1.2 shows the structure of the book. There is a logical progression in the chapters; they build on each other. It should be possible to cover all chapters in a

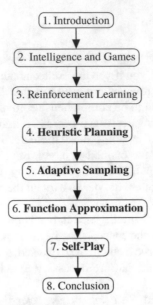

Fig. 1.2 Overview of the chapters of this book

one-semester course, possibly skipping the starred sections. Normally the chapters would be taught in sequence. Chapters 2 and 8 are less technical, and provide some reflection on intelligence and artificial intelligence. They can be combined towards the end, putting the technical material first.

All links to web pages were correct at the time of writing and have been stable for some time. The companion website for this book https://learningtoplay.net contains free updates, slides, and other course material that you are welcome to explore and use in your course.

Prerequisite Knowledge

In order to build up an understanding and to experiment with the algorithms, a general computer science background at undergraduate level is required. Some proficiency in programming is needed, preferably in Python, since that is the language that is currently used in the field of reinforcement learning, and the language that we use in this book. Also some background in undergraduate AI is beneficial, although we strive to be comprehensive and self-contained.

Chapter	Algorithm	Select	Backup	Eval
Chap. 4	alpha-beta	left to right	minimax	heuristic
Chap. 5	MCTS	adaptive	average	sample
Chap. 6	DQN	-	-	generalize
Chap. 7	self-play	adaptive	average	generalize

Table 1.1 Heuristic-Sample-Generalize

Experiment and Theory

As in many fields, progress in reinforcement learning is driven by an interaction between experiment and theory. Experiments are designed to better understand theory, and new theory is developed to explain experimental results. Reinforcement learning rests on a strong theoretical foundation in computational complexity and decision theory, some of which is introduced in Chap. 3.

However, many of the eye-catching advances in the field (Deep Blue, TD-Gammon, and most recently Atari and AlphaGo) are driven by experimental and engineering advances. There are some intuitions to explain results, but many theoretical questions remain. This state of affairs is reflected in the style of this book. In the later chapters we mention experiments and intuitions, but few formulas, lemmas, or proofs. Establishing a comprehensive theory of deep reinforcement learning is still future work.

1.3 Outline

We have almost come to the end of the introduction. Let us have a closer look at what we can expect in the remainder of this book.

This book covers the technologies behind the major AI breakthroughs in reinforcement learning in games; see Table 1.1. Chess, Atari, and Go required surprisingly diverse techniques. The methods in this book go from heuristic planning to self-play. First we describe methods that need domain-specific heuristics, and we end with a method that is able to generalize features in many domains, and to teach itself to do so. We will describe in detail heuristic methods, sampling, and generalization. Together the chapters tell a story of how AI progressed from artificial specific (or narrow) intelligence towards somewhat more general intelligence.

Figure 1.3 gives a related overview of the topics of this book, in terms of mappings between problems and methods that go from specific to general. The first chapters are specific in the sense that the methods make direct use of the structure of the problem to traverse board positions. The later chapters are more abstract, and the mapping between method and problem becomes less direct. Methods become adaptive, and learn features from examples of the problem domain, instead of directly traversing the problem itself. Self-play methods that teach themselves which examples to learn from, are described.

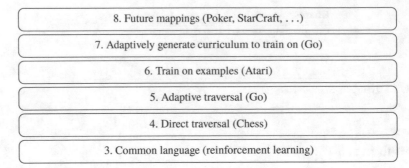

Fig. 1.3 Stack of chapters, with (from bottom to top) increasingly advanced mappings from problems to methods

The story of games research is the story of AI researchers who were learning how to make algorithms that learn to learn.

*Starred Sections

The chapters are organized from planning to learning to self-play. Figure 1.2 gives an overview of the chapters. The names of the four core technical chapters are printed in bold.

Sections and exercises whose name starts with a *star are advanced material, which is essential for understanding high-performing implementations, but may be skipped when in a hurry, without missing the main thread.

We will now describe the main topics of this book. Please refer to Table 1.1 and Fig. 1.3, since the concepts Heuristic-Sample-Generalize and (in)direct mappings between methods and problem spaces are important threads.

The Chapters

Let us now discuss the chapters in more detail. We will start in Chap. 2 with early thoughts on intelligence and intelligent machines. We then provide a brief historical overview of some of the important games and game playing programs, starting with the early designs of Claude Shannon, Christopher Strachey, and Alan Turing.

In the next chapter, Chap. 3, we introduce reinforcement learning. The concepts and formalizations of reinforcement learning are at the basis of the historic advances in artificial intelligence that we have recently witnessed. Concepts such as value function, policy function, and Q-learning are discussed in this chapter.

In Chap. 4, we introduce heuristic planning. In this chapter we discuss the principles of the search methods that are at the basis of AI breakthroughs in Checkers and Chess. Heuristic planning in games uses domain-specific knowledge to reduce the size of the state space, and then uses minimax planning to traverse that reduced state space. The planning methods of heuristic planning are simple and rigid, and it turns out that many enhancements are needed to achieve good performance in real game playing programs. We introduce enhancements that overcome some of the rigidity of the minimax approach.

In the next chapter, Chap. 5, we delve deeper into the principles of learning by trial and error. Major topics in this chapter are the exploration/exploitation trade-off and the concept of evaluation by random playout, leading to the Monte Carlo Tree Search (MCTS) algorithm. The algorithm in this chapter is variable-depth and variable-width by design, and great performance improvements, especially in 9×9 Go, are achieved with MCTS. The chapter ends with a discussion of enhancements of MCTS.

Then, we switch paradigms from planning to learning. Instead of *traversing* the states directly and finding good states, we now try to *generalize* features from the states. We start in Chap. 6 with a review of deep learning methods for supervised learning. Among many other things, convolutional networks are discussed, and the problem of overfitting. In 2012 deep learning methods caused a breakthrough in image recognition performance. Much of the current interest in artificial intelligence is caused by this breakthrough for which Bengio, Hinton, and LeCun received the 2018 Turing award. Section 6.3 looks at how these methods can be used in a reinforcement learning setting: generalization of features in deep neural networks for learning by trial and error, of which Deep Q-Networks (DQN) is the best known algorithm. Q-learning with function approximation and bootstrapping is in principle unstable, and important enhancements had to be developed to achieve stable training. With these enhancements, we find that deep reinforcement learning can be an effective way to improve on heuristic evaluation functions.

Chapter 7 combines planning and training to create self-learning systems. This is a long chapter in which the methods behind AlphaGo are explained, and AlphaGo's variants. AlphaGo Zero teaches itself to play Go from scratch. This kind of learning resembles human learning, creating much interest in the research community, and some self-play and self-learning variants and other related research are discussed.

Finally, we conclude in Chap. 8 by reflecting on artificial intelligence progress, and on the relation to natural intelligence. We discuss possible future research directions.

The appendices contain an overview of open-source deep learning environments that are suitable for experimentation, details on the AlphaGo implementations that were too detailed for the main text, the tournaments of AlphaGo against Fan Hui, Lee Sedol, and Ke Jie, pointers about learning to play and program Go and Chess, and some pointers to the Python programming language.

After this overview, let us begin our journey through the world of reinforcement learning and games.

Chapter 2
Intelligence and Games

As long as we have been around, humans have had dreams about artificial forms of intelligence, wondering if it would be possible to make intelligent machines. It is wonderful to live in a time where we are able to see the first realizations of these dreams appearing.

This chapter introduces the field of study of this book, artificial intelligence and games.

We will briefly touch upon the nature of intelligence, human and artificial. We will see that most AI researchers take a pragmatic, behavioristic approach to intelligence. Board games such as Chess and Checkers were used by the earliest computer science researchers to study reasoning processes. We will list the defining features of these games.

To give a broader understanding of the history of the field, we will then review some of the better known game playing programs, both old and new. The technical material with the algorithms that achieved all these accomplishments starts in the next chapter.

Core Problems

- What is intelligence?
- How can we measure intelligence?

Core Concepts

- Intelligence: embodied/computational; AI: symbolic/numerical
- Early work: Shannon, Turing, and Samuel
- Modern work: TD-Gammon, Chinook, Deep Blue, AlphaGo, and Libratus

© Springer Nature Switzerland AG 2020
A. Plaat, *Learning to Play*, https://doi.org/10.1007/978-3-030-59238-7_2

2.1 Intelligence

What is intelligence? Psychology provides various definitions of intelligence. Most definitions include recognition, reasoning, memory, learning, problem solving, and adapting to your environment. These elements are related to cognition.

In psychology most definitions implicitly assume that intelligence is human, and therefore embodied. Related to intelligence are intuition, emotion, self-awareness and volition, or *free will*. Humans have all of these capacities. However, artificial intelligence typically studies a limited set of capacities. Essential elements currently studied in AI are related to cognition, such as recognition, reasoning, memory, and learning [572]. Intelligent decision making is at the core of current AI research.

An important difference between human intelligence and artificial intelligence is that humans are intelligent beings. We are, we have an identity, and we are self-aware. Computers are not. Artificial intelligence research mostly studies intelligent behavior. Machines that exhibit intelligent behavior are generally not considered to *be* intelligent, just to *behave* intelligently, even programs that jokingly suggest that they have an identity by printing texts such as *Hello, World*. As Shakespeare wrote: "To be or not to be, that is the question."

We will now discuss cognition and intelligence in more depth.

2.1.1 Human Intelligence

Psychology teaches us that intelligence includes cognitive abilities, the abilities to learn, form concepts, and reason. These abilities allow us to recognize patterns, comprehend ideas, solve problems, plan, and use language to communicate. Cognitive abilities enable intelligent behavior. They also enable other capacities, such as conscious thought. There are two schools of thought on cognitive intelligence.

Embodied and Computationalist Intelligence

Experience and conscious thought are elements of embodied intelligence. The theory of embodied intelligence stresses our ability to *perceive* information, to use it as knowledge in adapting behaviors to an environment [718].

A rival theory is the theory of computationalism. Computationalism states that thoughts are a form of computation following a set of laws for the relations among representations. Computationalism regards the brain as a big computer [443]. Clearly, artificial intelligence, as part of computer science, studies intelligence through computations, and thus builds on computationalism.

Interestingly, the field of reinforcement learning has elements of both computationalism and embodiment. Reinforcement learning is all about learning in response to stimuli from an environment, both in AI and in psychology. It studies how agents act in an environment and learn from responses to alter their behavior, as in the embodied view of intelligence. Reinforcement learning is related to both schools, the school of embodiment and the school of computationalism.

We will now have a look at two similar approaches to artificial intelligence, a mathematical approach and a biological approach.

Mathematics and Biology

Artificial intelligence is the study of machines that exhibit behavior for which humans need intelligence. Main topics in the study of AI are cognitive functions such as learning and problem solving [572].

Artificial intelligence research is based on two fields of science: mathematical logic and biology [488]. One of the early ways of modeling thought processes is the top-down deductive approach that has come to be known as *symbolic AI*. Symbolic AI is inspired by mathematical logic. In symbolic AI logic, *reasoning* is used to draw inferences and conclusions from underlying facts and assumptions about the world. In this view, intelligence is considered to be equivalent to a top-down reasoning process. This school has yielded progress in expert systems, reasoning systems, and theorem proving systems. Well-known outcomes of this line of research are the STRIPS planner [213], the Mathematica and MATLAB computer algebra systems [110], the programming language PROLOG [147], and also semantic (web) reasoning [71, 17]. The material covered in the chapter on heuristic planning has grown out of the symbolic approach.

A second school of thought is the *connectionist* approach to AI. It purports that intelligence emerges bottom up, out of interaction processes between many small elements. Connectionism is inspired by biology. Examples of the successes of this approach are embodied intelligence (robotics) [101], Nature-inspired algorithms such as Ant colony optimization [183], swarm intelligence [361, 85], genetic algorithms and evolutionary strategies [220, 300, 27], and, last but not least, neural networks [278, 405]. This approach is also called the numerical, data driven, approach, because of the many numerical parameters of artificial neural networks. The material covered in the chapter on learning has grown out of the connectionist approach.

Thinking, Fast and Slow

The philosophical implications of the AlphaGo achievement are large. The realization that we are now able to create a machine that can learn to play such a tremendously challenging and rich game of strategy, beating the smartest professional players, is baffling. Indeed, for many researchers the goal of artificial intelligence research is to understand intelligence, and here we have made a tremendous step. It is now certainly the case, at least for the narrow domain of combinatorial board games, that we have succeeded in achieving learning and reasoning behavior beyond the human level, although it is not known how similar the artificial and human thought processes are.

In fact, it has often been argued that humans and computers think in very different ways.

Daniel Kahneman is a psychologist and winner of the Nobel Prize in Economics. In his works he combines psychology and economics. He has helped found the field of behavioral economics. In his book *Thinking Fast and Slow* [347] he presents topics of his most famous papers. Central in Kahneman's book are system 1 thinking, or fast, approximate, intuitive human thinking, and system 2 thinking, or slow, exact, reasoned human thinking. These two concepts fit well with our AI schools: learning/connectionist is related to system 1 thinking, and planning/symbolic is related to system 2 thinking.

It is interesting to note that Kahneman's system 1 and 2 suggests at least a crude similarity between artificial and human thought processes. At a few places we will highlight links between the methods described here and the concepts in Kahneman's book. Kahneman's book describes fast and slow thinking in human intelligence. In this book we focus on artificial intelligence (see also Chap. 8).

2.1.2 Artificial Intelligence

Let us now have a closer look at the main topic of this book, artificial intelligence. Artificial intelligence is old. There are indications that the first ideas on mechanical thought are as old as human thought, and are related to materialistic worldviews. The first recorded dreams of intelligent machines, which we now call robots, go back to Indian philosophies 1500 BC of Charvaka [443, 766]. In Greek the word "automaton" means *acting on one's own will*. In Greek mythology, Homer's *Iliad* describes automatons, self-operating machines, that open doors automatically. There are many more examples of automata in Greek mythology, such as an artificial person made of bronze, or watchdogs made of gold and silver. In Chinese texts mechanical engineers, or artificers, are described, as well as artificial wooden flying birds [481, 375].

By attempting to describe human thought as the mechanical manipulation of symbols, classical philosophers were the first to describe ideas of modern AI. This work on mathematical reasoning culminated in the invention of the digital computer in the 1940s. The advent of the first computers and the ideas behind it prompted scientists to start serious discussions on the possibility of creating an electronic brain.

The modern field of AI research was subsequently founded in the summer of 1956 at a workshop at Dartmouth College, New Hampshire (Fig. 2.1). Among those present were John McCarthy, Marvin Minsky, Nathaniel Rochester, Claude Shannon, Allen Newell, Herbert Simon, Arthur Samuel, John Nash, and Warren McCulloch. These would all become leaders of AI research in the following decades.[1] There was much optimism then, and many predicted that human-level machine intelligence would be achieved within 20 years (this was in 1956) [469, 443]. Eventually, however, it

---

[1] Some would become known for other fields, such as information theory and economics.

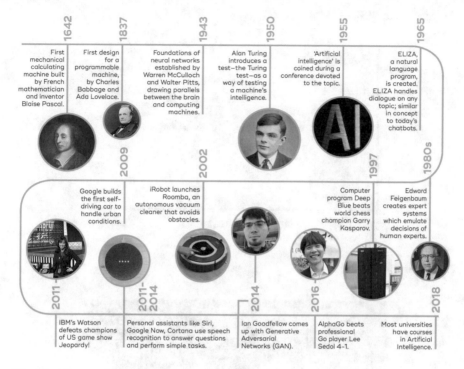

Fig. 2.1 A history of AI [327]

became clear that they had underestimated the difficulty of this project. An AI winter followed in which funding for AI research all but dried up (Fig. 2.2 [419]). Despite the funding drought, progress was made, and another period of inflated expectations followed (about knowledge representation and expert systems), followed by another winter. Achievements in the 1990s (Deep Blue, deep learning, Watson) heralded the current AI summer that we are still enjoying. After 2000 interest in AI has been high again, because of machine learning successes in search, vision, speech, and robotics. In fact, many other unexpected inventions did happen in industry, such as in search engines (Google and Baidu), in social networks (Facebook and Tencent), in recommender systems (Amazon, Alibaba, and Netflix), and in multi-touchscreen communicators (Apple, Samsung, and Huawei).

In 2018 the highest recognition in computer science, the Turing award, was awarded to three key researchers in deep learning: Bengio, Hinton, and LeCun (Fig. 2.3).

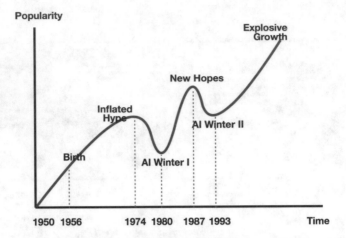

Fig. 2.2 AI winters [419]

Fig. 2.3 Geoffrey Hinton, Yann LeCun, and Yoshua Bengio

2.1.3 Intelligent Behavior

In contrast to some parts of psychology, AI is traditionally less interested in defining the essence of intelligence ("being intelligent") as it is in behaving intelligent, with a strong focus on creating intelligent systems. The AI approach is a pragmatic approach.

AI researchers are interested in machines that exhibit reasoning, knowledge, planning, learning, communication, perception, and the ability to interact with the physical environment and with humans. The focus is on behavior; by which methods

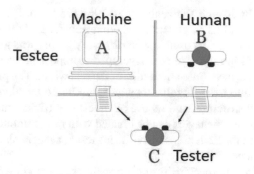

Fig. 2.4 Turing test [700]

the machines exhibit this behavior is considered less relevant. Consciousness and self-awareness are not (yet) on the mainstream AI research agenda, and simulating the human brain is not part of typical AI research.

Note that the strict separation between behavior and being is becoming somewhat less strict. The focus on behavior of AI fits the school of symbolic AI especially well, where intelligence is based on human logic, and not on human hardware. The other school, connectionism, is emphatically inspired by biology and neurology, i.e., a simulation of human hardware to achieve intelligent behavior.

Behavior: Turing Test

In 1950 Alan Turing proposed a test for how to determine if a machine exhibits intelligence. The machine passes the test when its behavior is indistinguishable from that of a human. In the Turing test a human evaluator engages in a natural language conversation with a human and with a machine (Fig. 2.4). The evaluator is aware that one of the two participants is a machine, and both participants are separated from one another by a screen. Participants are restricted to text only, such as through keyboard and screen (speech technology is deemed too hard). If the evaluator cannot tell which conversation is machine-generated and which is human, then the machine is considered to have passed the test. Note that the machine may make mistakes as long as they are mistakes that humans would also make. The Turing test is an imitation game. It might even be the case that making deliberate mistakes is a good idea, for example, when the domain would be a game of Chess, then a Chess machine could be identified by its being much stronger than a human would be.

The paper that introduced the Turing test was titled: "Computing Machinery and Intelligence" [700]. It opens with the words: "I propose to consider the question, 'Can machines think?' " and is a classic in AI.

The Turing test has been highly influential, but is also widely criticized. One of the first criticisms was exemplified by the Eliza experiment. Eliza was a computer program developed by Joseph Weizenbaum in 1966 [754]. The program had a list of keywords for which it had responses in which it transformed the user's input in a certain way. If no keyword was used, a generic "witty" reply was given, sometimes reusing part the user's input. Eliza was developed to appear like a psychotherapist, allowing the program to have little knowledge of the real world. The program was able to fool some people into believing that they were talking to a real person. However, its simple rule-based structure, and its use of superficial tricks, only succeeded in suggesting that intelligent behavior can be created with rather unintelligent means.[2] Eliza's success showed the limitations of the Turing test as a mechanism for identifying true artificial intelligence.[3]

Another noteworthy approach to Turing's question became known as the Loebner Prize. The Loebner Prize provided an annual platform for practical Turing tests. It was named after Hugh Loebner, who provided the prize money.

The first Loebner Prize competition in 1991 was again won by a mindless program that misled interrogators into making the wrong identification by such means as imitating human typing errors. It generated much controversy in which the term *artificial stupidity* was used [619].

A problem of the Turing test is that it does not directly test if the computer behaves intelligently, but rather if humans think it behaves like another human being. Turing tests have since taught us that human behavior and intelligent behavior are not the same thing. The Turing test can fail to identify intelligent behavior correctly because some human behavior is unintelligent, and because some intelligent behavior is inhuman (such as performing complicated mathematical sums quickly and correctly). The Turing test requires deception on the part of the computer; it does not require highly intelligent behavior, in fact, it discourages it, to prevent the computer from appearing to be inhumanly smart.

For these reasons, other tests of intelligence have been devised, such as tests for the ability to play games.

Before we take a look at those games, we will look at what kinds of artificial intelligence have been created.

Specialized and General Intelligence

Humans are good at many different things. Our intelligence is a general kind of intelligence; it allows us to cook, read, argue, do mathematics, and enjoy a movie. Studying artificial ways of being intelligent in all these domains is a daunting task. Machine intelligence researchers typically limit themselves to a single domain, and artificial intelligence is almost always narrow or special intelligence. Ever since the start of AI, games have played an important role. The rules of a game limit its scope, making it better suited as a first object of study than the full complexity of reality.

---

[2] Some would go so far to say that some unintelligent humans behave in a more human way than intelligent humans, confusing the discussion even more.

[3] The genealogy of Eliza and a list of programs that implement it can be found here http://elizagen.org/index.html.

Artificial *general* intelligence (AGI) would be the intelligence of a machine that can perform any intellectual task that a human can. AGI is the holy grail of AI research, and a favorite topic in science fiction and future studies. AGI is sometimes called *strong AI*, although that term is used by some other researchers to mean machines that experience consciousness [613]; see also Sect. 7.2.3. As of 2017, one study found that over forty organizations worldwide are doing active research on AGI [41].

It should be noted, of course, that most humans also have special intelligence abilities. Some humans are better at playing Chess and weaker at Tennis, and very few humans are equally good in all kinds of intelligence (if such a thing could even be measured). In terms of definitions, AGI is even less well defined than AI.

Drosophila melanogaster

In 1965, the Soviet mathematician Aleksandr Kronrod called Chess the *Drosophila melanogaster* of artificial intelligence [401]. *Drosophila melanogaster* is a type of fruit fly that is used by developmental biologists in genetics experiments as a model organism; because of its fast reproduction cycle it allows quick experiments. Also, by using *Drosophila*, biologists hope to learn about biological processes in general, beyond the particular species. Similarly, by using Chess, AI researchers hope to learn about processes of intelligence in general, beyond the particular game.

Such an experimenter's tool with quick turnaround times is useful in AI research. Chess was a convenient domain that was well suited for such experimentation. It is clearly a game for which humans need intelligence, requiring many years of dedication and study to achieve proficiency.

In addition to having a limited scope, a second advantage of games is the clarity of the rules. Possible actions are well defined by the rules, and the end of a game is also well defined. In this, games differ from real-world activities, such as preparing a meal, performing a dance, or falling in love, where goals and rules are often implicit and less well defined. Combinatorial games are thought to abstract from nonessential elements. Games allow researchers to focus on reasoning processes, processes that are assumed to capture the essence of intelligence. Thus, in games it is easier to achieve good performance than in other real-world tasks, a clear advantage for researchers [554].

Clear Performance

Games also allow for a clear and undisputed way to measure progress. Game rules define win and loss, and the intelligence of programs can be measured by letting them play against each other or against humans. Many games have rating systems, such as in Tennis, where the best of the world are ranked based on how many wins have been scored against other players. An often used measure is the Elo rating, a system devised by the Hungarian-American physicist Arpad Elo. The basis of the Elo rating is pairwise comparison [196]. In Chess, a beginner starts around 800, a mid-level player is around 1600, and a professional, around 2400.

Anthropomorphization

In the original Turing test *any* question can be asked of the machine. It is a test for general intelligence, the kind of intelligence that humans have. As with the *Drosophila*, limiting the scope of our domain to a single game clearly cannot be used for the general Turing test; all we can hope for is to achieve special intelligence, the kind of intelligence needed to win a certain game. Still, achievements in specific intelligence, such as by Deep Blue, Watson, and AlphaGo, attract large publicity. This may be in part because the human mind generalizes easily, and anthropomorphizes[4] easily. When we see a device do something in a particular domain for which a human must be incredibly smart, then we automatically assume that the device must *be* smart, and will do as well in another domain *because that is what a human would do*. It is easy for us to forget that the machine is not a human, something that writers of science fiction books and Hollywood movies eagerly exploit. Current machine intelligence is almost always highly specialized, which is quite unhuman like.

In Chap. 8 the issues of artificial and human intelligence will be revisited, including the topics of learning, and specialized and general intelligence. By then, we will have acquired a deep understanding of how to create specialized artificial intelligence in games.

2.1.4 Machine Learning

Machine learning is the field of research that studies algorithms that learn relations that were not explicitly preprogrammed, such as training an algorithm with a set of images in order to classify them. Machine learning encompasses both symbolic and connectionist methods. Machine learning algorithms find patterns, categorize data, or make decisions. Machine learning consists of three groups of learning problems: supervised learning, reinforcement learning, and unsupervised learning [81].

In supervised learning a (typically large) database of labeled examples exists, from which the type of relation between example and label is inferred. The labels have to be provided beforehand, by humans, or by other means. Chapter 6 covers supervised learning in detail.

In reinforcement learning there is no database of labeled examples; interaction is the key. In reinforcement learning an agent can interact with an environment, which returns a new state and a reward value after each action. The reward value can be positive or negative. By probing the environment, the reinforcement learning agent can learn relationships that hold in the environment. Reinforcement learning

---

[4] Treat as if human.

problems are often modeled as Markov decision processes [659]; see Chap. 3. Most games can be modeled as reinforcement learning problems. In addition to Chap. 3, Chap. 6 also covers reinforcement learning in detail.

Unsupervised learning algorithms find patterns in data without the need for human labeling. Typical unsupervised algorithms cluster data based on inherent properties, such as distance.

Reinforcement Learning in Games

In this book we study reinforcement learning algorithms in games. Reinforcement learning problems are interesting in that some problems are best solved by symbolic methods, while for others connectionist methods work best. In the chapter on self-play, we see how the two methods in AI join to achieve great success.

Thus, the work in this book draws on both schools of thought. Planning is closely related to symbolic AI, and learning to connectionism. Reinforcement learning is related to both computationalism and embodied intelligence. The breakthroughs of Chess are related to symbolic AI. Breakthroughs in Atari are related to connectionism. Breakthroughs in AlphaGo (and other self-play programs) in Chap. 7 rely on both schools of thought, and their success is a success of an integrated approach to AI, expressed in a reinforcement learning framework. For other combined approaches, see [705, 233].

After having looked at artificial intelligence in some depth, it is time to look at games.

2.2 Games of Strategy

Games come in many shapes and sizes. Some are easy, some are hard. Before we will look at game playing programs, we first describe the combinatorial games that are used frequently to study artificial intelligence. In the literature on games the characteristics of games are described in a fairly standard taxonomy.

2.2.1 Characteristics of Games

Games are used in artificial intelligence because they provide a challenging environment to play them well. The complexity of games is determined by a number of characteristics. Important characteristics of games are: the number of players, whether the game is zero-sum or non-zero-sum, perfect or imperfect information, turn based or simultaneous action, what the complexity of taking decisions is, and what the state space complexity is. We will discuss these characteristics now in more detail.

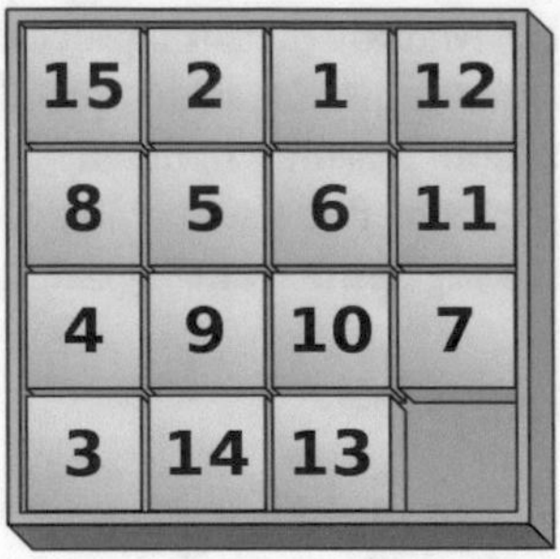

Fig. 2.5 15 Puzzle [304]

Number of Players

One of the most important elements of a game is the number of players. One-player games are usually called puzzles. The goal of a puzzle is to find a solution while following the rules of the puzzle. Well-known examples are mazes, Sudoku, mathematical problems such as the traveling salesperson problem (TSP), and the 15-puzzle [304, 381] (Fig. 2.5). Typical optimization problems are to find the shortest (lowest cost) solution of a problem instance.

Two-player games are "real" games. Most games in this book are two-player games; these have been studied the most in AI. The game play in two-player games is often competitive, zero-sum: my win is your loss. Keen reasoning and calculation often play a large role in these games, providing satisfaction to the players when a hard problem is solved. Quite a number of two-player games exist that provide a nice balance between being too easy and too hard for players, and for computer programmers. Many multiplayer games are still highly challenging for AI. Examples of two-player games that are popular in AI are Chess, Checkers, Go, Othello, and Shogi. These games will all be described in a little more detail shortly.

Multiplayer games are played by three or more players. Psychology, collaboration, and hidden information (and bluffing) often play a large role in these games. Much of the fun of playing these games may be related to social aspects. The game play can be competitive and collaborative, since players may collude in different phases to obtain their goals. Many card games are multiplayer games. Well-known examples of multiplayer games are the card games Bridge and Poker, and strategy games such as Risk, Diplomacy, StarCraft, and Defense of the Ancients (DOTA).

Zero-Sum vs. Non-Zero-Sum

An important aspect of a game is whether it is competitive or collaborative. Many two-player games are competitive: the win (+1) of player A is the loss (−1) of player B. These games are called *zero-sum* because the sum of the wins for the players remains a constant zero. Competition is an important element in the real world, and these games provide a useful model for the study of strategy and conflict, in practice, and especially in theory. The field of game theory has important links to economics and political science. The classic work is Von Neumann and Morgenstern's 1944 book *Theory of games and economic behavior* [730, 731], which laid the foundation for economic game theory. Many more modern and accessible works have been published since then, such as [163]. Classical game theory analyzes strictly rational behavior; the classical *homo economicus* is assumed to always act rationally. Many years later behavioral economics married psychological insight with economics. Amongst others, Kahneman and Thaler have written popular and accessible accounts [347, 680].

In contrast, in collaborative games the players win if they can create win/win situations. Again, the real world is full of opportunities for collaboration, and these games can be studied to hone our understanding of collaboration intelligence. Examples of collaboration games are Bridge, negotiation games such as Diplomacy [383, 168], management simulations such as Hexagon [190], or board games such as Magic Maze. Collaboration also occurs frequently in multiplayer games such as Poker and Risk.

Perfect vs. Imperfect Information

In perfect information games all relevant information is known to all players. This is the case in typical board games such as Chess and Checkers. In imperfect information games some information may be hidden for some players. This is the case in typical card games such as Bridge and Poker, where not all cards are known to all players.

A special form of (im)perfect information games are games of chance, such as Backgammon and Monopoly, in which dice play an important role. There is no hidden information in these games, and these games are therefore sometimes considered to be perfect information games, despite the uncertainty present at move time.

Turn-Based or Simultaneous-Action

In turn-based games players move in sequence. In simultaneous-action games, players make their moves at the same time. Simultaneous-action games are considered imperfect information, since players hold secret information that is relevant for a player at move time.

Chess, Checkers, and Monopoly are examples of turn-based games. StarCraft and Diplomacy are simultaneous-action games.

Decision Complexity

The difficulty of playing a game depends on the complexity of the game. The decision complexity is the number of end positions that define the value (win, draw, or loss) of the initial game position (see Chap. 4 for a theoretical explanation of *critical tree*). The larger the number of actions in a position, the larger the decision complexity. Games with small board sizes such as Tic-Tac-Toe (3×3) have a smaller complexity than games with larger boards, such as Gomoku (19×19). When the action space is very large it can be treated as a continuous action space. In Poker, for example, the monetary bets can be of any size, defining an action size that is practically continuous.

State Space Complexity

The state space complexity of a game is the number of legal positions reachable from the initial position of a game. State space and decision complexity are normally positively correlated, since games with high decision complexity typically have high state space complexity. As we shall see in Chap. 4, determining the exact state space complexity of a game is a nontrivial task. For most games approximations of the state space have been calculated.

In general, games with a larger state space complexity are harder to play ("require more intelligence") for humans and computers.

Zero-Sum Perfect-Information Games

Now that we have seen several important aspects of games, let us look at concrete examples of zero-sum perfect-information games.

Chess and Go are two player, zero sum, perfect information, turn based, discreet action games.

To study strategic reasoning in AI, two-player zero-sum perfect-information games are frequently used. Strategies, or policies, determine the outcome of these kinds of games. This was the first class of games tried by AI researchers.

2.2.2 Examples of Games

We will now give examples of games that have played an important role in artificial intelligence research. Table 2.1 summarizes the games and their characteristics.

Chess

Chess (Fig. 2.6) is a two-player zero-sum perfect-information turn-based game, played on an 8×8 board with 64 squares and 32 pieces, many with different move rules. The pieces move and can be captured. The goal of Chess is to capture the king. It has a state space complexity estimated to be 10^{47}. The number of actions in a typical board state is around 35. It is a game where material balance (the number and importance

Name	board	state space	zero-sum	information	turn
Chess	8×8	10^{47}	zero-sum	perfect	turn
Checkers	8×8	10^{18}	zero-sum	perfect	turn
Othello	8×8	10^{28}	zero-sum	perfect	turn
Backgammon	24	10^{20}	zero-sum	chance	turn
Go	19×19	10^{170}	zero-sum	perfect	turn
Shogi	9×9	10^{71}	zero-sum	perfect	turn
Poker	card	10^{161}	non-zero	imperfect	turn
StarCraft	real-time strategy	10^{1685}	non-zero	imperfect	simultaneous

Table 2.1 Characteristics of games

Fig. 2.6 Chess

of the pieces that the sides have) is quite important for the outcome of the game. The ability to reason over deep tactical lines in order to capture a piece is important. Chess has been used as a testbed of AI research since the early days of AI.

Computer players are typically based on heuristic planning and consist of a search function (that looks ahead) and an evaluation function (that scores the board position using heuristics). A heuristic is a rule of thumb that captures domain knowledge. In Chess a useful heuristic is to count material balance (which side has more pieces) and mobility (which side has more legal moves) and center control.

Chess is a tactical game in the sense that substantial changes in the static score of a position are present in the state space. Such sudden changes occur for example when an important piece, such as the queen, is captured. Chess also has "sudden death:" the game can end abruptly when the king is captured (checkmate). Tactical situations (i.e., large changes between static evaluation between positions) can typically be dealt with by searching, or looking ahead.

Fig. 2.7 Checkers

Checkers

Checkers (Fig. 2.7) is also a zero-sum perfect-information turn-based game, played on an 8×8 board with 24 pieces. (North American and British Checkers is played on an 8×8 board. In most other countries the board size is 10×10. In British English the game is called Draughts.) The pieces move diagonally (only on the dark squares) and can be captured. All pieces move in the same fashion. The number of actions in a typical board position is around 3. The goal of Checkers is to capture all the opponent's pieces. Ordinary pieces move only forward, until they reach the other side of the board, where they are promoted to kings, which can move backward as well. As in Chess, material balance is a good indicator (heuristic) for the chance to win, with mobility a good second indicator.

The state space of Checkers is estimated to be 10^{18}. This state space is just small enough for the game to have been mathematically solved in recent years: it has been proven by traversing all relevant lines of play that perfect play by both sides yields a draw [589]. This computation took months of computer time by a state-of-the-art research team.

Computer players for Checkers and Chess have a highly related design. Many of the techniques for search and evaluation functions that work on Checkers also work in Chess.

Shogi

Shogi (Fig. 2.8) is a zero-sum perfect-information turn-based game, sometimes described as Japanese Chess. Shogi is played on a 9×9 board, with 40 pieces. Pieces can be captured, and when they are, they may be returned to the board as piece for

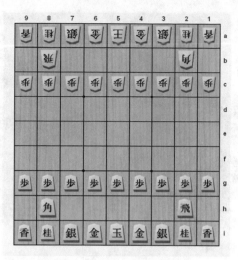

Fig. 2.8 Shogi

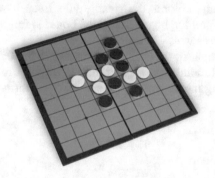

Fig. 2.9 Othello

the capturing side. The number of actions in a typical board position is around 92. The state space complexity of Shogi is significantly larger than Chess, 10^{71}, because of the reintroduction of pieces, and the larger board size, among others.

Important heuristics for Shogi are material balance and mobility. Techniques that work in Chess and Checkers playing programs often work in Shogi as well.

Othello

Othello (Fig. 2.9) is a zero-sum perfect-information turn-based game, played on an 8×8 board. Othello is also known as Reversi. Othello is a disc flipping game. The

Fig. 2.10 Go

number of actions in a typical board position is around 10. When a disc is placed adjacent to an opponent's disc, and there is a straight line to another friendly disc, the opponent's discs change color to the friendly side. In each move one disc is placed. Discs are never taken off the board. When the board is full the game stops, and the side with the most discs wins.

The state space complexity of Othello is estimated to be 10^{28}. Traditional heuristics such as material and mobility work to a limited extent. More advanced statistical and machine learning methods were needed for breakthrough performance [113] (Sect. 2.3.4).

Go

Go (Fig. 2.10) is a zero-sum perfect-information turn-based game, played on a 19×19 board. It is also played on smaller boards, for quicker and easier games for teaching, 9×9 and 13×13. Go originated in East Asia, and is popular in Korea, Japan, and China. In Go, stones are placed on intersections on the board. The number of actions in a typical board position is around 250. Surrounded stones are captured, although this occurs infrequently among strong players. The board is large, and the state space complexity of Go is also large: 10^{170}.

In Go, the objective in the game is to acquire territory, intersections that the opponent cannot claim. No effective heuristics have been devised for Go to calculate this territory efficiently for use in a real-time game playing program. Approaches as in Chess and Checkers failed to produce anything but amateur-level play in Go. Sampling-based methods (Monte Carlo Tree Search) and deep reinforcement learning caused a breakthrough (Chaps. 5 and 7).

Capturing stones occurs less frequently in Go than in Chess. Go is a more strategic game: stones, once placed, do not move, and typically radiate influence all the way to

Fig. 2.11 Backgammon

the end of the game. Strategically placing stones to later work together is an important concept in Go. Sudden death (checkmate in Chess) does not exist in Go. Strategic implications of a move are long term, and are typically beyond the horizon of a search or look ahead. Long-term effects are typically dealt with by the evaluation function.

Backgammon

Backgammon (Fig. 2.11) is a zero-sum turn-based game of chance. Backgammon is one of the oldest and most popular board games, often played for money. It is played on a board as in the figure. Dice are used to determine the number of moves that a player can make. Each side has 15 pieces. The objective is to be the first to move all pieces off the board. The number of actions in a typical board position is around 250.

Backgammon is a game of skill and luck. The state space complexity of Backgammon is estimated at 10^{20}. Computer player BKG achieved some success in 1970–1980 with a heuristic planning approach [68, 69]. Later TD-Gammon used a small neural network for temporal difference learning, and achieved world champion level play [675] (see the next section).

Poker

Poker (Fig. 2.12) is a non-zero-sum imperfect-information turn-based card game of chance. Betting is an integral part of the game play. It is used to signal the quality of a hand of cards to the other players (or to mislead them). Poker is a multiplayer game. The action space is large due to the betting, and varies greatly for different versions of the game. The difficulty of play is in estimating the quality of a hand with respect to others, and has psychological aspects, to ascertain if players are bluffing: placing high bets on weak hands, trying to scare other players.

The state space of No-Limit Texas Hold'em, a popular Poker variant, has been estimated between 10^{18} [77] and 10^{161} [103, 336]. There are many Poker variants, and this number can differ from variant to variant.

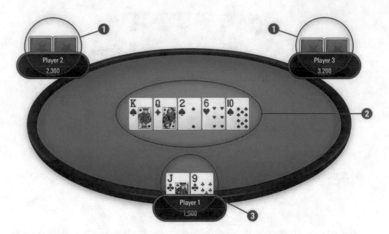

Fig. 2.12 Poker

Fig. 2.13 StarCraft [725]

Poker is an imperfect-information game (the hidden hands 1 in the figure). Because of this it is closer to some decision making situations that are common in the real world, than games such as Chess and Checkers.

Most computer Poker players are based on a detailed analysis of the quality of the hands using a methods called counterfactual regret analysis [779, 104].

StarCraft

StarCraft (Fig. 2.13) is a non-zero-sum imperfect-information simultaneous action real-time strategy game. It is a multiplayer game. The goal of StarCraft is to gather resources, create buildings, develop new technologies, and train attack units, which then must prepare for and fight battles. StarCraft combines imperfect information with multiplayer aspects, long-term strategy, and short-term tactics. Armies have to be built up (strategy), and battles have to be played (tactics). The imperfect-information aspect is that the game map is only partially visible, and the actions of the other players are not all known.

It is a highly popular, highly complex game. The number of actions in StarCraft positions has been estimated to be between 10^{50} and 10^{200} [496]. The state space complexity of StarCraft has been conservatively estimated by these authors at 10^{1685}, which is a very, very large number.

Of all the games that are used in AI, the complexity of the actions in StarCraft is one of the highest, and the decision making comes closer to real-world decision making than in other games. As AI methods are improving, the interest in StarCraft is growing.

2.2.3 Early Game Playing Programs

Now that we have studied the characteristics of some combinatorial games, it is time to have a look at the research field of computer game play.

In order to get a good understanding of the field, let us start with a short overview of some of the better known game playing programs in the history of AI. Even before computers were powerful enough to run game playing programs, there were paper designs of game playing programs. First we discuss two hypothetical game players, and then we continue with the first real game playing programs.

As an aside, please note that there is a common approach in all these attempts. A search function does look ahead, and a heuristic evaluation function scores the board positions. Together the two functions form the search-eval architecture, which we will study in detail in Chap. 4.

Claude Shannon 1949

Claude Shannon (1916–2001) was an American mathematician, electrical engineer, and cryptographer. Shannon is primarily known as the father of information theory.

In 1949 Shannon presented a paper titled "Programming a Computer for playing Chess." The paper describes a design of how to program a computer to play Chess based on position evaluation and move selection. The paper describes strategies for restricting the number of possibilities to be considered. Shannon's paper is one of the first articles published on the topic [618].

Fig. 2.14 Ferranti Mark 1

Fig. 2.15 Alan Turing

Alan Turing 1950

In 1948 Alan Turing (1912–1954, Fig. 2.15) worked with David Champernowne on a
Chess program for a hypothetical computer. They named their program Turbochamp.
In 1950, the program was finished. In 1952, Turing tried to implement it on a Ferranti

Fig. 2.16 Arthur Samuel

Mark 1, Fig. 2.14, but the computer was unable to execute the program, so he ended up executing the program by hand, flipping through the pages of the algorithm and carrying out its instructions on a chessboard. Reportedly, this took about half an hour per move. The program is the first to have played a full Chess game, even though it was executed on paper and by hand [701]. Turbochamp had an evaluation function and a search function, the design that is still used in today's programs.

Christopher Strachey 1951

Christopher Strachey (1916–1975) was a preeminent computer scientist at Oxford, well known for his work on denotational semantics and programming language design. In 1951, Christopher Strachey wrote a Checkers program for the Ferranti Mark 1 computer of the University of Manchester. It could play a complete game of Draughts (Checkers) at reasonable speed [648].

Arthur Samuel 1959

Arthur Samuel (1901–1990, Fig. 2.16) started in 1949 to write a Checkers program for the IBM 701 computer. It was among the world's first successful self-learning programs, adapting coefficients in the evaluation function based on the outcome of the search [577].

The main driver of the program was a search tree of the board positions reachable from the current state. To reduce memory consumption Samuel implemented a version of what is now called alpha-beta pruning. He used a heuristic evaluation function based on the position on the board to prevent having to search to the end of the game. He also used a method to memorize search results, and later versions used supervised learning from professional games and from self-play. Around the 1970s the program had progressed to amateur level [588].

2.3 Game Playing Programs

The playing strength of game playing programs has increased steadily since the early days. Computer hardware has become much more powerful, and better algorithms have been found. Most of these algorithms are described in this book.

For the pioneers the challenge was to create a program that could successfully play a game to the end. We will now skip a few years. The level of play has increased greatly, and now the challenge has become to beat human champions. We will pick up around 1990, where some programs started playing at world champion level.

2.3.1 TD-Gammon 1992

At the end of the 1980s Gerald Tesauro worked on Backgammon programs. (Figure 2.11 showed a Backgammon board.)

His programs were based on neural networks that learned good patterns of play. His first program, Neurogammon, was trained using supervised learning. It achieved an intermediate level of play [673]. His second program, TD-Gammon, was based on temporal difference learning and self-play, a form of reinforcement learning (see Chaps. 3 and 6). Combined with hand-crafted heuristics, in 1992 it played at world-class human championship level, becoming the first computer program to do so in a game of skill [677].

TD-Gammon is named after temporal difference because it updates its neural net after each move, reducing the difference between the evaluation of previous and current positions. In Tesauro's previous program Neurogammon an expert trained the program by supplying the "correct" evaluation of each position. The neural network used a single hidden layer with 80 units. In contrast, TD-Gammon initially learned knowledge-free, or *tabula rasa*. Tesauro describes TD-Gammon's tabula rasa self-play as follows: "The move that is selected is the move with maximum expected outcome for the side making the move. In other words, the neural network is learning from the results of playing against itself. This self-play training paradigm is used even at the start of learning, when the network's weights are random, and hence its initial strategy is a random strategy" [676].

The self-play version used the raw board encoding directly, without any hand-crafted heuristic features. It reached a level of play comparable to Neurogammon: that of an intermediate-level human Backgammon player. After adding a simple heuristic search it reached world-class level.

TD-Gammon's success inspired many other researchers to try neural networks and self-play approaches, culminating eventually in recent high-profile results in Atari [461] and AlphaGo [623, 626], Chaps. 6 and 7).

A modern reimplementation of TD-Gammon in TensorFlow is available on GitHub TD-Gammon.[5]

---

[5] https://github.com/fomorians/td-gammon

2.3.2 Chinook 1994

The Checkers program Chinook was the first computer program to win the world champion title in a competition against humans. It was developed by Canadian computer scientist and Chess player Jonathan Schaeffer. Based on his experience in Chess, Schaeffer decided to write a Checkers program, believing that the technology existed to achieve world championship level.

Chinook's architecture follows the standard search-eval approach of computer Chess, based on alpha-beta search and a hand-crafted heuristic evaluation function (see Chap. 4). Both functions were highly enhanced, well tested, and highly tuned [590, 591]. Apart from meticulous testing and tuning, Chinook derived much of its strength from its endgame databases. These endgame databases contained perfect knowledge for any board position with 8 or fewer pieces on the board.

Schaeffer started development in 1989. At first, progress came swift. In 1990 Chinook won the right to play in the human World Championship by being second to Marion Tinsley in the US Nationals. Tinsley, the current World Champion, was an exceptionally strong player who had reigned supreme for a long time in Checkers.

In 1994 Chinook was declared the Man–Machine World Champion. In 1995, Chinook defended its Man–Machine title in a 32-game match. The final score was 1–0 with 31 draws for Chinook. At the time Chinook was rated at a very high 2814 Elo. After the match, Chinook retired from competitive playing. Later, Schaeffer and his team used Chinook to solve Checkers, proving in 2007 that with perfect play by both sides, Checkers is a draw [589].

Chinook's win is made all the more impressive because of the opponent it faced: Dr. Marion Tinsley. Tinsley, a professor of mathematics, played Checkers at a level that was unheard of. He was world champion from 1955–1958 and 1975–1991 and never lost a world championship match, and lost only seven games in his 45-year career, two of which to Chinook [588]. He withdrew from championship play during the years 1958–1975, relinquishing the title during that time. It was said that Tinsley was to Checkers what Leonardo da Vinci was to science, what Michelangelo was to art, and what Beethoven was to music [436]. Schaeffer wrote a book about his experience, in which he recalls one particular event [588]. In one game from their match in 1990, Chinook made a mistake on the tenth move. Tinsley instantly remarked, "You're going to regret that." And, yes, after they played on, Chinook resigned after move 36, fully 26 moves later, when it saw its loss. Schaeffer looked back into the database and discovered that Tinsley picked the only strategy that could have defeated Chinook from that point and that Tinsley was able to see his win an implausible 64 moves into the future [588].

2.3.3 Deep Blue 1997

If the Checkers events caused excitement, then Chess did even more so. In 1985 Feng-hsiung Hsu, a PhD student at Carnegie Mellon University, started work on a

Fig. 2.17 Garry Kasparov

Fig. 2.18 Excitement in 1997. Game 6, Caro Kahn. Kasparov resigned after 19 moves

Chess program that, after much development, showed enough promise for IBM to become involved. After quite some more years of development, in 1996 performance had improved enough for IBM to sponsor a match against the human world Chess champion Garry Kasparov (Fig. 2.17).[6] The match took place at the ACM Computer Science Conference in Philadelphia. On February 10, 1996, Deep Blue won its first game against human champion Kasparov, making Chess history. However, Kasparov went on to win three games and draw two, winning the six-game match by 4–2.

A year later, in May 1997, the rematch was played in New York at the 35th floor of the Equitable Center (Fig. 2.18). An upgraded version of Deep Blue played

---

[6] Pictured speaking at the Turing centennial conference in Manchester. Image credit: Creative Commons.

Kasparov again, this time capable of evaluating 200 million positions per second, twice as fast as the 1996 version. Kasparov was defeated $3\frac{1}{2}$–$2\frac{1}{2}$ in a highly publicized match. Deep Blue became the first computer system to defeat a reigning world Chess champion in a match under standard Chess tournament time controls. Several accounts of the match, its historical significance, and the technology behind it, have been written [593, 119, 310, 309, 416, 483].

Deep Blue started out as a hardware design project, when Feng-hsiung Hsu wanted to see if he could create a special-purpose VLSI Chess move generator chip. This project evolved into a full-fledged Chess program, which was named Deep Thought, after the fictional computer in Douglas Adams' *The Hitchhiker's Guide to the Galaxy*, that computed the answer to life, the universe, and everything.[7]

The design of Deep Blue followed the standard search-eval architecture, with quite a number of special enhancements. To start with, the evaluation function used 480 specially developed hardware chips, allowing it to evaluate 200 million positions per second in parallel. The search algorithm was also heavily parallelized, running on a 30-node IBM RS/6000 system. Deep Blue would typically search to a depth of 6–8 moves and to a maximum of more than 20 moves in some situations.[8] The opening library was provided by grandmasters Miguel Illescas, John Fedorowicz, and Nick de Firmian. Deep Blue had an endgame database of positions with 5–6 pieces.

Deep Blue's evaluation chips were highly customizable, containing 8000 individual parts, and a database of master games was used to tune their weights [309]. The success of Deep Blue was rightfully billed as the success of brute force, due to the impressive number of 200 million evaluations per second. However, the fact that the evaluation weights were initially tuned by supervised learning, and not by hand, would equally allow a claim to a victory due to machine learning (although it did not use neural nets, nor did Deep Blue use any deep learning).

In its time, Deep Blue, with its capability of evaluating 200 million positions per second, was the fastest computer to face a world Chess champion. Since then, the focus has shifted to software, rather than using dedicated Chess hardware. Chess algorithms have progressed, and modern Chess programs such as Stockfish, Houdini, and Deep Fritz are more efficient than the programs of Deep Blue's era. Today less hardware is needed to achieve the same performance. In a November 2006 match between Deep Fritz and World Chess Champion Vladimir Kramnik, the program ran on a computer system containing one dual-core Intel Xeon 5160 CPU, capable of evaluating only 8 million positions per second, but searching to an average depth of 17 to 18 moves in the middle game, thanks to fast heuristics and aggressive search extensions (Chap. 4). Stockfish is currently one of the strongest Chess programs. It is open source, available on GitHub here.[9]

---

[7] Which, as you may know, is 42.

[8] To be precise, 6–8 moves for a side. In official Chess terminology a move is one half-move by white plus one half-move by black. So what we call 6–8 moves should really be called 3–4 moves if we would follow official Chess terminology.

[9] https://github.com/official-stockfish/Stockfish

2.3.4 Logistello 1997

After the massive team effort for Chess, a year later a one-person effort achieved impressive results in the game of Othello. The program is named Logistello. It was written by Michael Buro and was a very strong player, having beaten the human world champion Takeshi Murakami with a score of 6–0 in 1997. The best Othello programs are now much stronger than any human player.

Logistello's evaluation function is based on patterns of discs, and has over a million numerical parameters which were tuned using advanced logistic linear regression [113, 116, 117].

2.3.5 AlphaGo 2016

After the 1997 defeat of the Chess world champion, the game of Go (Fig. 2.10) became the next benchmark game, the *Drosophila* of AI, and research interest in Go intensified significantly.

Traditionally, computer Go programs followed the conventional Chess design of a minimax search with a heuristic evaluation function that was influence based. The GNU Go program is a good example of this approach [450]. This Chess approach, however, did not work for Go, or at least not well enough. The level of play was stuck at mid-amateur level for quite some time.

In a sense, the game of Go worked very well as *Drosophila*, in that new AI approaches were developed, and many researchers produced interesting findings. New algorithms have been developed, such as Monte Carlo Tree Search, and impressive progress has been made in deep reinforcement learning.

In 2015–2017 the DeepMind AlphaGo team, headed by David Silver, played three matches in which it beat all human champions that it played. There was even a book written analyzing the Go-theoretical innovations that AlphaGo has unlocked for human Go masters [778]. To get an appreciation of the achievement of AlphaGo, and to introduce the program, we will now have a closer look at the matches that it played, quoting some of the commentary that was written about the matches. Please go to Appendix C for a record of all games played in the Fan Hui tournament, the Lee Sedol tournament, and the Ke Jie tournament. First we discuss the Fan Hui games, then the Lee Sedol games, and finally the Ke Jie games. Fig. 2.19 shows the players and some of the AlphaGo team members.[10]

Fan Hui

The games against Fan Hui were played in October 2015 in London as part of the development effort of AlphaGo. Fan Hui is the 2013, 2014, and 2015 European Go

---

[10] Image credit Hassabis and Silver: DeepMind; Hui: Tristan Fewings/Getty Images.

Fig. 2.19 Fan Hui, Lee Sedol, Ke Jie; Demis Hassabis, David Silver and Aja Huang (left-to-right, top-to-bottom)

Champion, then rated at 2p dan. He described the program as very strong and stable. "It seems like a wall. I know AlphaGo is a computer, but if no one told me, maybe I would think the player was a little strange, but a very strong player, a real person."

Lee Sedol

The games against Lee Sedol were played in May 2016 in Seoul as part of a highly televised media circus. Although there is no official worldwide ranking in international Go, in 2016 Lee Sedol was widely considered one of the four best players in the world. Lee Sedol has been a 9p dan professional Go player since 2003. When he played AlphaGo, he had 18 international titles, and was confident that he would win against the computer.

To his surprise, the match ended in a 4–1 win for AlphaGo, with the program playing very strong games. The games against Lee Sedol attracted a large amount of media attention, comparable to the Kasparov–Deep Blue matches two decades earlier. A movie was made of AlphaGo, which can be found here.[11]

The match started with game 1, which was a win for AlphaGo. Then, in game 2, AlphaGo played a move on the right-hand side of the board that shocked spectators (Fig. 2.20). Commentators said that it was a very strange move; many thought that it was a mistake. Lee Sedol took nearly fifteen minutes to formulate a response. Fan

---

[11] https://www.alphagomovie.com

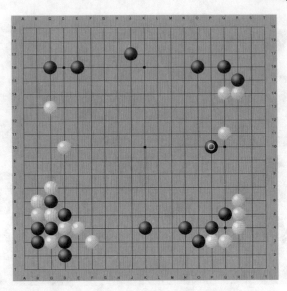

Fig. 2.20 "Speechless" move 37 by AlphaGo in game 2 (played on P 10)

Hui explained that, at first, he also could not believe his eyes. But then he saw the beauty in this rather unusual move. Indeed, the move changed the course of the game, and AlphaGo went on to win. At the post-game press conference Lee Sedol was in shock. He said: "Yesterday, I was surprised," referring to his loss in game 1. "But today I am speechless. If you look at the way the game was played, I admit, it was a very clear loss on my part. From the very beginning of the game, there was not a moment in time when I felt that I was leading."

Fan Hui gives more commentary, showing why this move looks so profound from a human perspective. He writes: "Black 37 is one of the two moves from this match sure to go down in Go history. This move proved so stunning that, when it appeared on the screen, many players thought the stone had been put down in the wrong place."

"On seeing Black 37, I wrote down the following: 'Here?! This goes beyond my understanding. Globally, there's nothing wrong with it, it's going in the right direction [...] and AlphaGo always pays special attention to coordinating the stones. It seems anything is possible in Go! Everyone will be talking about this move! A human would never dare play it, it's too difficult to estimate. But AlphaGo can. Perhaps this move is a sign of its confidence.' "

"This move made a deep impression on me during the game. I experienced first confusion, then shock, and finally delight. It reminded me of an old Chinese saying: 'A beginner plays the corners, an average player the sides; but a master controls the center.' These days, due to the convergence of strengths and the pressure of competition, something close to the opposite is true, with most players focusing on the corners and sides. In contrast, AlphaGo's talent for central control is second to none. Perhaps, through AlphaGo, we too can become the 'masters' of which the proverb speaks."

"Returning to the game, we may say that Black 37 casts an invisible net across the board. Together with the lower side, Black's shoulder hit creates potential all across the center. Although it helps White make territory on the right, the presence of White means that a Black invasion there would not have been valuable anyway. Of course, Black should be reluctant to give away fourth-line territory too easily, but one must give to get."

"After the match, when I examined the data back at DeepMind, I saw that AlphaGo had not even been thinking about 37 only a few moves before. It had been expecting a different move, and its data indicated that a human player would hardly consider the shoulder hit a possibility. It was only when White played 36 that AlphaGo discovered 37, and boldly decided that this move would work even better."

"The pace of the game was much slower than the previous day, so Lee had already gone out to smoke before 37. The minute he caught sight of AlphaGo's reply, he stared blankly at the board. Then he smiled, sat down, and started thinking. The longer he thought, the more serious his expression became, while the clock ran down little by little" [319]. And indeed, this game was also won by AlphaGo.

Lee continued to play three more games in the match, winning game 4 by a beautiful move, but losing the match 1–4, the first time in history that a Go champion of his caliber had lost a match to a computer program.

Ke Jie

A year later another match was played, this time in China, against the Chinese champion. Ke Jie was ranked number one in the Korean, Japanese, and Chinese ranking systems at the time of the match. He was also first among all human players worldwide under Rémi Coulom's ranking system [150].

On 23–27 May 2017 a three-game match was played in Wuzhen, China. The match was won 3–0 by AlphaGo. AlphaGo was subsequently awarded a professional 9-dan title by the Chinese Weiqi Association.

As preparation for this match the team had organized an online 60-game tournament against top pros, from 29 December 2016 to 4 January 2017. This version of AlphaGo ran on a strong machine that used four specially developed tensor processing units (TPU). TPUs are a kind of GPU, specially developed by Google for fast and efficient tensor processing. They are described in Sect. B.1. This version of AlphaGo achieved a very high Elo rating of 4858 against the online pros [626]; it showed that the program was 3 stone stronger than the version that defeated Lee Sedol. They named this match version *AlphaGo Master*. It was a refined and further developed version of AlphaGo, although the basic architecture was unchanged, with a combination of supervised and reinforcement learning (even though the researchers were, at the time, already working on a redesign, AlphaGo Zero).

In the rest of the book we will have a look at the methods that were used to achieve these results. Chapter 5 covers the search algorithm, Chap. 6 covers deep learning, and Chap. 7 goes in depth into self-play.

Appendix D contains links to tutorials on the rules of Go and on learning to play.

2.3.6 Poker 2018

In contrast to games of perfect information such as Chess, Checkers, and Go, Poker is a game of imperfect information. It is a card game in which some of the cards are hidden from the player. The set of possible actions is large, posing a challenge for search-based AI approaches. This has held back the development of strong Poker programs for some time.

Recently, however, impressive progress has been made by groups from the University of Alberta [92, 93, 470] and Carnegie Mellon University [579, 103]. Programs DeepStack and Libratus have defeated some of the strongest human Poker players in one-on-one play [105]. A year later they published equally strong results for multiplayer Poker, with the Pluribus program [104] defeating top players in six-player Poker.

Research in computer Poker is an active field, with versions of research programs being licensed for commercial entertainment purposes. Section 8.2.3 provides more information on the methods for Poker.

2.3.7 StarCraft 2018

StarCraft is a popular real-time strategy game with strong human champions. Researchers have become interested in using the game as a test bed for AI. Since 2010 academic competitions have been organized that stimulated research [692, 496]. In 2017 a Python interface to the game was created to facilitate its use in AI research [727].

In 2018 DeepMind's player AlphaStar played two-person test matches against some of the world's strongest players, which it won [725]. Research into multiplayer methods for StarCraft is becoming quite an active field. Section 8.2.4 provides more information on the challenges that StarCraft poses for AI and looks into further research.

Summary

We have covered a lot of ground in this chapter. We have discussed elements of intelligence, and mentioned that most AI researchers take a behavioristic approach to intelligence. For AI researchers "to be or not to be" is not the question; most take the pragmatic approach of duck-typing: "If it walks like a duck and quacks like a duck, then it must be a duck."

We have looked at characteristics of games, and discussed the important concepts *zero sum* and *perfect information*. We have also had a look at historical approaches to game playing programs, and we have listed modern successes, where computer programs have achieved a level of play beyond that of the strongest human players.

This chapter discussed key aspects of AI: recognition, reasoning, memory, and learning. AI takes a behavioristic approach to intelligence, which is operationalized with the Turing test, introduced by Alan Turing in 1950. We then proceeded with a brief history of AI, starting with the 1956 Dartmouth College workshop. A list of ambitious goals for AI were formulated, which turned out to be overly ambitious, causing AI funding winters. However, after research picked up by the turn of the millennium, a number of AI technologies (such as search, social networks, deep learning, and recommender systems) had deeply affected society, and AI summer arrived.

Games have been a favorite test-bed for AI research. Games such as Chess and Go have been called the *Drosophila* of AI, after the fruit fly from genetics research. An important difference between human intelligence and artificial intelligence is that human intelligence is general, or broad, while artificial intelligence is special, or narrow. Human intelligence can solve many problems; an AI program can solve only one, such as playing good Chess. Research is under way into artificial general intelligence.

The chapter provided a short overview of important designs and programs. We listed the early designs by Shannon, Strachey, Turing, and Samuel. The programs featured were TD-Gammon (Backgammon), Chinook (Checkers), Deep Blue (Chess), Logistello (Othello), AlphaGo (Go), Libratus and DeepStack (Poker), and AlphaStar (StarCraft).

Games are a favorite experimenter's tool for AI. Many breakthroughs in intelligence and learning have taken place in a variety of games, each with their own characteristics.

The early designs established some of the basic algorithms and approaches, such as the search-eval architecture, minimax, alpha-beta, heuristics, and learning. Computers were not yet powerful enough to reach strong levels of play. The later programs all did, using highly enhanced versions of the original blueprints, as well as new techniques, such as deep learning.

It is now time to prepare ourselves for the four core chapters of this book that look in detail at the methods that have been developed by researchers. We will do so by first discussing the reinforcement learning paradigm, as a common language for the four following chapters.

Historical and Bibliographical Notes

We conclude each chapter with a brief summary of entry points to the scientific literature. The works mentioned here may be more accessible than some of the more technical papers.

In this chapter we now list a few such works.

An excellent, popular, and all-encompassing standard textbook of AI is by Russell and Norvig [572]. If you have taken an undergraduate course in AI, chances are that you already own a copy.

Artificial intelligence and search are also used to generate content for computer games [693]. An excellent text on how to use artificial intelligence for creating entertaining and believable computer games is Yannakakis and Togelius [770], which also covers procedural content generation and game design.

Insightful and entertaining accounts have been written about the human and scientific side of writing world champion-level game playing programs. Schaeffer's account of how he and his team created Chinook is memorable, not just because of his inside story, but also because of the picture that it paints of Marion Tinsley, the amazing Checkers champion [588].

Much has been written about the Chess match between Deep Blue and Garry Kasparov. Feng-hsiung Hsu's account gives the story behind their "quest to build the mother of all Chess machines." It is an awe-inspiring story of this moment in the history of Chess-playing intelligence versus computer programming intelligence [309].

A good reference on how computers play Chess is [416], and Chap. 4 covers many of the techniques that are used in Chess programs.

OpenSpiel is a library for reinforcement learning in games. It provides a wealth of high-quality implementations of algorithms [399]. A link to OpenSpiel is here.[12] Appendix A contains more environments relevant to research in reinforcement learning and games.

A popular psychology book is *Thinking Fast and Slow* by Kahneman [347]. Kahneman is one of the founders of the field of behavioral economics, and his approach to intelligence fits well with the search-eval architecture that is prevalent in artificial intelligence in games.

---

[12] https://deepmind.com/research/open-source/openspiel

Chapter 3
Reinforcement Learning

The field of reinforcement learning studies the behavior of agents that learn through interaction with their environment. Reinforcement learning is a general paradigm, with links to trial-and-error methods and behavioral conditioning studies. In this chapter we will introduce basic concepts and algorithms that will be used in the rest of the book.

It is customary to use Markov decision processes (MDPs) as the formalism to model reinforcement learning. MDPs are a suitable paradigm to model the games that we use as benchmarks of intelligent behavior. Reinforcement learning and Markov decision processes allow solution methods for games to be formalized concisely and precisely. Our language will be mathematical in nature, but links to agent behavior, and behavioral studies, are never far away.

To start, let us summarize the core problem and concepts that will be covered in this chapter.

Core Problem

- How can an agent learn from interaction with an environment?

Core Concepts

- Agent and environment
- State, action, policy, and reward
- Value function, credit assignment, exploration/exploitation, and exact/approximate

The reinforcement learning paradigm consists of an agent and an environment (Fig. 3.1). The environment is in a certain state s. At time t, the agent performs action a, resulting in a new state in the environment. Along with this new state comes

© Springer Nature Switzerland AG 2020
A. Plaat, *Learning to Play*, https://doi.org/10.1007/978-3-030-59238-7_3

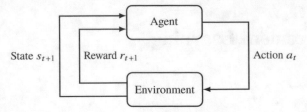

Fig. 3.1 Reinforcement learning: agent and environment [659]

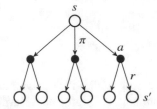

Fig. 3.2 Backup diagram with MDP tuple [659]

reward value r (which may be positive or negative). The goal of the agent is to learn how to maximize the rewards that the environment returns. To this end the agent learns a function, called policy π. It can improve (reinforce) this policy by interacting repeatedly with the environment (note that taking an action—sampling from the environment—may be costly).

3.1 Markov Decision Processes

Reinforcement learning problems can be modeled as Markov decision processes (MDPs). Markov decision problems are an important class of problems that have the Markov property: the next state depends only on the current state and the actions available in it (no memory of previous states or other information is necessary) [306]. The no-memory property is important because it makes reasoning about future states possible using only the information present in the current state. If previous histories would all influence the current state, then reasoning about the current state would be much harder or impossible. MDPs are named after Russian mathematician Andrey Markov (1856–1922) best known for his work on stochastic processes.

Where board games use the terms *board position* and *move,* the mathematical formalisms of MDP and reinforcement learning talk about *state* and *action.*

A Markov decision process is a 5-tuple (S, A, P, R, γ):

- S is a finite set of legal states of the environment; the initial state is denoted as s_0.
- A is a finite set of actions (if the set of actions differs per state, then A_s is the finite set of actions at state s).

- $P_a(s, s') = \Pr(s_{t+1} = s' | s_t = s, a_t = a)$ is the probability that action a in state s at time t will lead to state s' at time $t + 1$ in the environment.
- $R_a(s, s')$ is the reward received after action a transitions state s to state s'.
- $\gamma \in [0, 1]$ is the discount factor representing the difference between future and present rewards.

Figure 3.2 shows the MDP tuple s, a, p, r as well as s', π, and how the value can be calculated. The root node at the top is state s, where policy π allows the agent to choose between three actions a, which, following distribution p, can each end up in two states s', with their reward r. In this way the value of the root can be calculated, by a backup procedure [659]. (The value of γ is 1, in this tiny example.)

Deterministic board games such as Chess and Go can easily be formulated as MDPs with $\gamma = 1$ (future outcomes (lookahead) are as important as present outcomes) and $P = 1$ (actions predictably lead to one future state).[1]

Terminology

Reinforcement learning and MDPs introduce a new formal terminology for board games. The board configuration is called state s, a move is action a, and the score of an end position is the reward R (typically win, loss, or draw). In reinforcement learning a strategy for a player (all the moves from positions leading to a certain end position and outcome) is called a *policy*. In games such as Chess and Go, actions lead deterministically to one state (in Poker and Backgammon they can stochastically lead to different states, see [659]). The state space of a game is the set of all states that are reachable from the initial board position or state.

The state space is easily visualized as a directed graph. Figure 3.3 shows a partial graph of a position in the well-known game of Tic Tac Toe (also known as Noughts and Crosses, or Three in a Row). This new diagram is a simplification of the diagram in Fig. 3.2, since $p = 1$ actions directly lead to a single successor state s'. Most trees in this book are of the new, simpler, type.

Graphs introduce yet another terminology. States/boards are nodes in the graph, actions/moves are links, and terminal states are leaves. Note that the graph in Fig. 3.3 does not have cycles, and is a tree (artificial intelligence is full of "trees," all growing upside down, with the root at the top). Such a graph of the state space of a game is often called a game tree. In general, MDPs and game graphs may contain cycles, although most games have rules to prevent never-ending game situations. Another difference between graphs and trees are transpositions: nodes that have more than one parent. Transpositions are identical board positions that can be reached by different move sequences. Section 4.3.3 discusses transpositions in more detail. A tree does not contain transpositions: in a tree only one path exists between any two nodes, and all children have exactly one parent. Graphs can have transpositions: in a graph, child

---

[1] To be precise, only versions of Chess and Go that do not use rules to prevent repetition, such as the 50-move rule and the ko-rule. The repetition-prevention rules require memory and thus violate the Markov property.

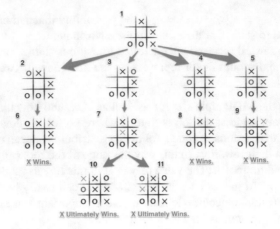

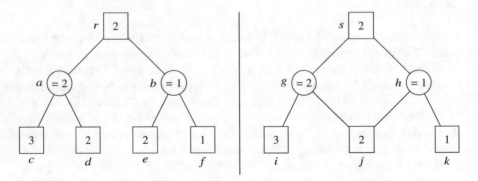

Fig. 3.3 Tic Tac Toe game tree

Fig. 3.4 A tree and a graph; node j is a transposition

nodes may be shared between parents, and there are more ways than one to reach a certain position from the root. See Fig. 3.4 for an example of a tree and a graph with a transposition. Nodes in Fig. 3.4 are either squares or circles. Squares indicate the max (first) player is to move, and circles indicate the min (second) player is to move. The value of a max node is the maximum of its children, while the value of a min node is the minimum of its children (see Sect. 4.1.2).

A score function is defined for the leaves of the game tree/graph to tell whether the game has been won, lost, or drawn. In reinforcement learning terminology we say that the reward is known. If we look at the graph in Fig. 3.3 again, and we want to find the value of a nonterminal board position, all we have to do is work upwards from the leaves of the tree, and determine the values of the parent nodes, carefully taking the max or min, until finally the value of all nodes in the tree is known. At that point we know if the initial position of the game is won or lost if both players play perfectly.

Now that we have discussed basic terminology we are ready to look at two central elements in reinforcement learning: the policy function and the value function.

3.2 Policy Function, State-Value Function, Action-Value Function

In reinforcement learning two functions are usually associated with the states: the policy function and the value function. Furthermore, this value function exists both for states and for actions.

3.2.1 Policy Function

Of central importance in reinforcement learning is the concept of *policy,* or π. The policy function π associates states with actions. A deterministic policy $\pi: s \mapsto a$ returns one action for each state. A stochastic policy $\pi(a|s)$ gives the probability of taking action a in state s.

For two-person games the goal of reinforcement learning and MDPs is for the agent to find an optimal policy $\pi^\star$ that gives an action $a = \pi^\star(s)$ that should be chosen in each state s that leads to a win for the first player. Finding the optimal policy function is also known in engineering as solving the *optimal control problem* [659].

3.2.2 State-Value Function

The state value function $V(s)$ returns the expected value of state s; it is the discounted value of the expected future rewards of a state. In leaves, the "expected" value is equal to the reward $V(s) = R(s)$. The expected value $V(s)$ of a state s is determined by the current policy, and should therefore be written $V^\pi(s)$. Many solution methods exist to efficiently determine value functions and policy functions. Finding the value function solves the *estimation problem.*

In the next chapter, Chap. 4, we will discuss methods that efficiently determine this root value, and, by extension, the optimal policy $\pi^\star$, the tree of actions that leads to it.

3.2.3 Action-Value Function

The action value $Q(s, a)$ is the value of taking action a in state s under policy π. Writing it more precisely as $Q^\pi(s, a)$, the function takes action a and then takes policy π for the remainder. The value of the $Q^\pi(s, a)$ function is equal to the value function when taking action a in state s:

$$Q^{\pi}(s, a) = V_a^{\pi}(s).$$

The final value of state s is given by the value function V^{π}, after the fact, when all computations have been done. The $Q^{\pi}(s, a)$ function gives the value of a single action a, and is important during the calculation. The Q-value can be computed for intermediate single action values. Important algorithms such as Q-learning and DQN are named after this action-value function.

3.2.4 Implementing Functions

It is common to discuss value and policy problems in terms of functions. Functions map input values to output values, and are sometimes called mappings.

At this point it is useful to consider that value and policy functions can be implemented in different ways. The most basic and easy to implement situation is when for a function $f(x) \mapsto y$ a closed-form mathematical formula is known, such as $f(x) = x + 5$. The formula can be implemented straightforwardly as a procedure that takes its input arguments and runs some code to calculate the return value: `def f(x): return x+5`. This is the *code* approach.

A slightly more complicated situation is the following. There are nonlinear functions $f(x) \mapsto y$ that can not be expressed as a closed-form mathematical formula, or for which no such formula is known. However, when a database of input/output pairs is available, then we can impement the mapping as an array, list, or dictionary in most programming languages: `def f(x): return table[x]`. This is typically the case in machine learning problems, where the resulting function is to be learned by looking at examples. When the number of examples is manageable, they can be stored in memory. The function is then implemented as a lookup table. This is the *database* approach.

For most real-world machine learning situations we have an even more complicated situation, where the database is too large to fit in memory, or the training set must generalize to cover unseen examples from the test set that are not present in the training database. In this case the function can be learned with machine learning methods, although the function values will necessarily be approximated. The function mapping can be implemented as a parameterized (neural) network that takes as input a state, and produces as output a value. This is what is used in many real-world machine learning situations. Since the function is approximated using a set of parameters θ, it is often written as $f_{\theta}(x) \mapsto y$. This is the *function approximation* approach. Chapter 6 is dedicated to function approximation.

3.3 Solution Methods

Now that we have introduced the basic elements and terminology of reinforcement learning, it is time to discuss solution methods, methods that help us find the optimal values and policies.

In this section we will introduce many building blocks of reinforcement learning: the Bellman equation to recursively compute root values when the transition function is known, the exploration/exploitation trade-off to find optimal paths, temporal-difference learning to find the policy by sampling, the value iteration and policy iteration solution methods, and on- and off-policy methods for learning the optimal policy.

The methods will be introduced one by one. At the end of the chapter full algorithms are described that combine all these fundamental concepts.

We will now start with two essential elements of reinforcement learning: Bellman recursion and the exploration/exploitation trade-off.

3.3.1 Bellman Recursion

Games consist of actions by players. For each action that the player makes, the optimal policy of the board position must be found. (Or, equivalently, the optimal value must be found.) In the previous section we discussed Tic Tac Toe and how the optimal policy and the value of a position depend on the rewards, or leaf values. We mentioned how the value of the root can be found by recursively traversing the tree upwards, working backwards, computing the values of inner nodes. This recursive solution method described informally in the previous section can be described formally with the Bellman equation. Figure 3.5 gives an artistic impression of the concept of recursion, known as the Droste effect: a picture of a picture of a picture within a picture etc. Richard Bellman showed that discrete optimization problems can be described as a recursive backward induction problem [54], using what he called dynamic programming. The Bellman equation shows the relationship between the value function in one state and the next state.

The Bellman equation of the expected value for being in state s and following policy π is

$$V^{\pi}(s) = R(s, \pi(s)) + \gamma \sum_{s'} P(s'|s, \pi(s))V^{\pi}(s'),$$

where R is the reward function and γ is the discount rate. The value of a state is equal to the reward of that state, following policy π, and the discounted sum of the values of its successors. Before a node has been searched, it is not yet known which child is the best successor. The Bellman equation defines a recursive relation on how to compute the expected value of the initial state s_0. Note that for games such as Chess and Checkers the search space is defined implicitly by the rules of the game and the initial board position, of which we desire to know the optimal policy and the expected value

Fig. 3.5 Recursion: Droste effect

(win, draw, or loss). For common two-person zero-sum perfect-information games the Bellman equation simplifies greatly: $\gamma = 1$, and R is commonly chosen to be $+1$ for win, -1 for loss, and 0 for draw, and also for intermediate nodes. The expected value therefore depends recursively on the rewards at leaf nodes. The probability of transitioning from state s to s' under perfect information in the optimal policy is 1. In perfect-information game playing algorithms the Bellman equation reduces to a simple backup function.

Dynamic Programming

Dynamic programming was introduced by Bellman in the 1950s. It recursively breaks down problems into smaller subproblems that are then solved. Dynamic programming can be used to solve problems whose structure follows the Bellman equation. Dynamic programming works when the transition function P is known; it is a model-based planning method (Sect. 3.3.4). The key idea of dynamic programming is to use the value function to guide the search for good policies [659]. We will discuss two dynamic programming algorithms for solving reinforcement learning problems in Sect. 3.5. In the next chapter, we will see more methods.

```
def value_iteration():
    initialize(V)
    while not convergence(V):
        for s in range(S):
            for a in range(A):
                Q[s,a] = Σ_{s'∈S} P_a(s,s')(R_a(s,s') + γV[s'])
            V[s] = max_a(Q[s,a])
    return V
```

Listing 3.1 Value iteration pseudocode (based on [8])

Two dynamic programming methods to iteratively traverse the state space are value iteration and policy iteration.

Value Iteration

Value iteration methods directly improve the estimate of the optimal value function by traversing the state space. Pseudocode for a basic version of value iteration is shown in Listing 3.1. Value iteration converges to the optimal value function by iteratively improving the estimate of $V(s)$. The value function $V(s)$ is first initialized to random values. Value iteration repeatedly updates $Q(s, a)$ and $V(s)$ values until convergence occurs (when values of $V(s)$ stop changing much). Value iteration has been proven to converge to the optimal values, but, as we can see in the pseudocode in Listing 3.1, it does so quite inefficiently by essentially enumerating the entire state space.

Value iteration methods help find the best action for each state by following the action that yields the optimal value function. This can work with a finite set of actions. However, convergence in large spaces is slow [8, 659].

Policy Iteration

Value iteration algorithms keep improving the value function at each iteration until the value function converges. However, most agents only care about finding the optimal control policy (the best move) and not its value.

In games with a low branching factor, such as Checkers, there are only few actions in a state. When there are also many different state values (which is the case in most game playing programs) then the optimal policy may converge before the value function. Directly updating the policy function will then converge faster than taking the route via the value function. Policy iteration methods directly improve the policy function. This approach is also useful when the action space is continuous (or stochastic).

Both value iteration and policy iteration can be used when there is prior knowledge about the model/environment. For both methods the MDP 5-tuple, especially the transition and reward function, must be known. When that is not the case, then other methods are needed, such as Q-learning (to be discussed shortly).

Approximate Solutions

An important choice in implementing reinforcement learning algorithms is which storage concept to use for the states, the actions, and the policy and value functions. For small state spaces, all states can be stored individually in a table, array, or tree. Small state spaces can be enumerated, and solutions can be exact.

Many reinforcement learning problems have state spaces that are arbitrarily large. For example, the number of possible images of even a small black and white picture is very large (the number of gray scale values raised to the power of the number of pixels). The number of instances encountered during training will be small in relation to the possible number of instances, and the trained policy should work well on unseen problems. The number of possible states is too large to be stored, so some form of generalization has to be used. Where exact methods store the function values in a table with an entry for each state/action pair, for large state spaces function approximation must be used. Artificial neural networks are popular methods.

Neural networks, or function approximators, are parameterized by a vector of weights θ. The length of the vector is much less than the number of possible states. States are *represented* by the weight vector. This has two advantages. First, the examples from the very large number of possible states can be stored efficiently in limited memory. Second, the example states are generalized according to some method, recording the generalization into the weight parameters, allowing unseen states to be recognized as belonging to some (hopefully appropriate) value or class.

In classification or other statistical tasks where unseen states must be classified or evaluated, generalization is a goal by itself. Through generalization the "essence" of the states is to be found. Generalization transforms a high-dimensional space to a lower-dimensional space.

In Chap. 6 approximation methods will be introduced. Deep Q-networks (DQN) will be discussed. DQN consists of a deep convolutional network for function approximation, which is trained by reinforcement learning using Q-learning (see page 58).

3.3.2 Exploration and Exploitation

Now that we know how to calculate the expected value of a state, we should look at how to do so efficiently. For each action to be taken in a state, let us maintain a table of numbers that represent the probability of winning for that action. As actions are performed, the value in the table begins to reflect more reliably the expectation of winning when taking that action.

Now the question is: Which action should we take? One approach is to always choose the action that has accrued the highest winning probability so far. This approach is called a *greedy* approach. Another approach is to sometimes try another action, temporarily ignoring the one with currently the highest winning probability, exploring a new successor state, in the hope of finding an untried action with an even higher overall winning probability.

The ϵ-greedy approach is to mostly try the best (greedy) action except to explore an ϵ fraction of times a randomly selected other action. If $\epsilon = 0.1$ then 90% of the times the best action is taken, and 10% of the times a random other action. The ϵ-greedy policy is an example of a *soft* policy: a policy with a finite probability of selecting any of the possible actions.

This choice between greedily exploiting known information and exploring unknown nodes to gain new information is called the exploration/exploitation trade-off. It is a central concept in reinforcement learning.

Let us look at the exploration/exploitation trade-off in more intuitive and concrete terms. Assume you have moved into a new neighborhood, which you do not yet know, and you want to find the route to the supermarket. After some trial and error, you have found a route, which you meticulously memorize. The greedy approach is then, when you need to go to the supermarket again, to always follow this same route. You exploit the knowledge that you have to the fullest, without ever investing the cost of trying out a possible new route (exploring). Trying out a different route will take some extra time and effort, but might pay off in finding a shorter route, which you can then use many times for as long as you live in the neighborhood.

Clearly, always exploiting might be the safe way, but it is likely to not find an optimal solution. How much to explore, and in what situations, is a fundamental topic in reinforcement learning that has been studied in depth in the optimization literature [299, 761] and in multi-armed bandit problems [22, 394] (see also Chapter 5).

Smart use of exploitation and exploration is at the basis of the breakthroughs in Go. In Chap. 5 we will discuss in depth the Monte Carlo Tree Search algorithm, MCTS, whose selection rule UCT uses bandit theory to find a good exploration/exploitation trade-off.

Temporal Difference

We have now discussed how to calculate the values of states when the policy function is known and how to then find the optimal policy for states. We are building up our tools to construct solution methods with which we can estimate the optimal policy and value of a game state, allowing us to construct a game playing program that can compute the best moves so that it can play a full game.

The Bellman equation calculates the value of states when a model P of the problem is known. For model-free problems (Sect. 3.3.4) we need another solution method, that can work by sampling.

Perhaps the best known solution method for estimating policy functions is temporal difference learning [658]. This method is the basis of TD-Gammon [676]. The temporal difference in the name refers to the difference that it calculates between two time steps, which it uses to calculate the value of the new time step.

The Bellman equation describes how $V(s)$ can be calculated using dynamic programming when the transition function P is known. It is a model-based planning method. TD is different: under the policy π it samples from the environment to adjust the current $V(s)$ estimate using a learning rate. TD does not need to know the transition function P and finds $V(s)$ by sampling.

TD works by updating the current estimate of the state $V(s)$ with an error value based on the estimate of the next state. It is, therefore, a bootstrapping method, where the update takes into account previous estimates:

$$V(s) \leftarrow V(s) + \alpha[R' + \gamma V(s') - V(s)].$$

Here s is the current state, s' the new state, and R' the reward of the new state. Note the introduction of α, the learning rate. The γ parameter is the discount rate. The last term $-V(s)$ subtracts the value of the current state, so that TD computes the temporal difference. Another way to write the update rule is $V(s) \leftarrow \alpha[R' + \gamma V(s')] + (1-\alpha)V(s)$ as the difference between the new TD target and the old value. Note the absence of P in the formula; TD is model-free.

Now, in order to arrive at a full reinforcement learning algorithm, we also need a control method. TD gives us a learning rule for value updates, the error part of trial and error. For a full reinforcement learning algorithm we also need a control method, which tells us which nodes to choose for expansion, the trial part of trial and error. Two such control methods are SARSA,[2] yielding on-policy TD control, and Q-learning, yielding off-policy TD control. SARSA and Q-learning are discussed more fully in Sect. 3.5.

3.3.3 Actor-Critic

SARSA and Q-learning learn the value function of a state in order to find the optimal policy. Value function methods work well when there is a finite set of actions. They work less well in continuous or stochastic environments, such as robotics, where arm movements or distance to drive are continuous choices.

In addition to finding the value function, to then find the best action, it is also possible to try to compute the optimal policy directly, without first going through the intermediate step of calculating values. Williams [759] introduced the REINFORCE policy gradient algorithm. Direct policy evaluation can be more efficient in continuous or stochastic environments and when there are many different reward values. Converging to the value may then take a long time.

A first challenge for policy gradient algorithms is how to find reliable information on which action is best. Of course there is the reward function, which is known in

---

[2] The name of the SARSA algorithm is a play on the MDP symbols as they occur in the action value update formula: s, a, r, s, a.

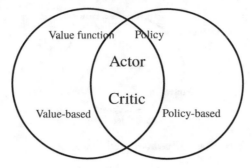

Fig. 3.6 Value and policy in Actor-Critic

end states. However, it is not known in intermediate states, and the more intermediate steps have to be taken between an action and a reward, the more unreliable this end signal is. Statistics can be called to the rescue, by taking many samples, which is computationally problematic. In large problems, policy gradient methods may suffer from low sample efficiency, since many samples are needed for reliable reward information [659, 262].

At this point you may ask if it would be possible to combine the value-based approach and the policy-based approach. After all, value functions can backup reward functions reliably. If reward values are unreliable in large problems, might value function methods be used to provide a more reliable signal for the value of the actions? Indeed this is possible, and this approach is called Actor-Critic [657, 660]. The actor is the policy method; the critic is the value method. Each uses its own separate method, typically a neural network. The critic network calculates the action value function for each state, and the actor the policy function for each state. In Actor-Critic, value functions (not unlike SARSA or Q-learning) are used to calculate more reliable values of states or actions more efficiently than sampling many rewards, in large problems.

Actor-Critic interleaves a policy function (actor) and a value function (critic). These algorithms have been studied widely [377, 364, 659, 706, 378, 491]. This combination of the value/policy idea is shown in Fig. 3.6.

SARSA and Q-learning do not have an explicit policy representation; they are critic-only algorithms. Actor-Critic alternates policy evaluation with policy improvement steps. Actor-Critic methods combine the best of both worlds: better convergence than value methods, and better policies due to value learning and reduced variance. Actor-Critic methods are quite popular. Two well-known methods, asynchronous advantage Actor-Critic (A3C) and proximal policy optimisation (PPO), will be introduced in Sect. 6.4.7, where we will discuss advanced actor-critic methods in the context of function approximation—A3C is an improvement over the popular Deep Q-Network (DQN) algorithm.

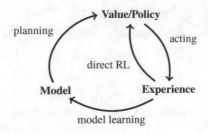

Fig. 3.7 Model-free and model-based methods [659]

3.3.4 Model-Free and Model-Based Methods

A basic distinction in reinforcement learning is between model-free and model-based methods (such as temporal difference and value iteration) [345]. Model-free methods learn a value and policy function directly from the observations (Fig. 3.7, the inner loop). Model-based methods, on the other hand, first need an intermediate model of the transition probabilities. This model can be given by the rules of the problem, or it can be learned. To use the model then another reinforcement learning algorithm is used to find the value and policy function, often an exact planning algorithm [371, 743, 524]. Model-based methods follow the outer loop in the figure. Model-free methods are also known as direct methods.

Some reinforcement learning methods are model-based, such as dynamic programming, and others are model-free, such as TD. Model-based methods can be used when a model of the environment exists, when transition and reward functions are known. This can be a statistical model, a simulator, or the rules for the dynamics of the environment, such as we have in games.

When a model is available, it can be used to do look-ahead planning, as we shall do in the next chapters on planning. When no model is available, methods must be used to first learn a model of the environment, often using sampling. The chapters on learning discuss deep reinforcement learning methods that start with no model and create a model. Finally, combinations of model-based and model-free methods, of planning and training, are discussed. AlphaGo is perhaps the best known example of this combined approach [623]. Section 7.3.5 further discusses model-free and model-based reinforcement learning.

Let us now look at another central concept in reinforcement learning: that of on-policy and off-policy learning methods for model-free learning.

3.3.5 On-Policy Learning and Off-Policy Learning

We will now discuss two model-free solution methods, methods that work when the transition function of the MDP is not known.

Reinforcement learning is concerned with learning a policy from actions and rewards. The agent selects an action, and learns from the reward that it gets back from the environment; or, in terms of the Tic Tac Toe tree of Fig. 3.3, the value of the root is learned by downward selecting an action, and by backing up the value that is returned. Note that the policy determines the downward action selection, and the subsequent learning takes place in the backup of the reward value.

Normally, the learning takes place by backing up the value of the action that was selected by the policy: the learning is *on-policy*. It turns out that there is an alternative. If the learning takes place by backing up values of another action, not the one selected by the policy, than this is known as *off-policy learning*. This makes sense when the policy explores by selecting a non-optimal action (i.e., it does not perform greedy exploitation). On-policy learning would then have to backup the value of the non-optimal exploration action (since otherwise it would not learn on-policy). Off-policy learning, however, is free to backup the value of the best action instead, and not the inferior one selected by the exploration policy. Thus, in the case of exploration, off-policy learning can be more efficient, by not stubbornly backing up the value of the action selected by the policy, but of the best action instead. (In the case of an exploiting step by the policy, on-policy learning and off-policy learning are the same.)

All learning methods face a trade-off: they try to learn the best target action from current behavior that is known so far (exploitation), and they choose new (most likely non-optimal) behavior in order to explore and be able to find actions that are better than the current best actions. Thus, in principle, there are two policies: first, the behavior policy that is used for actual action selection behavior (sometimes exploring), and second, the target policy that is learned by backing up values. The first policy performs *downward* selection to expand states, the second *upward* value propagation to update the target policy.

Recall that the $Q(s, a)$ function computes the expected value of (downward) selecting action a in state s. On-policy learning and off-policy learning update the $Q(s, a)$ function by backing up values (upward) from their successor actions (which can be implemented as an array, or lookup table). When the algorithms sample the state/action pairs often enough, the algorithms are proven to converge to the correct values.

On-Policy

In on-policy learning a single policy function is used for (downward) action selection and for (upward) value backup towards the learning target. On-policy learning updates values directly on this single policy. The same policy array is used for exploration behavior and for the incumbent optimal target policy.

The update formula is

$$Q(s_t, a_t) \leftarrow Q(s_t, a_t) + \alpha[r_{t+1} + \gamma Q(s_{t+1}, a_{t+1}) - Q(s_t, a_t)].$$

On-policy learning selects an action, evaluates it, and moves on to better actions. A well-known on-policy approach is SARSA. On-policy learning starts with a starting policy, samples the state space with this policy, and improves the policy by backing up values of the selected actions. Note that the term $Q(s_{t+1}, a_{t+1})$ can also be written as $Q(s_{t+1}, \pi(s_{t+1}))$, highlighting the difference with off-policy learning. Since SARSA is on-policy, it updates its Q-values using the Q-value of the next state s and the current policy's action. In a short while we will look at SARSA example code, and compare its behavior with off-policy learning.

The primary advantage of on-policy learning is that it directly optimizes the target of interest, and achieves stable learning. The biggest drawback is sample inefficiency, since policies are estimated from the full rollouts. This may further cause large variance—if it goes in the wrong direction, there is no stabilizing other information to get it out.[3]

Off-Policy

Off-policy learning is more complicated. It uses two separate policy arrays: one for exploratory downward selection behavior, and one to update as the current target backup policy. Learning (backing up) is from data *off* the downward selection policy, and the whole method is therefore called off-policy learning.

The update formula is

$$Q(s_t, a_t) \leftarrow Q(s_t, a_t) + \alpha[r_{t+1} + \gamma \max_a Q(s_{t+1}, a) - Q(s_t, a_t)].$$

The difference from on-policy learning is that the $\gamma Q(s_{t+1}, a_{t+1})$ term has been replaced by $\gamma \max_a Q(s_{t+1}, a)$. The learning is from backup values of the best, not the actual, action.

The reason that Q-learning is off-policy is that it updates its Q-values using the Q-value of the next state s and the greedy action (not necessarily the selection policy's action—it is learning off the selection policy).

In this sense, off-policy learning collects all available information and uses it simultaneously to construct the best target policy. The best known off-policy algorithm is Q-learning [748]. It gathers information from (partially) exploring moves, it evaluates states as if a greedy policy was used, and it slowly reduces random exploration.

Differentiating On-Policy and Off-Policy Learning

To understand the difference between on-policy and off-policy learning, let us look at the update formulas. A way to differentiate on-policy and off-policy learning is to look how the backup formula depends on the next action a_{t+1}, which can be written

---

[3] See [475] for a discussion on variance reduction. To avoid large bias, SARSA can use on-policy data, or updates can be slowed.

as $\pi(s_{t+1})$. Q-learning is off-policy learning since it does not depend on the next action a_{t+1}, i.e., it does not depend on the policy π. No matter what a_{t+1} is, the $\max_a Q(s_{t+1}, a)$ part does not depend on a_{t+1}. $Q(s_t, a_t)$ is updated regardless of the future policy π starting from s_{t+1}. On the other hand, SARSA is on-policy learning because the term $Q(s_{t+1}, a_{t+1})$ in $Q(s_t, a_t)$ depends on the next actual action a_{t+1}, the one taken by following the policy $\pi(s_{t+1})$. The backpropagation learning in SARSA depends on the behavior policy.

To recapitulate, off-policy approaches can learn the value of the optimal target policy regardless of the selection policy, while in on-policy methods the agent learns the value of the policy whose actions it is following.

Off-policy learning is especially important when there is a database of previously stored trajectories (i.e., data in the form of tuples (s, a, r', s')). This data has been collected by previously applying some policy, and cannot be changed. This is a common case, for example for medical problems. To use this kind of data, only off-policy methods can be used.

Off-policy methods are more flexible in the type of problems they can be used for. Their theoretical properties, however, are different. If we compare Q-learning with SARSA, the difference is in the max operator used in the Q-learning update rule. The max operator is nonlinear, which can make it more difficult to combine the algorithm with function approximators. With function approximators (neural nets), on-policy methods are usually more stable.

Off-policy learning can be problematic since the Q-values tend to overestimate (because of the max operator). Off-policy learning that strays too far off the selection policy may get lost (or rather, become inefficient). In Chap. 6 we will cover learning stability of off-policy methods in more depth, including methods that limit the amount of off-policy learning.

We will now look at an underlying topic that permeates all of machine learning and that has been mentioned a few times already: sample efficiency.

3.3.6 Sample Efficiency

An algorithm is sample efficient if it gets the most out of every sample and efficiently learns a function with only few samples of the environment.

Model-free methods often require many environment samples to converge on the policy. A problem of model-free methods is that once a sample has been used, it is thrown away, and a new sample is sought.

Model-based algorithms use the samples of the environment more efficiently. They use the samples to build a transition model of the environment, which is then used internally to find the policy. Model-based methods are often more sample efficient, using the model to converge quickly to an optimum with few samples, provided that the predictions from the transition model are good [743, 465, 524]. Constructing accurate transitions models can be difficult in practice, and most good results so far have been achieved with model-free methods (unless a transition model is provided by the application domain).

SARSA and Q-learning, two model-free methods, are effectively performing random search in the environment, not using information from previous samples to guide the search. A drawback of on-policy learning is that it samples from its own target policy, which may lead to myopia, or tunnel vision, sampling a local part of the search space. When an algorithm learns only a part of the search space, learning can be unstable.

In off-policy learning old samples may be used, not related to the target policy. This may prevent myopia, but on the other hand not using all samples of the behavior policy may also lead to low sample efficiency.

Several methods have been proposed to improve sample efficiency of model-free methods. One such method is importance sampling [247, 474, 747], which samples from a distribution that overweights the important region. In this way the target is sampled heavily (as in on-policy) but the rest is not neglected completely (as in off-policy, preventing myopia).

3.4 Conclusion

We have now discussed in depth many elements of the reinforcement learning paradigm, one of the major paradigms of machine learning. To conclude this chapter, let us discuss some differences from supervised learning.

Supervised Learning

Machine learning is the part of artificial intelligence that studies mechanical learning principles. Machine learning algorithms are algorithms to learn patterns from data [81, 572].

In its most basic classification form, machine learning works by looking at pairs of examples and labels (E, L). The task of the learning algorithm is then to associate the correct label with the correct class of examples, so that when it is shown a new example, it classifies it with the correct label. A well-known machine learning problem is to learn the classification of a large sequence of pictures (examples E) as either dogs or cats (labels L). Such a problem is an example of supervised learning where the labels play the role of supervisor in the learning process. If not all examples have labels, then supervised learning is only possible for the examples with labels. Supervised learning needs a database of (example, label) pairs. It will be treated in depth in Chap. 6.

Interaction

Note that trial and error (or *interaction*) is an essential aspect of learning by reinforcement. Like supervised learning, reinforcement learning is a kind of machine learning. But unlike supervised learning, in reinforcement learning there is no preexisting database with labeled states. All states to learn from will be generated during the learning process by interaction with the environment. By smartly choosing the agent's actions, the sequence of states may be generated to learn efficiently, without the need for a large database of examples.

Furthermore, in supervised learning we can never learn more than the examples in the supervisory database provide; the teacher provides an upper limit to what the pupil can learn. In reinforcement learning there is no teacher holding us back; only the world to explore.

Credit Assignment

Now, in supervised learning all examples are labeled. However, in reinforcement learning some actions may not return a reward, but future rewards must be propagated to previous states. In other words, state spaces in reinforcement learning may have a *sparse* reward structure. This is the case in most games, where only terminal states have a reward $\{-1, 0, +1\}$, and for all other states the reward value must be propagated backward from the terminal states. This is known as the credit assignment problem. Long-range credit assignment is a challenging problem. This too will be discussed in Chap. 6.

Dependency

There are more differences between supervised learning and reinforcement learning. Supervised learning has a database from which it draws examples to learn from; reinforcement learning generates its own learning examples through interaction with the environment. In reinforcement learning there is therefore a dependency between subsequent samples, since the learning algorithm influences its own learning examples. This may cause learning anomalies, cycles, and local maxima. Special care must be taken in reinforcement learning to not get stuck in local maxima, as we will see in Chap. 6.

MDP Tuple and Reinforcement Learning

We are approaching the end of this chapter. Let us look at how the principles that were covered apply to the different chapters further on in this book.

Reinforcement learning can formally be described by the 5-tuple of Markov decision processes. The remainder of this book will discuss many different rein-

Chapter	Name	MDP-tuple	Reinforcement learning
Chap. 4	alpha-beta	$(S, A, 1, R, 1)$	policy, backup
Chap. 5	MCTS	$(S, A, P, R, 1)$	pol, b/u, exploration/exploitation
Chap. 6	DQN	(S, A, P, R, γ)	pol, b/u, expl/expl, discount, off-policy
Chap. 7	self-play	(S, A, P, R, γ)	pol, b/u, expl/expl, discount, off-pol, self-play

Table 3.1 MDP tuple and reinforcement learning in the chapters

forcement learning methods in depth, from heuristic planning, adaptive sampling, to generalization (as we saw in Table 1.1). These methods will start simple, with some of the MDP tuples being constant at 1, in the early chapters. As the methods become more elaborate, the full tuple is used, and more reinforcement learning elements apply. Table 3.1 gives an overview of how the full generality of reinforcement learning develops throughout the chapters of this book, as the methods progress from simple search to advanced generalization methods with adaptive self-learning.

3.5 Practice

It is time to try the insights that we have discussed in practice with programming exercises. First are some questions to check your understanding of this chapter and the previous chapter. Each question is a closed question where a simple, one sentence answer is possible.

Questions

1. Name three important elements of intelligence.
2. What element of intelligence does computer game playing focus on?
3. Describe the symbolic approach to AI. Describe the connectionist approach to AI.
4. Who wrote the first Chess program?
5. When did Deep Blue beat Kasparov, in 1996 in Philadelphia or in 1997 in New York?
6. Describe the difference between strategy and tactics in a board game. Give an example game of each.
7. Describe the reinforcement learning model.
8. Give the 5-tuple of a Markov decision process.
9. What is a value function?
10. What is a policy function?
11. Describe in words the intuition of Bellman's equation.
12. Describe the exploration/exploitation dilemma. Can you give one simple algorithm for trading off exploration and exploitation?
13. Describe in words the intuition behind temporal difference learning.
14. Why is it sometimes necessary to approximate a solution?

15. What is the difference between on-policy learning and off-policy learning? Can you give one example algorithm for each?
16. Why is sample efficiency important?

3.5.1 Algorithms

Next, we will look at on-policy and off-policy algorithms and their behavior. How do on-policy learning and off-policy learning learn optimal policies for the Taxi environment? We will use SARSA as the on-policy learner, and Q-learning as the off-policy learner.

As we saw in the previous chapter, benchmarks are of great importance for progress in AI. To support AI progress, the organization OpenAI has provided an easy-to-use suite of benchmarks for scientists and students to use. It is called Gym, and has a Python interface. One of the classic examples in reinforcement learning is the Taxi problem, introduced by Dietterich [176]. We will use the Taxi example from OpenAI Gym.

Python is a programming language that is popular in artificial intelligence. It supports quick development, rich and flexible data structures, and many third-party packages have been written, ranging from numerical simulation, graphics, to machine learning. If Python is not present on your computer, please go to Appendix E to learn more about Python and how to install it on your computer.

Now please install Gym. Go to the webpage and the GitHub page of OpenAI Gym and have a look around to see what is there. OpenAI Gym can be found here,[4] and the Gym GitHub page can be found here.[5] You will see different sets of environments, from easy to advanced. There are the classics, such as Cartpole and Mountain Car. There are also small text environments. Taxi is there, and there is the Atari Learning Environment [53], which was used in the paper that introduced DQN [461]. MuJoCo is also available, an environment for experimentation with simulated robotics. (Our Taxi environment can be found in `gym/envs/toy_text`, in case you would like to have a look at how the environment is written.) Installing Gym on your computer is easy. Type `pip install gym` (or `pip3 install gym`) at a command prompt. You should also install numpy and matplotlib. Go to Spinning Up to get started with Gym.

The Taxi example (Fig. 3.8) is an environment where taxis move up, down, left, and right, and can pickup and drop off passengers. The Gym documentation describes the Taxi world as follows. There are four designated locations in the grid world indicated by R(ed), B(lue), G(reen), and Y(ellow). When the episode starts, the taxi starts off at a random square and the passenger is at a random location. The taxi drives to the passenger's location, picks up the passenger, drives to the passenger's destination (another one of the four specified locations), and then drops off the passenger. Once the passenger is dropped off, the episode ends.

---

[4] https://gym.openai.com

[5] https://github.com/openai/gym

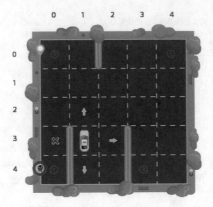

Fig. 3.8 Taxi world [351]

There are 500 discrete states, since there are 25 taxi positions, five possible locations of the passenger (including the case when the passenger is in the taxi), and 4 destination locations ($25 \times 5 \times 4$).

The environment returns a new result tuple at each step. There are six discrete deterministic actions for the Taxi driver:

0: Move south
1: Move north
2: Move east
3: Move west
4: Pick up passenger
5: Drop off passenger

There is a reward of -1 for each action and an additional reward of $+20$ for delivering the passenger. There is a reward of -10 for executing actions *pickup* and *dropoff* illegally. Please refer to Listing 3.3.

OpenAI not only provides environments, but also the other half of reinforcement learning, the agent algorithms. It provides baseline algorithms for learning policies of agent behavior. Code of all well-known reinforcement learning algorithms is present here[6] and here.[7]

SARSA

SARSA is the on-policy learning algorithm that we will use first. Its name comes from the tuple (s, a, r', s', a') that determines the next value of the $Q(s, a)$-function. We recall the on-policy update formula:

---

[6] https://github.com/openai/baselines

[7] https://stable-baselines.readthedocs.io/en/master/

```
# Q learning for OpenAI Gym Taxi environment
import gym
import numpy as np
import random
#Environment Setup
env = gym.make("Taxi-v2")
env.reset()
env.render()
# Q[state,action] table implementation
Q = np.zeros([env.observation_space.n, env.action_space.n])
gamma = 0.7    # discount factor
alpha = 0.2    # learning rate
epsilon = 0.1 # epsilon greedy
for episode in range(1000):
    done = False
    total_reward = 0
    current_state = env.reset()
    if random.uniform(0, 1) < epsilon:
        current_action = env.action_space.sample() # Explore
            state space
    else:
        current_action = np.argmax(Q[current_state]) # Exploit
            learned values
    while not done:
        next_state, reward, done, info = env.step(current_action)
                # invoke Gym
        if random.uniform(0, 1) < epsilon:
            next_action = env.action_space.sample() # Explore
                state space
        else:
            next_action = np.argmax(Q[next_state]) # Exploit
                learned values
        sarsa_value = Q[next_state,next_action]
        old_value = Q[current_state,current_action]

        new_value = old_value + alpha * (reward + gamma *
            sarsa_value - old_value)

        Q[current_state,current_action] = new_value
        total_reward += reward
        current_state = next_state
        current_action = next_action
    if episode % 100 == 0:
        print("Episode_{}_Total_Reward:_{}".format(episode,
            total_reward))
```

Listing 3.2 SARSA Taxi example, after [351]

$$Q(s_t, a_t) \leftarrow Q(s_t, a_t) + \alpha[r_{t+1} + \gamma Q(s_{t+1}, a_{t+1}) - Q(s_t, a_t)].$$

Listing 3.2 shows Python code for improving a policy in the Taxi world with the SARSA algorithm, adapted from [351]. The best policy found by SARSA can now

```
total_epochs, total_penalties = 0, 0
ep = 100
for _ in range(ep):
    state = env.reset()
    epochs, penalties, reward = 0, 0, 0
    done = False
    while not done:
        action = np.argmax(Q[state])
        state, reward, done, info = env.step(action)
        if reward == -10:
            penalties += 1
        epochs += 1
    total_penalties += penalties
    total_epochs += epochs
print(f"Results after {ep} episodes:")
print(f"Average timesteps per episode: {total_epochs / ep}")
print(f"Average penalties per episode: {total_penalties / ep}")
```

Listing 3.3 Evaluate the optimal SARSA Taxi result, after [351]

be used by following the best action values in the Q-table. When we evaluate the performance of our SARSA agent, we do not need to explore any more, since the best action is right there, in the Q-table.

Listing 3.3 shows the simple code to evaluate the SARSA Taxi policy. The number of illegal pickups/dropoffs is shown as penalty.

Q-Learning

Q-learning performs off-policy learning. We recall its update formula:

$$Q(s_t, a_t) \leftarrow Q(s_t, a_t) + \alpha[r_{t+1} + \gamma \max_a Q(s_{t+1}, a) - Q(s_t, a_t)].$$

Listing 3.4 shows Python code for finding a policy in the Taxi world with the Q-learning algorithm.

Again, Listing 3.3 can be used to evaluate the Q-learning Taxi policy. On average, Q-learning tends to find better policies than SARSA [659].

Exercises

1. Experiment with Taxi world. Download Gym, and perform the SARSA and Q-learning steps described before. Running ready-made SARSA and Q-learning code is nice, but you get a better idea of how the Taxi world works by tracing a few steps of the simulator by yourself. Do so and add code to allow you to print (render) each step, step by step. Watch the taxi move in its world.

```
# Q learning for OpenAI Gym Taxi environment
import gym
import numpy as np
import random
#Environment Setup
env = gym.make("Taxi-v2")
env.reset()
env.render()
# Q[state,action] table implementation
Q = np.zeros([env.observation_space.n, env.action_space.n])
gamma = 0.7    # discount factor
alpha = 0.2    # learning rate
epsilon = 0.1 # epsilon greedy
for episode in range(1000):
    done = False
    total_reward = 0
    state = env.reset()
    while not done:
        if random.uniform(0, 1) < epsilon:
            action = env.action_space.sample() # Explore state
                space
        else:
            action = np.argmax(Q[state]) # Exploit learned values
        next_state, reward, done, info = env.step(action) #
            invoke Gym
        next_max = np.max(Q[next_state])
        old_value = Q[state,action]

        new_value = old_value + alpha * (reward + gamma *
            next_max - old_value)

        Q[state,action] = new_value
        total_reward += reward
        state = next_state
    if episode % 100 == 0:
        print("Episode_{}_Total_Reward:_{}".format(episode,
            total_reward))
```

Listing 3.4 Q-learning Taxi example, after [351]

2. In Taxi world, which is better: SARSA or Q-learning? How do you know? On which criteria do you measure algorithm quality?
3. The environment is initialized randomly each time. This makes it hard to compare the two algorithms if each run is different, and it complicates debugging. Make a deterministic version of the algorithm comparison, where each starts at the same configuration.
4. How many runs do you need to do to get statistically significant results for $p < 0.05$ (if necessary, see a basic text on statistics or experiment design such as [37])?
5. Experiment with different values for ϵ, α, and γ. Which are better? Experiment with decaying values for ϵ, α, and γ.

6. Go to Gym, and look for the Mountain Car example. Compare SARSA and Q-learning. Which learns faster, and what about the solution quality?

Summary

This has been a challenging chapter, let us summmarize what we have seen. We have introduced many abstract formal concepts from reinforcement learning, to lay the ground work for understanding the algorithms in the following chapters. At the end you have been invited to experiment with the algorithms.

We started with the introduction of the concepts of agent and environment, and introduced states, actions, and rewards, which are the basis of the agent-environment interaction. In reinforcement learning the agent learns through interaction with an environment, by trial and error. Markov decision processes are a powerful and popular formalism. In processes with the Markov property, the distribution of future states depends solely on the current state, not on the states preceding it, i.e., there is no memory, which simplifies the mathematical analysis of Markov processes.

Two related central elements in reinforcement learning are the value of a state and the policy: the list of actions to be taken when in a state, defining a future behavior (strategy). Policies can be implemented as arrays, functions, mappings, or lists, and all these terms are used in the literature. The Bellman equation is a central concept in reinforcement learning. It recursively defines the value of a state based on the reward of its successor states. Bellman introduced the concept of dynamic programming for model-based reinforcement learning (planning). Other important algorithms that we covered are Temporal Difference learning, SARSA, and Q-learning for model-free reinforcement learning.

Reinforcement learning algorithms typically gradually build up information about the best actions to be taken in a state. Greedy algorithms always exploit the available information by following the action with the highest expected reward. Other algorithms may explore new or under explored actions, with a larger uncertainty, to possibly find better answers. A well-known simplistic approach is the ϵ-greedy approach, which chooses to exploit in $1 - \epsilon$ occurrences and chooses to explore in ϵ times.

On-policy learning backs up state values for the current downward behavior selection policy, off-policy learning backs up state reward values for the best policy independent of the downward behavior policy it follows. Q-learning is a model-free off-policy method.

We discussed exact and approximate methods. Exact methods are suitable for small state spaces; approximate methods are used when the state space is very large. In fact, the state space may be so large that almost all of the states that we see at test time are new, and cannot have been trained on. Approximation methods must be able to generalize well. Lookup tables are well-known exact data structures; neural networks are well-known approximation data structures.

Historical and Bibliographical Notes

The literature on reinforcement learning and games is rich and varied. This section will provide more pointers to interesting works.

Game playing programs solve reinforcement learning problems. Reinforcement learning is an old and large and rapidly expanding field. This chapter has only introduced the bare minimum. Two excellent comprehensive treatments of the field are the books by Sutton and Barto [659] and Bertsekas and Tsitsiklis [74]. Sutton and Barto divide reinforcement learning into exact tabular methods and approximate methods. This distinction maps nicely to Kahneman's categories of thinking slow and thinking fast, and Shannon and Turing's search-eval architecture.

Q-learning was introduced by Watkins [748]. Kaelbling provides a widely cited review of reinforcement learning [345]. Kaelbling has also contributed greatly to robotics, planning, and hierarchical reinforcement learning (Sect. 7.3.5). She received the 1997 IJCAI Computers and Thought award. For a review of reinforcement learning in robotics see [371].

A popular lecture series on reinforcement learning is by David Silver here.[8] Lecture notes of Sergey Levine's course on deep reinforcement learning at Berkeley are available here.[9]

---

[8] http://www0.cs.ucl.ac.uk/staff/d.silver/web/Teaching.html
[9] http://rail.eecs.berkeley.edu/deeprlcourse/

Chapter 4
Heuristic Planning

Combinatorial games have been used in AI to study reasoning and decision making since the early days of AI. An important challenge in decision making is how to search large state spaces efficiently. The methods in this book are organized around four main paradigms (and chapters). The first paradigm that we study for decision making is heuristic planning. It is a model-based paradigm. Heuristic planning uses a human-inspired approach: it is believed that when playing a board game such as Chess, most human players (1) try to look ahead a few moves in their mind, and then (2) try to assess if they like the situation that they arrive at, and play the move they liked best. Heuristic planning formalizes this concept, using a search function and a heuristic evaluation function.

A heuristic is a domain-specific rule of thumb. As a rule of thumb, it works most of the time, but not always. Being domain specific, a heuristic is not general; it only works in certain games, often exploiting a game-specific feature. Scientists, who strive for general methods, have a love-hate relationship with heuristics. They are often too successful to ignore for a specific problem, but the domain specificity limits their general applicability. Much of the efforts for generalization and feature discovery that have been so successful in deep learning (see Chap. 6) are driven by the desire to transcend domain-specific heuristics.

A first implementation of the look-ahead idea is the minimax algorithm. Minimax has been highly successful, especially since many more or less general enhancements have been developed over the years. We will cover some of these enhancements in depth, such as alpha-beta, iterative deepening, and transposition tables.

Heuristic planning has been quite successful in tactical games, such as Chess, Checkers, and Othello. Planning and heuristics are basic concepts of AI. Future chapters will introduce different paradigms, but often elements of good old heuristic planning will appear.

© Springer Nature Switzerland AG 2020
A. Plaat, *Learning to Play*, https://doi.org/10.1007/978-3-030-59238-7_4

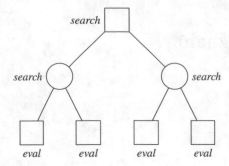

Fig. 4.1 Search-Eval architecture in a tree

Core Problems

- How can we search a large state space efficiently?
- How can search effort be directed to promising areas of the state space?

Core Concepts

- Search function
- Heuristic evaluation function
- Critical tree, alpha-beta pruning, and move ordering

First we will discuss the basis of heuristic planning: the search-eval architecture. Then we delve deeper into computing the size of the state space, and discuss basic search and evaluation functions. We continue with an analysis to find the smallest part of the state space must be traversed to find the optimal policy. Finally, we discuss search enhancements, such as alpha-beta and transposition tables, and evaluation function enhancements, such as end-game databases.

4.1 The Search-Eval Architecture

Let us start with the basic architecture of heuristic planning. Traditional Chess-style game playing programs consist of a search function and an evaluation function. Together these two functions form the search-eval architecture. The transition function P is known in these games; all successor states can be generated in each board position by following the game rules. Finding the optimal policy is done by generating all successor states and performing a look-ahead *search*. Searching the state space exhaustively is infeasible. The size of the state space of Chess is 10^{47}, too large to search fully. Therefore, after the initial state has been searched to a certain search depth, the search tree is chopped off. A heuristic evaluation function is called before the end of the game at a fixed distance from the root. See Fig. 4.1 for an illustration, where the root node is shown at the top.

The root represents the initial state s_0, the board position for which we wish to find the optimal policy, and the value. One level deeper we see two inner nodes, the children of the root, and at depth 2 we see four leaf nodes, which are not searched further, but where the evaluation function is called to determine a heuristic leaf value. In the square nodes it is the player's turn to move, and in the circle nodes the opponent's. Square nodes are max nodes; circle nodes are min nodes.

The search-eval architecture is a simple architecture. It consists of two functions: a search function and an evaluation function. The search function traverses the states one by one. It is an exact function. The evaluation function returns a heuristic value of the state on which it is called. It is an approximate function.

Note that the introduction of a heuristic evaluation function changes the range of values of the value function. The values for the full state space are determined by the terminal states, whose value can be $\{-1, 0, +1\}$ for loss, draw, and win (as viewed by the first player). A heuristic returns more values, typically in a more fine-grained range such as $[-16,000, +16,000]$. Positive values indicate an advantage for the first player; negative values indicate a disadvantage. Section 4.1.3 provides more details on evaluation functions.

Exact Search and Approximate Eval

Finding the optimal policy in a game of skill requires searching through the state space. For small state spaces, methods that traverse the states one by one are suitable; they give precise answers. They are unsuitable for large state spaces, since traversal would take too long. The alternative, approximation methods, do not traverse the state space at all. Instead, they approximate the value of a single state directly. Approximation methods use combinations of *features* of the state. Examples of features are heuristics such as material balance—which side has more and better pieces—or mobility (Sect. 4.1.3). In later chapters we will encounter other approximation methods, such as sampling in Chap. 5 and generalization by neural nets in Chap. 6.

Exact methods are precise but slow. Approximation methods are imprecise but fast. The search-eval architecture provides a framework for the two approaches to work together and achieve the best of both worlds: exact search methods traverse a part of the state space, calling the approximation methods to evaluate states at their search horizon. Together they find a good approximation of the value function without taking too long.

The goal of exact and approximate methods is the same: to determine the value function (and the optimal policy). Researchers have developed search and eval functions that together are strong enough to achieve a level of play that beats the best humans in Chess and Checkers. The first ideas for the search-eval architecture go back to Shannon [618] and Turing [701].

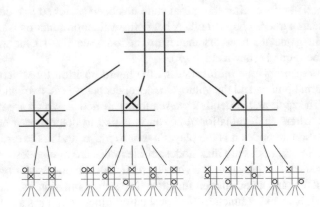

Fig. 4.2 Tic Tac Toe game tree (part)

One could ask the question why search has to be used, what is it that the heuristics miss that search has to be used at all? The reason that the search function is necessary is that the evaluation function misses game dynamics. An evaluation function provides a static assessment of a state, but cannot foresee the effects of dynamics caused by captures and other tactical play. Evaluation functions only work well in quiet (stable) positions (see also quiescence search in Sect. 4.4.2). The exercises at the end of this chapter will provide an opportunity to experiment with the search and the evaluation function to develop an understanding of the search-eval interplay.

On the other hand, the evaluation function is necessary because the search space is too large to search completely. Let us now look in more detail at the size of the state space.

4.1.1 State Space

Searching for the best action of a state is hard because the state space of possible successors (and successors of successors of . . .) is so large. Let us try to see how large it is. An often used measure to bound the size of the state space is to calculate how many legal states would be traversed if all successors are evaluated. In general, finding the exact state space size of games is a surprisingly challenging problem that has generated many interesting research papers [618, 589, 86, 6, 225, 330, 308, 326, 698].

For small games, such as Tic Tac Toe, the state space is small enough to enumerate with a computer. See Fig. 4.2 for an impression of a depth-2 tree of how the possible states are enumerated. To compute the size of the Tic Tac Toe state space, we note that there are 9 squares on the board that can be either empty, cross, or circle. Thus there are $3 \times 3 \times \ldots \times 3 = 3^9 = 19,683$ possible board configurations. However, this is an overestimation of the reachable state space, since it contains unreachable and illegal positions. When we remove illegal positions we come to 5,478 states. When we remove symmetric positions (rotations and reflections) there are only 765 positions left [585].

Beyond Tic Tac Toe, for more challenging games such as Chess or Go, calculating the precise number of legal and reachable game positions is harder. For Chess the size of the state space is often approximated as 10^{47}, and for Go on the standard 19×19 board this number is 10^{170} [6, 734, 698].[1]

Note that the state space size is different from the game tree size. The former is the game *graph*; the latter is the game *tree*. The same position from the graph can occur in many different lines of play that constitute the tree. These shared positions are called transpositions. The difference between the game graph and the game tree is large [618, 6, 527, 527]. For Tic Tac Toe an upper bound for the former is $3^9 = 19,683$ (pieces on squares), while for the latter it is $9! = 362,880$ (different full game sequences of moves).

An essential element of Chess and Checkers programs is the transposition table, a cache of positions, preventing the generation of states that have already been searched before. In Sect. 4.3.3 we will go deeper into transposition tables and their advantages.

Code

Listing 4.1 gives an example in Python code of a very small tree, with one max node (the root), three min nodes, and nine leaves. This code is meant to be easy to understand; clearly, more efficient ways of coding a tree are possible. In a short while we will provide an algorithm to compute the value of the tree by looking at the leaf values, and later on by looking at the material (pieces). This tree is shown in Fig. 4.4. The values at the leaves $(6, 1, 3, 3, \ldots)$ stand for the heuristic value of the leaves, where 6 is better than 3. The values themselves have no special meaning; they were chosen for explanatory purposes. Again, squares are max nodes, and circles are min nodes.

4.1.2 Search

How can we determine if a position is won, lost, or drawn, and how can we find the best move that leads to this outcome? In a two-player zero-sum game players are always assumed to choose moves that lead to the best successor positions. Let us assume that all values of states in the tree are viewed from the first player. If node n represents the position of which we wish to determine the value, then the value of node n is the maximum of the value of its children C_n. The value of these child nodes

---

[1] John Tromp published in 2016 that the exact number of legal Go states is 208168199 381979984 69947863 33448627 7028652 24538845 3054842 56394568 209274196 127380153 78525648 45169851 9643907 25991601 5628128 54608988 831442712 971531931 75577366 20397247 064840935. Tromp used advanced combinatorial methods in his calculations [697].

```
# a small tree, to be searched by the minimax algorithm
leaf_node1 = {'type': 'LEAF', 'value': 1, 'material': 3}
leaf_node2 = {'type': 'LEAF', 'value': 2, 'material': 4}
leaf_node3 = {'type': 'LEAF', 'value': 3, 'material': 2}
leaf_node4 = {'type': 'LEAF', 'value': 4, 'material': 9}
leaf_node5 = {'type': 'LEAF', 'value': 5, 'material': 1}
leaf_node6 = {'type': 'LEAF', 'value': 6, 'material': 7}
min_node1 = {'type': 'MIN', 'children' : [leaf_node6, leaf_node1,
      leaf_node3], 'material': 2}
min_node2 = {'type': 'MIN', 'children' : [leaf_node3, leaf_node4,
      leaf_node2], 'material': 7}
min_node3 = {'type': 'MIN', 'children' : [leaf_node1, leaf_node6,
      leaf_node5], 'material': 1}
max_node1 = {'type': 'MAX', 'children' : [min_node1, min_node2,
      min_node3], 'material': 3}

root = max_node1
```

Listing 4.1 Small tree code

is determined analogously, although here the moves are made by our opponent, who chooses positions that will minimize the outcome for us. Next it is our move again, and we choose the position that maximizes our winning probability. This alternating of maximizing and minimizing is the reason the procedure is called *minimax*.[2]

In Fig. 4.3 a Tic Tac Toe tree is drawn with values. Figure 4.4 shows a more abstract minimax tree, where nodes are drawn as squares (max) and circles (min). By following the values we can see how the values of the nodes are determined.

Listing 4.2 gives example code for the minimax algorithm. The minimax function will determine the value of a node by taking the minimum of the value of the children of the min nodes, and the maximum of the values of the children of the max nodes. In the case of the tree in Listing 4.1, the value of nodes min_node1 and min_node3 is both 1, and the value of min_node2 is 2. The maximum of 1 and 2 is 2, so the minimax value of the root is 2.

Search Tree

The minimax procedure recursively traverses the entire game tree (Listing 4.2). Minimax is a *backtracking* procedure. It starts at the root, and does a depth-first traversal of the tree by calling itself recursively for each child node. When a child has been searched, it backtracks up (returning its value) and searches down the next child, going down-up-down-up through the tree. Minimax is a trial-and-error procedure,

---

[2] Note that minimaxing is a kind of self-play. Since our opponent uses the same algorithm as we do, in minimax we play against ourselves; our opponent is just as smart as we are. This kind of minimax self-play is a different kind of self-play than the one in Chap. 7, where a self-play loop is used to train a neural network evaluation function to learn to play a game from scratch.

```
INF = 99999

def eval(n):
    return n['value']


def minimax(n):
    if n['type'] == 'LEAF':
        return eval(n)
    elif n['type'] == 'MAX':
        g = -INF
        for c in n['children']:
            g = max(g, minimax(c))
    elif n['type'] == 'MIN':
        g = INF
        for c in n['children']:
            g = min(g, minimax(c))
    else:
        error("Wrong_node_type")
    return g

print("Minimax_value:_", minimax(root))
```

Listing 4.2 Minimax code

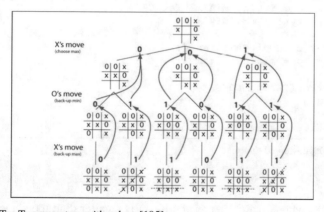

Fig. 4.3 Tic Tac Toe game tree with values [195]

as all reinforcement learning procedures are. The trial element is trivial: try all successors. The error part is the backup rule. Minimax does not explore; all learning is on-policy. The values that are backed up are those of the nodes that were selected.

The nodes that are actually traversed during a search procedure are referred to as the *search tree*. The tree version of the full state space is also known as the game tree. Since minimax recursively traverses all nodes in the state space, the search tree is identical to the game tree. In the rest of this book we will see many examples

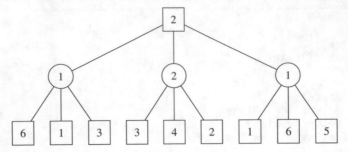

Fig. 4.4 Minimax tree of Listing 4.2

```
INF = 99999

def heuristic_eval(n):
    return n['material']

def minimax(n, d):
    if d <= 0:
        return heuristic_eval(n)
    elif n['type'] == 'MAX':
        g = -INF
        for c in n['children']:
            g = max(g, minimax(c, d-1))
    elif n['type'] == 'MIN':
        g = INF
        for c in n['children']:
            g = min(g, minimax(c, d-1))
    else:
        error("Wrong node type")
    return g

print("Minimax value: ", minimax(root, 2))
```

Listing 4.3 Depth-limited minimax

of procedures whose search tree is significantly smaller than the game tree while they still are able to find the value of the root. Minimax does a full-depth full-width expansion of the game tree. For regular trees, where all nodes have the same number of children, the number of leaves of the game tree is w^d, where w is the width of the nodes (the number of children of a node) and d is the depth of the tree. For the tree in Figure 4.4 the width is 3 and the depth is 2, so the number of leaves is $3^2 = 9$. The size of the game tree is exponential in the depth parameter, and is dominated by the number of leaves. A useful approximation of the size of the tree is therefore w^d, and also of the running time of the minimax procedure, since it visits every node.

Now that we have looked at the search function, it is time to look at the heuristic evaluation function.

4.1.3 Eval

Calling the minimax function on a Chess position, whose game tree is of size 10^{47}, would take too long to compute its value.[3] In order to reduce the size of the search tree, the search depth can be reduced.[4] To do so, even the earliest Chess and Checkers programs (Turing, Samuel) used a heuristic evaluation function as an approximation of the true value of a position. The heuristic is based on domain knowledge, provided by domain experts. In Chess and Checkers, the most important heuristic is material balance (the number and the importance of the pieces on the board).

Instead of traversing the tree to the depth where the game ends due to an end-game position, the heuristics create artificial leaves, at a much shallower search depth. The deeper search is artificially limited, and a heuristic is called to statically evaluate whatever position happens to occur at that depth.

A basic assumption of heuristic planning is that deeper searches provide better approximations of the optimal policy and the value of the root. Listing 4.3 adds depth limiting to our Python code of minimax. New is parameter d. The parameter is decremented in the recursive call of the function. The eval function no longer uses the score at the leaves, but takes a heuristic value of the node whenever the depth parameter is 0. The heuristic eval in the example code is quite straightforward; it uses the material value of the node (see Listing 4.1).

Domain Knowledge

A heuristic is a function that encodes domain-specific knowledge. To be useful in practice, a heuristic must be such that it can be computed efficiently. For example, in Chess, having two pawns is better than having one pawn, and the queen is more valuable than the rook. For many years heuristic evaluation functions have been a central piece of combinatorial search. In fact, they are so important that the field has been called heuristic planning. (See, for example, the title of Judea Pearl's seminal work [511].)

A heuristic evaluation function in general takes the form

$$h(s) = c_1 \times f_1(s) + c_2 \times f_2(s) + c_3 \times f_3(s) + \ldots + c_n \times f_n(s),$$

where $h(s)$ is the heuristic function of the state, $f_i(s)$ are the feature terms such as material balance, mobility, or center control, and c_i are the coefficients, the weights that signal the importance that a feature has in the total evaluation function.

In Chess and Checkers material balance is the dominant factor in the strength of a position. For this reason, the heuristic evaluation function of Listing 4.3 uses the material field of the nodes defined in Listing 4.1.

---

[3] Even if node evaluation would take a very fast one nanosecond, it would still take 10^{38} seconds, or 3×10^{30} years, which is about 10^{20} times the estimated age of the known universe.

[4] Also the width of the tree can be reduced. With forward pruning fewer children are expanded at inner nodes. See Sect. 4.3.5.

Heuristic evaluation functions are linear combinations of features. A typical Chess evaluation function consists of the following features: material, mobility, king safety, and center control. The evaluation function is static (it applies to a single position). Tactical aspects such as captures are taken care of by the search. To search as many positions as possible, speed of evaluation is important. For that reason heuristics are often optimized for speed, not for accuracy.

Heuristic Approximations

Heuristic evaluations are, in almost all games, crude approximations of the value of the states. They capture static elements of a position, and lack insight into the dynamics. Achieving good play requires extra work either on heuristics or on understanding dynamics with search algorithms. In reinforcement learning theory the two approaches (exact planning and function approximation) are often treated as mutually exclusive approaches. In most board games, however, they are studied together out of necessity, due to the low quality of play of heuristic evaluation functions without search, and conversely the low quality of play of search without heuristic evaluation functions.

A further problem with the heuristic values is that their unreliability is not smoothed in any way by the minimaxing. Minimax applies a sequence of max operations, which tends to exacerbate noise or errors in the heuristic estimates. This effect, where deep minimax searches of noisy values enlarge the noise, is called search pathology (since deeper searches are supposed to give more reliable results). Nau, Pearl, and others have studied search pathology [479, 510, 44, 760, 573]. In practice, search pathology does not occur frequently. In any case, alternatives to minimax have been proposed that back up probability distributions instead of single point values (Sect. 4.3.8).

In tournament Chess and Checkers programs the heuristic evaluation function is a highly advanced piece of code, using many features. The features are typically manually chosen, and manually optimized and tuned. This feature engineering is quite labor intensive. The search space is large, and finding the precise state at which unwanted behavior occurs may be difficult. It may even be unclear if solving a problem in one part of the play does not introduce a weakness in another part. To achieve world championship level, the teams behind Chinook and Deep Blue spent years refining their heuristics.

A further downside of a heuristic is, of course, that it is domain specific; e.g., a piece of Chess code that assigns the queen 900 points is of no use in Checkers, which does not have queens.

Heuristics in Practice

Today, many Chess programs are open source, including some of the top programs, such as Stockfish [559].[5] To get an idea of just how extensive current state-of-the-art

---

[5] The name Stockfish may seem strange for a Chess program. The authors Romstad and Costalba state that it reflects their two countries : "produced in Norway and cooked in Italy."

heuristic evaluation functions have become, you may want to have a look at the Stockfish source at GitHub, which can be found here.[6]

Stockfish has a conventional evaluation function with manually designed features and manually tuned weights. In other games evaluation functions based on machine learning have been successful, such as Othello (Logistello [114]), Backgammon (Neurogammon [673]), and of course Go. Despite some effort to automate tuning of weights by Samuel [577] and the Deep Blue team [309], in Chess and Checkers most programs use manual evaluation functions. Some papers describe success in evolving coefficients of manual features [161], and in AlphaGo both the features themselves and the coefficients are learned [623, 626, 625]. (Table 6.5 in Sect. 6.4.8 lists game playing programs that use machine learning.)

Machine learning evaluation functions have the advantage of being more general and easier to debug. At the end of this chapter we will revisit machine learning evaluation enhancements. But first, we will explore in more depth how the minimax function works.

4.2 State Space Complexity

The state space of two-agent zero-sum perfect-information games has a minimax structure. This structure follows directly from the fact that the value of a state is determined by the value of the best successor state (since we assume that rational players always play the best move). The minimax state space is redundant; only a small part of the state space (the optimal policy) defines the value of the initial state. We will now do a theoretical analysis to find the size of the optimal policy. This analysis will show us that there is an exponential amount of redundancy in the tree, which allows us to create much more efficient search algorithms.

Width and Depth

Let us start with a regular fixed-width fixed-depth tree. The size of this tree is dominated by the number of leaf nodes, which is w^d for width w and depth d. In Fig. 4.4 we see a tree with $w = 3$ and $d = 2$ (the root node is depth 0).

Critical Path

Figure 4.5 shows a different minimax tree, $w = 2$, $d = 3$, with leaf values, and values at the inner nodes. Recall that the leaf values are typically integer values from a heuristic score, for example in the range $[-16,000, +16,000]$. As usual, the root is a max node; its value is the maximum of its child values, and the children of the root

---

[6] https://github.com/official-stockfish/Stockfish

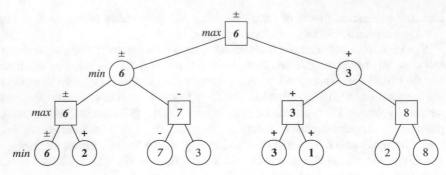

Fig. 4.5 ± *Critical path*, **+ max solution tree**, *- min solution tree*

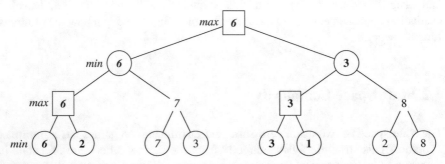

Fig. 4.6 Max solution tree: upper bound determined by all children at max nodes, a single child at min nodes

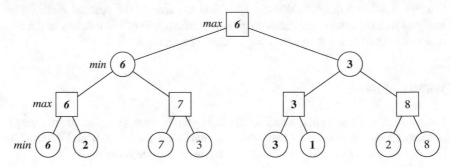

Fig. 4.7 Min solution tree: lower bound determined by all children at min nodes, a single child at max nodes

are min nodes, whose value is the minimum of their child values, as can be seen in the example tree. The path of bold, italic number 6s is called the *critical path,* the path of nodes whose value is equal to the value of the root.

Solution tree	Value	# children at max node	# children at min node
Max	upper bound	all	1
Min	lower bound	1	all

Table 4.1 Solution trees and bounds

Critical/solution trees
Critical tree = max solution tree $\cup$ min solution tree
Critical path = max solution tree $\cap$ min solution tree

Table 4.2 Critical tree and path

Critical Tree

We will now analyze the lower bound of the size of the tree that needs to be expanded to determine the value of the root.

As we shall see, not all nodes in the minimax tree play a role in determining the value at the root. In fact, only a small fraction of the tree nodes do so. Let us try to construct the smallest possible subtree that defines the minimax value. By the definition of the maximum function that takes the highest of its inputs, at max nodes, the highest child determines the value of the parent node. All other children are unnecessary; they are noncritical nodes that are "dominated" by their critical sibling. Likewise, at min nodes, only the lowest-valued child determines the value of the node.

So, it would seem that we only need to expand a single child to know the value of a node. There is a complication, however. If we only expand one child, then we do not know for certain what the value of a node is. Even if it is the critical child, since we have only seen one child so far we do not yet know if there is another, better child. At a max parent, the single expanded child creates a *lower bound* on the minimax value, since expansions of subsequent children can only increase the value upwards. Likewise, a min node whose children have been partly expanded has an upper bound on its final value, since subsequent expansion can only lower the value further.

A partly expanded max node defines a lower bound on the minimax value. Lower bounds of *min* nodes, however, require all children of that min node to be expanded (since, if it were partly expanded, then expansion of another child could lower the value further, and the lower bound evidently was not a lower bound).

Likewise, a partly expanded min node is an upper bound on the min node value. Upper bounds of *max* nodes, however, require all children of that max node to be expanded.

Now we have enough information to construct the smallest tree that defines the minimax value. If we wish to have an upper bound at the root node, then we need a tree where at least *one* child of the min nodes is present, and *all* children of all max nodes are present. Figure 4.6 shows such a tree. This tree is called a max solution tree in the literature, the tree determining an upper bound [164, 522]. In a max solution tree, all children at the max nodes are included, and one child at the min nodes.

Conversely, if we wish to have a lower bound at the root node, then we have to construct a tree where at least one child of all max nodes is present, and all children of all min nodes. Figure 4.7 shows such a tree, which is called a min solution tree, a tree determining a lower bound in a minimax tree. In a min solution tree, all children at the min nodes are included, and one child at the max nodes (Table 4.1).

The minimax value of a position is, of course, defined by two solution trees of equal value: one min solution tree defining a lower bound of the same value as the upper bound defined by its max solution tree. The intersection of the min solution tree and the max solution tree is the critical path. Figure 4.5 contains such an intersection of a min solution tree and a max solution tree. The union of the two solution trees is called the critical tree, or the proof tree (see Table 4.2). It is the smallest tree that proves the value of the position.

The critical path is the optimal policy of optimal actions in each state, the critical tree proves its value. An optimal algorithm to find the optimal policy would search no more than the critical tree. The critical tree proves that the minimax value is not less than the value of the min solution tree, and not larger than the value of the max solution tree. Every algorithm that wishes to find the minimax value has to traverse at least this critical tree, otherwise it has not seen enough of the tree to determine its value for certain [369].

The size (or rather, the number of leaf nodes) of a max rooted max solution tree is $w^{\lceil d/2 \rceil}$, or the square root of the size of the minimax tree, where $\lceil x \rceil$ rounds up x to the nearest integer. The number of leaves of a max rooted min solution tree is $w^{\lfloor d/2 \rfloor}$. The reason that the size of the solution trees is determined by *half* of the search depth is interesting to see. As the minimax tree grows down from the root the number of nodes is multiplied at each depth by w, but in a solution tree it is intermittently multiplied by 1, and then by w, and by 1, and by w, and so on. If w_d is the branching factor at depth d, then the number of leaves of the depth-3 minimax tree of Fig. 4.5 is $2_1 \times 2_2 \times 2_3 = 8$. The number of leaves of the max solution tree of Fig. 4.6 is $2_1 \times 1_2 \times 2_3 = 4$. The number of leaves of the min solution tree of Fig. 4.7 is $1_1 \times 2_2 \times 1_3 = 2$.

Likewise, the number of leaves of the critical tree (the union of the two solution trees) is $w^{\lceil d/2 \rceil} + w^{\lfloor d/2 \rfloor} - 1$, the square root of the size of the minimax tree, $\sqrt{w^d}$. Thus, the size of the critical tree that defines the minimax value is the square root of the size of the minimax tree.

In order to determine the value of a minimax tree with 1,000,000 leaves, at least 1000 leaves have to be examined. A bad algorithm would expand a million nodes, an optimally good algorithm a thousand. In the same time that minimax would search to depth 5, an optimal algorithm would search to depth 10, double the depth.

In Listing 4.2 we have seen an $O(w^d)$ algorithm for traversing the tree and finding the minimax value.

Name	Principle	Applicability	Effectiveness
alpha-beta	backward pruning	all minimax games	$w^d \rightarrow \sqrt{w^d}$
iterative deepening	iterate search depth	with TT: move ordering	helps alpha-beta
transposition table	cache of states	with ID: move ordering	helps alpha-beta
null window	alpha-beta cutoffs	all minimax games	more cutoffs
forward pruning	variable width	domain specific	variable
capture moves	ordering	games with captures	good
killer moves, HH	ordering	domain specific	good
backup rule	probability	imperfect info	imperfect info feasible

Table 4.3 Search enhancements

Conclusion

We have now looked in depth at the part of the state space that defines the minimax value. It is now time to look at enhancements to the basic minimax algorithm.

In Sect. 4.3.1 we will describe alpha-beta, a best-case $\sqrt{w^d}$ algorithm for traversing the tree to find the minimax value.

4.3 Search Enhancements

The previous sections provided us with the basic building blocks for heuristic planning in games, with the search-eval architecture and the minimax algorithm. We have seen that theoretically it is possible to find the best move with a thousand node expansions, where minimax would do a million. We will now discuss search enhancement methods with which we can approach optimal efficiency.

Minimax is a fixed-width fixed-depth algorithm that is too inefficient to achieve high performance. The heuristic function is domain dependent. In the enhancements in this section and the next, we will see a trend towards variable-depth search and generalization of the evaluation function (foreshadowing a bridge to the next chapter on adaptive sampling).

An important role in search enhancements is played by the alpha-beta algorithm, which uses a powerful exponential pruning mechanism.

Table 4.3 gives an overview of the search enhancements that are presented in this section, to help you find your way in the myriad of terms and approaches. The effectiveness of the approaches depends to a large extent on the domain, hence the qualitative terms. The enhancements are presented in the order shown in the table.

Most search enhancements are related to alpha-beta, and improve its performance. The alpha-beta algorithm is the core of decades of high-efficiency game playing search. The difference between the best case and the worst case performance of alpha-beta is large, $\sqrt{w^d}$ versus w^d. This best case is achieved on well-ordered trees, where the best successor positions are the first that are expanded. On well-ordered trees alpha-beta can find many cutoffs. (On badly ordered trees it performs as badly as minimax.) Many of the search enhancements that we will now discuss have been developed to improve the successor ordering, in order to improve the performance of alpha-beta.

We will now start with the alpha-beta algorithm.

4.3.1 Alpha-Beta

Listing 4.4 shows the alpha-beta algorithm. Let us see how alpha-beta works, to understand how it finds the true minimax value without searching the entirety of the tree.

Alpha-Beta Window

Alpha-beta maintains a *window* on the value of a position. The window consists of two bounds, named α and β. The α and β bounds together form lower and upper bounds on the possible value of the position, or node, that the algorithm searches.

At the root node, alpha-beta starts out with an $\langle \alpha, \beta \rangle$-window with the widest possible window, which we write as $\langle -\infty, +\infty \rangle$.[7] Alpha-beta is a recursive algorithm to find the minimax value of a node. In order to find this value of a node, it calls itself recursively, to find the values of the children of the node in order to compute its own value. Each call to alpha-beta uses the latest (tightest) version of the window. The window for recursive calls is updated with the results of the child nodes. When, at a node n, the window collapses (the bounds become equal) the subtree below n does not have to be explored since then the value of node n is known, and thus the search of n is stopped. Alpha-beta is then said to *cut off* the search of the remaining children of n. The alpha-beta cutoff is the central mechanism to achieve the $w^d \rightarrow \sqrt{w^d}$ best-case potential.

Alpha-Beta Example

We will now look in detail at the code,[8] to see how alpha-beta traverses the same example tree of Fig. 4.8.[9] The root r is a max node, the level below the root are two min nodes, representing the two child positions of the player. Each of these has two

---

[7] Note that ∞ is shorthand for a number outside the range of numbers returned by the evaluation function. Also note that evaluation functions are assumed to return integer values.

[8] You will note that the code for the max and the min node is quite similar. A clever reformulation exists, NegaMax, that switches the point of view each time that it is called [217]. NegaMax has no code duplication and is functionally equivalent. The switching of sides complicates reasoning about trees, bounds, and values somewhat, and we do not use it in this book.

[9] The code shown is the so-called fail-soft version of alpha-beta, a version that may return values outside the $\langle \alpha, \beta \rangle$-window. This may seem odd, but is actually quite useful later on, when

```
INF = 99999

def alphabeta(n, a, b, d):
    if d <= 0:
        return eval(n) # return n['value']
    elif n['type'] == 'MAX':
        g = -INF
        for c in n['children']:
            g = max(g, alphabeta(c, a, b, d-1))
            a = max(a, g) # update alpha
            if a >= b:
                break # beta cutoff, g>=b
    elif n['type'] == 'MIN':
        g = INF
        for c in n['children']:
            g = min(g, alphabeta(c, a, b, d-1))
            b = min(b, g) # update beta
            if a >= b:
                break # alpha cutoff, a>=g
    return g

print("Minimax_value:_", alphabeta(root, -INF, INF, depth))
```

Listing 4.4 Alpha-beta

child positions (again max nodes) for which the opponent moves. These are leaf positions (it is a very small tree). The leaves have values 3, 6, 2, ·. Figure 4.8 shows an example tree and a detailed example run. Working through the example in the caption of the figure will show you how an alpha-beta cutoff works.

In this tiny example tree, only one node was cut off, but in larger trees, the maximum gain of alpha-beta is to cut off $w^d - \sqrt{w^d}$ leaf nodes. (So, in a $w = 10, d = 6$ tree with 1,000,000 leaves, 999,000 leaves can be cut off, searching only a critical tree of 1000 leaves. If minimax can see important capture moves three moves in advance, alpha-beta, in the best case, can see them six moves in advance, with the same computational effort.) Typical high-performance game playing programs come close to the best case; at the majority of the nodes (more than 90%) the first child is also the best child [416, 586].

Alpha-Beta Cutoff

In addition to the walk-through in the figure we will explain how alpha-beta cut-offs work intuitively. The concept of *cutoff* can be understood intuitively as follows. Let us assume we are the max player searching the value of a max node (as in Fig. 4.8).

---

we introduce narrow-window searches. The fail-hard version always returns a value inside the $\langle \alpha, \beta \rangle$-window, or equal to α or β.

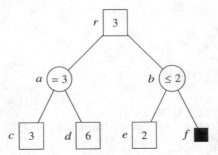

Fig. 4.8 Alpha-beta starts at the root, with a window of $\langle -\infty, +\infty \rangle$. In other words, alpha-beta is called with $n = r$, $a = -\infty$, $b = +\infty$. At the root it expands the max node's first child a. Node a is of type min, and min node a's first child, leaf node c is visited. Node c is a leaf node with value 3. Coming out of the recursion back in node a alpha-beta updates variables $g = \min(+\infty, 3)$ and $b = \min(+\infty, 3)$ to 3. It expands the second child of min node a, leaf node d. This node d is expanded with window $\langle -\infty, 3 \rangle$, a tighter beta bound. Its value is 6, coming back in a, alpha-beta updates the variables $g = \min(3, 6)$ and $b = \min(3, 6)$ to 3, finds no other children at a, and returns $g = 3$ to r. Back at the root r, alpha-beta updates $g = \max(-\infty, 3)$ and $a = \max(-\infty, 3)$ to 3. There is another child b, which it expands with window $\langle 3, +\infty \rangle$; it expands its first child b, finding leaf node e. The value of 2 is returned to parent b, who updates the variables $g = \min(+\infty, 2)$ and $b = \min(+\infty, 2)$ to 2. Now the if statement is tested and $3 \geq 2$ is true, so the break statement breaks out of the loop, returning the value of $g = 2$ to parent r, cutting off the expansion of child f. At parent r, the root, the variables are updated to $g = \max(3, 2)$ and $a = \max(3, 2)$ to 3. Alpha-beta is ready and returns $g = 3$ to the caller as the minimax value n *without having expanded all nodes of the tree.*

As we perform our look-ahead, we encounter child positions. Until all children have been searched, the values of the children seen so far provide a bound on the final value. In our case this intermediate value is a lower bound (since we are in a max node our value can only increase with each child value that comes in). In alpha-beta, this lower bound is recorded in the α value of the $\langle \alpha, \beta \rangle$-window as soon as the first subtree of the root has been searched. The α-value thus increases from $-\infty$ to the value of the best child c_α that we have seen so far. In the example tree, this c_α is node a, the first child of the root r. The alpha-beta window at root r, after a has been searched, is $\langle 3, +\infty \rangle$. So far, so good.

Now, we continue the search with child b with window $\langle 3, +\infty \rangle$. The positions that our opponent searches can only lower the values it finds, since our opponent is the minimizer. Thus, in min nodes, the intermediate search results are upper bounds. In min nodes, the search results update β of the $\langle \alpha, \beta \rangle$-window. As soon as the opponent finds child positions c_β equal to or below that good move c_α that we found in the previous paragraph, the search at our opponent's node can be stopped, since its remaining children cannot influence *our* value anymore. In the example this child is node e, whose value 2 causes the β bound to fall below α. For us, the remaining child positions have become irrelevant as soon as it has been proven that their min parent's value will be lower than the good move c_α. *The subsequent children of the min node are said to be cut off by the good child $c_\alpha = a$ of the max node that we found earlier and the strong reply move $c_\beta = e$ that the opponent found.*

After I have found a strong move $c_\alpha = a$, then a strong opponent's move $c_\beta = e$ can cut off the search for further opponent's moves. The reason is that my opponent's move $c_\beta = e$ is so strong (bad for the first player) that searching further for other children of b that are even worse for me is useless, since I will no longer play b, but choose instead to play my own strong move $c_\alpha = a$.

In considering my own move, as soon as I have identified a strong enough reply by my opponent to one of my options, I move on, cutting off the search for other replies to that option. If I have not yet found a strong counter-reply by my opponent, I continue searching for one in this option. If there is no strong reply, then I am happy, since I have found a position where my opponent has no strong replies to my move.

Move Ordering

Cutoffs are possible due to the intermeshing of maximization and minimization. The impact of alpha-beta on the development of early Chess and Checkers programs was large. Through this simple algorithmic trick programs could search twice as deep as before, achieving a much better quality of play.

It should be noted, however, that there is a catch. Alpha-beta is a left-to-right algorithm, and it can perform cutoffs only if the trees are well ordered. The example tree in Fig. 4.8 is well ordered: the root has two subtrees, one with value 3 and one with value ≤ 2. It is well ordered since the highest (best) child occurs first. If the subtrees had been ordered the other way around, then node b would have been expanded first, and leaf f would have been expanded, along with all other leaves, arriving at the same minimax value of 3. The ordering of successor positions does not influence the value of the position, but it does influence the efficiency with which alpha-beta can compute the value. Alpha-beta's worst case time complexity is still w^d.

There is always an ordering of the leaves on which alpha-beta achieves the best-case bound; this tree is called a perfectly ordered tree. In a perfectly ordered tree all children of max nodes are ordered high to low, and all children of min nodes are ordered low to high (or to be more precise, all that is needed is that the first child is the best child). Consequently, much research in move ordering heuristics has been performed. Two of the best-known heuristics are iterative deepening and transposition tables, which we will discuss next.

4.3.2 Iterative Deepening

Iterative deepening is a search enhancement that, together with transposition tables, can achieve excellent move ordering, allowing alpha-beta to achieve high efficiency. A basic assumption of the search-eval architecture is that looking deeper improves the quality of the answer. A shallow search provides a rough estimate of value and

```
def iterativedeepening(n):
    d = 1
    while not keypressed() and not time_is_up():
        f = minimax(n, d)
        d = d + 1
    return f
```

Listing 4.5 Iterative deepening

best move; a deeper search provides a better estimate. Likewise, a shallow search provides an approximation of the ordering for a deeper search.

In all practical applications of reinforcement learning, there is a time limit to the search. In typical Chess tournaments a move has to be produced every three minutes on average. The more time we have, the deeper we can search, and the better the playing strength will be. Thus it would be useful if we could stop our search at *any time* and produce a good answer [273]. Iterative deepening provides a solution. Instead of performing one large search to a certain fixed search depth d, iterative deepening performs a sequence of quick searches, starting with depth 0, increasing to depth d. It may seem wasteful to perform these $d - 1$ shallow searches, but due to the exponential nature of the search, the shallow searches take negligible time.

Iterative deepening is a technique to transform a standard fixed-depth depth-first search algorithm into an anytime algorithm, that can be stopped at any time and still have a useful answer available.[10]

In addition, when the search results (especially the best moves) of all the shallow searches are retained in a large cache (the transposition table), the move ordering of each subsequent $d + 1$ search will benefit from the shallower d searches.

Thus, iterative deepening has two advantages: (1) it transforms alpha-beta into an anytime algorithm, and, together with transposition tables, (2) it improves the move ordering for alpha-beta, increasing its efficiency.

The code of iterative deepening is simple; see Listing 4.5. A disadvantage of iterative deepening is that it expands more nodes: all node searches before the final interation are unnecessary. However, because of the exponential nature of the search space, this number is small compared with the nodes searched in the final iteration. Also, the search time of each iteration is difficult to predict in practice, since the size of subtrees is unknown beforehand. When an anytime algorithm is necessary, such as in a time-controlled tournament, the negligible extra time for the earlier iterations is traded off for the certainty of having a best move, when one is needed.

Though useful by itself, iterative deepening really shines when combined with transposition tables, since then it can improve move ordering for alpha-beta signifi-cantly.

---

[10] Note that for anytime behavior also the alpha-beta searcher must now be interruptible, and check for key-pressed or time-up conditions—not shown in the alpha-beta code in the listing.

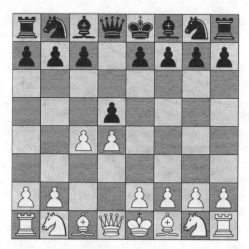

Fig. 4.9 Transposition: c4,d5,d4 or d4,d5,c4?

4.3.3 Transposition Tables

In many games there are positions that can be reached through multiple parent positions. For example, the position in Fig. 4.9 can be reached through the move sequence d4,d5,c4 but also through the move sequence c4,d5,d4. The position has two parent positions (d4,d5) and (c4,d5). Arriving at the same position through a different move sequence is called a transposition. So (c4,d5,d4) is a transposition for the state that we get by playing (d4,d5,c4). It is an identical state with a different move history.[11]

In Chess, the state space is not a tree but a graph. Searching a transposition is wasteful, and exponentially so. Tree traversal algorithms such as minimax and alpha-beta can be transformed to algorithms that traverse a graph efficiently through the addition of a cache or table. Such a cache or table is called a transposition table. The table stores positions and their search results, in order to prevent transpositions from being searched. Before a new node is searched, the graph algorithm checks if the search result is already known in the table. Search results can be stored in lookup tables (hash tables or dictionaries). For board games often the fast Zobrist hash function is used [780]. In Python, the Dictionary type is convenient to implement a transposition table.

The table entries typically contain an identification key, the search depth, the value, a best move, and an indication of whether the value is a bound or a full value. Entries are typically less than 100 bytes. A program that searches 100,000 nodes per second would need to store 1.8 GB to store the entire search tree for a three minute search. Typical cache replacement schemes such as least-recently-used or depth-first are often used when collisions occur.

---

[11] To transpose means to exchange.

Listing 4.6 shows how transposition table results are used to transform a tree search algorithms into a graph search algorithm. Two italic lines of code are added to the code. The two lines show basic versions of the use of lookup and store functions, returning the search value g, and the best move. In a real program more elements would be added. For one, real programs would use a null window variant of alpha-beta (to be discussed soon). The search results that are stored would be upper bounds, lower bounds, or minimax values. Note that in real programs not only the values of the best successor state would be stored, but also the actions leading to them. In this way, information on the *best action* in a shallower search depth is acquired, which will greatly help with move ordering to produce many alpha-beta cutoffs. Thus, even when a transpostion lookup for the necessary search depth fails to find an entry of the required depth, and a search ensues, this search will still use the best-move information stored in the table for the shallower search depth, in order to improve the tree ordering of the deeper alpha-beta search. For this reason, the Listing shows how best-move ttbm is inserted into the list of children, so that it is searched first.

Apart from the efficiency improvement due to the prevention of duplicate search of transposed states, it is these best actions of shallower searches that make transposition tables so important. In an iterative deepening search, at all inner nodes best action information will be present in the transposition table. In most situations search values and best moves are moderately stable between iterations: the previous search depth is a good approximation of the current search depth. The consequence is that the best action information from the transposition table from a previous search depth will frequently be the best action for a deeper search depth and therefore cause an alpha-beta cutoff at inner nodes.[12]

Together, iterative deepening and transposition tables allow for the search of a well-ordered tree and an efficient alpha-beta search, approaching the best case of alpha-beta in practice [592]. Note that this is an empirical finding, as pathological counter-examples can be constructed, but do not appear to occur frequently in practice.

4.3.4 *Null Window Search

Before we go on to more heuristics in the next section, we will look further into enhancements based on the alpha-beta window. The window is a powerful concept, with which more efficiency can be gained. The move ordering can be improved in order to approach a perfectly ordered tree, improving the number of cutoffs that alpha-beta can find. There is another way to achieve more cutoffs, and that is through null windows.

This is a starred section (*) that covers advanced material. If you only want to follow the big picture then this can be skipped (or skimmed). For an understanding of how heuristic planning can achieve good performance, to get an appreciation of the

---

[12] The opposite situation, where shallow searches are not good predictors for deeper searches, is considered to be pathological. See the works of Nau, Pearl, and others [479, 510, 44, 760, 573].

```
INF = 99999

def ttalphabeta(n, a, b, d):
    (hit, g, ttbm) = lookup(n, d)
            # find in transposition table for depth d
    if hit: # if not hit at this depth, still use tt-bestmove
        return g
    if d <= 0:
        g = eval(n) # return n['value']
        bm = ()
    elif n['type'] == 'MAX':
        g = -INF
        for c in ttbm+n['children']: # search tt-bestmove first
            gc = ttalphabeta(c, a, b, d-1)
            if gc > g:
                bm = c # save best-move information
                g = gc
            a = max(a, g) # update alpha
            if a >= b:
                break # beta cutoff, g>=b
    elif n['type'] == 'MIN':
        g = INF
        for c in ttbm+n['children']:  # search tt-bestmove first
            gc = ttalphabeta(c, a, b, d-1)
            if gc < g:
                bm = c # save best-move information
                g = gc
            b = min(b, g) # update beta
            if a >= b:
                break # alpha cutoff, a>=g
    store(n, g, d, bm)  # store in transpostition table
    return g

print("Minimax value: ", ttalphabeta(root, -INF, INF, depth))
```

Listing 4.6 Use of transposition table

amount of complexity and effort that went into current state-of-the-art game playing programs, please read on.

Narrow Windows, Bounds, and Solution Trees

Alpha-beta searches with a wide window, which causes cutoffs at internal nodes, returning the minimax value at the root node. The tighter the window, the more cutoffs. So far we have only considered alpha-beta as a routine that searches with a wide window at the root. At most inner nodes, alpha-beta is called with a tighter search window. Let us have a closer look at what happens: how much of the tree is searched, and how should we interpret a return value that falls outside the alpha-beta

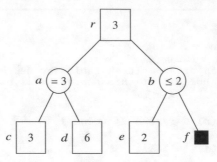

Fig. 4.10 Alpha-beta starts at the root with narrow window $\langle -\infty, 2 \rangle$. In other words, alpha-beta is called with $n = r, a = -\infty, b = 2$. At the root it expands first child a. Node a's first child, leaf node c, is visited. Coming out of the recursion back in node a, alpha-beta updates variables $g = \min(+\infty, 3)$ to 3 and $b = \min(2, 3)$ to 2. No cutoff happens since $-\infty \not\geq 3$. We then expand the second child of min node a, leaf node d. Its value is 6; coming back in a, alpha-beta updates the variables $g = \min(3, 6)$ and $b = \min(3, 6)$ to 3, finds no other children at a, and returns $g = 3$ to r. Back at the root r, alpha-beta updates $g = \max(-\infty, 3)$ and $a = \max(-\infty, 3)$ to 3. Now a cutoff happens, since $3 \geq 2$. The root returns the value 3, a lower bound since the max node has unexpanded children. Let us also try a second narrow window, this time with a high window: $\langle 4, +\infty \rangle$. At the root, node a and leaf c are expanded, which returns 3 at node a. There a cutoff happens, since $4 \geq 3$. Min node a returns upper bound 3 to the root. There, no cutoff happens since $3 \not\geq +\infty$ and node b is expanded, with window $\langle 4, +\infty \rangle$. Node e is expanded and returns 2, which causes a cutoff in b since $4 \geq 2$, and upper bound 2 is returned to the root, which returns $\max(3, 2) = 3$. This value is an upper bound, since the two children returned upper bounds. After two narrow window passes we now have an upper bound and a lower bound of equal value 3.

window with which it was called? Figure 4.10 shows the familiar tree, whose minimax value is 3. In the figure we will traverse the tree now two times, first with a narrow alpha-beta window $\langle -\infty, 2 \rangle$ just below that minimax value, and second with a narrow window $\langle 4, +\infty \rangle$ just above the minimax value, to show what happens when the return value falls outside the alpha-beta window. Please follow the example in the figure, and refer to the alpha-beta code in Listing 4.4.

The lower narrow window $\langle -\infty, 2 \rangle$ yields as return value a lower bound $3 \leq v$ on the minimax value (future child expansion can still increase the value at max nodes, hence the value so far is a lower bound on the final return value). As we can see, the subtree expanded so far is a min solution tree (all children of min nodes, not all of max nodes). The higher narrow window $\langle 4, +\infty \rangle$ yields as return value an upper bound $v \leq 3$ since the min children of the root returned upper bounds, as only some of their children were expanded. The tree traversed in this second pass for this upper bound is a max solution tree (all children of max nodes, some of min nodes). The first (low) window yielded lower bound $3 \leq v$, and the second (high) window yielded upper bound $v \leq 3$. Since, in this case, the lower and the upper bound are equal, we have found the minimax value $3 \leq v \leq 3$ and the proof tree is the union of the min solution tree and the max solution tree.

Post-condition and Bounds

A narrow window causes more cutoffs, but returns a bound if the return value is outside the window. Can we construct useful search algorithms using only bounds?

We will now formalize these notions in the alpha-beta post-condition, in order to see if we can create a useful and efficient algorithm based on the narrow window idea. We know that alpha-beta returns the minimax value if it is called with the window $\langle -\infty, +\infty \rangle$. When the return value falls outside the window, then the return value bounds the minimax value.

The post-condition of $g = $ alpha-beta(n, α, β) is as follows [369, 526]:

1. $\alpha < g < \beta$: the window was right, g is the minimax value of the tree rooted in n. Alpha-beta has traversed at least the nodes in a critical tree, the union of a max and a min solution tree.
2. $g \leq \alpha$: the window was too high, g is an upper bound on the minimax value of the tree rooted in n. Alpha-beta has traversed at least the nodes in a max solution tree whose value is an upper bound g on the minimax value.
3. $\beta \leq g$: the window was too low, g is a lower bound on the minimax value of the tree rooted in n. Alpha-beta has traversed at least the nodes in a min solution tree whose value is a lower bound g on the minimax value.

This post-condition allows the construction of the ultimate in efficient decision procedures: the null window search, or NWS. A null window of $\alpha = \beta - 1$ guarantees[13] that alpha-beta performs the most efficient search possible, at the cost of returning only a Boolean answer: the minimax value is either above or below the input window. Finding the minimax value with the NWS decision procedure requires a sequence of NWS calls. There are two main algorithms in the literature, Scout, which uses NWS recursively, and MTD(f), which uses NWS iteratively from the root.[14] Scout is also known as principal variation search [217].

Scout

Scout [509, 548] works on the assumption that the first child of a node is the best child. This first child is called the *principal variation*. Assuming such a well-ordered tree, Scout searches the first child with a wide window, and then uses NWS to check efficiently if the other children are indeed inferior. If not, they are searched with a wide window, to find the value. Listing 4.7 shows the code.

---

[13] We assume that all values are integer values, so with $\alpha = \beta - 1$ there is no room for an integer value to fit in the window. A null window of $\alpha = \beta$ would not work, since alpha-beta would return immediately and not traverse any nodes. The term "one window" would perhaps have been better, but history has decided otherwise.

[14] The efficiency gain for null windows versus wide windows depends to a large degree on the quality of the move ordering. Experiments with tournament quality programs yielded differences of around 20% in leaf count, increasing with search depth [525, 526]. For badly ordered trees the difference is much larger.

```
INF = 99999

def eval(n):
    return n['value']

def scout(n, a, b):
    if n['type'] == 'LEAF':
        return eval(n)
    elif n['type'] == 'MAX':
        g = -INF
        for c in n['children']:
            if c == n['children'][0]:
                g = max(g, scout(c, a, b)) # first child wide
                    window
            else:
                g = max(g, scout(c, a, a+1)) # other children nws
                if g >= a+1:
                    g = max(g, scout(c, g, b)) # if better, wide
                        window
            a = max(a, g) # update alpha
            if a >= b:
                break # beta cutoff, a>=b
    elif n['type'] == 'MIN':
        g = INF
        for c in n['children']:
            if c == n['children'][0]:
                g = min(g, scout(c, a, b)) # first child wide
                    window
            else:
                g = min(g, scout(c, b-1, b)) # other children nws
                if g <= b-1:
                    g = min(g, scout(c, a, g)) # if better, wide
                        window
            b = min(b, g) # update beta
            if a >= b:
                break # alpha cutoff, a>=b
    else:
        error("Wrong node type")
    return g

print("Minimax value: ", scout(root, -INF, INF))
```

Listing 4.7 Scout [509, 548]

```
def mtdf(n, f, d):
    ub - +INF
    lb = -INF
    while lb < ub:
        if f == lb:
            b = f+1
        else:
            b = f
        f = ttalphabeta(n, b-1, b, d)
        if f < b:
            ub = f
        else:
            lb = f
    return f
```

Listing 4.8 MTD(f) [526]

Transposition Table and Null Window Search

The re-searches may seem inefficient, and they would be, if alpha-beta would recompute search results for each search anew. (Node a and c in the example of Figure 4.10 are re-expanded.) Actual game playing versions of alpha-beta use transposition tables, large lookup tables in which all nodes and their search results are efficiently stored. Re-searching is therefore not more expensive, since no new nodes are expanded. The code in the listing omits the lookup and store calls, and the depth parameter.

MTD(f) and MTD-bi

MTD(f) [526] takes as input a first guess to the minimax value, and then iteratively calls a sequence of NWS decision procedures to home in on the minimax value. If the first guess is too high, then NWS will return a lower value, an upper bound, which is fed into the next NWS call, and a sequence of lower return values (upper bounds) follows, until the minimax value is found and NWS returns a higher return value (a lower bound equal to the previous upper bound). If the first guess is too low, the converse occurs.

In contrast to Scout, which uses some wide window searches, MTD(f) uses only NWS. Experimental comparisons showed indeed that MTD(f) expands even fewer nodes than Scout on average, although trees can be constructed in which either algorithm performs best [526, 523]. Even more so than Scout, MTD(f) relies on a well-functioning lookup table to store intermediate search results in, which requires care with inconsistencies in the tree.

Listing 4.8 shows the code for MTD(f). MTD(f) starts the search for the minimax value at a heuristic first guess, and then iterates in the direction of the minimax value based on the outcome of the null window search. When the granularity of the evaluation function is fine, the number of iterations can become large, and the overhead of traversing through the tree also increases.

An alternative approach is to use a binary search [370] to interpolate between the upper and the lower bound. That value can then be used as the pivot for the null window search, which will produce a new bound, and to repeat the binary search. This may result in fewer iterations of null window search to find the minimax value. This algorithm is called MTD-bi [526]. The idea of bisecting the search goes back to C* [149, 752] where it is used in end-game search. MTD-bi is used in Sunfish, a tiny fully functional Chess program in 111 lines of Python code (Sect. 4.6.1).

After this elaborate discussion of alpha-beta and related move ordering enhancements, it is time to discuss other enhancements that have been developed to improve the performance of heuristic planning.

4.3.5 *Heuristic Forward Pruning

If we want to search deeper, the first idea that often springs to mind is to only search "important" nodes. This method is called forward pruning, in contrast to alpha-beta's backward pruning. In forward pruning, the idea is to use domain-dependent heuristics to determine these important nodes. If for certain moves we can immediately see that they are not good, then they should not be searched. In early game playing programs this was used since compute power was so limited relative to the large number of subtrees to be searched. This is the approach taken in Go playing programs such as GNU Go, where the move generator generates only the "sensible" moves such as connect, corner, jump, and territory making moves. The disadvantage of heuristic forward pruning is that the static heuristics may be wrong, and valuable moves are missed, that only a search would reveal to be valuable. In practice it turned out that static board heuristics can all too easily miss deeper tactical game dynamics. As soon as compute power allowed, programmers of Chess and Checkers programs started to use full-width move lists.

Plain heuristic forward pruning misses too many dynamics in most games. In Section 4.4.3 further developments of forward pruning are introduced, named null move pruning [181] and Prob-cut [115].

4.3.6 *Capture Moves

Another ordering mechanism that is highly domain specific, but is often highly effective, is capture move ordering. For alpha-beta it is important to search an ordered sequence of moves. An obvious move ordering enhancement is to prioritize capture moves, since in many games the dominant factor of the heuristic evaluation function is material balance, e.g., how many pieces of a color are still on the board. It stands to reason that, in positions where among the available actions there are capture moves, those capture moves lead to a better position, and should be tried first.

Many Chess programs therefore employ a move generator that first generates capture moves, and if no cutoff has occurred, then the noncapture moves.

Note that this enhancement is heuristic; sometimes it fails, and a non-capture move is best. It uses domain-dependent knowledge, and only works in domains where captures are important and frequent. In Go, for example, captures are less frequent, and the capture enhancement is of no importance in this domain.

4.3.7 *Killer Moves and History Heuristic

Another well-known and effective enhancement is called the *killer move*. In many domains actions that are good actions in one position are also good in another position. For example, if I am in a position where I find a strong action, say by moving my pawn from e4 to f5 I can capture my opponent's queen, then the move pawn e4-f5 is likely to be a good move in many other positions, provided the board has not changed too much. This move is called a killer move. The enhancement works by recording moves that are so strong as to cause an alpha-beta cutoff, and then first trying these moves in subsequent positions [318].

A generalization of the killer move is the history heuristic, which adds counters to the moves that cause cutoffs, making the heuristic more refined. The history heuristic maintains a table indexed by *from* and *to* squares, and when there is a cutoff, the entry in the table is incremented, possibly weighted by search depth [587]. The history heuristic came out of basic experiments on the interplay of search and knowledge in Chess, one of the earlier works with a principled empirical approach to this question [586].

Killer moves are even easier to implement than the history heuristic, are more general than capture moves, and work in many domains. They are present in most Chess and Checkers playing programs. Killer moves were first described by Barbara Liskov, who would (much later) win the 2008 Turing award for work on object-oriented and type-safe programming. The history heuristic was developed by Jonathan Schaeffer, who would later lead the Chinook Checkers effort.

Most search enhancements focus on selection of moves as a way to improve efficiency.

To conclude our discussion of enhancements of the search function, we will look at a different element of the search, the backup rule.

4.3.8 *Backup Rules Other than Minimax

Most enhancements in this chapter are applicable to two-person zero-sum perfect-information games, games that can be modeled well in the minimax paradigm. For other games, different backup rules are needed. Interestingly, even for some zero-sum games a non-minimax backup rule works best, as we shall see in the next chapter on MCTS. In this section we will discuss alternative backup rules.

The minimax backup rule has dominated game playing research for a long time (1950–2006). For two-person zero-sum games with a single heuristic reward value it is intuitively appealing, since it follows the idea of how humans play a game in which they try to pick the best move.

For imperfect-information games or games of chance, such as card games or dice games, minimax is not an obvious choice. Researchers have tried to find work-arounds to force these games into the minimax paradigm, with limited success.

Statistical sampling can be used to cope with the randomness of the game. A disadvantage is that in order to get reliable outcomes, the number of samples must be high. Alternatives to minimax have been developed. Already in 1966 Michie published the Expectimax algorithm [445] for computing probabilities with the product rule. In 1983 Ballard published the *-minimax rule, which augmented the alpha-beta algorithm with chance nodes, allowing distributions to be propagated through the product rule (by multiplication) while still allowing the efficiency of cutoffs [33, 547]. Subsequent experiments are reported in [137, 478, 277]. Expectimax and *-minimax did not become popular after these experiments, although in 2013 Lanctot et al. [400] reported good results with a combination of Expectimax and statistical sampling.

In 1988 McAllester [441] introduced conspiracy number search as an alternative to alpha-beta, which is based on backing up the size of the subtree in addition to the value (how many nodes *conspire* to change a node's value). It thus explicitly searches for small subtrees. It did not become popular, but it did lead to the development of proof number search [7, 6], which is based on the search for Boolean values such as win/loss. Proof number search is often used for mathematically solving games, to determine the exact win/loss/draw value of a position—not its heuristic approximation. To solve a game, the state space is fully searched to the terminal states [557, 589].

The next chapter, on Monte Carlo Tree Search, will introduce the *averaging of statistical samples* as backup rule. MCTS and its backup rule did become quite popular and successful.

To summarize the different backup rules, minimax is an efficient algorithm for backing up scalar values. Expectimax works with probability distributions. Averaging works well for statistical sampling. For Boolean values such as win/loss, proof number search is an efficient algorithm.

4.3.9 Trends in Search

We are coming to the end of the section on search enhancements and will close with some conclusions.

Please refer to Table 4.3 on page 85. Minimax is a rigid fixed-width, fixed-depth algorithm, distributing the search effort equally over all parts of the tree, good or bad. The enhancements reported in this section all point to a trend of variable-width,

Name	Principle	Applicability	Effectiveness
search extensions	variable depth	domain specific	good
quiescence search	variable depth	domain specific	good
null-move search	variable depth	no Zugzwang	good
odd-even effect	move advantage	minimax games	unstable values
piece-square tables	evaluation coding	heuristic evaluation	efficiency
coefficient learning	machine learning	evaluation tuning	automated learning
end-game database	database	endgame	perfect knowledge
opponent modeling	different opponent	teaching	explore weaknesses

Table 4.4 Eval enhancements

variable-depth, using forward or backward pruning, and move ordering, to devote most of the search effort to the most promising part of the tree, to find the best move, disregarding bad moves as early as possible.

Furthermore, there is a trend towards generality, away from domain-specific heuristics, towards mechanisms such as the history heuristic, iterative deepening, and transposition tables, methods that work in many domains.

4.4 Evaluation Enhancements

After elaborating on the many search enhancements that have been invented, it is time to see how heuristic evaluation can be enhanced. Table 4.4 gives an overview of the evaluation function enhancements. The enhancements try to ameliorate the limitations of static heuristics with search extensions, and improve the evaluation function by smart implementations and databases. (The term Zugzwang, or forced moving, is explained in Sect. 4.4.3.)

4.4.1 *Search Extensions

The heuristic evaluation function computes a score of the static board position. These scores are then used in the search. Potentially important tactical dynamics in the position cannot be seen by a standard static evaluator, since the tactical problem is over the *search horizon*. It would help if this situation could be detected, and the search be extended somewhat to see the effect of the tactical dynamics. Singular extensions were devised by the Deep Thought team (the predecessors of Deep Blue) for Chess [10, 309]. There are many variations of search extension; all are based on domain-specific heuristics. Two of the best-known search extensions for Chess are check extensions and capture extensions. Positions that are in check or where some kind of capture happened are searched one level deeper. A problem with capture extensions can be that in positions where many capture opportunities exist, the search expands too much. For this reason partial depth extensions have been devised. Tuning the amount and type of search extensions is an important part of the tuning effort of game playing programs, especially in Chess, which is a highly tactical game.

Singular extensions are related in some sense to forward pruning. Forward pruning uses heuristics to restrict search to certain "good" moves. Search extensions do a full-width search up to a certain depth, and then use heuristics to extend certain positions for deeper search, combining full-width and selective search.

Multi-cut introduced search reductions [84]. Here a shallow search is used to determine if a cutoff is taken early in a node. Related to multi-cut are Prob-cut [115] and a pruning technique in Chinook [590] which uses a shallow search to identify nodes to terminate the search. Finally, search extensions are reported to reduce the problem of search pathology [349, 9, 608].

4.4.2 *Quiescence Search

Related to search extensions is quiescence search. Quiescence search [46] and search extensions both try to reduce the impact of the search horizon. It tries to distinguish between so-called *quiet* and *noisy* positions. A noisy position is a position whose value cannot be reliably estimated with static heuristics, for example, because of the presence of threats or other dynamics. Noisy positions should be searched deeper until a quiet position arises, that can more reliably be evaluated. Quiescence search is most often implemented by looking at differences between positions in the heuristic evaluation function. As with search extensions, getting quiescence search to work requires much experimentation to build up understanding of the effects of the static evaluation heuristics that are used in one's program [260, 348, 46, 583].

4.4.3 *Null-Move Heuristic

We will now discuss the null-move heuristic. A null move is a pass, not making a move, a position where the only difference with the successor position is which side is to move [45]. In some games passing is legal, such as in Go; in some games it is not, such as in Chess. Being allowed to move typically provides opportunities for improvement. If it is not, and all possible moves make a position worse, it is called *Zugzwang*, or forced moving. In this case the introduction of a pass move causes an unfair advantage to occur.

The null-move heuristic tries to get alpha-beta cutoffs cheaply by seeing if a pass creates a situation that is strong enough to cause a cutoff before the regular moves are tried. If a position is so strong that not moving already provides a cutoff, then it is a good idea to take that cutoff. In that case the cut off has been found without an expensive search.

Null moves typically work well, at least in Chess. (In other games, such as Othello, Zugzwang plays a bigger role, and null moves are not used, or in a different way [115].) The null-move idea has been developed further by extending zero-depth cutoff searches to small-depth cutoff searches, with success [248, 181, 286, 115, 97]. The ProbCut algorithm [115] in particular has been successful in Othello.

4.4.4 *Odd/Even Effect

As was noted before, in most positions having the opportunity to make a move is advantageous. If we are white, then positions with white to move are typically better than black-to-move positions. This fact causes pronounced swings in the score between search depths. The odd/even effect is caused by a simple statistical fact, that the expected value of the maximum of a distribution is greater than the expected value of the minimum of a distribution: $E(\max(\text{random}[-999, +999])) > E(\min(\text{random}[-999, +999]))$.

The odd/even effect is a statistical effect; it is possible to construct counter-example trees where the value at the node is stable as the search depth increases. This effect is also related to the search horizon. Many game trees have a pronounced odd/even effect, especially when the trees are fixed depth. As iterative deepening searches deeper (Listing 4.5) the scores at the root node go up and down as the leaf values switch between being minimized and maximized.

The odd/even effect occurs in "normal" trees, for non-Zugzwang positions, and without search pathology. The odd/even effect is not caused by search instability, but is a consequence of the min-max structure of the minimax tree [193].

The value swings do complicate empirical analysis and finding errors in programs, and comparing search results from different search depths becomes less reliable.

The odd/even effect can be reduced by search extensions, that transform the fixed-depth search into a variable-depth search. Another solution is to prevent the effect, using search extensions and shallow searches to extend and reduce depth in multiples of two.

4.4.5 *Piece-Square Tables

After discussing enhancements that are concerned with the search horizon, we will now look at the core of the evaluation function, the efficient computation of the heuristic value.

Piece-square tables are a popular method for creating efficient evaluation functions. They are used in many strong Chess programs [249]. A piece-square table is a table for each piece on each square for each color. Values for the piece × square × color combination indicate the value of the piece being on this square. Piece-square tables are efficient since moving a piece from a square to another amounts to subtracting the source value and adding the destination value to the heuristic evaluation score.

Piece-square tables are quite popular because of their efficiency. A well-known implementation of piece-square tables is by Fabien Letouzey in his open source program Fruit.[15]

Furthermore, piece-square tables are well suited for learning the evaluation function [47, 186], sometimes leading to surprising differences between manually tuned and machine-learned values. The creation of an evaluation function that encodes heuristics in a correct way and combines their values efficiently is a challenging problem. Let us look at how this can be automated.

4.4.6 Coefficient Learning

As has been noted before, tuning the coefficients of evaluation function terms (Sect. 4.1.3) by hand is a difficult and error-prone process. Recall the general form of the evaluation function:

$$h(s) = c_1 \times f_1(s) + c_2 \times f_2(s) + c_3 \times f_3(s) + \ldots + c_n \times f_n(s).$$

An alternative is to train the coefficients by supervised learning. This works by creating a large database of test positions from grandmaster games, of which the value or the best move is known. The difference between the evaluation of the state and the correct answer constitutes an error value. Then an iterative optimization process is used to adjust the evaluation function coefficients such that the sum of the error values is minimized.

Many authors report on machine learning methods that train the coefficients against databases of grandmaster games or in self-play [577, 42, 119, 539, 686, 222, 489, 230, 223, 162, 675]. Frequently, it is reported that the coefficients deviate considerably from hand-tuned coefficients (the machine-learned coefficients "work, but don't make sense"). Many Chess programmers have tried to find a middle ground by adjusting the coefficients to values that make intuitive sense, and also have low error scores, after they have been optimized by machine learning.

Most work in automated Chess evaluation optimization is in the automated tuning of the coefficient of the features. There is also some work that goes a step further, and tries end-to-end learning of evaluation functions directly from board positions, without the intermediate step of hand-crafted heuristic features [160, 626, 393]. This work is quite recent and often related to the work reported in Chap. 7.

We are coming to the end of this overview of evaluation function enhancements. There is one more to discuss: the endgame.

---

[15] The source code is available here: Fruit. http://arctrix.com/nas/chess/fruit/

4.4.7 End-Game Database

In Chess and Checkers the endgame is an important phase of the game. Inaccurate play can often result in loss of the game. It is also a phase of the game where few pieces are on the board, allowing the exact minimax value to be computed (without heuristic approximation). Sometimes highly "artificial" lines of play turn out to be the correct line of play, with nontrivial and counter-intuitive moves. Work on end-game databases was proposed early, e.g., by Bellman [55], and Thompson [684].

Much of the strength of world champion Checkers program Chinook came from the 8-piece end-game database [591]. Chess program Deep Blue used a database that contained 5-piece endings and some 6-piece endings.

End-game databases are often computed by retrograde analysis, working backwards from the end [205, 398, 684]. Retrograde analysis is used frequently in solving games (determining the outcome in the case of perfect play by both sides, by full enumeration of relevant parts of the state space). Games that have been solved are Nine Men's Morris [234], Awari [557], and Checkers [589].

Culberson and Schaeffer generalized end-game databases to pattern databases, to be used in all stages of a search [154, 380]. Pattern databases play an important role in the playout phase of MCTS-based Go programs (Sect. 5.2.1).

4.4.8 Opponent Modeling

The minimax procedure assumes that our opponent uses the same knowledge as we do. For perfect (non-heuristic) play, this is appropriate. When the values in the state space are heuristic evaluations, i.e., imperfect approximations of perfect play, then it may be reasonable to assume that our opponent has a different play style than we do. Also for teaching purposes it may be better to play other moves than the optimal policy. This *opponent modeling* can be used to exploit perceived weaknesses in the opponent's play. Opponent modeling is often relevant in multiplayer imperfect-information games [80, 232].

4.4.9 Trends in Eval

We are now at the end of our discussion of heuristic evaluation enhancements. Let us see if we can find a common trend in the enhancements.

Heuristic evaluation functions are domain specific. One would think that enhancements of evaluation functions trend towards more specific knowledge. This is not the case. The techniques that are used to enhance evaluation functions trend towards finding automated methods for feature creation: retrograde analysis for creating end-game databases, machine learning of coefficients or piece-square tables, and some variations trying to overcome the search horizon problem. In many cases, the heuristic knowledge is compartmentalized in features that are created with automated methods. Furthermore, many game programmers use automated testing whenever a change is made to the code base. Even in search extensions and quiescence search, whose implementations typically involve domain specifics, there have been efforts towards general methods [46].

The overall trend in evaluation function enhancements is that enhancements start as domain specific, and then work is being undertaken towards automated methods and automated learning.

4.5 Conclusion

Determining the strength of Chess programs is of great importance. The playing strength of a program can be determined by playing tournaments, and by computing a rating based on the outcome and the strength of the opponent. A well-known internet tournament is the Top Chess Engine Championship (TCEC), where strong computer Chess programs are compared and a rating is calculated. TCEC can be found here.[16] In computer Chess the Elo rating is frequently used to compare playing strength.

The Elo rating was introduced by Arpad Elo (Sect. 2.1.3). It is calculated using tournament outcomes. For each game, the winner's rating increases, and the loser's rating decreases. The change depends on the difference between the original ratings. A win by a stronger program increases its rating by less than a surprise win by a weaker program. If player 1 has a rating R_1 and player 2 has a rating R_2 then the expected score of player 1 is $E_1 = \frac{1}{1+10^{(R_2-R_1)/400}}$. If the actual score of player 1 was S_1 then the new rating of player 1 is $R_1' = R_1 + K(S_1 - E_1)$, where K is a constant that determines the maximum adjustment per game. It is typically set from 16 for master players to 32 for weak players.

Code for computing the Elo rating can be found at BayesElo.[17]

Search-Eval and System 1 and System 2

We have come to the end of this chapter on heuristic planning. The search-eval architecture was originally inspired by the way in which humans are thought to play a game. Can we see a relation between the heuristic planning methods and human thinking as it is described by Kahneman?

Since the earliest days of game playing research, the search-eval architecture has been the cornerstone of game playing programs. The architecture is simple. The search function traverses possible game positions, and the evaluation function scores the position with a heuristic value function. In the early days of Turing's and Shannon's papers, when search-eval was conceived [701, 618], the search and eval functions

---

[16] https://tcec.chessdom.com/live.html

[17] https://github.com/ddugovic/BayesianElo

Chapter	Algorithm	Select	Backup	Eval
Chap. 4	alpha-beta	left to right	minimax	heuristic
Chap. 5	MCTS	adaptive	average	sample
Chap. 6	DQN	-	-	generalize
Chap. 7	self-play	adaptive	average	generalize

Table 4.5 Heuristic-Sample-Generalize

were quite straightforward. The heuristic function was the most basic function that worked, and the search function was a minimax(-like) function to traverse the nodes in standard depth-first order. This simple model proved quite versatile and amenable to successive refinements. Over the years many enhancements were introduced, and performance has reached world champion level in games such as Chess and Checkers. These enhancements are very important—they elevate the level of performance from being barely able to follow the rules to World Champion beating programs.

Table 4.5 gives an overview of the different paradigms in this book. The entry for Chap. 4 shows the heuristic search approach in reinforcement learning. The focus of this chapter has been on full-width search and manually crafted heuristic evaluation functions, and value backup via the minimax rule.

As the table indicates, in the following chapters different, more adaptive, techniques will be introduced. In Chap. 7 this will culminate in functions that are able to self-learn to play a game as complicated as Go with only the rules of the game known to the program.

At the time when early AI researchers such as Turing, Shannon, and Samuel discussed Chess playing computers, it was believed that by developing better Chess programs we would learn how human thought worked, and we would learn about human intelligence. When 40 to 50 years later Deep Blue finally beat Kasparov, this belief had changed. It was said that brute force had won over human intellect. We had not learned about how humans think, but we had learned how to make a fast computer search many positions.

Kahneman's view on human thinking as consisting of fast and slow points in another direction. Perhaps Chess computers do operate in a way that is related to the way that humans think. Humans have a fast, heuristic, system 1, and a slow, deliberative, system 2. This corresponds to Chess computers that have a fast heuristic evaluation function, and a slow planning function that painstakingly reasons through some of the possible positions. In this sense there is a correspondence to how humans and computers think or play Chess. The search-eval architecture is not only an architecture to organize the functions of a Chess program in a clean way; it also fits how Kahneman describes that humans play and think. Perhaps, at a high level, Turing and Shannon's dream of creating a mechanical model of thought has succeeded after all.

Of course the "brute force" argument is not without merit. Computers calculate fast and deep. It is true that computers always blindly follow their program, and do not deviate. Human system 2 thinking is not so perfect, and is easily distracted by system 1 associations. Indeed, computers can search many more positions than humans can.

Computer Chess has also taught us that writing error-free heuristic programs is hard. It has taken four to five decades of research by a dedicated community of researchers for artificial intelligence to rise to the challenge. Too much of this time has been spent in frustration removing errors from and improving heuristic evaluation functions that were hard to understand and hard to debug.

Conceptually the way in which computers and humans play Chess may be highly related. In the details, there are important differences.

Let us now review this chapter, and get our hands dirty with exercises about a concrete Chess program.

4.6 Practice

Questions

Below are some questions to check your understanding of this chapter. Each question is a closed question where a simple, one sentence answer is possible.

1. What is a heuristic?
2. Why is an exponential state space problematic?
3. How can you search an exponential search space efficiently?
4. What is the role of a search function?
5. What is the role of an evaluation function?
6. Why is minimax a form of self-play?
7. Why is minimax recursive?
8. What is the number of leaves of a regular tree of width w and depth d?
9. What is the critical tree?
10. What is the number of leaves of a regular tree that proves the value at the root?
11. What is a solution tree?
12. What is material balance?
13. What is Elo?
14. What is forward pruning?
15. What is backward pruning?
16. Draw a tree with an alpha-beta cutoff.
17. What causes the performance of alpha-beta to go from worst case to best case?
18. What is a transposition?
19. How do iterative deepening and transposition tables help the performance of alpha-beta?
20. What is a null window?
21. What is a null move?
22. What is a killer move?
23. What is a search extension?
24. How can you use supervised learning in a Chess program?

4.6.1 Sunfish—Chess in 111 lines of Python

Chess programs are often large pieces of code. For Chess, there are many open-source programs available that allow study of the code. However, the size of the codes typically requires a large investment of study time. There are also a few short Chess programs. For example, the program Micro-Max, by Harm Geert Muller, is a minimalist Chess program in 133 lines of C code, in less than 2000 characters (not counting comments). Another example is Sunfish, a Chess program in 111 lines of Python. Sunfish was written by Thomas Ahle. Although the name is similar to Stockfish, Sunfish was inspired by Micro-Max. You can download it from GitHub here.[18] The entire program code fits in a single file, `sunfish.py`.

The program consists of a heuristic evaluation function based on piece square tables (Sect. 4.4.5). It uses null window search algorithm MTD-bi (Sect. 4.3.4) enhanced with iterative deepening, transposition tables, null moves, and killer moves. Sunfish is small enough to play around with and study, to learn how a real working Chess program functions.

The small size and organization of the code also allow easy modification. Things to try are, for example, changes to the piece-square table, to see the effect on playing style of a different evaluation function (see the Exercises).

4.6.2 Implementation: New or Make/Undo

You may have noticed that the alpha-beta code in the figures lacks implementation details such as board manipulation and move making. These "details" are actually quite important for creating a working program. Recursive game playing programs call the search routine with the current board state, often indicated with parameter n for the new node. This board can be created and allocated anew in each search node, in a clean value-passing style (local variable). Another option is to pass a reference to the board, and to apply a `makemove` operation placing the stone on the board before the recursive call, and an `undomove` operation removing the stone from the board when it comes out of the recursion (global variable).

This reference-passing style may be quicker if allocating the memory for a new board is an expensive operation. It may also be more difficult to implement correctly, if capture moves cause many changes to the board, which must be remembered for the subsequent undo. Sometimes the incremental evaluation calculation is also incorporated into the makemove/undomove routines, for even more efficiency.

For parallel implementations in a shared memory at least all parallel threads must have their own copy of a value-passing style board. (On a distributed memory cluster the separate machines will have their own copy of the board by virtue of the distributed memory.)

---

[18] https://github.com/thomasahle/sunfish

Exercises

1. Download and install Sunfish and BayesElo for Python. Play your first game against Sunfish. Write a script that performs a tournament of two identical instances with the same time controls of Sunfish. Suggestion: 10 seconds per move. Look at the games. Do they make sense? [Only if you know how to play Chess] Does Sunfish at this time setting look like a strong program to you? Try different settings.
2. Setup BayesElo to allow you to run a tournament between two programs to determine their playing strength.
3. Running tournaments costs compute time. How long should a tournament be? How many games are needed for results to be statistically significant? Add confidence intervals or error bars to the graph showing the standard deviation of the Elo rating.
4. Make a change: halve the playing time of the second player. How does the Elo rating change?
5. Read part 1 of Kahneman [347], on the two systems (less than a hundred pages of reading. Part 2 is about heuristics, but not the kind we have used here in our evaluation functions). How is the thinking of a computer chess program related to human thinking? Is minimax like system 1 or system 2? Is heuristic evaluation like system 1 or system 2?

Sunfish implements null-window search, null moves, iterative deepening, transposition tables, and killer moves. Throughout this chapter it was often claimed that certain enhancements work well. Using the Sunfish and Elo code, the following exercises are to create a graph showing the effect of individual search enhancements. In the exercises we study the influence of search enhancements and evaluation heuristics. The baseline is standard Sunfish with all enhancements and all heuristics. Keep in mind how many runs of a program you need to get statistically significant results [37].

1. Try the following: Replace MTD-bi by MTD(f) (see Listing 4.8). How is performance influenced? If the tournaments take too long to run, what can you do to get quicker results?
2. Replace the null window search by wide-window alpha-beta. How is performance influenced?
3. Replace the move ordering heuristics: put killer moves last in the move list that is generated by the move generator.
4. Show the Elo rating of the program without enhancements. Remove killer moves, then remove null moves, then try removing the transposition table and iterative deepening. Are the enhancements related?
5. Study the code of the piece-square tables. Make a change to one of the squares, describe in words the intended meaning, and compare the difference in play.
6. Create test positions that contain Zugzwang (every move makes your position worse; not moving is advantageous). Check if turning off null moves improves performance.

Summary

In this chapter we introduced heuristic plannning reinforcement learning algorithms. The main problem for thesse algorithms is the size of the state space. We have calculated the size of the state space, and found that for most games a standard minimax enumeration of the full state space is infeasible. Heuristic methods are introduced that can artificially reduce the state space. Static board evaluation functions do not capture game dynamics, and search remains necessary. Thus we arrived at a solution architecture consisting of two functions: the search-eval architecture.

The search functions covered in this chapter have been conceptually simple, in the sense that they are directly based on maximization and minimization of the reward values: I try to maximize my outcome; my opponent tries to minimize my outcome. We have discussed the minimax procedure, and have looked at the concept of the critical tree, the smallest set of nodes that has to be searched to be certain of the value of the state space. This smallest tree concept has then been used to arrive at efficient search algorithms. The efficiency of both the search and the evaluation function can be greatly enhanced with general and domain-specific enhancements. We covered a wide range of enhancements, both search enhancements and eval enhancements. The first search enhancement is alpha-beta, an algorithm that can search twice as deep as minimax, if the tree is optimally ordered.

Achieving world champion level of performance with alpha-beta required researchers and game programmers to invent many search enhancements. For alpha-beta cutoffs to work effectively, the tree must be ordered. Perhaps the most important enhancements for alpha-beta are iterative deepening and transposition tables. They work together by storing best-move information of previous searches. In this way, alpha-beta searches a tree that is reasonably to well ordered by the previous iterations. Null windows improve the effectiveness of alpha-beta even further.

Another important area is relaxing full-width search. A basic approach is heuristic forward pruning. For Chess, it was found that a better approach is to use a mix of full-width and selective search (extensions and reductions).

On the eval side, we discussed quiescence, search extensions, piece-square tables, null moves, end-game databases, and evaluation function learning. The first few levels of the tree are searched full width, so that no move is left untried, and after a certain depth extensions (or reductions) are used.

A popular heuristic is null-move pruning, where before the legal moves an extra pass move is searched to a shallow depth. If a position is so strong that even passing yields a cutoff, then it is safe to take the cutoff.

Researchers have a large imagination, and many ideas have been tried. Not all have been successful in the minimax framework and in the games in which they have been tried. Among them are forward pruning (in Chess and in Go), different backup rules (such as star-minimax), Monte Carlo evaluation (such as in Go), and neural network evaluation (in Chess and in Go). Interestingly, as we will see in the upcoming chapters, although these did not work in Chess all these ideas have been used eventually to achieve a high level of play in different frameworks or games.

We noted a trend towards variable-depth search and automation in evaluation. Enhancements typically start with an idea to exploit a domain-specific feature (such as the killer move, or hand-tuned coefficients). After some more research, often a more general version arises, that performs even better (such as the history heuristic, or machine-optimized evaluation coefficients).

In the next chapter we will continue the trend towards more generally applicable methods and more selective search. We will see how Monte Carlo evaluation, a different backup rule, and selective search together form an algorithm that works well in domains in which minimax and heuristics do not work.

Historical and Bibliographical Notes

One of the earlier works in heuristic planning is Pearl's book *Heuristics* [511] (he would later co-author *The Book of Why*, on his work on causation [512]). Minimax is described in most standard artificial intelligence undergraduate texts, such as Russell and Norvig [572], although without solution trees. There is an extensive literature on solution trees, see [390, 522, 645, 511, 526].

One of the first open-source Chess programs is Crafty [325]. Chess programs have always used the most compute power that was available, and many have stimulated research into parallel programs, where multiple processors search the state space collectively. Deep Blue used special hardware and software for parallel search. Parallel Chess has also stimulated the development of research into parallel programming environments, such as Cilk [412]. The parallel Cilkchess program achieved some success in its days. Fruit is an influential open source program by Fabien Letouzey; the well-known open-source program GNU Chess is now based on Fruit [413].

The Chess programming wiki contains a wealth of information on null moves, search extensions, transposition tables, and many, many, other things.[19]

Alpha-beta is reported to have been reinvented independently by several authors, among them McCarthy, Samuel, Brudno, Richard, Hart, and Levine [485]. John McCarthy won the 1971 Turing award for work on AI. A seminal analysis of the alpha-beta algorithm is Knuth and Moore [369]. This analysis was without the benefit of the concept of solution trees, which were introduced in later publications on Stockman's SSS* algorithm [645, 511, 522]. The relation between SSS*, solution trees, critical trees, and alpha-beta is described in [526, 523].

Killer moves were described by Barbara Liskov (Huberman) in her 1968 thesis [318]. The history heuristic is described in Jonathan Schaeffer's thesis and subsequent paper [587]. An overview paper of search enhancements is [594]. A paper on search versus heuristics is [342]. Null moves are described by Donninger [181]. Buro introduced Probcut [115]. Search pathologies, where searching deeper gives worse quality answers, were introduced by Nau. They have been further studied by Pearl, Beal, and others [479, 510, 44, 760, 573].

---

[19] https://www.chessprogramming.org/Main_Page

Chapter 5
Adaptive Sampling

The previous chapter discussed heuristic planning. We saw the basic search-eval architecture, and the many enhancements that it needed for high performance. The search enhancements were necessary to overcome limitations of fixed-depth fixed-width minimax search. Many of the evaluation enhancements focused on alpha-beta cutoffs and the search horizon.

The two main challenges that are addressed in this chapter are (1) adaptive node selection and (2) evaluation of states for which there is no efficient heuristic evaluation function.

In minimax, all parts of the tree are searched equally, no matter how unpromising. The enhancements attempted to fix this, to allow the search to focus on promising parts of the state space. This approach worked very well for games in which tactical play is important, such as in Chess, Checkers, and Othello, where a single capture move can often change the static score significantly. For other games, notably Go, this approach did not work. Go is more strategic in nature, moves can have hidden long-term effects that are not easily found with a short tactical search as in Chess. For Go, researchers did not find efficient heuristics for variable-depth and variable-width search, nor for value estimation of states.

Addressing these two problems led to a new algorithm, based on a new paradigm. In this chapter the new algorithm, Monte Carlo Tree Search (MCTS) [151, 108], is introduced. MCTS combines three techniques: (1) it performs adaptive exploration (it is not fixed-width fixed-depth), (2) it uses sampling to determine an evaluation (it does not use heuristics), and (3) it uses averaging as backup function of the statistics to aid node selection (it does not minimax). MCTS works well for Go and many other applications, although for games such as Chess, Checkers, and Othello, alpha-beta with a heuristic evaluation function performs better [108].

Core Problems

- How to focus search effort where it is needed?

© Springer Nature Switzerland AG 2020
A. Plaat, *Learning to Play*, https://doi.org/10.1007/978-3-030-59238-7_5

- What if there is no efficient heuristic function?

Core Concepts

- UCT adaptive node selection
- Monte Carlo sampling
- Average as backup rule

First we will discuss the history and the challenges that led to the creation of Monte Carlo Tree Search and how, after decades of minimax, a different paradigm emerged. Then we discuss the algorithm, including the UCT selection rule, that governs the exploration/exploitation trade-off. Finally, we discuss MCTS enhancements such as RAVE and playout pattern databases.

5.1 Monte Carlo Evaluation

When Kasparov was defeated in 1997 by Deep Blue, many computer game researchers went looking for their new *Drosophila melanogaster*, a new test bed to help make progress in understanding intelligent reasoning.

Another game of strategy, the game of Go, became the focus of much research effort. Creating a player for Go seemed a daunting task. The branching factor of Chess is around 35 in the middle game; for Go it is around 200. The average length of a Chess game is 80 moves by a player; for Go it is closer to 250. The state space of Chess is estimated to be 10^{47}; for Go it is 10^{170}.

Go programs of around that time played at amateur level. They were designed like Chess programs but with forward pruning because of the high branching factor: a highly selective alpha-beta search, and heuristic evaluations based on the concept of territory, as humans are assumed to do [472]. The program GNU Go is a well-known example of this approach; typical designs of that time are described by Müller, Chen and Chen, Boon, and Kierulf et al. [472, 134, 87, 363]

Since a full-width look-ahead search is infeasible due to the branching factor, most early Go programs used aggressive forward pruning-based heuristics: (1) generate a limited number of heuristically likely candidate moves,[1] and (2) search for the optimal policy in this reduced state space [472]. A problem with this approach is that too many good candidates are missed. For evaluation, territory was calculated for each leaf. Such a territory computation used slow flooding-style algorithms and life/death calculations, much slower than the piece-square tables in Chess, necessitating the highly selective search. A different approach was needed.

In 1993, inspired by work on randomized solutions for the traveling salesperson problem, physicist Brügmann wrote a 9×9 Go program based on simulated anneal-

---

[1] Such as: play in corner, connect via 2-point jump, and break ladder.

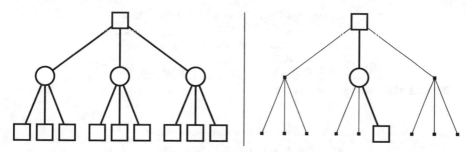

Fig. 5.1 Searching a tree vs. searching a path

ing [109], and in 1990 Abramson explored random evaluations in Othello [5]. These programs did not have a heuristic evaluation function, but played a series of so-called *Monte Carlo playouts*: random moves until the end of the game was reached, where the position was scored as win or loss. The playouts were repeated many times, and results were averaged for each top-level move.

This approach differs fundamentally from the minimax approach, where all moves at each node are searched, resulting in an exponential search of a *tree* of size w^d, from which the best child is chosen. In Brügmann's program, instead, the program searched a number of linear *path*s of size d (Fig. 5.1). Instead of using the minimax function, the program took the average of the scores. In contrast to the heuristic knowledge-based programs of the time, this program had no heuristic knowledge. Although the program did not play great Go, it played better than random. The field of computer Go generally considered this attempt at connecting the sciences of statistical mechanics and artificial intelligence to be a curiosity. The hand-crafted knowledge-based programs of the time performed better. For ten years not much happened with Monte Carlo Go.

Then, in 2003 Bouzy and Helmstetter experimented again with Monte Carlo playouts, again finding that a program can play somewhat reasonable Go moves without a heuristic evaluation function [90].

Three years later, with the introduction of Monte Carlo Tree Search (MCTS), a breakthrough occurred: a new kind of recursive tree search was added to the Monte Carlo playouts. Rémi Coulom introduced MCTS as a tree-based algorithm [152, 153, 151].[2] Rules for node selection, expansion, playout, and backup were specified.

The early works by Brügmann [109] and Bouzy and Helmstetter [90] showed that averaged random playouts do provide at the least an indication of the quality of a position. A "flat" algorithm, with playouts at the root only, did not provide great results, but a recursive, tree based version, combined with a smart exploration/exploitation selection rule, did.

Two of the first Monte Carlo programs were Sylvain Gelly's MoGo [239] and Rémi Coulom's Crazy Stone [151]. Crazy Stone and MoGo were instantly successful, and many other new Go playing programs were written based on MCTS [152, 130, 129,

---

[2] Following work by Chang et al. [127], Auer et al. [23], and Cazenave and Helmstetter [125].

Chapter	Algorithm	Select	Backup	Eval
Chap. 4	alpha-beta	left to right	minimax	heuristic
Chap. 5	MCTS	adaptive	average	sample
Chap. 6	DQN	-	-	generalize
Chap. 7	self-play	adaptive	average	generalize

Table 5.1 Heuristic-Sample-Generalize

Chapter	Name	MDP-tuple	Reinforcement learning
Chap. 4	alpha-beta	$(S, A, 1, R, 1)$	policy, backup
Chap. 5	MCTS	$(S, A, P, R, 1)$	pol, b/u, exploration/exploitation
Chap. 6	DQN	(S, A, P, R, γ)	pol, b/u, expl/expl, discount, off-policy
Chap. 7	self-play	(S, A, P, R, γ)	pol, b/u, expl/expl, discount, off-pol, self-play

Table 5.2 MDP tuple and reinforcement learning in the chapters

473, 201, 40, 235, 553, 408]. Since the introduction of MCTS the playing strength of programs improved rapidly to the level of weak master (2-3 dan) and stronger on the small 9×9 board.

MCTS is also successful in other domains, and there has been great research interest. Browne et al. [108] provide an extensive survey, referencing 240 publications.

Reinforcement Learning

In this chapter we look deeper into MCTS. First, let us see how MCTS fits into the general picture of reinforcement learning methods for games (Table 5.1). MCTS is a reinforcement learning algorithm, as are heuristic planning algorithms. In the Introduction we mentioned three basic paradigms: heuristics, sampling, and generalization. MCTS represents the sampling method. All three methods are reinforcement learning methods, and with MCTS we see the second main paradigm of reinforcement learning.

Likewise, in Chap. 3, the Markov decision process 5-tuple was introduced. Table 5.2 repeats the table from that chapter. We see how the exploration/exploitation trade-off is an integral part of MCTS, in contrast to minimax, where domain-specific enhancements were needed to achieve variable-depth search. With MCTS, we are using more elements of the MDP tuple in the core of the paradigm.

5.2 Monte Carlo Tree Search

We will now look at the MCTS algorithm in depth. MCTS consists of four operations: select, expand, playout, and backpropagate (Fig. 5.2). Note that the third operation (playout) sometimes goes by the names *rollout*, *simulation*, and *sampling*. Back-

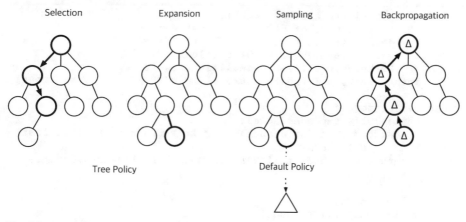

Fig. 5.2 Monte Carlo Tree Search [108]

propagation is sometimes called *backup*. Select is the downward policy trial part, backup the upward error/learning part of the algorithm. Soon, we will discuss the operations in order.

Iteration vs. Recursion

As in heuristic planning, in MCTS the state space is tree shaped, starting from the initial state s_0, using the rules of the game to generate successor states. Unlike in heuristic planning, where the tree is built by recursively adding subtrees, in MCTS the state space is traversed iteratively, and the tree data structure is built in a step by step fashion, node by node. MCTS is a mix between a tree and a path algorithm. A typical size of an MCTS search is to do 1000–10,000 iterations. In MCTS each iteration starts at the root s_0, traversing the tree down to the leaves using a selection rule, expanding an extra node, and performing a playout. The result of the playout is then propagated back to the root. During the backpropagation, statistics at all internal nodes are updated. These statistics are then used in future iterations by the selection rule to go to the currently "most interesting" part of the tree.

The statistics consist of two counters: the win count w and the visit count v. During backpropagation, the visit count v at all nodes that are on the path back from the leaf to the root are incremented. When the result of the playout was a win, then the win count w of those nodes is also incremented. If the result was a loss, then the win count is left unchanged.

The selection rule uses the win rate w/v and the visit count v to decide whether to exploit high-win-rate parts of the tree or to explore low-visit-counts parts. An often used selection rule is UCT (Sect. 5.2.4). It is this selection rule that governs the exploration/exploitation trade-off in MCTS.

```
def monte_carlo_tree_search(root):
    while resources_left(time, computational power):
        leaf = select(root) # leaf = unvisited node
        simulation_result = rollout(leaf)
        backpropagate(leaf, simulation_result)
    return best_child(root) # or: child with highest visit count

def select(node):
    while fully_expanded(node):
        node = best_child(node)      # traverse down path of best
            UCT nodes
    return expand(node.children) or node # no children/node is
        terminal

def rollout(node):
    while non_terminal(node):
        node = rollout_policy(node)
    return result(node)

def rollout_policy(node):
    return pick_random(node.children)

def backpropagate(node, result):
    if is_root(node) return
    node.stats = update_stats(node, result)
    backpropagate(node.parent)

def best_child(node, c_param=1.0):
    choices_weights = [
        (c.q / c.n) + c_param * np.sqrt((np.log(node.n) / c.n))
            # UCT
        for c in node.children
    ]
    return node.children[np.argmax(choices_weights)]
```

Listing 5.1 MCTS pseudo-Python [108, 157]

5.2.1 The Four MCTS Operations

Let us now look in more detail at the four operations. Please refer to Listing 5.1 and Fig. 5.2. As we see in the figure and the listing, the main steps are repeated as long as there is time left. Per step, the activities are as follows [108].

Select

In the selection step the tree is traversed from the root node down until a leaf is reached where a new child is selected that is not part of the tree yet. At each internal state the selection rule is followed to determine which action to take and thus which state to explore next. The UCT rule is the best-known selection rule [373].

The selections at these states constitute the policy π of actions in the look-ahead simulation leading to the state that currently is the best.

Expand

Then, in the expansion step a child is added to the tree. In most cases only one child is added. In some MCTS versions all successors of a leaf are added to the tree [108].

Playout

Subsequently, during the playout step moves are played in self-play until the end of the game is reached.[3] (These node are not added to the MCTS tree, but their search result is, in the backpropagation operation.) The reward r of this simulated game is +1 in case of a win for the first player, 0 in case of a draw, and −1 in case of a win for the opponent. Originally, playouts were random (the Monte Carlo part in the name of MCTS) following Brügmann's [109] and Bouzy and Helmstetter's [90] original approach. In practice, most Go playing programs improve on the random playouts by using databases of small 3×3 patterns with best replies and other fast heuristics [239, 152, 129, 622, 154].

Small amounts of domain knowledge are used after all, albeit not in the form of a heuristic evaluation function.

Backpropagation

In the backpropagation step, reward r is propagated back upwards in the tree, through the nodes that were traversed down previously. Note that two counts are updated: the visit count, for all nodes, and the win count, depending on the reward value.

MCTS is on-policy: the values that are backed up are those of the nodes that were selected (except for RAVE, at the end of this chapter).

---

[3] Note that this self-play is like the self-play in Chap. 4 where in minimax and alpha-beta the opponent moves for finding the best reply are found by the same algorithm. Unlike minimax, here only one, randomly chosen, successor is played out: a path, not a tree. In Chap. 7 we will see a different kind of self-play, where AlphaZero uses self-play loops to train a neural network evaluation function from scratch.

Code

Many websites contain useful resources on MCTS, including example code (see Listing 5.1).[4] The pseudocode is from an example Tic Tac Toe program (only the main methods are shown). The MCTS algorithm can be coded in many different ways. Listing 5.1 [157] follows the survey paper of Browne et al. [108]. The four main operations of MCTS are clearly indicated.

5.2.2 Policies

At the end of the search, after the required number of iterations has been performed, or when time is up, MCTS returns the value and the action with the highest visit count.[5] The action of this initial state s_0 constitutes the policy $\pi(s_0)$ (Sect. 3.2.1).

It should be pointed out that there are multiple policies in MCTS, and the word "policy" is used to describe these different kinds. During the MCTS look-ahead simulation a second policy was used. The actions selected by the selection rule in the tree form a selection policy. Additionally, the actions in the playout phase are also a policy. This third type of policy is sometimes called the *default policy*.

5.2.3 Example

Let us illustrate the working of MCTS with an example. Figure 5.3 gives an example of a few MCTS iterations. (The UCT formula is described in the next subsection.) In the example we see how MCTS traverses the state space in iterations, how the UCT formula adapts between exploiting high win values and exploring unseen parts of the tree, and how the statistics are averaged in the backpropagation phase.

5.2.4 UCT Selection Rule

The adaptive exploration/exploitation behavior of MCTS is governed by the selection rule. One of the most popular selection rules is the UCT formula.

UCT was introduced in 2006 by Kocsis and Szepesvári [373]. The paper provides a theoretical guarantee of eventual convergence to the minimax value. The selection

---

[4] https://int8.io/monte-carlo-tree-search-beginners-guide/

[5] An alternative would be to return the action with the highest win rate. However, the visit count takes into account the win rate (through UCT) and the number of simulations on which it is based. A high win rate may be based on a low number of simulations, and will thus be high variance. High visit count will be low variance. High visit count implies high win-rate with high confidence, high win rate may be low confidence [108].

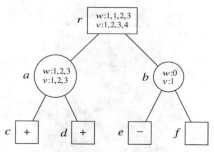

Fig. 5.3 MCTS starts at the root, does not select a move because there are no children in the tree, but expands a random child. Assume a is expanded. Then a random playout is performed at node a. Assume node d is the first node in the playout. In this tiny state space, the random path that is played out consists only of node d and is a terminal node. The value at node d is a win, so backpropagation increments all win values of the path to the root by 1 (nodes a, r) and also the visit counts. The second iteration starts at root r, where there are unexpanded children, so it expands a node, which is node b. At b a playout is performed, which ends up at, say, e, whose value is a loss. This gets propagated (no win values change, and the visit counts of b, r are incremented). Next, the third iteration starts. At the root all children are expanded, so we select a child. We select a since its UCT value is $1/1 + 1 \times \sqrt{\ln 2/1} = 1.83$, and b's value is $0/1 + 1 \times \sqrt{\ln 2/1} = 0.83$. There are unexpanded children so it expands a node, assume it picks node c, a win. The values are updated (a's win and visit count are incremented to 2 and 2, r's to 2 and 3). Next, the fourth iteration selects node a since the UCT value of a is $2/2 + 1 \times \sqrt{\ln 3/2} = 1.63$ and b is $0/1 + 1 \times \sqrt{\ln 3/1} = 1.04$. It finds that there are unexpanded children of a in the tree, so it expands child d, a win, and updates the win and visit values of d, a, and r accordingly. It continues with more iterations until time is up.

rule was named UCT, for Upper Confidence bounds for multi-armed bandits applied to Trees.

The exploration/exploitation trade-off is central in many reinforcement learning algorithms. The selection rule determines the way in which the current values of the children influence which parts of the tree will be explored more. The UCT formula is

$$\text{UCT}(j) = \frac{w_j}{n_j} + C_p \sqrt{\frac{\ln n}{n_j}},$$

where w_j is the number of wins in child j, n_j is the number of times child j has been visited, n is the number of times the parent node has been visited, and $C_p \geq 0$ is a constant (the tunable exploration/exploitation parameter). The first term in the UCT equation, the win rate, is the exploitation term. A child with a high win rate receives through this term an exploitation bonus. The second term is for exploration. A child that has been visited infrequently has an exploration bonus. The level of exploration can be adjusted by the C_p constant. A low C_p does little exploration; a high C_p has more exploration. Section 5.3.1 goes deeper into the choice for values for C_p. The selection rule then is to select the child with the highest UCT sum (the standard argmax function).

Fig. 5.4 A multi-armed bandit

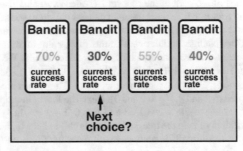

Fig. 5.5 Explore or exploit? [763]

The UCT formula balances *win rate* ($\frac{w_j}{n_j}$) and *"newness"* ($\sqrt{\frac{\ln n}{n_j}}$) in the selection of nodes to expand.[6] Many alternative selection rules have been proposed. Alternatives for UCT are variants such as Auer's UCB1 [22, 23, 24] and P-UCT [561, 440]. Most rules are based on bandit theory, which we will briefly touch upon next.

Multi-armed Bandit Problem

The work on UCT and upper confidence bounds (UCB) is based on bandit theory, a topic well studied in the field of stochastic scheduling and decision theory [23, 357, 127]. The theory provides a systematic means to optimize the search strategies to explore more promising parts of the tree, while still ensuring exploration. Seminal work has been done by Lai [394, 395], proving important optimality results.

A multi-armed bandit is a mathematical model whose name refers to a casino slot machine, but with more than one arm (Fig. 5.4). Each arm can have a different payout.

---

[6] The square-root term is a measure of the variance (uncertainty) of the action value. The use of the natural logarithm ensures that, since increases get smaller over time, old actions are selected less frequently. However, since logarithm values are unbounded, eventually all actions will be selected [659].

The probability distribution of the payout of the arms is also not known. As arms are played, the player gets more information as to their payout probability. However, each play also costs money. The multi-armed bandit problem then is to select the best arm in as few tries as possible (Fig. 5.5). Multi-armed bandit theory thus analyzes situations of short-term cost versus long-term gain.

Consider the following situation: One arm gives 10 dollars with probability 0.1, while another gives 1000 dollars with probability 0.002. After 50 tries, the first arm probably yielded some win, whereas the second probably did not. You may then want to play mostly the first arm, but this is not optimal in the long run, since the expected reward of the second one is actually twice as high. But to learn this, you will need to sample the second arm for quite a while.

Multi-armed bandits have a classic reinforcement learning exploitation/exploration trade-off: should I play the arm that I know to give high payout so far, or should I play arms whose payout I do not know but may have higher payout? In a paper Lai and Robbins [394] construct an optimal selection policy (optimal in the sense that it has maximum convergence rate to the arm with the highest mean) for a case where the reward distributions of the arms is known. An active field of research subsequently studied relaxations of this condition.

In MCTS the multi-armed bandit problem is applied in a recursive setting, in a tree of decisions. Each state is a bandit, and each action (child) is an arm.

5.2.5 The Impact of MCTS

Before 2006, mainstream game programming research was based on heuristic planning. The minimax backup rule was the main paradigm, spawning a large effort to formalize and code heuristic human knowledge. The conventional wisdom was that human knowledge should be captured in heuristics, and that no move should be missed (due to the tactical nature of the popular perfect-information games that were used at the time). There was no overarching principle behind the many heuristic enhancements, except that they should be efficient to code, and a means to make the search more selective should be tried, in order to overcome the horizon problem.

When MCTS was introduced, it provided an elegant framework for selective search, amenable to theoretical analysis and successful in practice. MCTS follows a different, non-exponential paradigm. Minimax is based on searching all successor states and is an inherently exponential tree searcher, with a $\sqrt{w^d}$ best-case time complexity for alpha-beta. MCTS is a sampling algorithm. It searches paths from the root to the terminals, not trees. This non-exponential principle circumvents the need for the plethora of heuristic search enhancements trying to curtail the exponential time complexity of minimax. Equally important, the sampling also removed the need for heuristic evaluation.

The success of the new approach of selective playout sampling created a paradigm shift in the world of computer game playing. In Go, and in many other games, it turned out that some moves *can* be missed, or rather, that *most* moves can be missed,

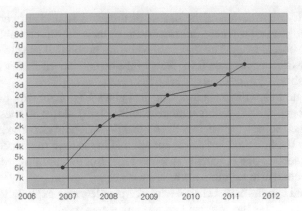

Fig. 5.6 Performance of MCTS programs [235]

as long as on average a reliable picture of the state space emerges. The paradigm changed from an exponential $O(w^d)$ to a polynomial $O(d)$ complexity. Exponential worked for Chess; polynomial worked for Go.[7] The new paradigm worked so well that no human knowledge in the form of heuristics was needed (or at least, initially).

The dominant language of the field changed with the introduction of MCTS. The graph-based language of nodes, leaves, and strategies changed to state, action, and policy.

Applications of MCTS

The introduction of MCTS improved performance of Go programs considerably, from medium amateur to strong amateur. Where heuristics-based GNU Go played around 10 kyu, Monte Carlo programs progressed to 2-3 dan[8] in a few years' time.

On the small board, 9×9, Go programs achieved very strong play. Figure 5.6 shows a graph of the improvements in the performance of Go programs on the large 19×19 board [235]. Performance did not improve much beyond the 4-5 dan level, despite much effort by researchers. It was thought that perhaps the large action space of the 19×19 board was too hard for MCTS. Many enhancements were considered, for the playout phase, and for the selection. One of the enhancements that was tried was the introduction of neural nets. As we will see in Chap. 7, in 2015 this became successful.

---

[7] In practice, both minimax and MCTS are made into anytime algorithms that produce a best move when stopped. For minimax, iterative deepening transforms it into an anytime algorithm; for MCTS, the algorithm is already an anytime algorithm that performs an iteration of playouts.

[8] Absolute beginners in Go start at 30 kyu, progressing to 10 kyu, and advancing to 1 kyu. Stronger amateur players then achieve 1 dan, progressing to 7 dan, the highest amateur rating for Go. Professional Go players have a rating from 1 dan to 9 dan, written as 1p–9p.

Name	Principle	Applicability	Effectiveness
expl/expl	expl/expl/N	small/large searches	all MCTS
RAVE	statistics sharing	early phase	all MCTS
play-out db	small patterns	domain specific	domain dependent
adaptive expl/expl	variable C_p	general	all MCTS
parallelism	parallel search	general	all MCTS

Table 5.3 MCTS enhancements

MCTS revolutionized the world of heuristic search. Previously, in order to achieve best-first search, one had to find a domain specific heuristic to guide the search in a smart way. With MCTS this was no longer necessary. Now a general method existed that could find the promising parts of the search without a domain-specific heuristic, just by using statistics of the search itself.

MCTS quickly proved successful in other games, both two agent and single agent: for video games [130], for single player applications [584], and for many other games such as EinStein würfelt nicht [429], Settlers of Catan [666], Havannah [428], Amazons [367], and mathematical games such as the Voronoi game [91].

5.3 *MCTS Enhancements

Basic MCTS already showed much promise, and researchers immediately found ways to improve performance of the basic algorithm further. They focused on action selection and on playout. We will discuss some of these enhancements. Table 5.3 shows the MCTS enhancements that we will discuss.

First we will discuss tuning of C_p, the exploration/exploitation parameter, and then we will discuss RAVE, a method to speed up the distribution of statistics at the early stage of an MCTS search. After that, we will discuss playout databases, adaptive C_p, and parallelism.

5.3.1 Exploration/Exploitation

The search process of MCTS is guided by the statistics values in the tree. MCTS discovers during the search where the promising parts of the tree are. The tree expansion of MCTS is an inherently variable-depth and variable-width search process. To illustrate this we show a picture of a snapshot of the search tree of an MCTS optimization from [388, 722]. In Fig. 5.7 we see that some parts of the tree are searched more deeply than others. The tree in the illustration is part of an expression optimization problem in a symbolic algebra system [721].

An important element of MCTS is the exploration/exploitation trade-off that can be tuned with the C_p parameter. The effectiveness of MCTS depends on the choice

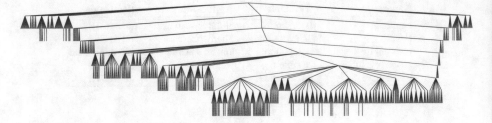

Fig. 5.7 Adaptive MCTS tree [388]

of this parameter. Typical initial choices for Go programs are $C_p = 1$ or $C_p = 0.1$; programs that use RAVE found $C_p = 0$ to works best [108], although in AlphaGo we will see highly explorative choices such as $C_p = 5$. In general, when compute power is low, C_p should be low, and when more compute power is available, more exploration (higher C_p) is advisable.

Kuipers et al. [388, 722] have performed experiments to plot the relation between C_p and the number of MCTS node expansions N. When C_p is small, MCTS favors parts of the tree that have been visited before and are known to be good; when C_p is large, unvisited parts of the tree are favored. Figure 5.8 shows four plots of an optimization for a large symbolic algebra polynomial. The plots show results from a large number of optimization runs, all starting with a different random seed. On the y-axis the number of operations of the optimized polynomial is shown; the lower this number is, the better. The lowest number found is close to 4000. This minimum is achieved in the case of $N = 3000$ iterations for a value of C_p with $0.7 \leq C_p \leq 1.2$. Dots above this minimum represent a suboptimal search result.

For 300 iterations per data point (left upper panel), some structure is visible, with a minimum emerging at $C_p \approx 0.4$. With more tree expansions (see the other three panels) the picture becomes clearer, and the value for C_p for which the best answers are found becomes higher; the picture appears to shift to the right. For low numbers of tree expansions (see again upper left panel) there is almost no discernible advantage of setting the exploration/exploitation parameter at a certain value. For 1000 iterations (see upper right panel) MCTS works best when exploitative (the left part of the plot achieves the lowest number of operations). As the number of iterations N is larger (the two lower panels) MCTS achieves better results when its selection policy is more explorative, to try to get out of local minima. For the graphs with iterations of 3000 and 10000 the range of good results for C_p becomes wider, indicating that the choice between exploration/exploitation becomes less critical.

For small values of C_p, such that MCTS behaves exploitatively, the method gets trapped in one of the local minima as can be seen from scattered dots that form "lines" in the left-hand sides of the four panels. For large values of C_p, such that MCTS is more explorative, many of the searches do not lead to the global minimum as can be seen from the cloud of points on the right-hand side of the four panels. For intermediate values of $C_p \approx 1$, MCTS balances well between exploitation and

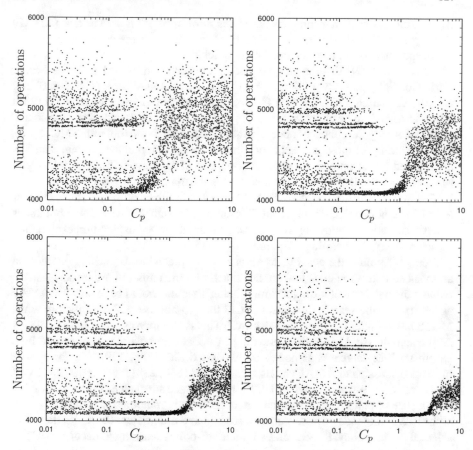

Fig. 5.8 Scatter plots of C_p for N = 300, 1000, 3000, and 10,000 node expansions per MCTS run. Each dot is one MCTS run to optimize a large polynomial. Lower is better. Exploitation (small C_p) works best in small trees (N = 300), exploration in large trees (N = 10, 000) [388]

exploration and finds almost always an ordering that is very close to the best one known [388, 722].

5.3.2 Selection: RAVE

We will now look at another enhancement. One of the best known enhancements to MCTS is RAVE, or rapid action value estimation. RAVE addresses the problem that initially, at the start of the search, all visit and win rate counts of the nodes are zero and MCTS is expanding with little guidance of where to go. The early part of MCTS thus unfolds in the dark. The sooner search information is available throughout the tree, the better the children that will be selected and the more efficient the search will be. Two closely related techniques have been developed: all moves as first (AMAF) and rapid action value estimation (RAVE). They allow for the node statistics (win count and visit count) to be updated more quickly.

Already in [109] Brügmann gives the first description of AMAF in his Monte Carlo Go. Gelly and Silver [236] report on the use of AMAF in MCTS, combining it with tree search and UCT, in a Go program. Helmbold and Parker-Wood [288] also find AMAF to be effective in Go. An AMAF update of the win and visit counts updates not only the counts of nodes on the playout path to the root of the MCTS tree, but also siblings of those nodes that occurred at *any* position in the playout. Statistics are updated for all actions of a state that occurred in the playout. Since playouts tend to touch about half the board for a side, this means that many extra nodes in the MCTS tree are updated by AMAF. AMAF works in the backup operation, in order to influence node selection in the UCT formula. Through AMAF many more nodes receive the statistics, allowing UCT to make a more informed exploration/exploitation decision. AMAF is learning off-policy.

Being off-policy, the cost of AMAF is a loss of precision. Branching out the win and visit statistics to nodes that are not exactly on the path, but are loosely related, reduces the precision of the algorithm. A better situation would be to only use AMAF at the start of the search, as warm up, and then to not use AMAF anymore when MCTS has sufficient statistics to work well. This is the approach that RAVE follows. At the start it use AMAF-like spreading of updates, whose use is governed by a parameter that decreases as nodes are expanded. See [288, 129, 108] for a more in-depth discussion of AMAF and its variants, and [236, 238] for their variant RAVE. Gelly and Silver further extend the UCT formula to take advantage of prior knowledge, making use of pattern databases that are trained from grandmaster games.

In RAVE the nodes whose statistics are updated are not just the nodes that were selected by the policy. RAVE causes limited off-policy learning to occur in MCTS.

5.3.3 Playout: Pattern Database

Another enhancement concerns the playout phase. Sinnce the playout phase chooses moves randomly, playouts are quick and no heuristic has to be devised. However, should such quick heuristics exist, they will almost surely achieve better play than random moves.

Most Go programs replace random playouts by heuristics or databases of small (often 3×3) patterns. The patterns are learned off-line by supervised machine learning from grandmaster games. These patterns check each position in the 3×3 pattern around where the last move was played.

Gelly et al. [239, 237] describe how pattern databases are used for better playouts in MoGo, achieving grandmaster performance on the small 9×9 Go board.

5.3.4 Adaptive Exploitation/Exploration

The C_p parameter of MCTS governs the exploration/exploitation trade-off. Ruijl et al. [568] describe a scheme in which C_p decreases towards zero over the course of the search, starting out favoring exploration, and becoming more exploitative towards the end of the search. This focuses search effort towards building deeper trees towards the end. This is beneficial in an application where large formulas are optimized with MCTS [568, 569, 567].

Such adaptive parameters are also used in simulated annealing, ϵ-greedy exploration, and other reinforcement learning methods.

5.3.5 Ensembles and Parallelism

One way to improve performance without actually having to change the algorithm is to parallelize it. A parallel algorithm can run faster when parallel hardware is available, such as a multi-core or cluster computer.

MCTS consists of many search iterations starting at the root. These searches are semi-independent. Through the win and visit counts the iterations communicate search results. The searches can in principle be run independently, altough the individual iterations miss out on some of the accumulated win and visit statistics in the other iterations. Nevertheless, MCTS appears quite well suited for speedup through parallelization. Indeed, most large Go programs run the iterations in parallel.

Traditionally, the literature identifies three approaches to parallelization: root parallelism, tree parallelism, and leaf parallelism [131, 454]. In root parallelism, processors perform MCTS searches independently, not sharing a tree (thus reducing synchronization and communication, at the cost of less efficient searches because of less win/visit statistics).

In tree parallelism the tree is shared, at the cost of more synchronization and communication, but also leading to a more efficient search [614].

Leaf parallelism again shares no information, and performs independent playouts in parallel [556].

Mirsoleimani et al. [452, 456] provide a unified view on tree and root parallelism, solving some of its problems, and allowing hybrid versions of root and tree parallelism to be created with pipeline parallel MCTS.

Although root parallelism may seem inefficient due to the lack of sharing of information, there is an interesting relation with ensemble search. Fern and Lewis [208] and Mirsoleimani et al. [451] study ensembles of independent MCTS searches, in which the tree is searched independently, in relation to exploration. Ensembles of MCTS searches explore more of the tree than a single MCTS search does, because the searches are independent. Root parallel searches are also independent; they share no information, just as ensemble search. Thus, if one would like to achieve a certain exploration/exploitation balance in a parallel setting, all one has to do is to use root parallelism with a reduced C_p parameter. The reduced C_p dials back the exploration of each individual search, and one gets more exploration inherent in the independent (ensemble or parallel) searches.

5.3.6 Rollout Algorithms

We are at the end of this section on MCTS enhancements. There is a final observation to be made, which is not an enhancement, but more a philosophical curiosity.

Alpha-beta and MCTS are usually regarded as algorithms from different classes, of an almost incomparable nature. Alpha-beta is a recursive depth-first tree traversal algorithm. MCTS is a path-traversal algorithm, iteratively invoked until the search budget is exhausted, starting from the root and returning to it after each pass. Alpha-beta is rigid left-to-right; MCTS is inherently adaptive and selective, using UCT.

MCTS is part of a family of *rollout* algorithms [73]. In rollout algorithms the starting point is a base policy, whose performance is evaluated in some way, possibly by simulation. Based on that evaluation, an improved policy is obtained by one-step look-ahead.

In 1995, Rivest [555] published an iterative approach for approximation of the minimax value, with good results. Twenty years later, inspired by MCTS, Huang [311] presented a rollout formulation (path-based) of alpha-beta. In this formulation the algorithmic structure of the rollout version of alpha-beta and MCTS look strikingly similar. The two differences are the selection rule (trial) and the type of values that are backed up (error). Alpha-beta has a left-first selection rule; MCTS selects the child with the highest UCT value. Alpha-beta backs up upper bounds and lower bounds; MCTS backs up node counts and win counts.

Listing 5.2 shows MCTS in compact pseudo-Python (after [311]). Listing 5.3 shows alpha-beta rollout code in pseudo-Python (after [311]).[9]

Huang's formulation is important because it elegantly captures the difference between these two important algorithms in a single algorithmic framework. His formulation also highlights that the two algorithms have more in common than previously assumed, even though they come from different paradigms.

5.4 Practice

Below are some questions to check your understanding of this chapter. Each question is a closed question where a simple, one sentence answer is possible based on the text in this chapter.

---

[9] Note that the code is pseudo-Python. It looks like Python, but, for the sake of compactness, some essential functions are missing, such as initializations of counters and bounds, tree manipulation code, and max and min functions for all children. The listings contain some code duplication to highlight similarity of algorithmic structure.

```
# python-like pseudo-code of MCTS. After [Huang 2015]
def mcts(root, budget):
  while root.n < budget:
    g = rollout(root)
  return g


def rollout(s):
  if s.isleaf():
    g = playout(s)
  elif s.ismax():
    c_select = s.argmax_c(c.avg + cp * sqrt(log(s.n)/(2*c.n)))
    g = rollout(c_select)
    s.avg = s.n/(s.n+1)*s.avg + 1/(s.n+1)*g
    s.n   = s.n + 1
  elif s.ismin():
    c_select = s.argmin_c(c.avg - cp * sqrt(log(s.n)/(2*c.n)))
    g = rollout(c_select)
    s.avg = s.n/(s.n+1)*s.avg + 1/(s.n+1)*g
    s.n   = s.n + 1
  return g
```

Listing 5.2 Rollout MCTS in pseudo-Python [311]

```
# python-like pseudo-code of alpha-beta. After [Huang 2015]
def alphabeta(root):
  # all bounds should be initialized to (-inf, +inf) (not shown)
  while root.lb < root.ub:
    rollout(root, root.lb, root.ub)
  return root.lower


def rollout(s, alpha, beta):
  if s.isleaf():
    s.lb = s.playout()
    s.ub = s.playout()
  elif s.ismax():
    c_select = first([c for c in s.child() if max(alpha, c.lb) <
        min(beta, c.ub)])
    rollout(c_select, max(alpha, c_select.lb), min(beta, c_select
        .ub))
    s.lb = max([c.lb for c in s.child()])
    s.ub = max([c.ub for c in s.child()])
  elif s.ismin():
    c_select = first([c for c in s.child() if max(alpha, c.lb) <
        min(beta, c.ub)])
    rollout(c_select, max(alpha, c_select.lb), min(beta, c_select
        .ub))
    s.lb = min([c.lb for c in s.child()])
    s.ub = min([c.ub for c in s.child()])
  return
```

Listing 5.3 Rollout alpha-beta in pseudo-Python [311]

Questions

1. How are Go players ranked?
2. What is the difference between tactics and strategy in games?
3. What is the difference between exponential and polynomial time complexity? Can you name an algorithm for each?
4. What are the four steps of MCTS?
5. Describe two advantages of MCTS over rigid heuristic planning.
6. How is MCTS recursive?
7. Describe the function of each of the four operations of MCTS.
8. Give the UCT formula.
9. How does UCT achieve trading off exploration and exploitation? Which inputs does it use?
10. When C_p is small, does MCTS explore more or exploit more?
11. For small numbers of node expansions, would you prefer more exploration or more exploitation?
12. What does RAVE do?
13. What is the role of pattern databases in the playout phase?
14. Give three ways in which the performance of MCTS can be enhanced.
15. What is a rollout algorithm?

Exercises

For the exercises in this chapter we will use two code bases: Browne et al. [108] and Michi. The MCTS implementation of Browne is simple, clear, and well suited to learn MCTS with. The example code implements Othello and Nim, but not Go. The Michi implementation does implement Go. It is a minimalist implementation of an MCTS Go program.

1. Implement MCTS, for example from here.[10] Familiarize yourself with the code, and implement a game of Othello.
2. Study the impact of search effort. Make a graph of Elo rating on the y-axis and N the number of node expansions on the x-axis (play different N numbers of node expansions against each other).
3. Study the impact of exploration and exploitation. For a fixed search budget, plot Elo rating for four different C_p values: $\{0.1, 0.7, 1.0, 3.0\}$.
4. Implement a Hex game player with MCTS. See the Hex page[11] for information. See also [106, 280, 314].
5. Go to Michi[12] and download the code. Play a game against the computer on 9×9 and on 19×19. Who won? Is your computer fast enough for the big board?
6. Do the preceding Othello exercises (1–3) also for 9×9 Go.

---

[10] https://int8.io/monte-carlo-tree-search-beginners-guide/

[11] https://www.maths.ed.ac.uk/~csangwin/hex/index.html

[12] https://github.com/pasky/michi

Summary

In this chapter the dual challenges of (1) rigid search and (2) lack of an efficient heuristic evaluation function were addressed. We introduced a new paradigm, the adaptive sampling paradigm, with the MCTS algorithm. Where minimax needed enhancements and tweaks to focus the search effort on the important part of the state space, MCTS is inherently selective. The most popular selection rule is UCT, which provides a good exploration/exploitation trade-off. UCT is based on a large body of bandit theory.

The development of MCTS was driven by Go, which emerged as the new *Drosophila* of AI, after Deep Blue beat Kasparov in Chess.

The fact that MCTS does not need a heuristic evaluation function allows it to work for Go, and for other domains for which no efficient heuristic function was found. MCTS caused a breakthrough in Go performance, achieving master level play on the small 9×9 board.

Traditionally, MCTS has four operations: select, expand, playout, and backup (although we also showed a more compact rollout formulation, providing a link to alpha-beta [311]).

As before, enhancements are important to achieve the highest possible performance. Two well-known enhancements are RAVE, to speed up the propagation of node statistics in the first part of the search, and databases of small patterns in the playout operation.

The previous chapters focused on model-based reinforcement learning. Heuristic planning and adaptive sampling need a simulator with the rules of the game as the transition function.

Historical and Bibliographical Notes

MCTS was first developed for Go. Soon other games and optimization applications were also found to benefit from the flexible adaptivity of MCTS and especially from the fact that no domain-specific heuristic evaluation function was needed. See for some examples [108, 20, 130, 630, 388, 129, 466, 467].

A highly cited survey on MCTS is Browne et al. [108]. It has more than 200 references to papers on MCTS and provided a wealth of knowledge on MCTS, highly recommended. Coulom introduced the MCTS algorithm [151], and he implemented it in his program Crazy Stone. Gelly et al. wrote another Monte Carlo-based program, MoGo [239, 235], which was successful in tournaments against other programs, and against human Go players. Gelly and Silver published an influential paper on pattern databases and AMAF/RAVE [236, 238].

Of prime importance in MCTS is the selection rule, which gives it adaptive selectivity. UCB1 and UCT are selection rules based on bandit theory, derived in [373, 22]. In their seminal 2006 paper, Kocsis and Szepesvári introduce UCT [373]. Most Go programs use some form of parallel search. There has been quite some research into parallelization of MCTS; see, e.g., Chaslot et al. and Mirsoleimani et al. [131, 456]. Ensemble MCTS is related to parallel MCTS and exploration; see [208].

On-line there are many resources to be found for programming a computer Go program. At Senseis there is much information on how to write your own Go program.[13]

---

[13] https://senseis.xmp.net/?ComputerGoProgramming

Chapter 6
Function Approximation

The previous chapter featured evaluation by random playouts. In this chapter we try to improve upon random playouts, using function approximation methods. The aim of this chapter is ambitious: we focus on large, high-dimensional, *end-to-end*, problems; actions must be found for states without hand-crafted intermediate heuristic features.

Deep learning is a method to approximate an objective function by automated discovery of features. This objective function can be a regression function, a classifier, a value function, or a policy function. Classification functions are used in supervised image recognition tasks, and value and policy functions are used in reinforcement learning in games.

Deep learning has been quite succesful in image recognition, yielding methods that classify images better than humans. In games, deep learning has found policy functions that play vintage Atari arcade games as good or better than humans. Deep learning is a driving force of the AI revolution.

End-to-end learning means that we learn output labels and actions directly from raw pixel inputs, un-preprocessed, without intermediate hand-crafted heuristics. End-to-end learning is computationally intensive. Progress has been made possible by advances in compute power in CPUs and especially in GPUs around the turn of the millennium. Furthermore, around that time large datasets of hand-labeled data were created, providing the necessary training data. Finally, algorithmic advances solved key problems in deep learning. Together with the increase in compute power and big data these developments enabled the deep learning revolution.

To quote one of the central works of this area, Mnih et al. [461]: "Recent breakthroughs in computer vision and speech recognition have relied on efficiently training deep neural networks on very large training sets. The most successful approaches are trained directly from the raw inputs, using lightweight updates based on stochastic gradient descent. By feeding sufficient data into deep neural networks, it is often possible to learn better representations than hand crafted features."

© Springer Nature Switzerland AG 2020
A. Plaat, *Learning to Play*, https://doi.org/10.1007/978-3-030-59238-7_6

Core Problem

- Can we find end-to-end value/policy functions for high-dimensional problems?

Core Concepts

- Automated feature discovery through deep learning
- Convolutional neural network (CNN) and deep Q-network (DQN)
- Overfitting and stable learning

Many of the advances in deep reinforcement learning started in supervised learning. Therefore the first part of this chapter is devoted to an introduction to the advances in deep supervised learning. A good understanding of deep learning is important in modern reinforcement learning; we will spend quite some effort on this topic.

6.1 Deep Supervised Learning

Towards the end of Chap. 3, in Sect. 3.3.1 we discussed ways to approximate functions when the state space becomes so large that it is unlikely that states, when tested, will have been seen before in training. Statistical learning theory provides a framework for machine learning methods such as supervised learning and reinforcement learning [572, 227].

Supervised learning is the task of learning a regression or classification function that maps an input to an output based on example input-output pairs [572, 250, 81]. Our goal is to solve the inverse function problem: find a function to fit its outputs. For example, the training set may be a set of pictures, labeled with a description, such as *CAT* or *DOG*. Because the learning process learns a function from an explicit set of labeled training data it is called *supervised*, since the labels supervise the learning process.

6.1.1 Generalization and Features

Supervised learning is a basic and widely studied problem in artificial intelligence. A wide range of algorithms exist for supervised learning: support vector machines, linear regression, Bayesian classification, decision trees, random forests, nearest neighbor, and artificial neural networks, to name just a few [572, 81, 272].

Since around 2010 artificial neural networks have achieved impressive results in image recognition, speech recognition, and game playing. We will focus on deep neural networks in this chapter.

Chapter	Algorithm	Select	Backup	Eval
Chap. 4	alpha beta	left to right	minimax	heuristic
Chap. 5	MCTS	adaptive	average	sample
Chap. 6	DQN	-	-	generalize
Chap. 7	self-play	adaptive	average	generalize

Table 6.1 Heuristic-Sample-Generalize

We will first discuss learning as a generalization task, and then how generalization can be viewed as a feature discovery task.

Learning as Generalization from Training Set to Test Set

Learning is the adaptation of behavior from experience. Supervised learning is closely related to generalization, which is the formulation of common properties in instances of data. Table 6.1 shows (again) the main paradigms of this book, to show how generalization is contrasted to the other paradigms.

Supervised learning learns a continuous regression or a discrete classification function. Regression finds the relation between examples and a continuous variable; classification finds the relation between examples and a set of discrete classes.[1]

A standard method in machine learning to assess the quality of a categorization algorithm is to divide the dataset into a training part and a test part (k-fold cross validation) [81]. A typical split is 90% of the data for the training set, and the remaining 10% for the test set. The algorithm is trained on examples from the training part. The quality of the resulting approximation function is then tested on the remaining (unseen) 10%, to see how well it generalizes. If the percentage of correct predictions on the test set is about the same as on the training set, then the approximation generalizes well to the test set. If not, the training process may have underfitted or overfitted (captured too little of the signal or too much of the noise, see Sect. 6.1.7).

Deep learning provides methods to generalize over data to approximate regression and classification functions. It does so by discovering common features. Let us see how this is achieved.

Generalization as Feature Discovery

Generalization can be achieved through the discovery of common features. Traditionally, feature discovery is a labor-intensive task. Common features in a dataset are painstakingly identified by hand, by one by one looking at the examples in the dataset, and by writing small algorithms that recognize the features. For image data, such

---

[1] Also in continuous regression problems the test examples will not be seen at training time, and approximation is necessary.

hand-identified features are typically simple features such as lines, squares, circles, and angles. These features can then be used in decision trees to construct recognizers to classify an image.

As we shall see in the next subsections, deep learning has allowed this manual process to be automated. We have just described machine learning as a generalization task. By finding commonalities we can group the instances into a smaller number of higher-level concepts. These concepts are more abstract, more general, than the many lower-level instances.[2]

In the context of image recognition the commonalities are called features, and the process of learning higher-level abstractions is called representation learning [405]. Deep nets can perform feature recognition through a layered hierarchy of increasingly abstract representations [293, 405]. Today deep learning is one of the core technologies that is used in automated function approximation.

From a scientific point of view, the hand crafting and hand tuning is undesirable as it is hard to reproduce. Hand crafting depends on expert knowledge, in contrast to the training of approximators by an optimization algorithm such as stochastic gradient descent, which can be reproduced easily by running the algorithm again.

Furthermore, and most importantly, the hand-crafted heuristics do not generalize well to other domains, whereas deep feature recognizers have been shown to work well in many domains (although they typically have to be retrained for each domain).

Finally, there may be problem domains where our domain intuition fails to come up with efficient features. We may not understand our own human interpretations well enough to come up with efficient algorithms. This was the case in Go, as we saw in the previous chapter.

End-to-End Learning

End-to-end learning, or classification directly from high-dimensional raw pixel data, is computationally quite demanding, as opposed to learning based on intermediate (lower dimensional) hand-crafted features. You may recall that in Chap. 4 heuristic value functions were used to search the large state spaces of Chess and Checkers (Sect. 4.1.3). Automated tuning of features was discussed as a hybrid method between hand-crafted heuristic functions and end-to-end feature learning. The features themselves are still hand crafted, but the coefficients (weights) c_i of the features in the polynomial evaluation function $h(s) = c_1 \times f_1(s) + c_2 \times f_2(s) + c_3 \times f_3(s) + \ldots + c_n \times f_n(s)$ are learned by supervised learning. The difference is that the features in the Chess evaluation function are manually designed heuristics, combined in a linear function whose coefficients are manually tuned, whereas the features in a deep net are trained (generalized) on a large set of examples in an automatic training process.

We will now see in more detail how neural networks can perform automated feature discovery. First we will describe the general architecture for shallow artificial neural networks.

---

[2] Feature discovery is related to dimensionality reduction, a technique that can be used for visualization of complex data [564, 672, 433].

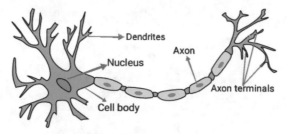

Fig. 6.1 Biological neuron [732]

6.1.2 Shallow Neural Network

The architecture of artificial neural networks is inspired by the architecture of biological neural networks, such as the human brain. Neural networks consist of neural core cells that are connected by nerve cells (see, for example, [49]). Figure 6.1 shows a drawing of a biological neuron, with two nuclei, an axon, and dendrites [732].

Figure 6.2 shows a simple fully connnected artificial neural network, with an input layer, an output layer, and a single hidden layer. A neural network with a single hidden layer (or a few, 2–3) is called shallow. When the network has more hidden layers, it is called deep.

Just as computer Chess, neural networks research has a long history, and much work was done before they were successful. Already in 1943 McCulloch and Pitts [444] provided a computational model for neural networks. The history of the development of neural networks is quite interesting and rich, with high ups and deep downs. Training neural networks is a problem that has been studied by many researchers. The 2018 Turing award was awarded to Bengio, Hinton, and LeCun for their work in this area (Fig. 2.3). Section 6.5 provides pointers to some of the literature.

The most popular training method is based on gradient descent, of which the stochastic version performs very well in deep neural networks. Much research has been done on algorithms for efficient gradient descent [756]. Stochastic gradient descent (SGD) and backpropagation have allowed the training of multi-layer networks, paving the way for deep learning's success.

Stochastic Gradient Descent and Backpropagation

We will now discuss the networks and their training algorithms in more detail.

Neural networks consist of neurons and connections, typically organized in layers (as in Fig. 6.2). The neurons act as functions that process their input signal as a weighted combination of inputs, producing an output signal. This function is called an activation function. Popular activation functions are the rectified linear unit (ReLU: partly linear, partly zero), the hyperbolic tangent, and the sigmoid or logistic function $\frac{1}{1+e^{-x}}$ (these will be discussed in more detail shortly). The neurons are connected by

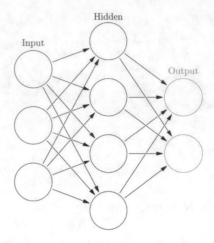

Fig. 6.2 A shallow neural network

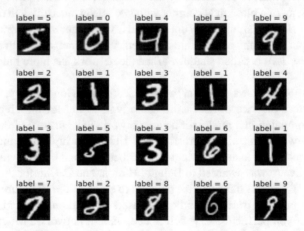

Fig. 6.3 Some MNIST images

weights. At each neuron j the incoming weights ij are summed $\sum$ and then processed by the activation function σ. The output o of neuron j is therefore: $o_j = \sigma(\sum_i x_i w_{ij})$ for weight ij of predecessor neuron x_i. The outputs of this layer of neurons are fed to the inputs for the weights of the next layer.

In supervised learning, a network is trained on a set of example pairs (x, z): inputs x and labels, or targets, z. Typical examples are images of pictures or digits, in which case the labels are the correct digit (Fig. 6.3).

The neural network is a parameterized function $f_\theta(x) \to y$ that converts input to output. The behavior depends on the parameters θ. Training the network is adjusting the weights such that the required input-output relation is achieved. This is done by minimizing the error (or loss) function that calculates the difference between the output y and the network target z.

The training process consists of training *epochs,* individual passes in which the network weights are optimized towards the goal. When training starts, the weights of the network are initialized to small random numbers. Each epoch consists of a forward (recognition, usage) pass and a backward (training, adjustment) pass. The forward pass is just the regular recognition operation for which the network is designed. The input layer is exposed to the input (e.g., the image), which is then propagated through the network to the output layers, using the weights and activation functions. The output layer provides the answer, by having a high value at the neuron corresponding to the right label (such as CAT or DOG, or the correct number).

The backward pass uses the difference between the forward recognition outcome and the true label. At the output layer the propagated value y is compared with the other part of the example pair, the label z. The difference with the label is calculated, yielding the *error.* Two common error functions are the mean squared error $\frac{1}{n} \sum_i^n (z_i - y_i)^2$ (for regression) and the cross-entropy error $- \sum_i^M z_i \log y_i$ (for classification of M classes). See, for example, Goodfellow et al. [250] for much more on error functions.

Training stops when the error function has been reduced below a certain threshold for a single example, or when the loss on an entire validation set has dropped sufficiently. More elaborate stopping criteria will be discussed later in relation to overfitting.

Then, in the backward phase, this error is propagated back to the input layer, adjusting the weights in the direction so that the error becomes smaller. This method uses the gradient over the weights, and is called gradient descent.

Most neural nets are trained using a stochastic version of gradient descent, or SGD [642], that samples the gradients. SGD speeds up the process and introduces some noise, reducing overfitting. Goodfellow et al. [250] provide more details.

Especially in image and speech recognition impressive results have been reported by deep networks [57]. Popular variants of SGD are AdaGrad [189] and Adam [365], methods that adaptively change the learning rate and momentum of the backpropagation. The theory and practice of gradient descent algorithms is quite elaborate and subtle. Many articles and books have been written on the subject of gradient descent; see, for example [250, 279, 294, 82, 405].

Now that we have discussed essential concepts of shallow neural networks, we will turn to deep learning

6.1.3 Deep Learning

There has been quite some theoretical work on the question of which functions can be represented with neural networks.[3] Some functions can only be represented with

---

[3] The universal approximation theorem states that a feed-forward network with a single hidden layer containing a finite number of neurons can approximate a wide variety of continuous functions [156].

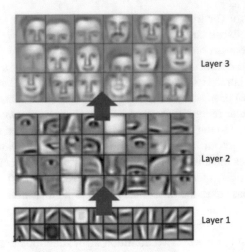

Fig. 6.4 Layers of features of increasing complexity [409]

an architecture of at least a certain depth [62, 61, 276]. For complex tasks such as image recognition single-layer networks do not perform well, or need preprocessing with hand-coded feature recognizers. A breakthrough in end-to-end (direct image) recognition was achieved only when multi-layer networks were introduced and when ways were found to train them efficiently [602, 405].

LeCun, Bengio, and Hinton [405], explain how multiple hidden layers in networks learn increasingly abstract representations. In deep learning, each layer transforms its input data into a more abstract representation. The hierarchy of network layers together can recognize a hierarchy of low-to-high level concepts [405, 409]. For example, in face recognition (Fig. 6.4) the first hidden layer may encode edges; the second layer then composes and encodes simple structures of edges; the third layer may encode higher-level concepts such as noses or eyes; and the fourth layer may work at the abstraction level of a face. Deep feature learning finds what to abstract at which level on its own [60], and can come up with classes of intermediate concepts, that work, but look counterintuitive upon inspection by humans.

For deep learning architectures to perform recognition tasks at a level comparable to human performance, a number of problems had to be solved, that we will now discuss.

Although it states that simple neural networks can represent a variety of interesting functions when given appropriate parameters, the theorem does not say how those parameters can be learned. Learning may take very long, and may take an impractical number of neurons in the hidden layer.

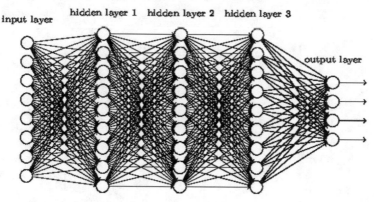

input layer   hidden layer 1   hidden layer 2   hidden layer 3

output layer

Fig. 6.5 Three fully connected hidden layers [574]

6.1.4 Scaling Up

The development of deep learning benefitted greatly from efforts in handwriting recognition. The standard test set for handwriting recognition was MNIST (for Modified National Institute of Standards and Technology). Standard MNIST images are low-resolution $x \times y = 32 \times 32$ pixel images of single handwritten digits (Fig. 6.3). Of course, researchers wanted to process more complex scenes than single digits, and higher-resolution images. To achieve higher accuracy, and to process more complex scenes, networks needed to grow in size and complexity.

There are three ways in which networks can grow. We assume that the layers have the same width as the input size. First, the width $x \times y = n$ of the network can be increased, by having more neurons in each layer. Second, the depth d of the network can be increased, by having more layers. And third, the complexity of the network can be increased, by using a more complex type of processing at the neurons, and a different interconnection structure.

As you might expect, all three were necessary, in unexpected and nontrivial ways.

Increasing Width: Slow Learning and Overfitting

Simply increasing the width n of a fully connected network of depth d increases the network size $s = n^2 \times d$. This is not a scalable solution (Fig. 6.5). More width creates three problems. First, in a fully connected network it causes a quadratic increase in weights and the same holds for the training time. Second, overfitting becomes a problem, since after increasing the capacity of the network, the (quadratically higher) number of parameters $n^2 \times d$ may become greater than the number of observations, in which case the network will overfit: it will perfectly memorize training examples, and be unable to correctly generalize to different test examples. Figure 6.6 illustrates overfitting, which will be described more fully in Sect. 6.1.7. Third, only increasing

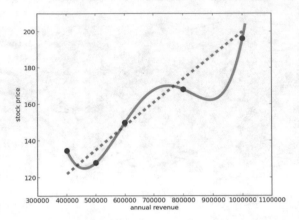

Fig. 6.6 Overfitting: does the curvy red line or the straight dashed blue line generalize the information in the data points best?

the width does not address the problem that some complex functions can only be approximated with a network of a certain depth [62, 61, 276].

Increasing Depth to Prevent Weights Increase

Increasing the width of a fully connected network runs into problems since the number of weights increases quadratically. Let us look what happens when we increase the depth d of the network.

As the depth increases, the number of weights $s = n^2 \times d$ increases linearly (Fig. 6.5) and so does the training time. The overfitting problem also increases linearly. And, complicated functions can be approximated better by the deeper network.

Therefore, increasing the depth of the network is a way forward. However, it does not solve all our problems. If we want to approximate a function, especially one with a high-dimensional input such as for higher-definition images, then at least our input layer has to have a correspondingly high number of inputs. So, we still have not completely solved the problem of the increasing number of weights of fully connected networks. The number of weights just keeps increasing with high-resolution input, causing long training times, overfitting, and exploding and vanishing gradients (to be discussed shortly).

For our solution we need the third element: a different connection structure. Therefore, instead of fully connected networks, we will now look at convolutional networks, and related improvements.

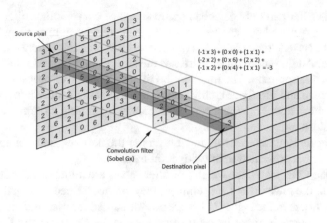

Fig. 6.7 Convolutional filters [250]

6.1.5 Convolutional Neural Nets

As we wish to process higher-resolution images, increasing n or d increases the number of weights too rapidly, leading to unacceptably long training times and overfitting when the network is fully connected.

The solution lies in the third element: using a different (sparse) interconnection structure. Convolutional neural nets (CNNs) take their inspiration from biology. Early work on monkey and cat visual cortexes indicated that neurons respond to small regions in the visual field [316, 317]. The visual cortex in animals and humans is not fully connected, but locally connected, in a receptive field.

The connectivity pattern of CNNs resembles the animal visual cortex [316, 439]. A CNN consists of convolutional operators or filters. A typical convolution operator has a small *receptive field* (it only connects to a limited number of neurons, say 5×5), whereas a fully connected neuron connects to all neurons in the layer below. Convolutional filters detect the presence of local patterns, or features. The next layer therefore acts as a feature *map*. A CNN layer can be seen as a set of learnable filters (or kernels), invariant for local transformations [250].

Convolutional Filter

In Fig. 6.7 we see an example filter. Filters can be used to identify certain features. Features are basic elements such as edges, straight lines, round lines, curves, and colors. To work as a curve detector, the filter should have a pixel structure with high values indicating a shape of a curve. By then multiplying and adding these filter values with the pixel values, we can detect if the shape is present. The sum of the multiplications in the input image will be large if there is a shape that resembles the curve in the filter.

Now this filter can only detect a certain shape of curve. Other filters can detect other shapes. A filter layer can be visualized in an activation map, showing where a specific filter (layer) fires. Larger activation maps can recognize more elements in the input image. Adding more filters increases the size of the network, which effectively is a large activation map. The filters in the first network layer process ("convolve") the input image and fire (have high values) when a specific feature it is built to detect is in the input image. Training a convolutional net is training a filter that consists of layers of subfilters.

By going through the convolutional layers of the network, increasingly complex features can be represented in the activation maps.

Before the CNN starts, the weights or filter values are initialized to random values. The filters in the lower layers are "empty"; they are not trained to look for edges and curves. The filters in the higher layers are not yet trained for eyes and mouths. During training, the filters in these layers take on their task as recognizers for respective representations.

Once they are trained, they can be used for as many recognition tasks as needed. A recognition task consists of a single quick forward pass through the network.

Let us spend some more time on understanding these filters.

Shared Weights

In CNNs the filter parameters are shared in a layer. Each layer thus defines a filter operation. A filter is defined by few parameters but is applied to many pixels of the image; each filter is replicated across the entire visual field. These replicated units share the same parameterization (weight vector and bias) and form a feature map. This means that all the neurons in a given convolutional layer respond to the same feature within their specific response field. Replicating units in this way allows for features to be detected regardless of their position in the visual field, thus constituting the property of translation invariance.

This weight sharing is also important to prevent an increase in the number of weights in deep and wide nets, and to prevent overfitting, as we shall see later on.

Real-world images consist of repetitions of many smaller elements. Due to this so-called *translation invariance*, the same patterns reappear throughout an image. CNNs can take advantage of this. The weights of the links are shared, resulting in a large reduction in the number of weights that have to be trained. Mathematically CNNs are constraints on what the weight values can be (some zero, some have to be equal). This is a significant advantage of CNNs, since the computational requirements of training the weights of many fully connected layers would be prohibitive. In addition, statistical strength is gained, since the effective data per weight increases.

Deep CNNs work well in image recognition tasks, for visual filtering operations in spatial dependencies, and for feature recognition (edges, shapes) [406].[4]

---

[4] Interestingly, this paper was already published in 1989. The deep learning revolution happened twenty years later, when publicly available datasets, more efficient algorithms, and more compute power in the form of GPUs were available.

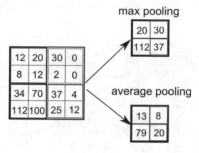

Fig. 6.8 Max and average 2 × 2 pooling [250]

CNN Architecture

Convolutions recognize features—the deeper the network, the more complex the features. A typical CNN architecture consists of a number of stacked convolutional layers. In the final layers, fully connected layers are used to then classify the inputs.

In the convolutional layers, by connecting only locally, the number of weights is dramatically reduced in comparison with a fully connected net. The ability of a single neuron in a CNN to recognize different features, however, is less than that of a fully connected neuron.

By stacking many such locally connected layers on top of each other we can achieve the desired nonlinear filters whose joint effect becomes increasingly global, as more layers are added.[5] The neurons become responsive to a larger region of pixel space, so that the network first creates representations of small parts of the input, and from these representations create larger areas. By stacking convolutional layers on top of each other, they can recognize and represent increasingly complex concepts without an explosion of weights.

Max Pooling

A further method for reducing the number of weights is pooling. Pooling is an operation related to convolving. Pooling is a kind of nonlinear downsampling (expressing the information in lower resolution with fewer bits). Typically, a 2 × 2 block is down sampled to a scalar value (Fig. 6.8). Pooling reduces the dimension of the network. The most frequently used form is max pooling. It is an important component for object detection [142] and is an integral part of most CNN architectures.

Max pooling also allows small translations, such as shifting the cat by a few pixels, or scaling, such as putting the cat closer to the camera.

---

[5] Nonlinearity is essential. If all neurons performed linearly, then there would be no need for layers. Linear recognition functions cannot discriminate between cats and dogs.

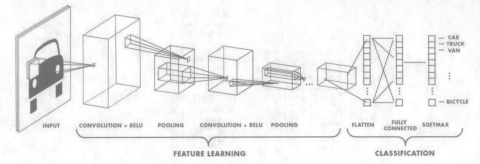

Fig. 6.9 Convolutional network example architecture [574]

A typical CNN architecture consists of an architectures of multiple layers of convolution, max pooling, and ReLU layers, topped off by a fully connected layer (Fig. 6.9).[6] Section 6.2.1 will discuss more concrete examples of well-known CNN architectures.

6.1.6 Exploding and Vanishing Gradients

The deep convolutional architectures solved the problem of processing higher-resolution and more complex scenes by controlling the number of weights organized in layers of filters. However, the deep architectures brought a new problem. The popular training algorithm, backpropagation, in combination with the conventional sigmoid activation function and deep networks, suffers from the vanishing gradient problem.

Gradients

The vanishing gradient problem was one of the problems that held back progress in multi-level neural networks for some time.

The backpropagation algorithm computes the gradient of the error function by the chain rule of composite functions. Originally, most neural networks used the sigmoid function as their activation function. The problem is that the derivative of the sigmoid function $\frac{1}{1+e^{-x}}$ on the domain $[0, 1]$ is a value between 0 and 0.25. Backpropagation multiplies these values with the weights for each layer, starting from the output layer and working backwards to the input layer. Each time that a value between 0 and 0.25 is multiplied by the weights, the derivative gets smaller, approaching zero for the deepest layers. Long products of many layers thus yield a low gradient value at the

---

[6] Often with a soft-max function. The soft-max function normalizes an input vector of real numbers to a probability distribution $[0, 1]$.

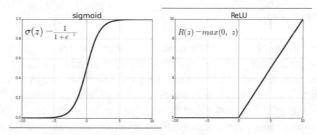

Fig. 6.10 Sigmoid and ReLU

deep layers. This means that neurons in the earlier layers learn much more slowly than neurons in later layers [297, 296].

The result is that gradient descent with a traditional activation function (sigmoid or tanh) cannot learn over many layers. For the deepest layers the gradients are vanishing to zero, negating the use that an extra layer would give.

The gradient in deep neural networks is unstable, tending to either explode or vanish in earlier layers. This instability was a fundamental problem for gradient-based learning in deep neural networks.

Multiple solutions to the vanishing gradient problem have been found. One solution is to model the network as a multi-level hierarchy of networks pretrained one level at a time [599]. Hinton's work on training deep networks addresses this problem [293].

Let us look at two more solutions.

ReLU

Since the problem of vanishing gradients is caused by the derivative of the activation function, alternative functions were proposed. Traditionally the activation function of neurons is a well-differentiable function such as tanh or the sigmoid function. A simpler activation functions is the ReLU function (short for rectified linear unit). The definition of ReLU is $f(x) = \max(0, x)$. Over the positive part of its input ReLU is linear, otherwise it is zero. See Fig. 6.10. ReLU is a simple function that is quick to calculate, is nonlinear, and removes negative values from the activations [386]. The major advantage of ReLU is that in deep networks it suffers much less from the vanishing gradient problem. Deep ReLU networks are much easier to train than sigmoid networks.[7]

---

[7] The derivative of the ReLU function has a discontinuity. This discontinuity has led to the introduction of soft-ReLU, which replaces the sharp transition from 0 to linear with a small smooth part.

Batch Normalization

Another solution to the vanishing gradient problem is batch normalization. Batch normalization periodically rescales the data. It performs a batch standardization and assures that each batch is in a safe area, taking the gradients away from the zero, the one, or infinity. This technique was introduced in [328]. At the cost of some extra computation, the effect of periodical normalization is manyfold. Training is sped up, overfitting is reduced, and, finally, the vanishing gradient problem is reduced substantially, since gradient values are normalized.

Batch normalization is at the moment the most powerful method to prevent overfitting.

6.1.7 Overfitting

Overfitting is a major problem in large neural networks. The intuition behind overfitting (and underfitting) is as follows. Let us assume that the training data represents a noisy signal, as most data generated by measurements of natural processes does. The learning process performs well, when the signal from the training data is learned, and the noise is disregarded. Only then will it generalize well to the test data. Underfitting occurs when the capacity of the network is too small to learn, model, or represent the signal, and a crude approximation results. Overfitting occurs when the capacity is so large that it learns even the noise in the training data (Fig. 6.6). Both underfitting and overfitting result in limited accuracy at test time.

Since the number of weights in deep networks is often in the millions, it is easily greater than the number of observations. In such a situation overfitting is a problem that reduces the generalization performance of the network. Overfitting is said to have happened when a trained model corresponds too closely to a particular dataset, and fails to reliably predict a future observation. The network has been fit to the particular training set, the signal and the noise, but not to the underlying structure of the data. Overfitting occurs frequently when a model has more parameters than the training dataset has examples.

Figure 6.6 illustrates this problem. The red curvy line perfectly fits all data points, but is unlikely to perform well on a separate test set. The dashed straight line is more likely to have caught the essence of the training domain, even though it misses some of the data points.

Overfitting can be prevented in a number of ways, some of which are aimed at restoring the balance between the number of network parameters and the number of training examples. We will discuss data augmentation and capacity reduction.

Another approach is to look at the the training process. Examples are regularization, early stopping, dropouts, and batch normalization.

Data Augmentation

Overfitting occurs when there are more parameters in the network than examples to train on. One possible solution is to increase the amount of data. This method is called data augmentation. The training dataset is increased through manipulations such as rotations, reflections, noise, rescaling, etc. A disadvantage of this method is that the computational cost of training increases.

Capacity Reduction

Another easy solution to overfitting lies in the realization that overfitting is a result of the network having too large a capacity; the network has too many parameters. A cheap way of preventing this situation is to reduce the capacity of the network, by reducing the width and depth of the network.

L1 and L2 Regularization

A standard method to try when we suspect that the network is overfitting, is regularization. Regularization involves adding an extra term to the loss function. The regularization term forces the network to not be too complex. The term penalizes the model for using too high weight values. This limits flexibility, but also encourages building solutions based on multiple features. Two popular versions of this method are L1 and L2 regularization [487, 250]. For different situations different preferred methods exist.

Early Stopping

Perhaps the easiest solution to overfitting is the early stopping solution. Early stopping is based on the observation that overfitting can be regarded as a consequence of so-called overtraining (training that progresses beyond the signal, into the noise). By terminating the training process earlier, for example by using a higher stopping threshold for the error function, we can prevent overfitting from occurring [121].

Finding the right moment to stop may take some experimenting [533, 534]. A convenient and popular way is to add a third set to the training set/test set duo which then becomes a training set, a test set, and a holdout validation set. The role of the training set and the test set remains the same. However, after each training epoch, the network is evaluated against the holdout validation set, to see if under- or overfitting occurs, and if we should stop training. Finally, the test set is used in the familiar former role to see how well the trained network generalizes to unseen instances. In this way, overfitting can be prevented dynamically during training [534, 81, 250].

Dropout

A popular method to reduce overfitting is to introduce dropout layers into the networks. Dropout reduces the effective capacity of the network by stochastically dropping a certain percentage of neurons from the backpropagation process [295, 643]. Dropout is an effective and computationally efficient method to reduce overfitting [250].

Batch Normalization

Batch normalization periodically normalizes the data [328], as we just mentioned. This has many benefits, including a reduction of overfitting.

6.1.8 Datasets and Networks

Now that we have discussed in depth the deep learning algorithms and their challenges and solutions, it is time to look at datasets and methods that have been instrumental in the progress of the field.

The algorithmic advances that were discussed in Sect. 6.1.2 were facilitated by the availability of large training sets of labeled examples. Deep learning has benefited from a number of *Drosophilas*. A well-known repository of datasets is the University of California at Irvine Machine Learning repository UCI.[8]

The MNIST database may well be the best known of these datasets. MNIST is a database of 60,000 handwritten digits provided by the National Institute of Standards and Technology. The original MNIST database is available at MNIST.[9] CIFAR is one of the most widely used set of images in machine learning and vision [385]. CIFAR-10 has also 60,000 images in 10 classes: airplanes, cars, birds, cats, deer, dogs, frogs, horses, ships, and trucks. Another major data set of central importance to deep learning is ImageNet [207, 172].[10] It is a collection of more than 14 million URLs of images that have been hand annotated with the objects that are in the picture. It contains more than 20,000 categories. A typical category contains several hundred training images.

The importance of ImageNet for the progress in AI is large. The availability of labeled images allowed algorithms to learn, and new algorithms to be created. ImageNet was conceived by Fei-Fei Li in 2006, and in later years she developed it further. Since 2010 ImageNet runs an annual software contest, the ImageNet Large Scale Visual Recognition Challenge (ILSVRC) [172]. Since 2012 ILSVRC has been won by deep networks, starting the deep learning boom in science and industry.

---

[8] https://archive.ics.uci.edu/ml/index.php
[9] http://yann.lecun.com/exdb/mnist/
[10] http://www.image-net.org

We will now mention some influential networks architectures. We will start with Yann LeCun's LeNet-5.

LeNet-5

Towards the end of the 1990s the work on neural networks moved into deep learning, a term coined by Dechter in [171]. Some twenty years after the introduction of deep convolutional neural nets by LeCun et al. [407] CNNs became highly popular. This paper introduced the architecture LeNet-5. LeNet-5 is a 7-layer convolutional neural net trained to classify handwritten MNIST digits from 32×32 pixel images. It is a successful network that was used commercially to recognize digits in banking checks. The paper has a thorough comparison of LeNet-5 with other methods such as principal component analysis (PCA).

At GitHub a modern Keras implementation of LeNet is available (and also of AlexNet and VGG).[11] The code straightforwardly lists the layer definitions, shown in Listing 6.1.

AlexNet

In 2012 Krizhevsky et al. published the AlexNet architecture [386] with breakthrough performance on the ImageNet dataset of 85% accuracy. They used a deep network of 8 layers. The first 5 layers were convolutional layers, some with max pooling, and 3 layers were fully connected layers. Krizhevsky et al. overcame problems of vanishing gradients and overfitting with ReLU, data augmentation, and L2 regularization, and effectively used the power of GPUs to train a large network. Their work caused many follow-up works showing even better performance, and attracted much attention, setting off the general interest in deep learning.

As we shall see shortly, deep networks have since grown further in size, with more layers, and different learning algorithms and connection structures. The number of weights in such networks is often in the millions, greater than the number of observations on which the network is trained. This makes overfitting an important problem, and many of the methods that we discussed previously have been developed because of these larger networks.

Crafting Neural Architectures

There is a flip side to the advantages of automated feature discovery with deep learning, since for many domains much time has to be spent finding a neural network architecture for the domain that works, before the training process results in features

---

[11] https://github.com/eweill/keras-deepcv/tree/master/models/classification

```python
def lenet_model(img_shape=(28, 28, 1), n_classes=10, l2_reg=0.,
        weights=None):

    # Initialize model
    lenet = Sequential()

    # 2 sets of CRP (Convolution, RELU, Pooling)
    lenet.add(Conv2D(20, (5, 5), padding="same",
            input_shape=img_shape, kernel_regularizer=l2(
                l2_reg)))
    lenet.add(Activation("relu"))
    lenet.add(MaxPooling2D(pool_size=(2, 2), strides=(2, 2)))

    lenet.add(Conv2D(50, (5, 5), padding="same",
            kernel_regularizer=l2(l2_reg)))
    lenet.add(Activation("relu"))
    lenet.add(MaxPooling2D(pool_size=(2, 2), strides=(2, 2)))

    # Fully connected layers (w/ RELU)
    lenet.add(Flatten())
    lenet.add(Dense(500, kernel_regularizer=l2(l2_reg)))
    lenet.add(Activation("relu"))

    # Softmax (for classification)
    lenet.add(Dense(n_classes, kernel_regularizer=l2(l2_reg))
        )
    lenet.add(Activation("softmax"))

    if weights is not None:
        lenet.load_weights(weights)

    # Return the constructed network
    return lenet
```

Listing 6.1 LeNet-5 code in Keras [407, 751]

that perform well. Some of the time previously spent hand crafting heuristic features is now spent hand crafting network architectures to automatically learn the features.[12]

TensorFlow

The deep learning breakthrough was caused by the co-occurrence of three major developments: (1) algorithmic advances that solved key problems in deep learning,

---

[12] Of course, research has now focused on ways to automate the hand crafting of network architectures. Section 7.3.3 describes ways to automatically generate appropriate network architectures for different domains in neural architecture search.

(2) the availability of large datasets of labeled training data, and (3) the availability of computational power (GPU).

The most expensive operations in image processing and neural network training are essentially operations on matrices. Matrix operations are some of the most well-studied problems in computer science. Their algorithmic structure is well understood, and for basic linear algebra operations high-performance parallel implementations for CPUs exist, such as the BLAS [180, 138].

Graphical processing units, or GPUs, were originally developed for fast processing of image and video data, largely driven by the video gaming industry. Modern GPUs consist of thousands of processing units optimized to process linear algebra matrix operations in parallel [578, 426, 641], offering matrix performance that is orders of magnitude faster than CPUs [493, 143, 662].

Neural network training packages support GPU parallelism. Well-known dedicated deep learning packages are Berkeley's Caffe [334], Facebook's PyTorch [508], Theano [64] which has been subsumed by Google's TensorFlow [1, 2], and its user-friendly add-on Keras [139]. Most packages have Python interfaces. Some machine learning and mathematical packages also offer deep learning tools, such as MATLAB and R.

TensorFlow provides high-quality implementations of many machine learning and neural network algorithms and operations. (A tensor is a multi-dimensional array, often used for transformations.) The programming concept of TensorFlow takes some getting used to. Programs are constructed as a data-flow graph in which the sequence of tensors defines the operations. A higher level, easier, interface is provided by Keras. Keras comes with TensorFlow, and is recommended for learning the packages.

Implementing a full working deep learning algorithm that performs well on a new problem is a challenging task. Many problems of backpropagation, gradient descent, overfitting, vanishing gradients, and numerical stability have to be solved. It is because of the free availability of high-quality deep learning methods that so much progress has been made in recent years. Advances in image recognition, speech recognition, game playing, automated translation, and autonomous vehicles are made possible in large part by these software suites. The free availability of high-quality implementations may be the fourth reason for the deep learning breakthrough. Appendix A contains overviews of machine learning packages.

Conclusion

We have discussed in depth methods for deep supervised learning. This has been a long section; many problems had to be overcome to achieve end-to-end learning. The deep learning breakthrough in image recognition was made possible only by the convergence of better algorithms, computational power, and large labeled datasets.

Name	Principle	Applicability	Effectiveness
AlexNet	CNN	image	improve
inception	net inside net	image	improve
residual	skip links	image	improve
GAN	generative-adversarial	image	robustness
RNN/LSTM	state	sequential proc	sequences

Table 6.2 Advanced network architectures

6.2 *Advanced Network Architectures

The breakthroughs in deep learning have prompted much further research in fascinating areas. Let us now look deeper at more advanced deep learning methods. Table 6.2 shows advanced network architectures that we will discuss. This is a starred section, with more advanced material, which may be skipped when in a hurry.

Much of the work in supervised learning is driven by image recognition tasks. Just as in game playing, the availability of clear benchmarks and competitions has facilitated progress. The ImageNet database [172, 571] has been at the center of this field. Guo et al. provide a review of the state of the art of visual recognition [268].

6.2.1 Examples of Concrete Convolutional Networks

As we saw, after the turn of the millennium two important developments happened: large databases of (hand) labeled images became available, and powerful GPUs became available and were used for training neural networks. Together, these two developments allowed major improvements in training speed and accuracy. Let us start by having a closer look at AlexNet.

AlexNet

The 2012 ImageNet database as used by AlexNet has 14 million labeled images. The network featured a highly optimized 2D two-GPU implementation of 5 convolutional layers and 3 fully connected layers. The filters in the convolutional layers are 11×11 in size.

The neurons use a ReLU activation function. In AlexNet images were scaled to 256×256 RGB pixels. The size of the network was large, with 60 million parameters. This causes considerable overfitting. AlexNet used data augmentation and dropouts to prevent overfitting.

Krizhevsky et al. won the 2012 ImageNet competition with an error rate of 15%, significantly better than the number two, who achieved 26%. Although there were earlier reports of CNNs that were successful in applications such as bioinformatics and

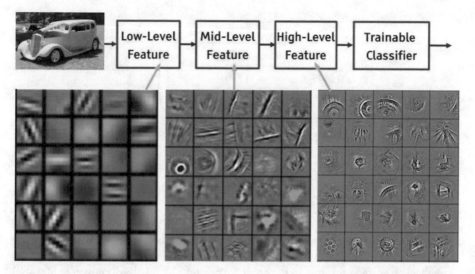

Fig. 6.11 ZFnet layers [774]

Chinese handwriting recognition, it was this convincing win of the 2012 ImageNet competition for which AlexNet has become well known.

AlexNet has become an important network architecture for research. Many resources are available for AlexNet. The original AlexNet code is available on GitHub at AlexNet.[13] Berkeley's Caffe project maintains a "model zoo" where multiple trained models are available, complete with Caffe code that can be studied. The AlexNet Caffe model is available on GitHub at BVLC AlexNet.[14] Also, as mentioned before, a Keras implementation of AlexNet, LeNet, and VGG is available at Models Keras.[15]

ZFnet

A year later a paper by Zeiler and Fergus [774] improved upon AlexNet. Their network has become known as ZFnet. The work also provided an enlightening explanation about how convolutional nets work, including a visualization of the inner layers (Fig. 6.11). In a sense, this allows a look into the brain of the neural net, to see what features it recognizes at which layer. Afterwards many papers have provided these kinds of insights into the hidden layers of their network.

Deep network layers learn a hierarchy of abstract features. The layers learn concepts of increasing generality [60, 405], creating a hierarchy of abstract concepts. The look into the "brains" of the net does not yield pictures that are easy to interpret. How

---

[13] https://github.com/akrizhevsky/cuda-convnet2

[14] https://github.com/BVLC/caffe/tree/master/models/bvlc_alexnet

[15] https://github.com/eweill/keras-deepcv/tree/master/models/classification

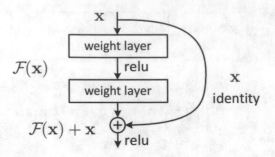

Fig. 6.12 Residual cell [281]

general are the concepts learned by self-play? What do they "look" like, can they be represented as a two-dimensional picture for us to interpret? A deeper understanding of these concepts might enable us to learn more complex representations, and thus achieve better local minima in the error function [520, 744]. Montavon et al. [468] provides an tutorial on methods for interpreting deep nets.

VGG

Simonyan and Zisserman [631] followed a different philosophy than AlexNet and ZFnet, with small filters (3×3) and a deep hierarchy of 16-19 layers. Their VGG net was also successful. VGG faithfully implements the idea behind deep nets as needing many layers (16) in order to build a hierarchical representation of visual data [405].

GoogLeNet

A further notable network is GoogLeNet [663], which is even deeper, with 22 layers. The new architecture and algorithms perform better than AlexNet, yet have 12 times fewer parameters, showing how strong the new architecture and algorithms are. The GoogLeNet architecture is about sparse networks, allowing a deeper network without increasing the total number of parameters. The network is built around *inception* modules. In previous architectures, convolutional layers were stacked sequentially on top of each other. Inception modules are small networks inside a network, where different sized convolutions are placed in parallel to each other. Through the inception modules sparse network structures were achieved, reducing training time. In addition to the inception modules, batch normalization was used to prevent vanishing gradients [664] and dropouts for regularization.

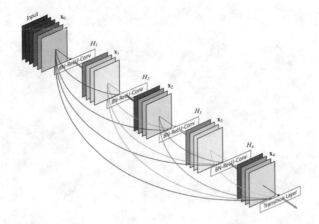

Fig. 6.13 Residual net [281]

Residual Networks

After inception modules, another important innovation is the residual network architecture, or *ResNets*. This was introduced in the 2015 ImageNet challenge, which He et al. won with a very low error rate of 3.57%. This error rate is actually lower than what most humans achieve: 5-10% [281]. ResNet has no fewer than 152 layers, and, as before, this is achieved through a *simpler* architecture with fewer connections (fewer parameters than VGG). The problem of vanishing gradients, which deep networks suffer from, is addressed with intermediate normalization steps.

The main contribution of ResNets is based on the following observation. The authors found that when adding more layers to their net, they were obtaining *lower* training accuracy. This is counterintuitive, since more parameters should allow the net to achieve at least the accuracy of the shallower net. The deep network suffered from degrading training accuracy due to reasons related to overfitting [281].

Residual nets introduce *skip links* to cure this degradation (Fig. 6.12). Skip links are connections skipping one or more layers, allowing the training to go directly to other layers reducing the effective depth of the network (Fig. 6.13). Skip links create a mixture of a shallow and a deep network, preventing the accuracy degradation and vanishing gradients of deep networks. Furthermore, He et al. note that normal layers have a harder time learning of an identity function, than learning a mapping to 0, and the skip layers allow the net to more easily learn an identity function.

Following up on ResNets, DenseNets were devised, building on the main insight behind residual nets, and achieving even more impressive results [312].

These architectural innovations have again caused important performance improvements. As a result, image recognition tasks now frequently exceed human performance [268, 178]. This is an active area of research, and better architectures are presented at the major machine learning conferences each year.

Fig. 6.14 Deep fake [769]

6.2.2 Generative and Sequential Architectures

In addition to mainstream image recognition architectures, there are other architectural innovations of different kinds of networks.

Generative Adversarial Networks

An active research area is deep generative modeling. Generative models are models from which a new example can be sampled. (A contrast to generative models are the regular discriminative models, which output a label, for classification. In a sense, a generative model is a discriminative model, but backwards.) There are several classes of generative models. An important and popular class that has made quite an impact is the generative adversarial network, or GAN [251].

It was found that if an image is slightly perturbed, and imperceptibly to the human eye, deep networks can easily be fooled to characterize an image as the wrong category [665]. This brittleness is known as the one-pixel problem [651, 665]. Deep networks are susceptible to adversarial attacks. The one-pixel problem has spawned an active area of research to understand this problem, and to make image recognizers more robust. (Adversarial attacks are also relevant to deep reinforcement learning; Sect. 7.1.4.)

Fig. 6.15 Deep dream [356]

GANs are generative models that generate adversarial examples. The purpose of adversarial examples is to fool the discriminator (recognizer). They are *designed* to cause a wrong classification. In GANs one network, the generator, generates an image, and a second network, the discriminator, tries to recognize the image. The goal for the generator is to mislead the discriminator, in order to make better discriminators.

In addition to making recognizers more robust against the one-pixel problem, one of the other uses of generative networks is to generate artificial photo-realistic images such as *deep fake* images [769]; see Fig. 6.14 and *deep dreaming*, Fig. 6.15[16] [356]. GANs have significantly increased our theoretical understanding of supervised training.

6.2.3 Sequential Processing

Image recognition has had a large impact on network architectures, leading to innovations in network architectures such as convolutional nets.

Other applications, such as time series analysis and speech recognition, have also caused new architectures to be created. Image recognition is a single-time-step modeling task. In contrast, speech recognition, text mining, and time series analysis concern sequential data that must be modeled. Such sequences can be modeled by recurrent neural nets. Some of the better known recurrent neural nets are Hopfield

---

[16] Deep Dream Generator https://deepdreamgenerator.com

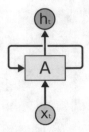

Fig. 6.16 RNN x_t is an input vector, h_t is the output/prediction, and A is the RNN [494]

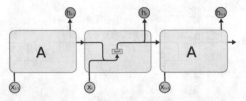

Fig. 6.17 Time-unrolled RNN neuron, with a tanh activation function; shown are the previous and next time steps as well [494]

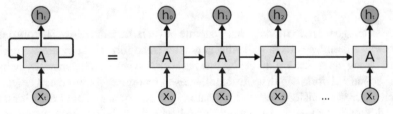

Fig. 6.18 RNN unrolled in time [494]

networks [303], recurrent neural nets (RNN) [72, 209], and long short-term memory (LSTM) [298].

Figure 6.16 shows a basic recurrent neural network. An RNN neuron is the same as a normal neuron, with input, output, and activation function. However, RNN neurons have an extra pair of looping input/output connections. Figure 6.17 shows the internal structure of an RNN neuron (a tanh activation function) with their loop connections unrolled as previous and next time steps. Through this structure, the values of the parameters in an RNN can evolve. In effect, RNNs have a kind of variable-like state.

To understand how RNNs work, it helps to unroll the network, as has been done in Figs. 6.17 and 6.18. The recurrent neuron loops have been drawn as a straight line to show the network in a deep layered style, with connections between the layers. In reality the layers are time steps in the processing of the recurrent connections. In a sense, an RNN is a deep neural net folded into a single layer of recurrent neurons.

Where deep convolutional networks are successful in image classification, RNNs are used for more demanding tasks, such as captioning challenges. In a captioning

The man at bat readies to swing at the pitch while the umpire looks on.

A large bus sitting next to a very tall building.

A horse carrying a large load of hay and two people sitting on it.

Bunk bed with a narrow shelf sitting underneath it.

Fig. 6.19 Captioning tasks [135]

task the network is shown a picture, and then has to come up with a textual description that makes sense [729]. Figure 6.19 gives examples of captioning tasks, from Chen et al. [135].

Captioning tasks are hard, and a computer succeeding in "seeing" an image and "interpreting" it with a caption that makes sense, describing what can be seen on the picture, can be a startling experience. Seeing one's own RNN learning to generate the first appropriate descriptions of images can be a satisfying experience for machine learning researchers (see the exercises at the end of this chapter). Interestingly, simple models can deliver surprisingly good results.

A step up from image captioning is video captioning, where a description has to be generated for a sequence of images [720].

The main innovation of recurrent nets is that they allow us to work with sequences of vectors. Figure 6.20 shows different combinations of sequences that we will discuss now. There can be sequences in the input, in the output, or in both. Karpathy has written an accessible and well-illustrated blog on the different RNN configurations [354]. The figure shows different rectangles. Each rectangle is a vector. Arrows represent computations, such as matrix multiply. Input vectors are in red, output vectors are in blue, and green vectors hold the state. Following Karpathy [354], from left to right we see:

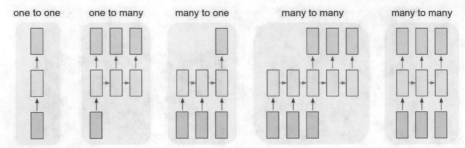

Fig. 6.20 RNN configurations [354]

1. *One to one*, the standard network without RNN. This network maps a fixed-sized input to fixed-sized output, such as an image classification task (picture in/class out).
2. *One to many* adds a sequence in the output. This can be an image captioning task that takes an image and outputs a sentence of words.
3. *Many to one* is the opposite, with a sequence in the input. Think for example of sentiment analysis (a sentence is classified for words with negative or positive emotional meaning).
4. *Many to many* has both a sequence for input and a sequence for output. This can be the case in machine translation, where a sentence in English is read and then a sentence in French is produced.
5. *Many to many* is a related but different situation, with synchronized input and output sequences. This can be the case in video classification where each frame of the video should be labeled.

State

Time series prediction is a difficult problem, for which sequential processing is well suited. Sequential networks are more powerful than fixed networks, which can only process a predetermined number of steps. Moreover, where normal deep networks represent a single stateless mathematical function mapping from input to output, RNNs combine the input vector together with the state from the previous time step to produce a new state vector, to be fed into the next time step. In this particular sense RNNs have state. The fact that RNNs have such state in addition to a learned function brings them closer to a conventional imperative computer program (such as a Python program with variables) [713, 4]. An RNN can be interpreted as a fixed program with certain inputs and some internal variables. In this way, RNNs are simple computer programs that do not have to be programmed, but learn their functionality by training. RNNs are appealing for building intelligent systems [241]. This is an active area of research.

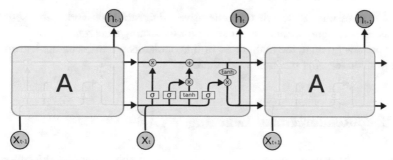

Fig. 6.21 LSTM [354]

Many different successful applications for recurrent neural networks have been found. Graves et al. describe speech to text processing [257]. Machine translation is described by Sutskever et al. [656]. Earlier work described text generation [654]. RNNs for video classification are described by Donahue et al. [179]. Mnih et al. describe RNNs for visual attention [460].

Long Short-Term Memory

Time series prediction is more complex than conventional regression or classification. It adds the complexity of a sequence dependence among the input variables.

LSTM (long short-term memory) is a more powerful type of neuron designed to handle sequences. Figure 6.21 shows the LSTM module, allowing comparison with the simple RNN of Fig. 6.17. LSTMs are designed for sequential problems, such as time series, and planning. LSTMs were introduces by Hochreiter and Schmidhuber [298].

RNN training suffers from the vanishing gradient problem. For short-term sequences this problem may be controllable by the same methods as for deep CNN (Sect. 6.1.6). For long-term remembering LSTM are better suited.

LSTM building blocks avoid the vanishing gradient problem by introducing skip connections that insert unchanged gradients between layers, just like residual nets. The skip links make LSTMS less susceptible to the vanishing gradient problem; this makes LSTMs better suited for large architectures.

LSTMs are frequently used to solve diverse problems [603, 256, 261, 242]. Researchers have experimented with LSTMs for creating hybrid architectures that combine planning and learning, with some initial success [629]; see also Sect. 7.3.5.

Conclusion

There has been a wealth of research into deep neural networks for image recognition (and beyond). Many complex deep architectures were created, and achieved impressive recognition results. Research on generative adversarial networks and sequence processing is a highly active area of supervised learning research.

Let us now go on to the main topic of this book, deep reinforcement learning, to see how deep learning methods work there.

6.3 Deep Reinforcement Learning

Deep reinforcement learning has shown inspiring results in artificial intelligence. Before the successes, there were quite some obstacles that had to be overcome. Methods from supervised learning were not as easy to transfer to reinforcement learning as some had hoped. There are challenges in generalization and learning convergence. In this section we will discuss these problems and the methods that have been found to address them. Table 6.3 summarizes some of the differences between supervised learning and reinforcement learning.

The need for deep reinforcement learning came out of the wish for improving performance beyond heuristics and sampling, beyond what can be achieved with (automated tuning of) hand-crafted features. End-to-end learning requires training in high-dimensional state spaces, far exceeding the capabilities of exact or heuristic planning methods, or of shallow networks or other conventional machine learning methods.

Let us now start at the beginning, with the need for end-to-end learning in a reinforcement learning context.

6.3.1 End-to-End Reinforcement Learning

The state space of problems for which hand-crafted features have been created is typically of manageable size. Much of the complexity of the problem domain is abstracted away by the hand-crafted heuristics. The heuristics translate raw board features into a small number of heuristic parameters, converting a high-dimensional state space to a low-dimensional state space. End-to-end learning does away with the hand-crafted heuristics, and takes the problem of learning from the raw inputs head on. The computational complexity of end-to-end learning problems is correspondingly higher.

In the previous section we saw the problems that had to be overcome in supervised learning to achieve end-to-end learning. Only after convolutional neural networks had been invented, and after solutions for overfitting and vanishing gradients had been found, did deep end-to-end supervised learning work.

In reinforcement learning a similar situation exists. Here the problem was the quality of the generalization and the convergence of the training process. Let us now see why stable deep reinforcement learning is such a difficult problem.

Supervised learning	Reinforcement learning
(example-label) or (example-number) pair	(state-action) or (state-reward) pair
database of ground truths	environment gives reward
static learning process	interactive learning process
fixed set of examples	changing and interdependent set of examples
dense: ground truth for all examples	sparse: rewards for some examples

Table 6.3 Supervised vs. reinforcement learning

Reinforcement learning is a form of machine learning, where just as in supervised learning, a function is learned from examples through generalization. The way in which these examples are presented to the learning algorithm, however, is different.[17]

First, supervised learning infers functions from a database of example-label pairs, where the ground truth is given. Reinforcement learning infers a function for state-action pairs (for the policy function) or state-reward pairs (for the value function). It has no fixed database of examples with ground truths. Positive or negative rewards are only provided after interaction with an environment. Actions by the agent determine the response from the environment. This interaction influences the learning process. The set of examples is not fixed, and may change from learning process to learning process. See Table 6.3 for a summary.

The second difference is that in supervised learning ground truths are present for *all* example-label pairs. The state space is dense. In reinforcement learning problems the state space is often sparse, the outcome of an action may only be known after many further steps, and the rewards are only available for some of the state-action pairs. For other state-action pairs the value or policy has to be inferred, propagated over a long distance of intermediate states before the reward of a state-action pair is known. This gives rise to the credit assignment problem, and, as we shall see next, to generalization problems and to learning instability.

Much research into the stability of reinforcement learning has been performed. We will discuss generalization to test sets, correlation between states, fluctuations in the data distribution, and the deadly triad.

Generalization to Test Set

The first problem we will look into is generalization. This problem concerns the ability to generalize training results to the *test* set.

Recall that a basic assumption for convergence in Q-learning and other reinforcement learning algorithms is that state-action pairs are sampled often enough. Clearly, this is not the case in large state spaces with sparse rewards, especially not when

---

[17] Also note that the functions to be learned are different. In supervised learning a classification or a regression function is typically learned. In reinforcement learning a policy or a value function is learned.

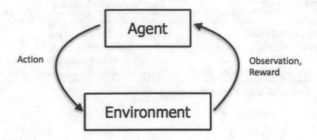

Fig. 6.22 Agent/environment loop [659]

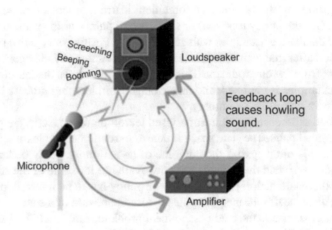

Fig. 6.23 Feedback loop

test samples are not part of the training set. The coverage of the training set can be problem. Even worse, the state-action pairs are not randomly distributed.

In supervised learning, data samples (states) are independent and are assumed to be distributed evenly over the state space. In the database of static images, there is no relation between subsequent images, and examples are independently sampled. Each image is separate (in contrast to a movie, where many inter-temporal relations between frames are present).

In model-based reinforcement learning a sequence of states is generated by a simulator or game playing program in an agent/environment loop (Fig. 6.22). The features of the states are often correlated, differing only by a single action, one move or one stone. Subsequent samples are correlated. Such a correlated training set may be myopic, covering only a part of the state space. The training set will not work well with standard supervised training algorithms. The algorithms may get stuck in local minima, and cycles may occur, which may turn into a feedback loop when state-action pairs and values are mixed due to function approximation (Fig. 6.23 illustrates a feedback loop in another domain).

To illustrate myopic learning, let us consider an example of correlated training in Chess. Imagine a program in which training got stuck in a loop with center control problems. Such a program knows much about center control but little about king safety, and therefore plays badly if it encounters a differently trained agent that can outplay it in the king safety domain. We can try to counter this effect, as we will see soon.

The low sample rate and correlations between subsequent states cause generalization problems. The end result is that deep reinforcement learning algorithms that are trained on sparse, correlated end-to-end states may not generalize well when they are tested on new problem instances.

In addition to the problems of loops and local optima, learning from correlated consecutive samples is inefficient. Little new information is contained in two states that are almost the same. The low learning efficiency translates into a smaller effective dataset; much training is done, yet little is learned. Randomizing the samples breaks these correlations and therefore reduces the probability of getting stuck.

Fluctuating Data Distribution

A further consequence of how samples are generated is that in reinforcement learning the data distribution may be fluctuating. In supervised learning the data set is fixed. In reinforcement learning output signals from the environment are infrequent or derived from other states, and may thus be "polluted" by old values, and are calculated using values that may be approximations.

Since in reinforcement learning training examples are generated in interaction with the environment, unstable training processes have consequences for the set of training examples. In reinforcement learning the size of the training set may vary, or may be infinite, as the training process itself influences which examples are generated.

This has two consequences, one undesired, one desired. In the short term, learning new behaviors may cause myopia or may get stuck locally by feeding on its own behavior as described in on-policy learning. This short-term training behavior can be smoothed with a replay buffer by providing data from a larger landscape [461].

In the longer term, learning new behaviors may actually be desirable. Forgetting bad behaviors can also be a way to escape ineffective parts of the state space. Thus, the replay buffer should not be too large. In Chap. 7 we will learn more about this in the context of self-play.

Function approximation may also cause problems with divergent training processes. For this, let us have a closer look at the so-called deadly triad.

Convergent Training: Deadly Triad

The learning process of deep reinforcement learning itself can be divergent.

The learning of Q-values may diverge, even if we assume that state-action pairs are sampled frequently enough. Tsitsiklis and Van Roy [699] showed in 1997 that combining off-policy reinforcement learning with nonlinear function approximaters (such as neural networks) could cause Q-values to diverge. Sutton and Barto [659] summarize three main reasons for divergent training: function approximation, bootstrapping, and off-policy learning. Together, these form the so-called *deadly triad* of instability. When these three techniques are combined, training can diverge, and value estimates can become unbounded.[18]

Function approximation may attribute values to states inaccurately. Whereas exact methods are designed to recognize individual states, neural networks are designed to recognize individual features of states. These features may be shared by different states, and values attributed to those features are shared also by other states. Function approximation may cause confusion or misidentification of states. In a reinforcement learning process where new states are generated on the fly, this sharing of values among states may cause loops or other forms of instability. If the accuracy of the approximation of the true function values is good enough, then states may be identified well enough to prevent most loops or divergent training processes.

Bootstrapping of values increases the efficiency of the training because values do not have to be calculated from the start, since previously calculated values are reused. Bootstrapping is at the basis of the recursive Bellman equation, of temporal difference, and of Q-learning. However, errors or biases in initial values may persist, and even spill over to other states as values are propagated, and error values become correlated between states. With function approximation, inaccuracies in values are almost guaranteed. Bootstrapping and function approximation can thus lead to divergent learning, and to training loops getting stuck in one area of the state space.

Off-policy learning uses a behavior policy that is different from the target policy that we are optimizing (Sect. 3.3.5). When the behavior policy is improved, the off-policy values may not ne improved, and the algorithm may not converge. Off-policy learning converges independently from the behavior policy, and converges generally less well than on-policy learning, especially when combined with function approximation [659].

The consequence of the deadly triad is that divergence may occur. In a divergent learning process Q-values do not converge, but diverge.[19]

---

[18] Actually, as Tsitsiklis and Van Roy [699] showed, already two of the three may be enough for instability. All three together increases the chance of divergent training more, unless special measures are taken.

[19] The deadly triad suggests us to use on-policy instead of off-policy learning, to improve the training convergence. However, when learning on-policy the target network determines the next data sample to be trained on. Mnih et al. [461] give an example of how on-policy learning also leads to training divergence. Assume that the maximizing action is to move left. With on-policy learning the training samples will be dominated by samples from the left-hand side; if, for some reason, the maximizing action then switches to the right, then the training distribution will also switch. In this way unwanted feedback loops may arise and the network will get stuck in self-reinforcing features.

For some time, most further research in reinforcement learning focused on linear function approximators, which have better convergence guarantees. Later, after the first positive results of DQN [461], experimental studies were performed to find out under which circumstances convergence in the face of the deadly triad can be achieved, causing many further techniques to be developed (Sect. 6.4).

Conclusion

The preceding challenges to achieve stable deep reinforcement learning might be summarized as problems of coverage, correlation, and convergence: a lack of coverage of the state space, too much correlation between subsequent states, and problematic convergence in training due to the deadly triad.

Although the theory suggests reasons why function approximation may preclude stable reinforcement learning, there were early indications to the contrary that stable training was possible in practice. TD-Gammon [675] used self-play reinforcement learning, achieving stable learning in a shallow network. Perhaps some form of stable reinforcement learning was possible, at least in a shallow network? TD-Gammon's training used a temporal difference algorithm similar to Q-learning, approximating the value function with a network with one hidden layer, based on heuristic features.

TD-Gammon's success prompted attempts with TD learning in Checkers [133] and Go [655, 144]. Unfortunately the success could not be replicated in these games, and it was believed for some time that Backgammon was a special case well suited for reinforcement learning and self-play [530, 606]. One suggestion was that perhaps the randomness of the dice rolls helped exploration and smoothing of the value function of the state space.

However, there were further reports of early successful applications of deep neural networks in a reinforcement learning setting, suggesting that stable deep reinforcement learning is possible [283, 576], prompting more work. The results in Atari (2013) and Go (2016) as well as further studies [710] have now provided clear indications that both stable training and generalizing reinforcement learning are indeed possible, and why.

So far, we have discussed reasons why deep reinforcement learning processes may suffer from instability. Deep reinforcement learning is a process where the training examples are influenced by the training process itself, introducing the possibility of divergent or self-reinforcing learning. We have also seen that, despite these reasons, some papers reported stable learning (in addition to TD-Gammon's success with shallow reinforcement learning).

As noted before, attempts to follow up on TD-gammon's success with neural nets and self-play in Checkers and Go were not successful at first. We will now discuss results where stable deep reinforcement learning was achieved on end-to-end reinforcement learning of Atari 2600 games on the Atari Learning Environment benchmark set (ALE) [53].

Fig. 6.24 Atari 2600 console

6.3.2 Atari 2600 Games

Let us look in more detail into the Atari 2600 experiments.

Learning actions directly from high-dimensional sensory inputs such as sound and vision is one of the long-standing challenges of artificial intelligence. In 2013, one year after the AlexNet success in supervised learning, a paper was published that took reinforcement learning a major step further. Mnih et al. [461] published a work on *end-to-end* reinforcement policy learning in Atari games. Their approach is end-to-end in the sense that they learn joystick actions directly from the visual state, the raw pixels, without an intermediate step of hand-crafted heuristic features. The network architecture and training algorithm were named DQN, for Deep Q-Network.

Mnih et al. applied deep learning to play 1980s arcade Atari 2600 games, such as Space Invaders, Pong, and Breakout, directly from the raw television screen pixels [53]. Figure 6.24 shows a picture of an Atari 2600 console.

Being able to close the loop from pixels to policy is a major achievement. In their original 2013 workshop paper Mnih et al. [461] were able to achieve human-level play for six games. In a follow-up article in 2015 they improved on their work and were able to achieve a level of play equal to humans for 49 of the games that were in the test set [462].

It should be noted that there are a few Atari games that proved difficult to achieve strong play at. Notably games that required more long-range planning because long stretches of the game do not give rewards, such as Montezuma's Revenge, were a problem. Delayed credit assignment over long periods is still hard. In 2020 a paper was published with success in 57 games using a meta-controller for learning in the different games [28].

In summary, a single architecture was able to successfully learn control policies for many different games. Minimal prior knowledge was used, and the neural network only processed the pixels and the game score. The same network architecture and training procedure was used on each game, although a network trained for one game could not play another game well.

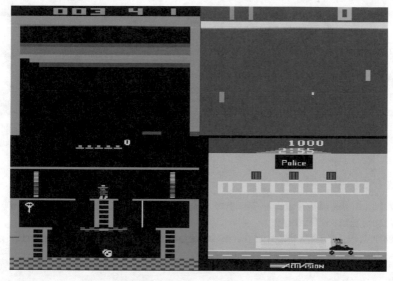

Fig. 6.25 Screenshots of 4 Atari Games (Breakout, Pong, Montezuma's Revenge, and Private Eye)

Arcade Learning Environment

The results by Mnih et al. stimulated much further work in the area of deep reinforcement learning. Successful end-to-end reinforcement learning created much interest among researchers, and many related algorithms were developed. Let us look into their methods and experiments.

The games that were used for DQN are from a standard benchmark set, the Arcade Learning Environment (ALE) [53]. ALE is a test-bed designed to provide challenging reinforcement learning tasks. Among other things it contains an emulator of the Atari 2600 console. ALE presents agents with a high-dimensional[20] visual input (210×160 RGB video at 60 Hz) of tasks that were designed to be interesting and challenging for human players (Fig. 6.25). The game cartridge ROM typically holds the game code (2-4 kB), while the console memory is small, just 128 bytes. This is not a typo, the console memory really is only 128 *bytes*. The actions can be input via a joystick, and a fire button (18 actions).

The original experiments were performed with seven Atari games. Training was performed on 50 million frames in total.

In their 2013 work [461] the neural network performed better than an expert human player on Breakout, Enduro, and Pong. On Seaqest, Q*Bert, and Space Invaders performance was far below that of a human. In these games a strategy must be found that extends over longer time periods. In their 2015 work [462] the net performed

---

[20] That is, high dimensional for machine learning. 210×160 pixels is not exactly high-definition video quality.

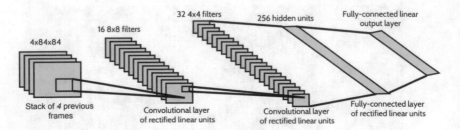

Fig. 6.26 DQN architecture [320]

better than human-level play in 29 of 49 Atari games. Again, games with longer credit delay were more difficult.

Let us look in more detail at the network architecture of the 2013 experiments.

Network Architecture

The Atari task is a control task: the network trains a behavior policy directly from pixel frame input. The task of processing raw frames involves a high computational load. Therefore, the 2013 training architecture contains a number of reduction steps. The network that is used consists of three hidden layers, which is simpler than what is used in most supervised learning tasks. Figure 6.26 shows the architecture of DQN.

The images are high-dimensional data. Since working with the full resolution of 210×160 with 128 colors at 60 frames per second would be computationally too intensive, the images are preprocessed. The 210×160 with 128 color palette is reduced to gray scale and 110×84 pixels cropped to 84×84. The first hidden layer convolves 16 8×8 filters with stride 4 and ReLU neurons. The second hidden layer convolves 32 4×4 filters with stride 2 and ReLU neurons. The third hidden layer is fully connected and consists of 256 ReLU neurons. The output layer is also fully connected with one output per action (18 actions for the joystick). The outputs correspond to the Q-values of the individual action. The network receives the change in game score as a number from the emulator, and derivative updates are reprocessed to $\{-1, 0, +1\}$ to indicate decrease, no change, or improvement of the score (Huber loss [38]).

To reduce computational demands further, frame skipping was employed. Only one in every 3–4 frames was used, depending on the game. For history, the net takes as input the last four resulting frames, allowing movement to be seen by the net. As optimizer RMSprop was used. A variant of ϵ-greedy is used, that starts with an ϵ of 1.0 (exploring) going down to 0.1 (90% exploiting).

The network architecture consists of convolutional layers and a fully connected layer. Recall that convolutional nets are shift-invariant feature recognizers. Fully connected nets allow $n \times m$ mapping. The feature recognizers together with the $n \times m$ mapping allow mapping of any feature (shape) to any action.

6.3.3 Decorrelating States

Let us now look in more detail at how stable learning was achieved. The focus of DQN is on breaking correlations between states. The DQN algorithm has two methods to achieve this: experience replay and infrequent weight updates. We will first look at experience replay.

Experience Replay

Recall that in reinforcement learning training samples are created in a sequence of interactions with an environment, and that subsequent training states are correlated. Thus the network is trained on too many samples in a certain area, and other parts of the state space remain unexplored. Furthermore, through function approximation, some behavior may be forgotten. When an agent reaches a new level in a game that is different from previous levels, the agent may forget how to play the other level.

DQN uses experience replay, with a replay buffer [420], a cache of previously explored states.[21] The goal is to increase the independence of training examples, by sampling training examples from this buffer. The next state to be trained on is no longer a direct successor of the current state, but one in a long history of previous states. In this way the replay buffer spreads out the learning over all seen states by sampling a batch of states at random, breaking temporal correlations between samples.

Experience replay improves on standard Q-learning in two respects, using randomization of the order in which samples are used to (1) break the correlations between consecutive samples; (2) prevent unwanted feedback loops, which would arise when the game makes moves in a certain area that it does not escape from, getting stuck in local areas of the state space. By averaging the behavior distribution over the previous states, experience replay smooths out training and avoids oscillations or local minima in the parameters.

Note that training by experience replay is a form of off-policy learning, since the target parameters are different from those used to generate the sample.[22] Off-policy learning is one of the three elements of the deadly triad. It is curious to see that this solution to stable learning is to use more of one of the causes of the deadly triad.

In practice, experience replay stores the last N examples in the replay memory, and samples uniformly when performing updates. A typical number for N is 10^6 [777]. A form of importance sampling might differentiate important transitions. Experience replay works well in practice in Atari [462]. However, further analysis of replay buffers has pointed to possible problems. Zhang et al. [777] study the deadly triad with experience replay, and find that larger networks resulted in more instabilities, but

---

[21] Originally experience replay is a biologically inspired mechanism [442, 495, 421].

[22] But since DQN uses ϵ-greedy exploration, in a percentage of the actions the behavior policy is used. DQN is a mix between on-policy and off-policy learning.

also that longer multi-step returns yielded fewer unrealistically high reward values. Indeed, in Sect. 6.4 we will see many further enhancements.

Infrequent Weight Updates

The second improvement in DQN is *infrequent weight updates.* Infrequent updates of the target weight values also reduce correlations and oscillations caused by loops and self-reinforcing features. This method works by using a separate network for generating the targets of the update of the Q value. Every x updates, the network Q is cloned to obtain a target network $\hat{Q}$, which is used for generating the targets for the following x updates to Q.

This second network improves the stability of Q learning, where normally an update that increases $Q(s_t, a_t)$ often increases $Q(s_{t+1}, a)$ for all a. This also increases the target, quite possibly leading to oscillations and divergence of the policy. Generating the targets using an older set of parameters adds a delay between the time an update to Q is made and the time the update changes the targets, breaking the feedback loop or at least making oscillations less likely.

6.3.4 Conclusion

It should be noted that the fundamental reasons for instability in reinforcement learning with function approximation still exist; the deadly triad has not evaporated into thin air, and states are still generated in an agent/environment loop. DQN and related algorithms have achieved stable learning for some games. Van Hasselt et al. [710] mention that divergence can be mitigated by using separate networks for bootstrapping, using multi-step returns, and prioritizing replay to reduce the overestimation bias. Many further advances to DQN have been found, as we will discuss further in Sect. 6.4.

The topic of this chapter is how deep learning enabled automated feature discovery to achieve true end-to-end machine learning, from pixels to labels and actions. We have seen how a combination of new algorithms, large training sets, and GPU compute power has enabled researchers to achieve breakthroughs in image recognition and game playing. These breakthroughs have resulted in applications that we use in our daily lives, and have inspired much further research (Sect. 6.4).

Let us take a step back and reflect on what has been achieved in supervised and reinforcement learning.

End-to-End Behavior Training

Both the works on Atari and ImageNet succeed in end-to-end training. It is interesting to compare end-to-end training in supervised and in reinforcement learning. The breakthroughs in image recognition with AlexNet [386] and other ILSVRC works rely on training on large labeled training sets. In these and later works, networks are trained directly from the raw inputs, using updates by stochastic gradient descent. The layered representations that are learned in this way are typically better representations than hand-crafted or heuristic features.

Mnih et al. learned an end-to-end behavior policy from raw visual input, also without any heuristics or intermediate features. The Atari 2600 games are games of skill. The games are difficult for humans, because they require dexterity and quick hand-eye coordination. Playing the games builds reflexes. The games are not so much designed as games of strategy (such as Chess, Checkers, Go, Backgammon, or Othello) where credit assignment is long and small differences between states can have large consequences, and where planning algorithms shine. The Atari 2600 games are reflex games (thinking fast, not slow) with mostly short temporal credit assignment, that could be learned with a surprisingly simple neural network. In this sense, the problem of playing Atari well is not unlike an image database categorization problem: both problems are to find the right answer (out of a small set) that matches an input consisting of a set of pixels. Apparently, mapping pixels to categories is not that different from mapping pixels to joystick actions, when the credit assignment problem has been overcome (see also the observations in [355]).

The algorithmic feat of breaking through the divergence and oscillation of reinforcement learning with feedback loops and off-policy function approximation, is highly imaginative, and has stimulated much subsequent research. Many blogs have been written on replicating the result, which is still not an easy task [38].

We will now turn to further developments of advanced deep reinforcement learning algorithms to address these challenges.

6.4 *Deep Reinforcement Learning Enhancements

As we have seen in Sect. 6.3.1, the stability of the training process is the main challenge in deep reinforcement learning. DQN showed that experience replay improves the training stability, enabling end-to-end learning in Atari. The Atari results have spawned much activity among reinforcement learning researchers to improve training stability further, and many refinements of experience replay have been devised. The algorithms in this section all aim to address the problems of coverage, correlation, and convergence, and largely succeed in doing so.

Many of the topics that are covered by the enhancements are older ideas that work well in deep reinforcement learning. DQN applies random sampling of its replay buffer, and one of the first enhancements was prioritized sampling [596]. It was found that DQN, being an off-policy algorithm, typically overestimates action values (due to the max operation). Double DQN addresses overestimation [711], and dueling DDQN introduces the advantage function to standardize action values [747]. Two effective actor-critic algorithms were introduced: A3C [459] and PPO [610]. The effect of random noise on exploration was tested [224], and distributional DQN

Name	Principle	Applicability	Effectiveness
double DQN	de-overestimate values	DQN	convergence
prioritized experience	decorrelation	replay buffer	convergence
distributional	probability distr	deep RL	generalization
random noise	parametric noise	deep RL	more exploration
actor-critic	value/policy interleave	A3C, PPO, dueling	stability, parallel

Table 6.4 Deep reinforcement learning enhancements

showed that networks that use probability distributions work better than networks that only use expected values [52].

In this section we will discuss these enhancements. Table 6.4 gives an overview of some of the deep reinforcement learning enhancements. The enhancements improve generalization to the test set and convergence of the training process. Just as we saw in Chap. 4 with heuristic planning, the basic concepts and algorithms in deep reinforcement learning are simple. And just as in heuristic planning, the basic ideas offer much room for further enhancement, to achieve better performance [594]. Interestingly, many of these enhancements are independent: the concepts do not interfere and can be used together.

In 2017 Hessel et al. published the Rainbow paper [290], in which they combined seven important enhancements. The paper is so called because the major graph showing the cumulative performance over 57 Atari games of the seven enhancements is multi-colored (Fig. 6.27).

The Rainbow paper summarizes some of them, and this section provides an overview of ideas and enhancements. The enhancements all use the same or similar benchmarks (ALE or Gym), and most algorithm implementations can be found on the OpenAI Gym GitHub site in the baselines.[23] This has stimulated research, resulting in the current abundance of ideas and algorithms, of which many play an important role in further research.

Reducing Correlation

The baseline algorithm of the methods described is DQN. The original DQN architecture is based on a simple neural network with two hidden convolutional layers and one fully connected hidden layer, a fully connected output layer,[24] and ϵ-greedy exploration. DQN further uses a combination of four techniques [461, 462]: an experience replay buffer for randomized sampling to break consecutive state correlations, a separate target weight network to break target value correlations, clipping rewards to $\{-1, 0, +1\}$, and skipping frames and reducing pixel resolution to reduce the computational load.

The following algorithms improve on various aspects of DQN.

---

[23] https://github.com/openai/baselines
[24] The 2015 architecture uses three hidden convolutional layers [462]

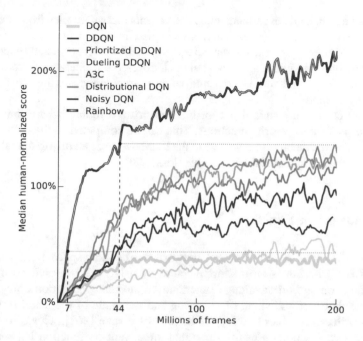

Fig. 6.27 Rainbow graph: performance over 57 Atari games [290]

6.4.1 Overestimation

Van Hasselt et al. introduce double deep Q learning (DDQN) [711]. DDQN is based on the observation that Q-learning may overestimate action values. They find that, in practice, such overestimations are common. On Atari 2600 games, due to the use of a deep neural network, DQN suffers from substantial over-estimations. Earlier Hasselt et al. [275] introduced the double Q learning algorithm in a tabular setting. The later paper shows that this idea also works with a large deep network. This DDQN algorithm not only reduces the overestimations but also leads to much better performance on several games.

DDQN was tested on 49 Atari games and achieved about twice the average score of DQN with the same hyperparameters, and four times the average DQN score with tuned hyperparameters [711].

6.4.2 Prioritized Experience Replay

Prioritized experience replay, or PEX, was introduced by Schaul et al. [596]. In the Rainbow paper its results are shown in combination with DDQN.

Recall that in DQN experience replay lets agents reuse examples from the past. In DQN experience transitions are uniformly sampled from a replay memory. Therefore, actions are simply replayed at the same frequency that they were originally experienced, regardless of their significance. Schaul et al. develop a framework for prioritizing experience. Important actions are replayed more frequently, and therefore learning efficiency is improved.

Schaul et al. use standard proportional prioritized replay, where the absolute TD error is used to prioritize actions. This can be computed in the distributional setting, using the mean action values. In the Rainbow paper all distributional variants prioritize actions by the Kullback-Leibler loss [290].

6.4.3 Advantage Function

Vanilla DQN uses a single neural network as function approximator. Dueling DDQN [747] improves on this architecture by using two separate estimators: a value function and an advantage function. An advantage function computes the difference between the value of an action and the value of the state. In this way it standardizes on a baseline for the actions of a state [262]. This allows better learning across actions. Results show that the advantage function leads to better policy evaluation when there are many similar valued actions.

6.4.4 Distributional DQN

DQN learns a single value, the estimated mean of the state value. Distributional Q-learning [52] learns a categorical probability distribution of discounted returns, instead of estimating the mean. This is in contrast to most reinforcement learning algorithms that model only the expectation of this value. Bellemare et al. use the distributional perspective to design a new algorithm which applies Bellman's equation to the learning of approximate distributions. Performance results of distributional DQN on Atari are good, showing the importance of the distributional perspective. Other relevant research into distributional perspectives is by Moerland et al. [463, 464].

Distributional reinforcement learning is an interesting and promising approach. Dabney et al. [158] report on experiments with mice that showed correspondence between distribution reinforcement learning algorithms and the dopamine levels in mice. It is hypothesized that the brain represents possible future rewards not as a single expected value, but as a probability distribution.

6.4.5 Noisy DQN

Noisy DQN [224] uses stochastic network layers for exploration. In NoisyNet parametric noise is added to the weights. This noise induces randomness in the agent's policy, increasing exploration. The parameters of the noise are learned with gradient descent along with the remaining network weights. The authors replace the standard exploration heuristics for A3C, DQN, and dueling agents (entropy reward and ϵ-greedy) with NoisyNet. The better exploration yields substantially higher scores for Atari.

6.4.6 R2D2

R2D2 [352] stands for Recurrent Replay Distributed DQN, and is built upon prioritized distributed replay and 5-step double Q-learning. It uses a dueling network architecture and an LSTM layer after the convolutional stack, see also [746, 263]. The RNN uses the recurrent state to exploit long-term temporal dependencies. They also find that RNN allows for better representation learning. R2D2 achieved good results on the 57 Atari games [352].

A recent benchmark achievement has been published as Agent57, the first deep reinforcement learning program that achieves a score higher than the human baseline on all 57 Atari 2600 games. Agent57 uses a meta-controller that adapts long- and short-term behavior of the agent, training for a range of policies, from very exploitative to very explorative [536].

6.4.7 Actor-Critic Approaches

Q-learning and value-based methods work well for discrete problem domains such as games. For continuous problem domains, such as robotics, policy methods are preferred. A challenge in policy methods is to find a reliable estimator for the quality of actions. A good way to achieve an accurate sense of the quality of actions is through the interleaving of value and policy methods, in an actor-critic approach (see also Sect. 3.3.3). There have been exciting advances in actor-critic, and some of the best performing algorithms on both games and robotics, such as PPO, are actor-critic.

Policy gradient methods caused recent breakthroughs in using deep neural networks for control, from video games, to 3D movement, to board games. Getting good results with policy gradient methods is challenging. They are sensitive to the choice of step size—too small, and progress is slow; too large and the signal is overwhelmed by the noise. When they lack good value estimates of the actions, they can have very poor sample efficiency, taking millions of time steps to learn simple tasks [609].

We will describe two main actor-critic algorithms: A3C and PPO.

A3C

A3C stands for Asynchronous Advantage Actor Critic [459] and is a parallel implementation of Advantage Actor-Critic (A2C), an actor-critic algorithm that uses the advantage function [659, 262].

In reinforcement learning, the amount of computational effort required for training is often substantial, and can be a prohibiting factor in achieving good results. Although the speedup provided by GPUs enabled much progress, the training times are still large. One way to speed up algorithms is to run parts of the search effort on multiple computers in parallel. Mnih et al. [459] present a method for parallel asynchronous gradient descent. The method allows implementation of different reinforcement learning variants, and related algorithms. One of these, an actor-critic algorithm called A3C, performs well.

A3C uses a multi-step bootstrap target [659, 658]. One of the effects of actor-critic is that it stabilizes training, just as experience replay. The parallel actor learners stabilize the controllers. The parallelism also decorrelates the samples into a more stationary process, since the parallel agents experience a variety of unrelated states. The Rainbow experiments include A3C and show its performance against advanced DQN algorithms, and in combination.

Proximal Policy Optimization

Another actor-critic algorithm is proximal policy optimization, or PPO [610]. PPO is an important algorithm that is successful in discrete action spaces (games) and continuous action spaces (robotics). PPO was not part of the Rainbow paper, which focuses mostly on value-based methods.

As we have seen [187] policy gradient estimates can have high variance and they can be sensitive to the settings of their hyperparameters. After the gradient is calculated, choosing the step size can be difficult: too small, and the algorithm is slow and sample inefficient; too large, and the algorithm overshoots and does not find the optimum. Several approaches have been proposed to make policy gradient algorithms more robust. One is to constrain the updates to a region, the so-called trust region. The trust region restricts the amount by which any update is allowed to change the policy. This approach is used in trust region policy optimization (TRPO [609]). In every iteration TRPO collects a batch of data and optimizes the surrogate loss subject to a constraint on how much the policy is allowed to change, expressed in terms of the Kullback-Leibler divergence. TRPO performs well, but uses expensive second-order derivative calculations, and a more efficient approach was sought.

Proximal policy optimization [610] is motivated by the same question as TRPO: how can we take the largest possible improvement step on a policy using the data we currently have, without stepping so far that we accidentally cause performance collapse. Where TRPO tries to solve this problem with a complex second-order method, PPO is a family of first-order methods to keep new policies close to the old. PPO methods are simpler to implement than TRPO, while performing as well in practice [284]. PPO trains a stochastic policy on-policy, in contrast to DQN, which is off-policy. This means that it explores by sampling actions according to the latest version of its stochastic policy.

While simpler than TRPO, the implementation of PPO is still complicated. OpenAI provides an implementation in its baseline.[25]

6.4.8 Enhancements in the Context of Game Playing Programs

To close this section on reinforcement learning enhancements, and to close this long chapter on deep learning, let us take a step back and look from a historical perspective at learning in games. We will look at how the various methods have been used in the context of game playing programs. We will discuss examples of database, supervised, and reinforcement learning. Some of the programs that we discuss will apply a form of self-play, a topic that will de explored more deeply in the next chapter.

Note that the simple minimax procedure already performs a kind of self-play. In minimax we determine our best move by calculating our opponent's best reply, which is based on our best reply, etc. In TD-Gammon and AlphaGo Zero style self-play we use a search-eval player to train our own evaluation function, by playing a small tournament against ourselves.

However, it can be difficult to get self-learning to work, because of instability in deep reinforcement learning training algorithms. When a supervised learning system does not learn, then we can try to find out why it is not learning certain examples by checking them one by one. A self-learning reinforcement learning system produces its own training examples, it can be unstable, and it can be hard to find out why a system is not learning, when there is no database of known knowledge that the system should have learned.

Therefore, we will see many examples of database learning, before we see self-play appear in game playing programs.

Earlier Works

Already in 1959 Samuel [577] introduced the idea of learning by self-play in his Checkers program. The coefficients of the heuristic function were updated towards the value of the search after black and white had each played one move. Today, more and more programs are based on end-to-end learning.

We will now have a look at previous game playing programs that used supervised and reinforcement learning. Table 6.5 lists notable works. The first column contains the name of the program, if given in the paper. The second column lists which game(s) the program plays. The third column is the planning algorithm, if applicable. The fourth column is the training algorithm, if applicable. CNN stands for convolutional

---

[25] https://openai.com/blog/openai-baselines-ppo/#ppo

Program	Game	Plan	Learn	Data	Net	Eval	Reference
Samuel	Check.	AlphaB.	coeff.	self-play	-	coeff. feat.	Samuel 1959 [577]
Chinook	Check.	AlphaB.	-	endgames	-	heur. feat.	Schaeffer 1992 [590]
Logistello	Othello	AlphaB.	regress.	patterns	-	coeff. pat.	Buro 1995 [113]
Deep Blue	Chess	AlphaB.	coeff.	manual	-	coeff. feat.	Hsu 1990 [310]
NeuroCh.	Chess	AlphaB.	TD(0)	db/self-play	1 layer	coeff. feat.	Thrun 1995 [686]
Neurogam.	B.gam.	-	FCN	games db	1 layer	coeff. feat.	Tesauro 1989 [673]
TD-gam.	B.gam.	AlphaB.	TD(λ)	self-play	1 layer	end to end	Tesauro 1995 [675]
-	Go	-	TD(0)	self-play	2 layer	end to end	Schraudolph [606]
MoGo	Go	MCTS	TD(0)	self-play	-	coeff/shape	Gelly 2008 [239]
NeuroGo	Go	-	FCN	games db	1 layer	coeff. feat.	Enzenberger [199]
Blondie24	Check.	AlphaB.	FCN	evo play	3 layer	end to end	Fogel 2001 [221]
Giraffe	Chess	AlphaB.	CNN	self-play	3 layer	end to end	Lai 2015 [393]
DeepChess	Chess	AlphaB.	FCN	games db	4 layer	end to end	David 2016 [160]
-	Atari	-	CNN	DQN	3 layer	end to end	Mnih 2013 [461]
ExIt	Hex	MCTS	CNN	self-play	15 layer	end to end	Anthony 2017 [15]
-	Go	MCTS	CNN	games db	5 layer	end to end	Clark 2015 [145]
DarkForest	Go	MCTS	CNN	games db	12 layer	end to end	Tian 2015 [691]
AlphaGo	Go	MCTS	CNN	games db	π:12C/1F	end to end	Silver 2016 [623]
				self-play	v:13C/1F		
AlphaGo Z.	Go	MCTS	ResNet	self-play	20 block	end to end	Silver 2017 [626]
					heads:π, v		
	Go				20 block		
AlphaZero	Chess	MCTS	ResNet	self-play	heads:π, v	end to end	Silver 2018 [625]
	Shogi						

Table 6.5 Evolution of planning, learning, and self-play in game playing programs

neural net, and FCN for fully connected net. The fifth column describes the data with which the learning took place. For supervised learning this is typically a database of grandmaster games, and for reinforcement learning a self-play loop is used, or databases with self-played games. The sixth column is the network architecture. Only the hidden layers are counted. For the older papers this is often a small number of hidden layers. After the advent of the use of GPUs in 2012 larger nets became feasible. The seventh column lists the evaluation method. This can be a linear combination of heuristic features, a system where the network learns the coefficients of heuristic features, or a full end-to-end learning system from raw board input. Last is a reference to a major work describing the approach of the program. Only the name of the first author is mentioned. Some programs were developed over many years by different authors. Please refer to the original papers for the often fascinating histories.

We will now discuss how the methods of these earlier programs developed.

Learning Shapes and Patterns

Game playing programs have been using many types of machine learning to improve the quality of play. For this reason, many early works focused on learning shapes and patterns. This learning was typically off-line, using months and months of training time. The Checkers program Chinook employed an end-game database that contained all board positions with 8 or fewer pieces. As soon as the database was reached by the search, perfect knowledge was available. The end-game database greatly contributed to the strength of Chinook [591]. In Chess, Deep Blue had a database that was accessed as soon as 5 or fewer pieces were on the board [119].

In Go, the emphasis of databases is on small local patterns. Stoutamire used hashed sets of patterns to find good and bad shapes [647]. Van der Werf used neural networks and automatic feature extraction to predict good local moves from game records [709, 708].

Supervised Learning

Many researchers have tried supervised learning with databases of grandmaster games. Tesauro's 1989 Neurogammon achieved good results in Backgammon with supervised learning of the coefficients of an evaluation function of handcrafted features. He used a single hidden layer [674].

In Go, Enderton used neural networks in the search in his Go program Golem, for move ordering and for forward pruning of selective search [198]. Enzenberger's NeuroGo used a neural network for position evaluation [199].

Much later, Maddison et al. published work on a 12-layer convolutional neural net for move prediction in Go [435], laying a foundation for the supervised learning of AlphaGo. Facebook's AI Research lab created Darkforest for end-to-end deep learning of Go positions and MCTS [691].

Reinforcement Learning

Supervised learning, as in Neurogammon, uses a database to learn from good moves. After the success with supervised learning in Neurogammon, Tesauro tried temporal difference learning from the raw board in a small neural network in 1992. This was further augmented with expert designed features, resulting in play at world class level. TD-Gammon's success was the first widely published success of self-play [676, 677].

In Go Schraudolph et al. [606] used temporal difference to learn position evaluation from board networks. They note that to be successful, networks should reflect the spatial organization of the input signals. Huang et al. [315] used self-play of 16 different players to learn opening strategies in Go.

Silver, in his PhD thesis [622], applied reinforcement learning to search in Go, and Silver et al. [627] and Gelly and Silver [237, 236, 235] studied reinforcement learning of local shape patterns. Silver et al. [628] further combined temporal difference learning in MCTS.

In Chess, Thrun's NeuroChess [686] tried temporal difference feature learning. Inspired by the progress in deep learning, in 2015 Matthew Lai tried end-to-end learning in Chess: he went beyond evaluation function weight tuning with Giraffe [393], using DQN, and self-play, including feature extraction and pattern recognition for end-to-end reinforcement learning. Giraffe reached master-level play. Lai later joined the AlphaZero team.

In some of the early works the small size of the networks limited success. In others the temporal difference learning or self-play is based on hand-crafted or heuristic features of the state space, possibly introducing bias or errors. End-to-end learning from the raw board or pixels requires more computational power. When first done successfully end-to-end (AlexNet [386], Atari [461, 462]) the papers generated much research interest.

Concurrent to the work by the AlphaGo team, Anthony et al. [15] worked on a similar idea for tabula rasa learning based on self-play, combining MCTS and DQN. The name of their work is ExIt, for Expert Iteration. They did not use Go, but Hex, a simpler game, to show their methods. They do make the link with Kahneman's work explicit, even in the title of their paper.

The relation between planning and training is also studied in model-based and model-free reinforcement learning (Sect. 3.3.4). The interplay between planning and training, and especially of model-based and model-free approaches, is an active area of research [15, 750, 506, 733, 414, 749].

6.4.9 Conclusion

Progress has been made in deep reinforcement learning by many researchers in a short period of time. The actor-critic algorithms and the Rainbow paper algorithms illustrate how much our understanding of deep reinforcement learning has improved. As in heuristic planning and in supervised learning, the presence of clear benchmarks was instrumental for progress. Researchers were able to see clearly which ideas worked, and to check if their intuition and understanding were correct. The earlier game playing programs, OpenAI's Gym [98], and the ALE [53] are responsible to a great extent for enabling this progress.

The next chapter will look deeper into self-play, a kind of reinforcement learning in which the environment is played also by the agent, and which takes performance of deep reinforcement learning to another level.

6.5 Practice

Below are some questions to check your understanding of this chapter. Each question is a closed question where a simple, one sentence answer is possible.

Questions

1. What is the difference between supervised learning and reinforcement learning?

2. What is the difference between a shallow network and a deep network?
3. Why is function approximation important in game playing?
4. What phases does a learning epoch have? What happens in each phase?
5. What is the difference between heuristic features and learned features?
6. What is MNIST? What is ImageNet? What is TensorFlow?
7. Name three factors that were essential for the deep learning breakthrough, and why.
8. What is end-to-end learning? Do you know an alternative? What are the advantages of each?
9. What is underfitting, and what causes it? What is overfitting, and what causes it? How can you see if you have overfitting?
10. Name three ways to prevent overfitting.
11. What is the difference between a fully connected network and a convolutional neural network?
12. What is max pooling?
13. Why are shared weights advantageous?
14. Describe the vanishing gradient problem. What are ReLU units?
15. Why is deep reinforcement learning more susceptible to unstable learning than deep supervised learning?
16. What is the deadly triad?
17. Why may reinforcement learning with function approximation be unstable?
18. What is the role of the replay buffer?
19. How can correlation between states lead to bad generalization?
20. How did AlexNet advance the state of the art in deep learning?
21. Name three architectural innovations/characteristics of AlexNet.
22. What is an inception modules? What is a residual network? What is the relation between the two?
23. What is a GAN?
24. What is an RNN, and how is it different from a deeply layered network?
25. What are the advantages of LSTM?
26. Why is the Rainbow paper so named, and what is the main message?
27. Why is PPO an actor-critic method?

Exercises

Let us now start with some exercises. Install TensorFlow and Keras (go to the TensorFlow page).[26] The exercises below are meant to be done in Keras.

1. Download and install TensorFlow and Keras. Check if everything is working by executing the MNIST training example. Choose the default training dataset. Run it on the training set, and then test the trained network on a testset. How well does it predict?

---

[26] https://www.tensorflow.org

2. Which optimizer does the MNIST example use? Try a different optimizer, an adaptive optimizer such as Adam, and compare it with simple Backprop. Does training speed improve?
3. OpenML is a research project to compare different machine learning algorithms with different datasets. Go to OpenML and download different datasets to see which problems may be harder to learn.[27]
4. The learning rate is a crucial hyperparameter. Always tune this one first. You may find that learning goes slowly. Try to increase the training speed by increasing the different learning rates. Does performance increase? Does the error function drop faster or slower? Can you explain your observations?
5. Explore options for cloud processing. The cloud provides ample compute power at cheap prices, often with free student or sign up bonuses. Go to AWS, the Google Cloud, Colab, or Microsoft Azure, and explore ways to speed up your learning.
6. One of the biggest problems of supervised learning is overfitting. Can you check if over- or underfitting occurred in your experiments? Create an experiment in which you force overfitting to occur. What will you do: change the size of the network, change the algorithm (change CNN, ReLU, dropout), or change a parameter (learning rate, dropout percentage, training time)? How can you see if overfitting has occurred? When has it been reduced?

Atari DQN Code

The Atari papers come with source code. The original DQN code from [462] is at Atari DQN.[28] This code is the original code, in the programming language Lua, without new developments. Before you start working with this code, it should be noted that DQN can be difficult to get working. There are many details to get right. In addition, the experiments often have to run for a long time, which means that debugging and improving is slow if you have just one GPU.

A better start is the TensorFlow implementation in Python of DQN for the Atari game Breakout, at Atari Breakout Code.[29] This will get you up to speed more quickly. The code is readable, and follows the concepts discussed in this chapter. However, the code is too large to cover in detail here.

To get really started with deep reinforcement learning, we suggest to use DQN and many of the other algorithms that are available at the OpenAI Keras RL library at Keras RL[30] [528, 241].

---

[27] https://www.openml.org

[28] https://github.com/kuz/DeepMind-Atari-Deep-Q-Learner

[29] https://github.com/floodsung/DQN-Atari-Tensorflow

[30] https://github.com/keras-rl/keras-rl

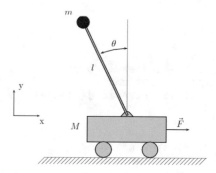

Fig. 6.28 Cartpole experiment [659]

Cartpole

OpenAI provides baseline implementations of important reinforcement learning algorithms [173]. A good implementation of DQN for the Atari Learning Environment is available. Installation instructions for Linux and macOS are provided.

Cartpole is a basic experiment in which an agent must learn to balance a stick on a cart by reinforcement learning. A nice video of a Cartpole experiment is Cartpole Video[31] (this is a real-life cartpole, as opposed to the simulated cartpole that is most often used in reinforcement learning experiments; Fig. 6.28). At OpenAI Cartpole baseline[32] working example code for the Cartpole experiment is available.

The high-level code is simple, as Listing 6.2 shows. To really understand what is going on you have to look into the implementations of deepq.learn, which implements DQN in a few hundred lines of code.

More Exercises

For the following exercises, if you have not done so, download and install Gym.

1. Go to the Mountain Car example, and run it. Experiment with different learning settings to understand their effect on the learning.
2. Try the same for Cartpole.
3. Install ALE. Train a player for Space Invaders. Did the training process work well? How do you find out if the trained player is a good player? Can you compute an Elo rating?
4. Identify the replay buffer in the code. Reduce the size, or otherwise turn it off. Does DQN still converge, what does it do to the quality of the player that is trained?

---

[31] https://www.youtube.com/watch?v=5Q14EjnOJZc

[32] https://github.com/openai/baselines/tree/master/baselines/deepq

```python
import gym

from baselines import deepq

def callback(lcl, _glb):
    # stop training if reward exceeds 199
    is_solved = lcl['t'] > 100 and
            sum(lcl['episode_rewards'][-101:-1]) / 100 >= 199
    return is_solved

def main():
    env = gym.make("CartPole-v0")
    act = deepq.learn(
        env,
        network='mlp',
        lr=1e-3,
        total_timesteps=100000,
        buffer_size=50000,
        exploration_fraction=0.1,
        exploration_final_eps=0.02,
        print_freq=10,
        callback=callback
    )
    print("Saving_model_to_cartpole_model.pkl")
    act.save("cartpole_model.pkl")

if __name__ == '__main__':
    main()
```

Listing 6.2 Cartpole code [173]

5. *Try a few other Atari games. Does DQN train well? Try Montezuma's Revenge. Does DQN work well? Have a look at the alternative deep reinforcement methods. How could you improve DQN to play well in Montezuma's Revenge? (This is a hard research question; see also [28].)

Stable Baselines

The Gym GitHub repository OpenAI Baselines[33] contains implementations of many algorithms covered here. You can easily download them and experiment to gain an insight into their behavior. Stable Baselines is a fork of the OpenAI algorithms; it has more documentation and other features. It can be found at Stable Baselines,[34] and the documentation is at Docs.[35] An implementation of the Rainbow paper in Torch

---

[33] https://github.com/openai/baselines

[34] https://github.com/hill-a/stable-baselines

[35] https://stable-baselines.readthedocs.io/en/master/

is available here.[36] The RL Baselines Zoo even provides a collection of pretrained agents, at Zoo.[37]

The open availability of TensorFlow, Keras, ImageNet, and OpenAI Gym/ALE allows for easy replication and, importantly, improvement of the works covered in this chapter. Keras implementations of VGG, ResNet are available in Keras.applications (see Keras Applications).[38] AlexNet is here: AlexNet,[39] GoogLeNet is here: GoogLeNet.[40]

*Advanced Exercises

Due to the advanced nature of some parts of this chapter, the following exercises are large, project sized. These topics and these exercises are fascinating, but answering these questions may require a substantial amount of research and work (potentially thesis size).

1. Reproduce the basic AlexNet, VGG, and ResNet results on ImageNet in Keras. Do deeper ResNets give better results? How do deeper ResNet impact training time?
2. Read GAN papers on how to generate artificial images [251, 356, 695]. Try to generate fake cat and dog images. Can you also use a discriminator to separate real images from fakes?
3. Use an RNN to perform a captioning challenge in ImageNet.
4. Read the Rainbow paper [290]. Go to the OpenAI baselines and download and run the code and perform an ablation study, leaving out the constituting methods one by one.

Summary

In this chapter we faced the challenge of finding function approximators for large, high-dimensional, state spaces. Deep learning allowed automated feature discovery for end-to-end learning. The field of function approximation with neural networks is large, rich, and deep. This chapter can only give a glimpse of the work that has been done.

The goal of function approximation is to find a reliable value function for large state spaces, so large that test examples have not been seen during training. In this way, the function approximators of this chapter are an alternative to the heuristic feature function of Chap. 4 and the averaged random values of Chap. 5.

---

[36] https://github.com/Kaixhin/Rainbow

[37] https://github.com/araffin/rl-baselines-zoo

[38] https://keras.io/applications/

[39] https://gist.github.com/JBed

[40] https://gist.github.com/joelouismarino

Training deep networks is not easy. Among the problems to be overcome are efficient training methods, overfitting, and vanishing gradients. Many solutions have been discussed, from ReLU, batch normalization (to prevent vanishing gradients) to dropouts (to prevent overfitting) to convolutional layers (to both reduce the number of weights and allow efficient translations and rotations) and we have discussed training methods such as stochastic gradient descent.

Function approximation blossomed when large labeled datasets became available *and* when the necessary computational power in the form of GPUs arrived. In addition to the datasets, easy-to-use free software packages such as TensorFlow and Keras have lowered the barrier of entry for research significantly. These packages have played a large role in the success of the field.

We also discussed deep reinforcement learning, where correlations between states cause divergent and unstable learning.

Deep supervised learning constructs complex features from example databases. The examples in these databases are independent, and training converges towards an optimum. In reinforcement learning states are correlated and the training process easily diverges. Two techniques, replay buffer and infrequent weight updates, have been introduced to decouple states enough to allow the training to converge.

Mnih et al. state the following in their paper [462]: "a single architecture can successfully learn control policies in a range of different environments with only very minimal prior knowledge, receiving only the pixels and the game score as inputs, and using the same algorithm, network architecture and hyperparameters on each game, privy only to the inputs a human player would have." This architecture, DQN, was demonstrated on Atari games to achieve end-to-end learning from the raw pixels on a wide variety of games that are challenging for humans.

For better feature discovery new methods such as VGG and ResNet have been introduced, achieving very high levels of performance on image recognition tasks. Recurrent neural nets, or LSTMs, are well suited for sequence processing, such as caption generation.

For reinforcement learning, many methods have been devised to improve generalization and to reduce divergence, and thus solve problems related to coverage, correlation, and convergence. The methods typically use two networks to break possible oscillations between the search and the target values, and they use a form of replay buffers. Many variants for better generalization and more stability have been developed since DQN, as the aptly named Rainbow paper documents. Among the promising methods are actor-critic methods, such as PPO.

Historical and Bibliographical Notes

Learning in Games

In game playing, the advantages of neural networks for function approximation were recognized early. Although the best known success of neural networks in games is undoubtedly AlphaGo, there has also been interesting work performed with supervised learning in games. Before we move deep reinforcement learning and AlphaGo, let us briefly look at the earlier approaches that have been tried.

Twenty years before AlexNet, in 1990, Tesauro published a paper on Neurogammon [674], his program for playing Backgammon. Neurogammon used supervised learning to train the coefficients of human-designed heuristic input features, by using 400 example games played by Tesauro himself. A later version of Neurogammon, TD-Gammon, used reinforcement learning to train the same heuristic input features. TD-Gammon achieved world-class human tournament level play [675, 676].

In 1996 Enzenberger created the NeuroGo [199] Go playing program. NeuroGo uses temporal difference learning and backpropagation to train the coefficients of manually crafted heuristics features. Its performance did not surpass that of heuristic programs of its time. In 1990 there was insufficient computer power for training of large networks, nor were there large databases of example games to achieve strong play.

In 1999 Chellapilla and Fogel [133, 221] used a fully connected network to evolve board features in Checkers, achieving good results. Maddison et al. [435] show how convolutional neural nets can be used in the context of Go to generate moves. Sutskever and Nair [655] used CNNs to learn from Go expert games.

Convolutional neural nets were also used in Go by Clark and Storkey [144, 145], who had used a CNN for supervised learning from a database of human professional games, showing that it outperformed GNU Go and scored wins against Fuego. David et al. [160] report on end-to-end deep learning in Chess, achieving results on par with Falcon and Crafty, two alpha-beta-based programs.

Deep Learning

Good review papers on deep learning are [602, 405]. In 1958 Rosenblatt [560] introduced the perceptron, a simple neural network for pattern recognition.

Much work has been done to formulate this backpropagation algorithm [756]. It allowed the training of multi-layer networks, paving the way for deep learning's success. In the 1980s McClelland and Rumelhart published an influential work coining the terms parallel distributed processing and connectionism [570]. However, support vector machines and other simpler classifiers became popular [88, 637]. They were easier to reason about and performed better [563]. Later, max pooling was introduced, and GPU methods were created to speed up backpropagation. The performance of neural nets was further plagued by the vanishing gradient problem, especially in deeper networks.

Among many other contributions to both the theory and practice of deep learning, Schmidhuber devised a hierarchy of networks that were pretrained one network at a time, to overcome this problem [599]. Other methods were later designed, such as ReLU threshold functions and batch renormalization [328].

There are many books on Keras and TensorFlow; see, e.g., [241].

NeuroGo [199] and Neurogammon [674] used small nets to learn the coefficients of heuristic evaluation functions of the state. They were written at a time when little compute power was available, nor had the necessary advances in deep learning training algorithms occurred, to learn features directly from the state.

Silver et al. [628] discuss the use of temporal difference search in Go, comparing MCTS with TD reinforcement learning. Matthew Lai [393] experiments with DQN in Chess.

Experience replay is an important technique for the success of deep reinforcement learning [461]. Related ideas can be traced to earlier works. Gradient TD methods have been proven to converge for evaluating a fixed policy with a non-linear value approximator [75]. Relaxing the fixed control policy in neural fitted Q learning algorithm (NFQ) has been reported to work for nonlinear control with deep networks [552]. NFQ builds on work on stable function approximation [252, 203] and experience replay [420], and more recently on least-squares policy iteration [392].

Pattern recognition research has created a wealth of machine learning algorithms, of which deep learning is just one. Other well-known and successful approaches are principal component analysis, decision trees, random forests, support vector machines, k-means clustering, Bayesian networks, Kalman filters, and hidden Markov models. Each of these methods works well in different situations. Good reference works on these methods are [81, 358], or more practically oriented works such as [241, 471].

Pointers to further work on recurrent networks (RNN and LSTM) can be found in [261, 256]. Important work on RNNs has been done by Sutskever [653], Mikolov [449], and Graves [254]. A more detailed explanation of LSTMs can be found in [298, 354].

For more theory on deep supervised learning the book by Goodfellow et al. is indispensable [250]. Goodfellow et al. [251] introduced generative adversarial networks, which spawned much follow-up research including dreamlike (but also curiously realistic) fake images.[41] Huang et al. [313] apply adversarial attacks to reinforcement learning policies.

---

[41] Perhaps GANs are the answer to the question posed by Philip K. Dick in one of his science fiction stories: "Do Androids Dream of Electric Sheep?" [174].

Chapter 7
Self-Play

This chapter is devoted to AlphaGo-style self-play. Self-play is an intuitively appealing AI method that has long been used by AI researchers in various forms, as we saw at the end of the previous chapter. The 2016 results showed, many years after TD-Gammon, how self-play can achieve world champion level play in a highly complex game. Self-play, as it is used in AlphaGo, combines MCTS and deep reinforcement learning, using approaches from both symbolic AI and connectionist AI.

In this chapter planning and learning come together. The previous chapter showed us how deep learning can achieve very high performance in image classification and Atari game play. In Chap. 5 we saw how the UCT formula provided effective adaptive node selection. Chapter 4 taught us the basics of searching large state spaces: the search-eval architecture, and enhancements.

We will now see how to combine these methods in a self-learning reinforcement learning system that is able to beat the strongest human Go players. This chapter covers self-play, the AlphaGo results, and future developments. The main problem that we discuss is how to achieve stable, high performance, self-play, in a very challenging state space.

First, we will explain the basic principle of self-play, and the reasons why stable self-play is difficult to achieve. We will also see that self-play is faster than pretraining with human grandmaster games, and why.

Second, we will look in more detail at the architecture of self-play programs. The AlphaGo experiments actually consist of a sequence of three programs. We will look at the designs of all three programs and at the experiments.

Third, we will look at future work. The AlphaGo results inspired much further work. At the end of the chapter we will look in more detail at directions for future research.

© Springer Nature Switzerland AG 2020
A. Plaat, *Learning to Play*, https://doi.org/10.1007/978-3-030-59238-7_7

Program	Planning	Learning	Input/output	Achievement
AlphaGo	MCTS	supervised & reinforcement	Go	beat human champions
AlphaGo Zero	MCTS	self-play	Go	learn tabula rasa
AlphaZero	MCTS	self-play	Go, Chess, Shogi	generalize three games

Table 7.1 AlphaGo, AlphaGo Zero, and AlphaZero

Core Problems

- How can we create training examples that allow training beyond the level of play of human grandmasters?
- How can we use function approximation to improve adaptive sampling?

Core Concepts

- Stable self-play: coverage, correlation, and convergence
- Curriculum learning

A Note on Names

In this chapter we will discuss three related programs, all with names that confusingly start with Alpha, and all developed by related researchers. Each program achieved an AI milestone that was published in a top journal. The programs are AlphaGo [623], AlphaGo Zero [626], and AlphaZero [625]; see Table 7.1.[1] We will discuss in this chapter which methods were used and which advances in reinforcement learning were achieved. These advances are mostly related to self-play. We will also discuss further developments related to self-play.

The main publications on the three Alpha-★ programs are [623, 626, 625]. Appendix B contains more technical details of the three systems.

We will now first describe self-play, as it is used in AlphaGo Zero, the strongest Go program on Earth.

7.1 Self-Play Architecture

We have seen in Sect. 6.4.8 that self-play has a long history in game playing programs (Table 6.5). As we mentioned in the previous chapter, self-play is quintessential artificial intelligence: a system that can teach itself to become more intelligent. By

---

[1] Work on a fourth program, AlphaStar, for StarCraft, is also under way [725]; see Sect. 8.2.4. Furthermore, a related program, AlphaFold, is successful in protein folding [490].

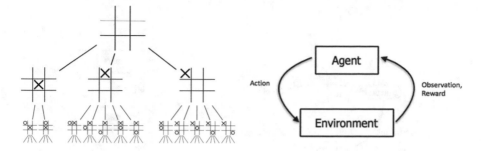

Fig. 7.1 Minimax tree and agent/environment loop

crafting a system in which intelligence emerges out of basic interactions, tabula rasa, from a blank slate, self-play comes very close to the original inspiration of the field.

Interestingly, if we go back to the original search-eval architecture, even simple minimax programs perform a kind of self-play, or self-lookahead (Fig. 7.1 left panel): since minimax uses the same algorithm for player and opponent it plays itself to find out what the best move is. MCTS also uses self-play in this way to find the best move.

7.1.1 Self-Play Learning

The kind of self-play that we discuss in this chapter goes a step further than finding the best move, however, and is used to create an entire self-*learning* program. Let us look at the familiar reinforcement learning loop of Fig. 7.1 (right panel). In this figure the agent learns a good policy by querying the environment (which actions are good in which states). In reinforcement learning, the environment is our opponent. If we perform the same trick as earlier in minimax, and replace the environment algorithm by the same agent algorithm then we have a self-learning "*self-agent*" system, a dragon biting its own tail.

The self-play design of AlphaGo Zero combines these two kinds of self-play: we add look-ahead to agent-self-learning and get a system that improves, through MCTS, its own training input.

We get a system as shown in Fig. 7.2: an agent system in which the training examples are generated by using the same system as the opponent. In each iteration a searcher creates higher-quality actions. MCTS improves the quality of the training examples in each iteration (left panel), and the net is trained with these better examples, improving its quality (right panel). By letting such a self-learning system play for a while it will teach itself an increasingly advanced level of play all the way to world champion.

This kind of self-play is used in AlphaGo Zero. The output of MCTS is used as input for the training of the network that is used as the evaluation function in that same

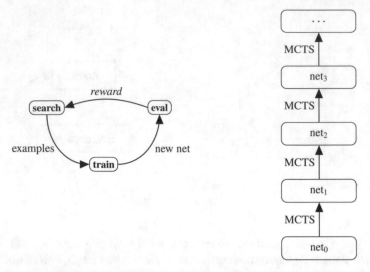

Fig. 7.2 Self-play loop improving quality of net

MCTS. An extra loop is wrapped around the search-eval functions to keep training the network with the game results, creating a learning curriculum.

To summarize, AlphaGo Zero self-play consists of the following elements:

1. Search: MCTS look-ahead using a policy input for selection and a value input for backup providing stronger examples
2. Eval: a neural network providing a policy output and a value output to be used in the search
3. Train: a training algorithm to improve the neural network with samples from the played games
R. Repeat the 3 steps to perform a self-play training curriculum

Self-Learning

Conceptually self-play is as simple as it is elegant: a training loop around a standard search-eval player with a neural network as evaluation function. Figure 7.3 and Listing 7.1 show the self-play loop in more detail. The numbers in the diagram refer to the line numbers in the pseudocode.

Let us perform an outside-in walk-through of this system using the code in Listing 7.1.

Line 1 is the main self-play loop. It controls how long the execution of the curriculum of self-play tournaments will continue. Line 2 executes the training episodes, consisting of tournaments of self-play games. Line 4 plays such a game to create (*state, action*) pairs for each move, and the outcome of the game. Line 5 calls MCTS to generate an action in each state. MCTS performs the simulations

```
1  for tourn in range (1, max_tourns): # curric. of max_tourns
        tournaments
2      for game in range(1, max_games): # play a tourn. of max_games
            games;
3          trim(triples) # if buffer full: replace old entries
4          while not game_over(): # generate the states of one game
5              game_pairs += mcts(eval(net)) # move is a (state,
                  action) pair
6          triples += add(games_pairs, game_outcome(game_pairs))
                  # add to buf
7      net = train(net, triples) # retrain with (state,action,outc)
            triples
```

Listing 7.1 Self-play pseudocode

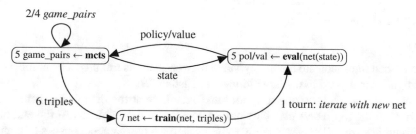

Fig. 7.3 A diagram of self-play

where it uses the policy net in UCT selection, and the value net at the MCTS leaves. Line 6 adds the outcome of each game to the (*state, action*)-pairs, to make the (*state, action, outcome*)-triples for the network to train on. Note that since the network is a two-headed policy/value net, both an action and an outcome are needed for network training. On the last line this triples-buffer is then used to train the network. The newly trained network is used in the next self-play iteration as the evaluation function by the searcher. With this net another tournament is played, using the searcher's look-ahead to generate a next batch of higher-quality examples, resulting in a sequence of stronger and stronger networks (Fig. 7.2 right panel).

Levels of Abstraction

The self-play loop looks elegant and simple, but contains an ingenious interplay of learning at different levels of abstraction. The levels of abstraction of AlphaGo Zero-like self-play are shown in Fig. 7.4. Looking at the figure for a moment can help us better understand self-play.

The structure of self-play is a straightforward onion-like system of functions (or loops) wrapped around each other (Fig. 7.4). The arrows in the figure point to the lower functions that are used by the higher function to generate the training examples.

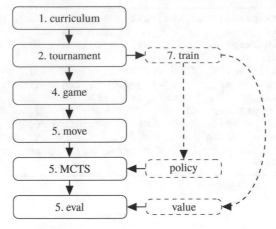

Fig. 7.4 Levels in self-play

The dashed lines indicate the policy/value network, and its training. The numbers in the figure correspond to the line numbers in Listing 7.1.

We can also peel the onion by looking outside-in at the data that is generated. Starting at the top, a self-play curriculum consists of tournaments. At the end of a curriculum a trained player is ready to be used. Each tournament consists of games (25,000 in AlphaGo Zero); at the end of the tournament the buffer is filled with example positions to train the network further. Each game consists of positions and moves; at the end of a game the *outcome* can be added to the moves (*state, action*) ready to be added to the buffer. Each move is computed by an MCTS search; at the end of the search a best action is returned, to be added to the list of pairs of the game buffer. Each MCTS search consists of simulations (1600 in AlphaGo Zero); at the end of each simulation another node is added to the MCTS tree.

Triple Recursion

The neural network of AlphaGo Zero is a single residual network with 19 hidden layers and two output layers: a value head and a policy head. Compared with the original AlphaGo, which had three networks, a striking element of AlphaGo Zero is the simplicity of this network architecture.

The policy and value are calculated in AlphaGo Zero using a single network. The relationship between the two heads goes back to Chap. 3, where policy functions and value functions were introduced. Policy and value are intimately related (good actions have high values and vice versa).

The simple and elegant network architecture allows a recursive, self-play training method. The training is triply recursive: it uses its own code three times. (1) The program self-improves the player in a curriculum of tournaments. (2) In each tournament the players perform self-play games, generating examples that are used to train the evaluation function. (3) In each game MCTS uses the same opponent model in its look-ahead, for itself and for the opponent, just as minimax. Listing 7.1 and Fig. 7.3 provide the code and the conceptual picture of this triply recursive training structure in line 1, line 2, and line 5 (the third level of recursion is implicit inside the MCTS look-ahead).

7.1.2 Self-Play and Search-Eval

Now that we have seen how it works conceptually, let us have a look at which techniques are used in self-play. All methods of the previous chapters come together in self-play. From Chap. 3 we see the concepts of policy and value functions. From Chap. 4 we see the search-eval architecture and we see shape enhancements and pattern databases. From Chap. 5 we see MCTS. From Chap. 6 we see deep supervised database learning, value function approximation, advanced generalization, exploration, and decorrelation techniques.

Self-play programs have a search function and an evaluation function just like all game playing programs. In AlphaGo Zero the search function is MCTS, and the evaluation function is a deep network. They are used in two phases: a training phase and a usage phase.

Evaluation

The eval function in end-to-end self-play is a deep neural net. The function approximator is trained, and is then queried during play (usage phase). Thus, eval has two roles:

1. While in the training phase, the eval network is the *learning element* of the self-play scheme
2. While in the usage phase, eval is a *policy/value function* to be queried for the policy and the value of the state

MCTS is an on-policy algorithm that makes use of guidance in two places: in the downward action selection and in the upward value backup. In AlphaGo Zero the function approximator returns both elements: a policy for the action selection and a value for the value backup. The neural network has two output layers, or heads: a policy head and a value head. The policy head of the net is used in the UCT action selection, and the value head of the net is used in the backpropagation of the leaf values of the MCTS tree. (These are the first and the last MCTS operation in Fig. 7.5.)

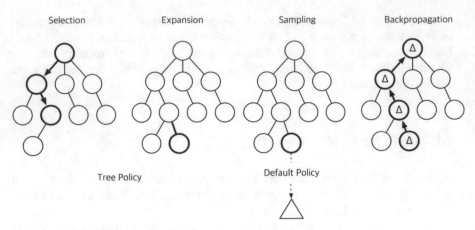

Fig. 7.5 Monte Carlo Tree Search [108]

Search

In self-play the search function also has two roles: to look ahead to generate examples in the training phase and to look ahead during actual play (usage phase). For both roles the look-ahead algorithm does exactly the same thing. It is only its *role* in the self-play scheme that is different during training and use:

1. While in the training phase, the search function generates the examples for the training. By looking ahead, it generates better quality examples for the training.
2. While in the usage phase, when self-play training has finished and the program is used for normal game play, the search function performs look-ahead using the net to find the best action in actual play.

The two phases are similar to the training and test phases in supervised learning.

We should note that the MCTS that is used in the three Alpha-⋆ programs differs from the MCTS from Chap. 5. MCTS is used inside the training loop, as an integral part of the self-generation of training examples, to enhance the quality of the examples for every self-play iteration.

Also, in the ⋆-Zero programs MCTS backups rely fully on the value function approximator; no playout is performed anymore. Only the selective statistics-based exploration/exploitation trade-off of MCTS is left. The MC part in the name of MCTS, which stands for the Monte Carlo playouts, really has become a misnomer for this network-guided tree searcher.

Furthermore, selection in self-play MCTS is different. UCT-based node selection now also uses the input from the policy head of the trained function approximators, in addition to the win rate and newness. Likewise, random playouts at the leaves are replaced by the value head of the deep function approximator. What remains is that through the UCT mechanism MCTS can focus its search effort greedily on the part with the highest win rate, while at the same time balancing exploration of parts of the tree that are underexplored.

The formula that is used to incorporate input from the policy head of the deep network is a variant of P-UCT [626, 466, 561, 440]. Let us compare P-UCT with UCT in order to see the difference. The original[2] UCT formula is [373]

$$\text{UCT}(a) = \frac{w_a}{n_a} + C_p\sqrt{\frac{\ln n}{n_a}}.$$

The P-UCT formula adds the policy head $\pi(s, a)$:

$$\text{UCT}(a) = \frac{w_a}{n_a} + C_p\pi(s, a)\frac{\sqrt{n}}{1 + n_a}.$$

P-UCT adds the $\pi(s, a)$ term specifying the policy function of the action a to the exploration part of the UCT formula.[3]

Dual-Headed Network

Let us look at a few concrete facts and numbers about the AlphaGo Zero self-play implementation, to get a feeling for the complexity of the problem [626].

AlphaGo Zero uses a dual-headed residual network. Policy and value loss contribute equally to the loss function. The network is trained with SGD. L2 regularization is used to reduce overfitting. The network has 19 hidden layers, and an input layer and two output layers, one for the value v estimation and one for the policy π distribution. The size of the mini-batch for updates is 2048. This batch is distributed over 64 GPU workers, each with 32 data entries. The mini-batch is sampled uniformly over the last 500,000 self-play games (replay buffer). The learning rate started at 0.01 and went down to 0.0001 during self-play.

For search AlphaGo Zero uses a version of on-policy MCTS that does not use random playouts anymore, Dirichlet noise is added to the P-UCT value at the root node, to ensure that all moves may be tried, increasing exploration. The C_p value of MCTS in AlphaGo is 5, heavily favoring exploration. In AlphaGo Zero the value depends on the stage in the learning; it grows during self-play. In each self-play iteration 25,000 games are played. For each move, MCTS performs 1600 simulations. In total over a three-day course of training 4.9 million games were played, after which AlphaGo Zero outperformed the previous version, AlphaGo.

More details can be found in Appendix B.2.

---

[2] Substituting a for the action for ease of comparison with the P-UCT terminology, where UCT originally uses n_j for the visit count of child j.

[3] Note the small difference under the square root (no logarithm; and addition of 1 in the denominator) also change the UCT function profile somewhat, ensuring correct behavior at unvisited actions [466].

7.1.3 Stable Self-Play through Exploration

Self-play has a long history in AI, yet the most recent successful self-play approach for training a machine learning system was TD-Gammon, 30 years ago. Now that we have seen the architecture of self-play, let us look at the performance and the challenges in achieving a strong level of play.

Self-play uses two forms of reinforcement learning: MCTS in both downward action selection and value backup, and DQN-like reinforcement learning to train the neural network with the MCTS results. One could say that self-play is reinforcement learning squared. The double reliance on reinforcement learning puts the quality of the generalization and convergence in the center, which may be the reason why it took so many years to achieve high-performance self-learning self-play.

Since all learning is by reinforcement, the training process must now be even more stable. The slightest problem in overfitting or correlation between states can throw off the coverage, correlation, and convergence. AlphaGo Zero uses various forms of exploration to achive stable learning. Let us summarize how stability is achieved.

- *Coverage* of the state space is improved by playing a (very) high number of games. The quality of the states is further improved by MCTS look-ahead. MCTS searches the state space for good training samples, improving the quality and diversity of the covered states. The exploration part of MCTS should make sure that enough new and unexplored parts of the state space are covered. Dirichlet noise is added at the root node and the C_p parameter in the P-UCT formula, that controls the level of exploration, has been set sufficiently high, around 4-5 (see also Sect. 5.3.1 and Appendix B.1).
- *Correlation* between subsequent states is reduced through the use of experience replay buffers and MCTS look-ahead, as in DQN and Rainbow algorithms.
- *Convergence* of the training is improved by using on-policy MCTS, and by taking small training steps. Since the learning rate is small there is little risk of divergence, although now convergence is quite slow and requires many training games.

By using these measures together, stable generalization and convergence are achieved. Although self-play is conceptually simple, achieving stable and high-quality self-play required slow training with a large number of games, and quite some tuning. There are many hyperparameters whose values must be set correctly. Although the values are published [626], the reasoning behind the values is not always clear. Reproducing the AlphaGo Zero results is not easy, and much time is spent in tuning and experimenting by efforts to reproduce the AphaGo Zero approach [531, 649, 679, 689, 775].

7.1.4 Curriculum Learning

As we will soon see in Sect. 7.2, AlphaGo and AlphaGo Zero use different training methods. AlphaGo uses a combination of supervised learning and reinforcement learning, while AlphaGo Zero is purely based on self-play. The result of self-play is not only *better* but also *faster* training, from weeks or even months for AlphaGo to days for AlphaGo Zero.

Why is self-play faster than a combination of supervised and reinforcement learning based on games databases? Self-play is faster because it follows a curriculum of examples that is ordered from easy to hard. This kind of learning is known as curriculum learning [477, 62, 626]. Let us see why learning an ordered sequence of examples is faster than learning many difficult concepts at once.

The training curriculum generated by self-players is a curriculum of examples from easy to hard. In easy examples the training error is small; for hard examples it is large. Problems that generate small errors train quickly; larger errors take more epochs to converge. In self-play the targets from the trainer are generated in lock step with the trainee. Both trainer and trainee grow in playing quality together.

In ordinary deep reinforcement learning the network is trained by solving a problem in one large step, using a set of examples that are not sorted from easy to hard. With examples that are not sorted on error value, the program has to achieve the optimization step from no knowledge to human-level play in one big, unsorted, leap, by optimizing many times over the samples. Overcoming such a large training step (from beginner to advanced) costs much training time.

In contrast, in AlphaGo Zero, the network is trained in many small steps, starting against an opponent that has just as little knowledge as we have ourselves, and will play moves that are just as easy as we do, which goes quickly. Subsequently, harder problems are generated and trained for, using the network that has already been pretrained with the easier examples.

Self-play naturally generates a curriculum with examples from easy to hard. As a consequence, training times go down and the ultimate playing strength goes up.

Training Speed

A curriculum strategy is faster because the learner spends less time with harder to predict examples. Weinshall et al. show in a theoretical analysis that curriculum learning is expected to significantly speed up learning, especially at the beginning of training [753]. Furthermore, they show that generalization is improved with curriculum learning, especially when the conditions for learning are hard: when the task is difficult, when the network is small, or when strong regularization is enforced. These theoretical result are supported by empirical evidence [62, 438, 202, 58].[4]

Weinshall et al. also note that curriculum learning is not often used in the real world, since it is hard to find situations where a teacher can rank the examples from easy to hard. In most supervised and reinforcement learning settings, there is no ordering from easy to hard available for the examples. This may have precluded the widespread adoption of curriculum learning.

---

[4] Also note the link with Hinton's unsupervised one-by-one pretraining of layers in a deep network, from simple concepts to complicated concepts [294]

Correlation Revisited

Having disussed curriculum learning, it is interesting to note the existence of a paradox concerning correlation. The problem is this: in the previous chapter we have seen that breaking correlations between examples improves state space coverage, preventing cycles and local minima, yet now curriculum learning show us that correlation between the difficulty of states achieves curriculum learning.

So: do we want correlation, or not? There must be enough diversity between states within each self-play iteration to allow good coverage, preventing myopic learning, to allow learning to progress in each iteration. Yet, for curriculum learning, examples should be ordered from easy to hard.

On state features subsequent states should be uncorrelated, but on a larger scale, on error values, they should be correlated.

In self-play, sorting on error values occurs implicitly by the learning scheme in which the examples are generated. Within the iterations, MCTS, replay buffer, and other methods are used to achieve a high level of exploration, as discussed previously.

Active Learning and Related Learning

Curriculum learning is a topic that has been studied outside deep learning as well. We will discuss three topics: active learning, adversarial attacks, and generative adversarial networks.

Active learning is a type of machine learning that is in between supervised and reinforcement learning. Active learning is relevant when labels are in principle available (as in supervised learning) but at a cost. Active learning performs a kind of iterative supervised learning, in which the agent can choose to query which labels to reveal during the learning process. Active learning is related to reinforcement learning and to curriculum learning, and is for example of interest for studies into recommender systems, where acquiring more information may come at a cost [616, 565, 159].

In Sect. 6.2.2 we saw that deep learning is susceptible to adversarial attacks, because of the one-pixel problem. In deep reinforcement learning this problem can also give rise to unwanted behavior [313]. Gleave et al. [246] study this problem further, showing the existence of adversarial policies in zero-sum simulated robotics.

Interestingly, recent work in generative adversarial networks (GANs) has suggested that the good performance of GANs may be due to curriculum learning. The generator and discriminator work in tandem, and in a well-tuned system generate a sequence of easy to hard training examples [620, 177]. Since the publication of the AlphaGo Zero results, and the interest in GANs, curriculum learning has attracted more attention. An overview of related work can be found in [755].

Human Learning is Curriculum Learning

Curriculum learning has been studied both in human learning and in deep learning. Most structured, supervised, human learning is guided by a curriculum [753]. When a human teacher presents examples, the order in which the examples are presented is rarely random. Tasks are typically divided by the teacher into smaller subtasks and ordered from easy to hard. This subtasking is called shaping [387] and studied in reinforcement learning, e.g., by Graves et al. [255].

Krueger and Dayan [387] note that in human and animal learning, curriculum learning is able to learn higher concepts that are beyond what can be found by trial and error. They use the term *shaping* for the creation of a curriculum of easy and hard targets.

In human learning children are taught easy concepts first. There is a reason that children start in first grade, and not in sixth. Using a neural network for language acquisition, Elman [194] argues for starting small, with a small network, and gradually increasing the difficulty of training examples and the network size. Multi-stage curriculum strategies improved generalization and show faster convergence.

Although curriculum learning has been studied in AI and in psychology it has not been popular in AI since in most training situations it is difficult to find well-sorted training curricula. However, it has been identified as a key challenge for machine learning throughout [457, 458, 742]. Due to the self-play results, curriculum learning is now attracting more interest in AI (see, e.g., [477, 755]).

7.2 AlphaGo

We have now taken an extensive look at self-play, the learning method that is used in AlphaGo Zero. We have looked at the architecture, we have looked at how stable learning was achieved, and we have looked at curriculum learning. Self-play builds on a long history of AI research, from Samuel's Checkers to Tesauro's TD-Gammon to AlphaGo Zero (Table 6.5).

Curiously, there was no straight line from TD-Gammon or the other programs to AlphaGo Zero's clean self-play design. First another program was created, AlphaGo, that used a more complex hybrid design with supervised learning, reinforcement learning with a database of self-play games, and multiple neural networks. This complex program beat the human champions. We will now describe the earlier AlphaGo approach in a starred section, for your comparison and historical insight and to see the continuity with previous research, although its design has now been superseded by the more elegant self-play design that achieves tabula rasa learning. Progress in science does not usually follow straight lines.

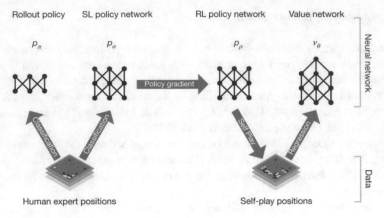

Fig. 7.6 AlphaGo networks [623]

7.2.1 *AlphaGo Architecture

In 2016 AlphaGo beat human world champions. What technology was used in AlphaGo to achieve such a strong level of play, ten years before most experts had expected this milestone to be reached?

It turns out that in AlphaGo there was no magic bullet, no single groundbreaking new technology that had been invented. In AlphaGo existing approaches were combined, both supervised and reinforcement learning, they were improved and refined, and a way was found for the different technologies to work together.

The AlphaGo design follows the search-eval architecture. For search, it employs a version of MCTS. For eval, three neural nets are used: a fast shape policy net for the MCTS playouts, a slow policy net for UCT exploration/exploitation selection, and a value net for the leaf values of the MCTS tree. In addition, the slow policy net is trained by supervised and by reinforcement learning, giving a total of four training methods for three networks. Figure 7.6 reproduces the familiar AlphaGo networks picture from [623].

After this high-level description, let us look in more detail into the AlphaGo methods.

First, we will discuss the supervised learning in AlphaGo. AlphaGo uses supervised learning to learn from grandmaster games. A database of 160,000 grandmaster games is used to train a slower selection policy network by supervised learning (28 million positions). The positions from grandmaster games consist of a board position and a best action (the move played by the grandmasters). This policy network is used in the MCTS selection operation. The supervised learning is used to pretrain the network to a certain (high) level of play, and then positions from self-play are used to improve it further.

Second, AlphaGo uses reinforcement learning for three networks: for two separate policy networks and for a value network. It trains the slow policy network against an "environment" that really is a database with games that were played against a copy of itself. This part of the training, against a database of self-play games, is often simply called self-play.

Third, a value network is trained based on a database of 30 million self-play positions. For the MCTS leaf values a mix is used of the value network and of the outcome of MCTS rollouts using the fast rollout policy network. The mixing of these values is governed by a new parameter λ. Note that in AlphaGo the random playouts of MCTS are replaced by playouts using the fast policy net.

Fourth, a game database is used to train a fast policy network by supervised learning. The fast policy network is trained with positions from separate games to prevent overfitting and loops due to correlation between subsequent game states.

To summarize, AlphaGo uses the four training methods to train three networks:

1. A "slow" selection policy net, first trained by supervised learning from grandmaster games, then further refined through self-play positions
2. A value net for position evaluation, trained by self-play positions
3. A "fast" rollout policy net trained by supervised learning from human games, used for MCTS playouts

7.2.2 AlphaGo Results

Let us now have a look in more detail at the performance that this complicated approach has achieved.

An early version of AlphaGo beat European champion Fan Hui in London in 2015 in a training match, while AlphaGo was still being developed. A year later, after the program had been developed further, it beat top-ranked Lee Sedol in Seoul in March 2016. In 2017, AlphaGo beat top-ranked Ke Jie in Wuzhen in May 2017.

Figure 7.7 (left panel) shows the Elo rating of AlphaGo compared with other programs[5] and compared with Fan Hui. AlphaGo is clearly superior. The graph indicates a playing strength of 5p dan. Quite some development and experimentation were needed for AlphaGo to reach the level of play that it did. Since publication of the article in 2016, AlphaGo has been further refined, and the performance has continued to improve. The version playing against Lee Sedol and Ke Jie was significantly stronger, at 9p dan.

We have seen that AlphaGo has three networks. Therefore, it is instructive to see how each network influences performance. Figure 7.7 (right panel) shows the impact of turning some of the three networks off. We see that each network has a significant contribution, and that the contribution of the networks is independent in the sense that they all complement and improve each other.

AlphaGo uses a significant amount of compute power, for training, but also during tournament play time. Therefore, it is interesting to see how more compute power influences playing strength. Figure 7.8 shows the impact of extra hardware

---

[5] GnuGo is a minimax-based program. Fuego, Pachi, and Zen are conventional MCTS programs without self-play or a neural net. Pale red is 4 handicap stones.

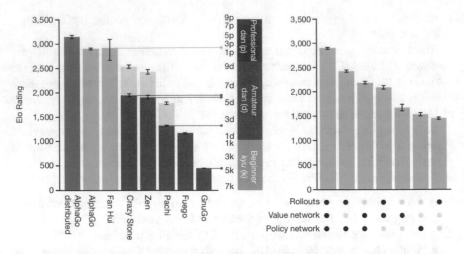

Fig. 7.7 AlphaGo Elo rating; Effect of individual networks [623]

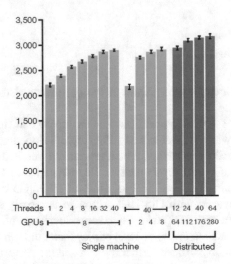

Fig. 7.8 Elo rating of Alphago distributed versions [623]

for the distributed version of AlphaGo. Clearly the use of more than one GPU is advantageous, as is the use of multi-threading. The use of a cluster of machines (dark blue, distributed) gives an increase in performance of around 200 Elo points. As preparation for the match against Ke Jie, AlphaGo used TPUs, specially developed tensor processing units from Google. TPUs are a kind of GPUs that are optimized for low precision, high throughput matrix operations (where GPUs are optimized for high-precision operations). Fig. 7.9 shows pictures of a CPU, a GPU, and a TPU.

Fig. 7.9 CPU, GPU, and TPU

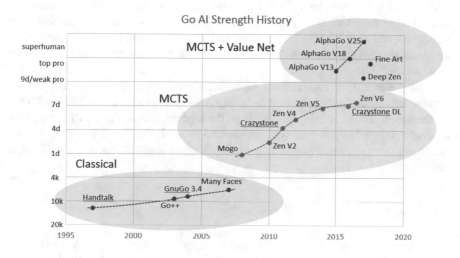

Fig. 7.10 Go playing strength over the years [12]

Playing Strength in Go

At this point it is interesting to compare programming paradigms of the different Go programs that have been written over the years (Fig. 7.10). The programs fall into three categories. First are the programs based on heuristic planning, the Chess-style programs. GNU Go is a well-known example of this group of programs. The heuristics in these programs are hand-coded. Their level of play was at medium amateur level. Then come the adaptive sampling MCTS-based programs, which reached strong amateur level. Examples of these programs are MoGo and Crazy Stone. Finally come the AlphaGo programs, of MCTS combined with neural nets. They reach super-human performance. The figure also shows the program Fine Art, by Tencent.

The figure clearly shows how the performance improved with the different paradigms.

7.2.3 Impact of AlphaGo

The AlphaGo results have caused quite an impact in AI and beyond. Let us first take a brief look at how science and society reacted to the AlphaGo breakthrough.

Popular Media

The Lee Sedol match of AlphaGo has had a large impact in the popular media. The idea of computers being "smarter" than highly intelligent human champions continued to attract attention, as much as it did in the days of Deep Blue–Kasparov. Artificial intelligence shot to prominence, and many AI researchers were interviewed on questions ranging from when we would see self-driving cars to the future of the human race.

Newspaper articles appeared on AlphaGo, a movie[6] was made, and many blogs were written by enthusiasts on how to build your own AlphaGo and AlphaZero. This, by the way, turns out to be quite doable on the algorithmic side (see Appendix A for a list of open-source self-play systems inspired by AlphaGo Zero), but acquiring the necessary computational power to train the function approximators is a significant challenge.

Impact on Go

It is interesting to see how human Go players respond to the matches, and to see the effect on the style of human play. Of course, there was sadness and melancholy when the human champions lost against the machines at this beautiful game, a hold-out of the supremacy of human intelligence. However, most reactions were positive, and not just for the achievement in artificial intelligence. Go players were enthusiastic about the innovations and new style of play that AlphaGo exhibited. See also the commentary by Fan Hui and Lee Sedol in Sect. 2.3.5. Players were eager to learn more about how they could improve their beloved game even more. Books have been written about the new Go theory that was created (see, for example, Zhou [778]). Furthermore, the publicity around the matches created much new interest in Go.

Impact on Science

The AlphaGo matches have also had quite an impact on society and science. The interest from society in artificial intelligence has increased significantly, with companies and governments investing in research labs. Also within science there has been much interest in multidisciplinary collaborations, to see how machine learning can

---

[6] https://www.alphagomovie.com

transfer to fields ranging from astronomy to the arts. Many collaborations between artificial intelligence and these fields are emerging.

Impact on AI

On the field of artificial intelligence itself the results have had a large impact as well. Machine learning has attracted many new talents, and especially reinforcement learning has benefited. Attendance at scientific conferences has increased manyfold, to the extent that some conferences started limiting attendance.

The use of the game of Go as a benchmark for intelligence has led to an increased interest in benchmarking and reproducibility [289, 329, 476, 323]. Popular suites are ALE [53], Gym [98], ELF [690], StarCraft [703, 374, 727], and Mario [353]. See also the list of frameworks in Appendix A. There is much interest in further challenges of self-play. The computational demands for learning by self-play are large. Wu reports on a list of improvements that speed up learning significantly [765].

Weak, Strong, and Ultrastrong AI

At this point it is appropriate to put the AlphaGo achievements in a more historical perspective. In 1988 Donald Michie defined three types of AI: weak, strong, and ultrastrong AI [446]. Michie's criteria were meant to discern various qualities of machine learning, beyond predictive performance. Michie's criteria stressed understanding, or comprehensibility, of learned knowledge. In weak AI the agent produces improved predictive performance as the amount of data increases. In strong AI the agent must also provide hypotheses, and explanations. Ultrastrong AI should be able to teach the hypothesis to a human.

Clearly, most of modern machine learning has only achieved weak AI according to Michie's criteria, AlphaGo included. For AI to be truly useful in society, it must achieve more. The current interest in explainable AI aims to achieve strong AI (see also Sect. 7.3.5).

7.2.4 AlphaGo Zero Results

After having discussed the AlphaGo results, let us now turn to the playing strength of its successor, AlphaGo Zero.

Playing Strength

In their paper Silver et al. [626] describe that learning progressed smoothly throughout the training. AlphaGo Zero outperformed the original AlphaGo after just 36 hours.

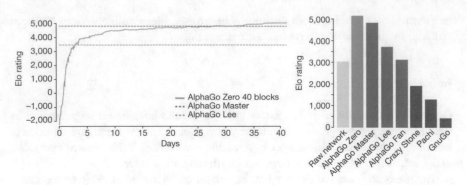

Fig. 7.11 Performance of AlphaGo Zero [626]

The training time for the version of AlphaGo that played Lee Sedol was several months. Furthermore AlphaGo Zero used a single machine with 4 tensor processing units, whereas AlphaGo Lee was distributed over many machines and used 48 TPUs. It is noted that the training did not suffer from the oscillations or catastrophic forgetting that have been noted in previous literature [219, 285]. Figure 7.11 shows the performance of AlphaGo Zero. Also shown is the performance of the raw network, without MCTS search. The importance of MCTS is large, around 2000 Elo points.

Tabula Rasa

AlphaGo Zero's reinforcement learning is truly learning from scratch. The paper notes that AlphaGo Zero discovered a remarkable level of Go knowledge during its self-play training process. This knowledge included not only fundamental elements of human Go knowledge, but also nonstandard strategies beyond the scope of traditional Go knowledge.

Joseki are standard corner openings that all Go players become familiar with as they learn to play the game. There are beginner's and advanced joseki. Over the course of its learning, AlphaGo Zero did indeed learn beginner to advanced joseki. It is interesting to study how it did so, as it reveals the progression of AlphaGo Zero's Go intelligence. Figure 7.12 shows how the program learned over the course of a few hours of self-play. Not to anthropomorphize too much, but you can see the little program getting smarter.

The top row shows five joseki that AlphaGo Zero discovered. The first joseki is one of the standard beginner's openings out of Go theory. As we move to the right, more difficult joseki are learned, with stones being played in looser configurations.

The bottom row shows five joseki favored at different stages of the self-play training. It starts with a preference for a weak corner move. After 10 more hours of training, a better 3-3 corner sequence is favored. More training reveals more, and better, variations.

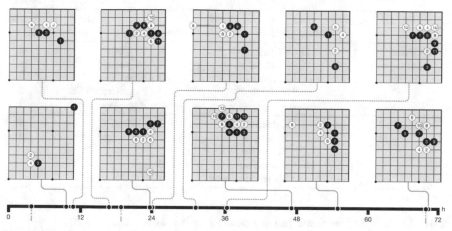

Fig. 7.12 AlphaGo Zero is learning joseki [626]

For a human Go player, it is remarkable to see this kind of progression in computer play, reminding them of the time when they themselves discovered these joseki. With such evidence of the computer's learning, it is hard not to anthropomorphize AlphaGo Zero (think of the computer as a human being).

7.3 *Self-Play Enhancements

We have looked more broadly at self-play, and have seen earlier programs that have tried self-play. AlphaGo Zero showed the large potential of this method. We will now look at enhancements to self-play, further developments, and directions for future research. First we will start with the third Alpha-★ program: AlphaZero.

7.3.1 General Play: AlphaZero

After defeating the best human Go players, and after having created the first tabula rasa self-learning Go computer, a third experiment was created concerning another long-standing challenge in AI: constructing a general game player. If AlphaGo Zero's architecture was able to learn Go from scratch, then perhaps it would be able to learn *any* game? A year after the AlphaGo Zero publication, another paper was published, showing how AlphaGo Zero's design could also learn to play Chess and Shogi [625, 624].

This publication showed that self-play was able to teach the same search-eval architecture (MCTS with 20 ResNet blocks) to learn Go, Chess, and Shogi, thus achieving a form of *general* tabula rasa learning, albeit limited to three games. The

Go		Chess		Shogi	
Feature	Planes	Feature	Planes	Feature	Planes
P1 stone	1	P1 piece	6	P1 piece	14
P2 stone	1	P2 piece	6	P2 piece	14
		Repetitions	2	Repetitions	3
				P1 prisoner count	7
				P2 prisoner count	7
Colour	1	Colour	1	Colour	1
		Total move count	1	Total move count	1
		P1 castling	2		
		P2 castling	2		
		No-progress count	1		
Total	17	Total	119	Total	362

Table 7.2 Different input planes (first set repeated 8 times to capture history) [625]

program, named AlphaZero, beat the strongest conventional players in Go, Chess, and Shogi (respectively AlphaGo Zero, the program Stockfish, and the program Elmo).

Note that there are differences. The hand-crafted input and output layers of the networks are different for each game. Table 7.2 shows these differences. The more complicated move patterns of Chess and Shogi cause the input planes to be significantly more elaborate than for Go (see the paper for details). Furthermore, the weights in the trained networks are also different. Strict transfer learning was not achieved: a trained Shogi net is not able to play Go well.

AlphaZero's achievement of a general game learning architecture is remarkable for more than one reason. First, it is remarkable that self-play is so powerful that it can learn from scratch *and* become so strong that it beats the current world champions. Second, it is remarkable that different games can be learned by the same network architecture. Perhaps, some kind of element of general learning must be present in the structure of the ResNets of AlphaZero, although the networks that are learned differ between games: a network trained for Chess cannot play Go well. Third, for Chess and Shogi all previous strong programs had been based on the heuristic planning approach of alpha-beta with domain-specific heuristics, but now they are beaten by a general learning approach using self-play function approximation (see also [544]).

Playing Strength

The Elo rating of AlphaZero in Chess, Shogi, and Go is shown in Fig. 7.13. Also shown is the Elo rating of the programs Stockfish, Elmo, AlphaGo Zero [626], and AlphaGo Lee [623].

We can see how AlphaZero is stronger than the other programs, all through learning by self-play. In Chess, a field that has benefited from work by a large community of

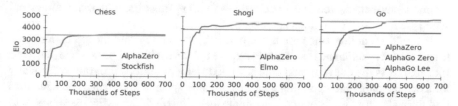

Fig. 7.13 Elo rating of AlphaZero in Chess, Shogi, and Go [625]

researchers for as long as computers existed, the difference is the smallest. For Shogi the difference in playing strength is larger.

Interestingly, AlphaZero slightly outperforms AlphaGo Zero. There are small differences between AlphaZero and AlphaGo Zero. AlphaZero updates the neural network continually, whereas in AlphaGo Zero the new net is only accepted if it wins 55% of the time against the old network. AlphaZero does not exploit Go symmetries. The paper does not provide other reasons for the differences.

Go, Chess, and Shogi

That AlphaZero can play three different games with one architecture is surprising. The three games, though all board games, are quite different. Go is a static game of strategy. Stones, once placed, do not move, and are rarely captured. Each stone played is therefore of strategic importance. In Chess the pieces move, it is a dynamic game where tactics are important, and the possibility of sudden death is an important element of play: in Chess it is possible to win in the middle of the game by capturing the king. No such concept exists in Go. Indeed, one element of human Chess play is to move the king to a safe position to reduce the level of stress in the game. Shogi, sometimes called Japanese Chess, is even more dynamic. Pieces, once captured, can be returned to the game, changing loyalty, creating even more complex game dynamics.[7]

As all top Chess programs, Stockfish follows the classic search-eval design of alpha-beta and a heuristic evaluation function, that we have seen in Sunfish (Sect. 4.6.1) and Deep Blue (Sect. 2.3.3). Among the enhancements of Stockfish are forward pruning, iterative deepening, transposition tables, quiescence, piece-square tables, null window, null move, history heuristics, search extensions, search reductions, an opening book, and an end-game database. Chapter 4 provides explanations on most of these enhancements. In Stockfish, all these enhancements have been refined, tested, and tuned, for many years [559].

The state space complexity of Shogi is substantially larger than Chess: 10^{71} versus 10^{47}. The strongest Shogi programs have recently started defeating human champions [704]. Elmo, one of these programs, is designed like a Chess program,

---

[7] Pieces are of the same color, but are wedge-shaped, and change orientation when switching sides.

around alpha-beta search and a heuristic evaluation function, with many tuned and tested game-dependent enhancements.

It would seem that since the move patterns, the tactics, and the strategies to be learned are very different, that it would require a different kind of program to play well. Indeed, this is the conventional approach: a developer crafts a program specifically for a certain game, incorporating all kinds of game-specific knowledge and heuristics into the code. For Go, the game is so subtle and difficult that no scientist was able to find successful heuristics, and knowledge had to be learned by machine learning from game databases (initially, in AlphaGo) or through self-play (eventually, in AlphaGo Zero).

The conventional game-specific approach has worked well for Chess, Shogi, and other games so far. AlphaZero is the first to show that it is possible to be general *and* strong.[8] Indeed, AlphaZero has shown that the differences in move patterns are not such that a different kind of program is needed to learn to play well.

One General Architecture

Although it would seem that the different kinds of games require a different program design, AlphaZero's results have proven this conventional wisdom wrong, at least for the learning of three board games. All that needed to be changed were the input and output layers of the function approximator. The self-play training algorithms, network architecture, search algorithm, most training hyperparameters,[9] and compute hardware are all the same. The self-play program was then able to learn to play the game beyond world class level. Perhaps the game dynamics of Go, Chess, and Shogi are less different than they seemed, but clearly the structure of self-play with ResNets is general enough to allow it to learn very different nonlinear value/policy functions.

It is this last aspect that makes the results so inspiring from an AI point of view, since it reminds us of how humans learn to play.

7.3.2 Training as Generalization

We will now look at other generalization methods, in particular, transfer learning.

The goal of machine learning is to build an approximation function based on examples. Many methods exist to train the approximator. Generalization is the process minimizing an error function over input examples. In some sense, all training is generalization.

---

[8] In Sect. 8.2.5 another approach is introduced, general game playing, or GGP. The general programs created by GGP generally trade off generality for playing strength.

[9] The learning rate decay scheme was slightly different for Go than for Chess and Shogi.

Sample Efficiency

The canonical deep learning case is training from zero knowledge, when the network parameters are initialized to random numbers. Training methods have been developed for efficient training yielding the lowest error function in as few training steps as possible. Since in reinforcement learning each training example is a costly sample from the environment, achieving high sample efficiency is important.

Model-based methods, such as planning, are more sample efficient than model-free methods. All they need to do to find a value of a state is to follow the model and lookup the value of the actions. Compared to planning, deep learning is not very sample efficient. Model-free methods have no model to follow and need to sample many states before the value approximates the true value.

Deep reinforcement learning is a model-free method that takes many samples to learn the features. Furthermore, the learning rate is set low for good convergence and generalization. In contrast to planning, however, deep learning is able to learn an evaluation function, which is something that planning cannot do. And although planning is sample efficient, it is inadequate for traversing exponentially large state spaces. For that, it needs a good evaluation function. An evaluation that is better than a heuristic, and better than averaged sampling. Function approximation can learn such a good function, and self-play can use planning to generate samples of increasing quality to continuously improve the learning evaluation function.

Self-play is thus not very sample efficient, because of the model-free evaluation function approximation, and because the model-based planning is stretched to perform many state space traversals to improve the quality of the learning targets. Without curriculum learning it would be worse.

Pretraining

Pre-training the network with another related task may increase sample efficiency. The network weights are no longer randomly initialized, but are such that the error is lower and training can progress with fewer samples.

Curriculum learning performs a sequence of pretraining steps. In each curriculum iteration the network is pretrained by the former iteration, creating an easier learning task with a low error.

Lifelong Machine Learning

It has been observed that most machine learning tasks currently start from zeroknowledge, and subsequently take a long time to learn. In contrast, in human learning experiments, subjects do not start from zero knowledge, and typically learn a new task quickly with few samples. Humans already have knowledge of related tasks. Lifelong machine learning studies methods to retain learned knowledge tasks that are trained from different domains over the lifetime of the system [687]. The goal is to selectively transfer that knowledge when learning a new task [621].

Transfer Learning

Transfer learning aims at improving the process of learning new tasks using the experience gained by solving similar predecessor problems [532, 688]. As humans, we make use of our past experience by not only repeating the same task in the future but also for learning completely new tasks. That is, if the new problem that we try to solve is similar to a few of our past experiences, it becomes easier for us. Transfer learning aims to transfer past experience of one or more source tasks and use it to boost learning in a related target task.

When we want to transfer knowledge, it can be transferred by initializing part of the network by other weights, for example, by transfering the entire network, and then retraining, or transferring some of the lower layers of a network.

Multi-task learning

Transfer learning is related to multi-task learning, where one network is optimized for multiple tasks that are related. The major task can be learned better through using the experience gained by other tasks. This approach is effective when the tasks have some commonality. In multi-task learning, related learning tasks are learned at the same time, whereas in transfer learning they are learned in sequence by different networks. Multi-task learning improves regularization by requiring the algorithm to perform well on a related learning task instead of penalizing all overfitting uniformly [204, 19]. The two-headed AlphaGo Zero network optimizes for value and for policy at the same time in the same network [500, 120]. Multi-task learning has also been applied to Atari games [360, 359].

Meta-learning

There are many forms of transfer learning [120, 500, 670]. Going beyond transfer of network parameter values, knowledge transfer can also include hyperparameter values, network architecture, or learning algorithms. Transfer learning is a form of meta-learning where the extent of domain adaptation is typically restricted to weight parameters, where in meta-learning other parts of the algorithm are also involved [95].

Meta-learning is sometimes described as "learning to learn" or selecting the best learning algorithm for a task. It is related to algorithm selection [551, 362] and hyperparameter optimization, and also to transfer learning. Although meta-learning work goes back to the 1980s [597, 175, 59, 95] there has been recent interest in the field [305, 717, 321], also because of work on zero-shot learning [397, 258, 767]. In few-shot or zero-shot learning new concepts are recognized after seeing only a few problem instances [767, 581, 549].

Normally a classifier is expected to correctly classify at test time new samples from classes that have been seen during training. A zero-shot classifier has seen no samples from the classes at training time. To be able to correctly classify the samples the classifier is given some information about the classes. This can be a natural text or structured description [305, 558]. RNN and LSTM are often used [546]. The information can also be a similarity measure between the classes.

This brings us to the question of similarity metrics between problems. High-dimensional discrete classes can be embedded in a lower-dimensional continuous vector. The zero-shot classifier can then predict a sample's position in that space, and the nearest embedded class is used as the predicted class [228]. In addition to being a similarity measure, low-dimensional representations also allow visualization, providing insight into the often high-dimensional state spaces of machine learning problems [520, 468, 433].

Model-agnostic meta-learning (MAML) is a recent meta-learning approach for few-shot learning [214]. MAML uses optimization-based meta-learning, and learns initial network representations that can then be fine-tuned using a few class examples. This work has spawned more interest in meta-learning [16, 50, 215, 776, 726, 543]. New benchmark suites for research on multi-task and meta learning have been introduced, Meta World [773] and Meta-dataset [696].

In meta-reinforcement learning Duan et al. [188] introduce RL^2, an approach in which the reinforcement learning algorithm itself is a target of a training process, and Wang et al. [741] explore the link between meta-learning and reinforcement learning, by having one reinforcement learning algorithm implement a second reinforcement learning algorithm.

Let us now look at hyperparameter optimization methods.

7.3.3 Hyperparameter Optimization

Deep learning and self-play systems typically have many hyperparameters, to control various aspects of the learning process. The AlphaGo Zero paper lists those presented in Table 7.3.

The effects of some of these hyperparameters may interfere with each other.Finding the optimal setting for all parameters is a daunting task, best left to machine optimization.[10] Many optimization algorithms have a large set of hyperparameters, and hyperparameter optimization is an active field of research. Well-known methods are exhaustive search [302], random search [65, 745], Bayesian optimization [66,

---

[10] Just as finding the best coefficients for an evaluation function of hand-crafted heuristics is best left to machine learning, and, for that matter, crafting the evaluation features themselves is also best left to machine learning, and crafting a curriculum of training positions is best left to self-play. Some would even say that crafting machine learning algorithms is best left to machine learning [492], but that is a topic for another book [274].

Hyperparameter	Value
self play games per iteration	25000
MCTS simulations	1600
exploration temperature	1 for first 30 moves, 0 afterwards
Dirichlet noise	$\eta = 0.03, \epsilon = 0.25$
resignation threshold	5%
regularization parameter	$c = 10^{0.4}$
mini batch size	2048, 32 per worker
self play positions	500,000
learning rate	annealed with momentum 0.9
CE loss/MSE weighting	equal in the loss function
optimization checkpoint	1000
self play evaluator	400
win margin for acceptance	55%
network architecture	19 residual blocks

Table 7.3 AlphaGo hyperparameters [626]

324, 685, 638], and evolutionary strategies [27, 112, 504, 715]. Some software packages for hyperparameter optimization are SMAC[11] [324], auto-sklearn[12] [210], Auto-WEKA[13] [382], scikit-learn[14] [513], irace[15] [427], and nevergrad[16] [545].

A parameter sweep of AlphaZeroGeneral (Sect. A) is Wang et al. [738, 739]. AlphaGo Zero optimized its hyperparameters with Bayesian optimization, AlphaZero used the same set of hyperparameters.

Network Architecture

The architecture of the network can also be regarded as a hyperparameter to be optimized. Among the decisions to make are the number and types of the layers, and the number and types of the neurons, whether to have ResNet cells, and how they are connected. Getting the architecture right for your problem can be a time-consuming problem, perhaps also best left to machine learning.

Neural Architecture Search is an active field of research, using methods that are related to hyperparameter optimization. Two surveys are [771] and [197]. Random search, Bayesian optimization [772], evolutionary algorithms [366, 714, 333, 448, 735, 26], and reinforcement learning [781, 521, 30] are popular methods.

---

[11] https://github.com/automl/SMAC3

[12] https://automl.github.io/auto-sklearn/stable/

[13] http://www.cs.ubc.ca/labs/beta/Projects/autoweka/

[14] https://scikit-learn.org/stable/

[15] http://iridia.ulb.ac.be/irace/

[16] https://code.fb.com/ai-research/nevergrad/

Network Optimization

An important element of all neural network function approximators is the optimization algorithm. Stochastic gradient descent has been the optimization algorithm of choice, although alternatives exist. Recently works report on evolution strategies as network optimizers, for example when derivates of the error function are not available [141, 575, 758]. An advantage of evolution strategies is that they are well suited for parallelization, providing possible speedups for the training phases of self-play.

Another alternative to SGD network optimization are distributional methods, where not just the expected value is optimized, but also the variance of the error [52, 463, 464] (Sect. 6.4.4).

7.3.4 Parallelism

A major problem of self-play is the large computational requirement, which translates to long training times. Self-play has three obvious areas where parallelism can be used for speedup. First of all, network training can be sped up. Here GPUs and TPUs are already used, and TensorFlow and other packages typically include support for parallel training.

Another option is to parallelize MCTS. We have already seen a few parallel MCTS approaches, such as tree parallelism and root parallelism, in Sect. 5.3.5. Even though their use is not trivial, implementation in current self-play can speed up training.

Furthermore, the tournament games of the self-play setup are all independent, and can be parallelized within the same self-play iteration. This should give an important speedup of self-play, filling the example buffer in parallel. Advances in this area will enable more experimentation and more insights into self-play processes.

7.3.5 Further Research

Self-play has been an active area of research in two-agent zero-sum games for many years. The AlphaZero results have reinforced the power of the paradigm, showing that TD-Gammon's success was not an exception. The successes have created much research interest in fundamental questions and applications of self-play.

However, there remain open questions to be answered. Among them are:

* The learning time for AlphaGo Zero is long; many games are generated to achieve good coverage, (de-)correlation, and convergence. How can self-play be made faster?
* Self-play works for two-agent board games. For which other domains can self-play work? Does self-play also work for other Markov decision problems, or for non-Markovian problems?

- Did AlphaGo/DQN self-play kill the deadly triad? How are overfitting and specialization related in reinforcement learning?
- Why do ResNets perform so well in self-play? Are there other architectures that work even better?
- Does self-play work well in imperfect-information games such as Bridge, Poker, and StarCraft?
- Are self-play results easy to transfer? How can concepts that are learned in one game be transferred to other games? (Note that in AlphaZero each game starts training from scratch.)
- Evolutionary strategies and related population-based methods have been successful in some studies. Will they play a role in (general) self-play?

The successes have prompted researchers to look at other domains, beyond two-agent zero-sum, to see if and how these questions can be answered and similar progress can be made. We will list some future research directions, noting relevant papers. We start with different kinds of problems, such as single-agent games, multi-agent problems, and then we continue with different ideas.

Single-Agent Games

Reinforcement learning is a natural training paradigm for two-agent games. Reinforcement learning is also used in multi-agent and imperfect-information games, such as StarCraft and Poker [285].

However, many optimization problems in science are single-agent optimization problems, such as navigation, the Traveling Salesperson Problem, the 15 puzzle, and the Satisfiablity Problem [572]. MCTS and neural networks have been used to solve single-agent combinatorial problems [466, 569, 728, 635]. Single-agent optimization problems, where the shortest solution must be found, can have especially sparse state spaces in which few reward signals are present. Learning in such sparse spaces is hard. A solution can be to introduce intermediate goals.

The advantage of self-play is that it creates a curriculum learning situation, which speeds up learning. Approximate reinforcement learning has been applied to TSP [379, 56, 231]. Xu and Lieberherr [768] also used self-play in combinatorial optimization. It can be expected that more research into single-agent self-play approximators will appear, attempting to benefit from the curriculum learning effect that is inherent in self-play approximators [438].

Multi-agent and Population-Based Methods

Two-agent games are typically competitive (zero-sum) games. Multi-agent games are often (partly) cooperative. They have been the subject of study for some time [425, 668, 146, 118, 501, 285, 431, 128].

Multi-agent games, real-time strategy games, and multiplayer online battle arenas model more aspects of real life. They are a logical next step beyond two-person zero-sum perfect-information games. Real-time strategy games also feature movement aspects that are closer to robotics than board games do.

Applying the recent progress in self-play with multi-agent cooperative games will be quite interesting, as we will see in the next chapter. Combinations of multi-agent and population-based approaches have shown great progress in StarCraft II and Defense of the Ancients 2 (DOTA). See Sect. 8.2.1 for more.

Sparse Rewards

Many real-world reinforcement learning problems are sparse problems: the reward information in state spaces is sparse, and credit assignment can be delayed for a long time. Furthermore, the action space may be large as well. An example of a game with sparse rewards is Montezuma's Revenge, an Atari game in which many actions can be taken without encountering a reward state or a change in value. This game requires more advanced strategic reasoning, presenting a challenging problem for many reinforcement learning methods (Sect. 6.3.2) [499, 538, 3]. The Go explore algorithm is specifically designed for exploration of sparse or deceptive reward environment. It uses a combination of remembering previously visited states, look-ahead, and exploring from promising states. It is reported to perform well in Montezuma's Revenge and in Pitfall [192].

Continuous Action Spaces

Many applications have large, continuous action spaces, possibly combined with imperfect information (see Poker and StarCraft in Sect. 8.2.3). We often encounter this in real life [418, 466, 184, 580]. Large discrete or continuous action spaces can be segmented or discretized [191]. Examples are prevalent in robotics, where an arm movement can be over a continuous angle; a good review of this field is [371].

Hierarchical Reinforcement Learning

One of the main challenges in reinforcement learning is scaling up classic methods to problems with large action or state spaces. A problem of model-free reinforcement learning is low sample efficiency; sample generation is slow, or samples are not used efficiently (see also Sect. 3.3.6).

After having seen how different parameters of the training process can be optimized, we will look at hierarchical reinforcement learning, a more principled idea to scale reinforcement learning to larger problem classes, by decomposing large problems into smaller ones.

Most reinforcement learning problems are specified at a low level of detail. The steps that we can make are small (move a single piece, perform a single movement

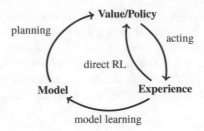

Fig. 7.14 Model-free and model-based methods [659]

of a robot arm). The advantage is that this allows for precision and optimality. The disadvantage is the large size of the state space.

In contrast, consider the following problem: In the real world, when we plan a trip from A to B, we use abstraction to reduce the state space, to be able to reason at a higher level. We do not reason at the level of footsteps we need to take, but we first decide on the mode of transportation. Hierarchical reinforcement learning tries to mimic this idea: conventional reinforcement learning works at the level of a single state; *hierarchical* reinforcement learning performs abstraction, solving subproblems in sequence. Temporal abstraction is described in a paper by Sutton et al. [661]. Despite the appealing intuition, work remains to be done, such as learning hierarchies automatically, and finding good benchmarks to show clear progress.

Flet-Berliac [218] provides a recent overview of hierarchical reinforcement learning, noting that planning research into hierarchical methods showed that exponential improvements in computation cost can be achieved with methods such as hierarchical task networks [155], macro actions [212], and state abstraction methods [368]. The promise of hierarchical reinforcement learning is summarized as: (1) to achieve long-term credit assignment through faster learning and better generalization, (2) to allow structured exploration by exploring with sub-policies rather than primitive actions, and (3) to perform transfer learning because different levels of hierarchy can encompass different knowledge.

Rafati and Noelle [541] learn subgoals in Montezuma's Revenge. Schaul et al.'s [595] universal value function approach suggests the use of function approximation for hierarchical reinforcement learning. Pang et al. [502] describe experiments with macro actions in StarCraft.

Model-Free and Model-Based Reinforcement Learning

Section 3.3.4 introduced model-free and model-based reinforcement learning, the inner and the outer loop of Fig. 7.14 [659]. Model-free reinforcement learning is quite successful. Most work in reinforcement learning is model-free (or *flat* reinforcement learning) without a transition model, tree, self-play, or planning (see, e.g., [14]). However, model-free reinforcement learning has low sample efficiency.

Long-range credit assignment and hierarchical structures are especially difficult to fold into flat (model-free) function approximators; some form of model, abstraction, and strategic reasoning is likely to be necessary. The option to use exact planning methods will also depend on the dimensionality of the problem. For high-dimensional problems approximation is a necessity; for low-dimensional problems exact methods will yield better answers. Can these be combined into a single architecture?

Network architectures can be created that combine planning and learning. RNN and LSTM networks are well suited for modeling sequential problems. There are studies on how look-ahead can be performed by neural networks, obviating the need for the often slow MCTS planning part [265, 264]. Schrittwieser et al. [607] report on MuZero, a system that combines model-based planning and model-free learning. MuZero learns a latent model that is used during planning on-line, for board games as well as Atari games. Kaiser et al. [350] learn a model for Atari games called SimPLe. Hafner et al. [271] use planning in latent space to learn dynamics in a system called PlaNet. This is an exciting research direction where more can be expected [743, 524].

Explainable AI

An important emerging research area in machine learning is explainable AI, or XAI. Explainable AI is closely related to the topics of planning and learning that we discuss in this book. When a human expert gives a recommendation, the expert can be questioned, and can explain the reasoning behind the advice. This is a very desirable property of an agent. Most clients receiving advice, be it financial, medical, or otherwise, prefer to receive a well-reasoned explanation with their advice, to see if they feel that they can trust the advice.

Most decision support systems that are based on symbolic AI can be made to provide such reasoning. Decision trees [540], graphical models [340, 404], and search trees are eminently suited for following the decision points of advice.

Connectionist approaches such as deep learning are more opaque. However, the accuracy of deep learning approaches has assured their popularity. The area of explainable AI aims to combine the ease of reasoning of symbolic AI with the accuracy of connectionist approaches [266, 182, 107]. Hybrid approaches combining aspects of planning and learning are among the techniques that hold promise. Soft decision trees [229, 292] and adaptive neural trees [669] are ways to distill knowledge from neural nets (that generalize well) into decision trees (that are highly interpretable). These works build in part on research on model compression [136, 111].

Another area of interest is the intersection of knowledge representation and reinforcement learning, also driven by the desire for decision support where the reasoning behind a recommendation is also provided. This field is related to learning Bayesian networks and belief networks [282, 480, 612, 165, 51, 678, 96, 21].

7.4 Practice

We have now come to the end of a chapter that covered many advanced topics, and provided pointers to even more research. Let us turn to practice now, to implementations.

First are questions to check your understanding of this chapter. Each question is a closed question where a simple, one sentence answer is possible.

Questions

1. What are the differences between AlphaGo, AlphaGo Zero, and AlphaZero?
2. What is the dan-rating of Fan Hui, Lee Sedol, and Ke Jie?
3. Which networks does AlphaGo have, and which training methods?
4. Which networks does AlphaGo Zero have, and which training methods?
5. What is a double-headed network?
6. What is the error function that is trained in a double-headed value/policy net?
7. What is a TPU, and how is it different from a GPU?
8. What is the Elo rating of AlphaGo in 2016 (approximately: around 2000, around 2500, or around 3000)?
9. Which three elements make up the self-play loop? (You may draw a picture.)
10. How is self-play recursive?
11. What is the network architecture of AlphaGo?
12. What is the network architecture of AlphaGo Zero?
13. What is tabula rasa learning?
14. How can tabula rasa learning be faster than reinforcement learning on top of supervised learning of grandmaster games?
15. What is the main result of the AlphaZero paper?
16. Name a top traditional Chess program.
17. Name a top traditional Shogi program.
18. Was the style of play of AlphaGo described by the Go community as boring or as exciting?
19. What decorrelation efforts does AlphaGo use?
20. What decorrelation efforts does AlphaGo Zero use?
21. What decorrelation efforts does AlphaZero use?
22. Explain similarities between planning, learning, system 1, and system 2.
23. What is curriculum learning?
24. What is transfer learning?
25. What is multi-task learning? Does AlphaGo have multi-task learning? Does AlphaGo Zero have multi-task learning?
26. What is meta-learning?
27. Describe three kinds of recursion in AlphaGo Zero-like self-play?
28. What is hyperparameter optimization, and how does it apply to reinforcement learning?
29. What is neural architecture search, and how does it apply to reinforcement learning?

30. What is hierarchical reinforcement learning? Name three approaches.
31. Why are games with sparse rewards difficult for reinforcement learning?
32. Why are domains with continuous action spaces difficult for reinforcement learning?
33. What is explainable AI?

7.4.1 Exercises

The AlphaZero General (A0G) code base is well suited for experimentation with self-play. We use it in the exercises of this chapter. A0G can be found at A0G.[17] Note that you also have to install TensorFlow and Keras. They are at tensorflow.org.

1. Install and run A0G Othello 6x6. Play against the computer to see if everything works. Look at the source code, especially at `Coach.py`. Can you see a relation with the code in Listing 7.1? What is an episode?
2. Observe the learning processes of the different games Tic Tac Toe, Connect4, and Gobang. See how self-learning progresses.
3. Vary learning rate, vary MCTS Nsims, vary iterations. How is performance impacted? How is learning time impacted?
4. A stable self-play process in A0G depends in part on the amount of exploration in MCTS. Vary the Cpuct constant, and observe if training is impacted adversely.
5. Try different net architectures. How is performance impacted?
6. Take a traditional alpha-beta Othello program, for example Othello.[18] Scc if A0G can learn a strong enough player to beat it.
7. Choose a simple game of your own preference, and implement it in A0G. Does it learn quickly?
8. *Implement Chess input and output layers in A0G, learn it tabula rasa, and play against Sunfish. You may want to have a look at LeelaZero Chess or ELF OpenGo for inspiration.
9. Play with tensorboard to look inside the brain/training process and try to understand the training process.
10. Implement hyperparameter tuning of A0G parameters.
11. *Write a hyperparameter optimizer for A0G, trying different net architectures. This is challenging and quite computationally intensive. How can you reduce the computational demands?
12. Can single-agent optimization problems benefit from self-play? Implement the 15 Puzzle in A0G, and Travelling Salesperson. See also [403, 768].
13. See if transfer learning of 4x4 Othello, to 6x6 to 8x8 works, and works faster. Are you seeing a curriculum learning effect?

---

[17] https://github.com/suragnair/alpha-zero-general
[18] http://dhconnelly.com/paip-python/docs/paip/othello.html

Summary

The challenge of this chapter was to combine planning and learning, to create a self-playing self-learning system. We described the performance of AlphaGo, AlphaGo Zero, and AlphaZero in depth. There was great interest in Go and AI from science and society.

Issues of coverage, correlation, and convergence (the deadly triad) were mostly overcome by the AlphaGo team through science and engineering, for which they received many accolades.

The main conceptual innovation of this chapter is self-play, a combination of planning and a training loop, a combination of MCTS and deep reinforcement learning. Self-play (Fig. 7.3) takes evaluation (system 1) and planning (system 2) and adds a third item, a learning loop, creating a self-learning search-eval system.

The self-play loop uses MCTS to generate high-quality examples, which are used to train the neural net. This new neural net is then used in a further self-play iteration to refine the network further (and again, and again, and again). Alpha(Go) Zero thus learns starting at zero knowledge, tabula rasa. And, just as impressively, the same self-play architecture can learn tabula rasa Chess and Shogi as well, defeating decades of heuristic refinement.

Self-play makes use of many reinforcement learning techniques. In order to ensure stable, high performance learning, exploration is important. MCTS is used for high-quality sampling. Exploration parameters in MCTS are set high, and convergent training is achieved by a low training rate. Because of these parameter settings many games have to be played. The computational demands of self-play are large.

MCTS has been changed significantly in the self-play setting. Gone are the random play outs that gave MCTS the name Monte Carlo, and much of the performance is due to a high-quality policy and value approximation residual network. (The name Deep Q Tree Search might be more appropriate.)

Reproducibility in science is of great importance to progress [289]. The impact of benchmarks and open-source algorithms in this respect is important. The reimplementations of the self-play results in A0G, ELF OpenGo, PhoenixGo, and Leela will stimulate experimentation and are of importance for progress towards general learning systems.

In this chapter we discussed enhancements of self-play, to understand why it works, and how its performance can be enhanced further. Self-play learns faster than a database approach. Self-play creates a natural curriculum learning situation, where the examples are ordered from easy to hard. We discussed the links between curriculum learning and transfer learning. The self-play success stimulates research interest in curriculum and transfer learning.

We also discussed further enhancements to self-play. Optimization of the network architecture and the training hyperparameters are active fields of research. Another field in which planning and learning come together is explainable AI.

Historical and Bibliographical Notes

Self-learning systems are exciting. Self-learning is a holy grail of artificial intelligence: the emergence of intelligent behavior out of basic interactions [411]. Machines that teach themselves how to play have intrigued researchers since the start of game playing research.

The work on AlphaGo is a landmark achievement in AI. Every AI researcher is encouraged to study it well. The primary sources of information for AlphaGo are the three AlphaGo papers by Silver et al. [623, 626, 625]. The papers contain a lot of information, and can be a bit overwhelming at times, especially the detailed methods sections. Many blogs and popular press articles have been written about AlphaGo that might be more accessible.

Do not forget to watch the AlphaGo movie. Although it does not go too deep into the details, it is a fascinating account of the match, and its significance in AI. It is at AlphaGo Movie.[19] There are also explanations on YouTube, for example at AlphaZero Explanation.[20]

A book devoted to building your own state-of-the-art self learning Go bot is *Deep Learning and the Game of Go* by Pumperla and Ferguson [537].

AlphaGo was not created in a vacuum. There is a large body of research of which we will now discuss some of the more notable papers. Pre-MCTS, there are works on shape and move prediction [644, 67]. In the contexts of MCTS, many researchers worked on combining MCTS with learned patterns, especially to improve the random roll outs of MCTS. Supervised learning on grandmaster games was used to improve playouts and also to improve UCT selection. Gelly and Silver et al. published notable works in this area [239, 627, 237], and others [63].

Patterns are also important in Othello. Around 1995 very good results were achieved by Logistello [113]. Logistello used logistic regression on patterns. The author also successfully introduced probabilistic depth reduction methods [115]. Graf et al. [253] describe experiments with adaptive playouts in MCTS with deep learning. Convolutional neural nets were also used in Go by Clark and Storkey [144, 145], who had used a CNN for supervised learning from a database of human professional games, showing that it outperformed GNU Go and scored wins against Fuego. In Chess, the program DeepChess by David et al. [160] performed end-to-end deep learning in Chess, achieving results on par with two alpha-beta-based programs. In Checkers, Blondie24 [133, 221] used a network to evolve board features, also achieving good results.

Tesauro's success inspired many others to try temporal difference learning. Wiering et al. and Van der Ree [757, 707] report on self-play and TD learning in Othello and Backgammon. The program Knightcap [42, 43] and Beal et al. [48] also use temporal difference learning on evaluation function features. Veness et al. [719] use self-play to learn evaluation function weights. They name their approach *search bootstrapping* and, referencing Samuel's Checkers program, describe it as follows: "The idea of

---

[19] https://www.alphagomovie.com

[20] https://www.youtube.com/watch?v=MgowR4pq3e8

search bootstrapping is to adjust the parameters of a heuristic evaluation function towards the value of a deep search." This sentence captures the idea of self-play, as used in AlphaZero, quite well. Arenz [18] applied MCTS to Chess.

Heinz also reported on self-play experiments in Chess [287]. In other games, Guo et al. [267] report on the use of MCTS to play Atari games; their combination of MCTS and DQN outperforms DQN on Atari.

In Poker impressive results have been published [92, 470] with combinations of planning and learning algorithms, most notably counterfactual regret minimization and self-play.

Since the AlphaGo results many other applications of machine learning have been shown to be successful. Complex combinatorics is of interest to theoretical physics [569, 503], chemistry, and pharmacology, specifically for retrosynthetic molecular design [615] and drug design [716]. Image recognition is of interest to experimental physics [32], biology [486], and medicine [166]. Decision support is of interest to medical decision making [307]. Reasoning and image analysis are of interest to smart industry [244, 335], linguistics, and humanities [646], and strategic reasoning is of interest to law, international relations, and policy analysis [25, 422, 712, 122]. Finally, the applications of robotics and reinforcement learning are of great interest to the cognitive and social sciences [337, 100]. Of particular interest are cheminformatics including drug design [615], theoretical physics, cognitive robotics, and law and negotiation.

For more information on hyperparameter optimization, see [66, 324]. A reference work on evolutionary strategies is [27]. To learn more about curriculum learning, see [755, 62, 438]. For more information on transfer learning, see [532, 688].

Ever since his paper on reinforcement learning for aerobatic helicopter flight [3]— there are videos on the web—Pieter Abbeel's work in robotics and in reinforcement learning has been influential.

The study of model-based reinforcement learning is an active area of research. Recent experiments are reported in [629, 667, 206, 750, 350, 271, 524].

Meta-learning and transfer learning are related, and active areas of research [226, 611, 724, 270, 269, 542, 639, 694, 321].

Hierarchical reinforcement learning is an active field of research with a long history. See for further reading for example [343, 519, 226, 437, 36, 31, 632, 389, 415, 650, 346, 723]. Applications of hierarchical reinforcement learning to self-play remain to be explored, see also [652].

Readable and insightful introductions into the field of abstraction in deep representation learning are [60, 405]. A good place to start for network visualization is the ZFnet paper [774]. Wang et al. [737] study the optimization target of a dual-headed self-play network in AlphaZeroGeneral.

Chapter 8
Conclusion

Computers are now faster at learning Go than humans: it takes AlphaGo Zero days to reach world champion level, for humans this takes years.

This chapter is about the future. We summarize the lessons learned in this book, to reflect upon where AI may go next.

In the previous chapters we have discussed in depth the methods that have been used to achieve artificial intelligence in games. The focus has been on single games, on narrow intelligence.

The purpose of this chapter is to see how narrow intelligence can be extended to general intelligence, or at least to some extent. We will approach this goal in three steps. First, in Sect. 8.1, we will analyze the methods of the previous chapters, to find common threads. Second, in Sect. 8.2, we will discuss new problem domains that expand our horizon beyond zero-sum perfect-information games. Then, in Sect. 8.3, we will compare human and artificial intelligence, and look into future methods of artificial intelligence.

Core Problems

- How are artificial and human intelligence related?
- What games can be used in our quest towards general intelligence?
- What are essential methods of intelligent decision making in games?

Core Concepts

- Specialized intelligence and general intelligence
- Sample efficiency, transfer learning, and population-based methods
- Multi-agent, imperfect-information games

© Springer Nature Switzerland AG 2020
A. Plaat, *Learning to Play*, https://doi.org/10.1007/978-3-030-59238-7_8

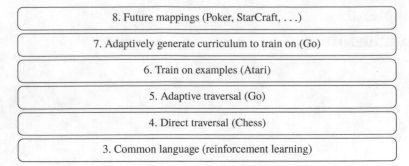

Fig. 8.1 Stack of chapters, with (from bottom to top) increasingly advanced mappings from problems to paradigms

8.1 Artificial Intelligence in Games

In this section we will review the methods that we have seen in the book so far. We will analyze them to see how they created an artificial kind of intelligence. We will look for common aspects in the hope that we can extend them to create new methods, to create an even more human kind of artificial intelligence, allowing better human-computer interaction and better human-computer understanding.

8.1.1 Summary of Paradigms

Figure 8.1 shows the structure of this book as a stack of chapters, with the paradigms building on top of each other. At the bottom is the reinforcement learning layer (3) that provides a common language and formalism for this book.

Planning

The paradigms start with being closely related to the state space. The methods in the second layer (4) in Fig. 8.1 directly traverse the state space, enumerating the states one by one. Basic undergraduate planning methods such as depth-first and breadth-first search are used [572].

Heuristics

When the state space is larger, the time complexity of full enumeration becomes prohibitive, and manually constructed features are introduced, based on heuristics. The heuristics are used in both backward and forward fashion: in evaluation functions (backward propagation) and in transition functions or move generation (forward pruning). Through these heuristics, depth-first and breadth-first search are transformed into best-first search: the heuristics guide node expansion towards parts of the tree that the heuristics deem best.

Heuristic planning combines the traversal algorithms with these heuristics and has been quite successful. This field of artificial intelligence has also been called heuristic search, or simply heuristics [511]. The Deep Blue–Kasparov match in 1997 marked the success of this approach.

Adaptive

Already with the heuristics enhancements arrived that softened the rigid depth-first fixed-depth expansion, when transpositions and search extensions were introduced, amongst many, many others. Going towards the next layer (5) in Fig. 8.1, we arrive at the adaptive paradigm. Node selection rules such as UCT based on exploration and exploitation provide a formal basis and greatly improve on the ad hoc forward pruning idea in many new domains.

Sampling

Furthermore, an alternative, non-minimax, backup rule is introduced. Averaging, together with a sampling evaluation function and UCT selection, provides a new search paradigm. The new paradigm works in domains with large branching factors where no efficient heuristic features have been found.

Together these methods constitute MCTS, which took the field of heuristic search into the realm of reinforcement learning, where methods are adaptive (i.e., they learn) and where methods balance exploration with exploitation. Through MCTS the application domain of combinatorial methods has expanded greatly.

Supervised Generalization

Still, the states that were explored in the state space are treated separately by MCTS. Commonalities between states, such as shared features, are not exploited explicitly. Even worse, in MCTS, in its most basic form, features of states are deliberately ignored, since node evaluation is solely based on random playouts. Moving to the next layer (6) in Fig. 8.1, this fact already suggests a further paradigm. This new paradigm, function approximation, opens up the states, looks at individual features, and uses methods to learn common features by training on examples of states.

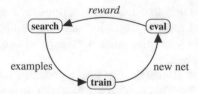

Fig. 8.2 Simplified self-play loop

Reinforcement Learning Generalization

The field of deep learning has introduced methods to learn features from examples, balancing generalization and overfitting. In supervised learning a fixed database of examples exists from which features must be learned. In reinforcement learning the training process generates the new examples as part of the training process. Because of this, there is a high degree of correlation between subsequent examples. In reinforcement learning special care must be taken to explore a sufficiently large and diverse part of the state space, since otherwise the training gets stuck in a local optimum, or the training process itself may even diverge (due to the deadly triad).

Self-Play

In the next layer (7) in Fig. 8.1, self-play is shown, which uses the generalization methods in a self-play setting. Here, the neural network is combined with MCTS. It is used for node selection, incorporating it in UCT, and for evaluation, replacing random playouts. In addition, the game playing program is used to generate the examples for the generalization process, which is used to train the evaluation features of the neural network, which is used by the program to generate the next (better) set of examples, etc.

Self-play is a highly recursive approach in which many aspects of the algorithm feed upon themselves (see also Fig. 8.2). Stability issues are plentiful, and various exploration methods must be used (and tuned well) for self-play to work. When it works, we find that it is quite an efficient way of training features, because of curriculum learning.

Other application domains and learning methods are shown in the next layer (8).

8.1.2 Summary of Methods

There are a few methods, or principles, that occur frequently in the paradigms of reinforcement learning that we have seen in different shapes and forms in this book. Let us now summarize these common principles.

Recursion and Bootstrapping

First of all is recursion. Recursion is the calling of a function by the same function with different parameters. It is used to traverse trees and graphs, it is the basis of Bellman's dynamic programming, and it is also behind the idea of self-play: reusing parts of the algorithm in a slightly different way to achieve your goal. Recursion is a standard way of traversing a state space, for example, to search for some optimal value, or for traversing the weights in a network to update them according to an error gradient.

Bootstrapping determines a state's value by making use of its previous values. Bootstrapping is often implemented using recursion, and dynamic programming makes use of this principle. Bootstrapping is at the basis of reinforcement learning, in Bellman's equation, defining the value of a state based on the discounted value of future actions. Minimax, the principle of using the same model for the player and the opponent, also finds the value at the root of the game tree by bootstrapping on the tree of child values.

Finally, bootstrapping and recursion feature three times in AlphaZero self-play, in the move selection of MCTS, in the generalization of the network for example states, and in the curriculum of games that are generated in a tournament against an identical copy of the player.

Optimization

This brings us to the next method that is used in all paradigms: optimization. Optimization is, again, everywhere. Optimization is used to find the best value, to find the best action, to find the best weights, and to find a global optimum.

Optimization is the principle of choosing the best item out of a set, preferably using some smart means or extra information to do so efficiently. All reinforcement learners and all game playing programs are nothing more than advanced optimizers, using many times the principle of optimization to select best actions, best states, best examples, best network architectures, and best training hyperparameters.

The principles of optimization and of bootstrapping work together in the search-eval architecture. Other examples exist, many exact algorithms use the principle of optimization, such as SARSA, A*, and depth-first search, and many other algorithms exist for the other three cells as well.

Optimization methods can also be used to approximate, for example, by using the features of states.

Exploration

Exploration is essential for stable deep reinforcement learning, to ensure broad coverage of the state space, to break through correlated subsequent states in reinforcement learning loops, and to ensure convergent training methods. Exploration is of crucial importance in MCTS, DQN, and PPO, and it is at the core of efficient simple reinforcement learning (such as Q-learning) and of stable deep reinforcement learning and self-play.

Search-Eval

The search-eval architecture provides a framework for the trade-off between exact planning algorithms and approximate learning algorithms. In two-player games the use of a combination of exact and approximate methods has proven to be essential for success, and all programs follow this model-based architecture. In self-play an extra learning loop is added to search-eval, to allow for the evaluation network to bootstrap itself on the search-eval examples.

Deep learning is a model-free method that takes many samples to learn the features. It is not very sample efficient because it lacks a model, although curriculum learning helps since examples are easy to learn. Deep learning is important because it is, in contrast to heuristic planning, able to learn an evaluation function. Planning and learning can be sequenced together to make a powerful model-based/model-free self-play system (which is not very sample efficient).

End-to-End

A final principle of this book is the progression of compute power, allowing larger and larger problems to be addressed. Where 60 years ago Samuel could only train coefficients of hand-crafted features, 30 years ago TD-Gammon could train end-to-end temporal difference learning on a small network, now AlphaGo can do tabula rasa end-to-end learning with a deep network. Being able to train end-to-end allows us to forgo hand-crafted features, with all their inherent errors and biases, achieving high performance and true (but still narrow) artificial intelligence.

8.1.3 On the Importance of Enhancements

The search-eval architecture provides a conceptual framework for game playing programs. To achieve a high level of performance, the enhancements, however, are as important. High-performing game playing programs from 1950-2006 were based on alpha-beta. Without transposition tables and singular extensions there would be no Deep Blue. Without fast playout patterns there would be no AlphaGo, without specific input layers no AlphaZero, without ReLU, dropouts, and GPUs, no deep learning Turing award, and without the replay buffer there would be no success in Atari. The enhancements are the result of deep understanding by the researchers of their domains. Understanding that is more specialized, and less general, than abstract principled frameworks such as minimax, reinforcement learning, or function approximation.

In addition to the elegant conceptual frameworks, deep, dirty, domain-specific understanding is necessary for progress in this field [594].

8.1.4 Towards General Intelligence

Let us revisit the problem statement from the Introduction.

What are the machine learning methods that are used in Chess and Go to achieve a level of play stronger than the strongest humans?

Various reinforcement learning methods have beaten human champions in Chess and Go, ranging from heuristic planning, adaptive sampling, function approximation, to self-play. All methods fit in the classic search-eval architecture, and all use variants of the principles of bootstrapping and optimization. Heuristic planning can achieve levels of play far surpassing human ability in Chess and Checkers. We have also seen how to combine planning and learning into a self-play system that learns to play from scratch, achieving even *higher* levels in Chess, Shogi, and Go.

Did we achieve intelligence? For these three games, we certainly passed the Turing test.[1] Systems were created that behave at a level for which a human would need super human intelligence. The intelligence is, however, single-domain intelligence. AlphaGo cannot play Shogi, and it cannot think of an entertaining joke.

Joining the two fields of symbolic AI and connectionist AI, AlphaZero showed that the methods generalize to three games, hinting at artificial general intelligence. However, it is more precise to speak of training three almost identical systems to become three different systems specialized in their own kind of special intelligence (since the net, once trained for Go, cannot play Chess). (GGP systems can play general games, but do not achieve performance close to AlphaZero; Sect. 8.2.5.)

8.2 Future *Drosophilas*

The reinforcement learning results in Atari and Go have inspired much further research. The use of concrete games, the *Drosophilas*, has stimulated progress in game playing greatly. In addition to the usual two-person zero-sum perfect-information games, researchers have looked for games that capture other elements of real life, such as non-zero-sum (collaboration) games, imperfect information, and multi-agent games. In this section we will review some of these aspects.

---

[1] Actually, since we far surpassed human play, an argument can be made that in doing so we *failed* the Turing test, since no human can play at this level.

8.2.1 Real-Time Strategy Games

Imperfect information games have been studied extensively in reinforcement learning [640, 344]. Multi-agent imperfect-information *Drosophila*s can be card games (such as Bridge and Poker) and real-time strategy games (such as Defense of the Ancients (DOTA) 2 and StarCraft). StarCraft has been studied for some time [727, 692, 703], as have DOTA 2 [185, 34, 497] and other RTS games [535, 402, 671, 332]. Easy-to-use Python interfaces have been created for StarCraft and DOTA 2. These games are highly challenging for current methods. They are multi-player, imperfect information, have large and continuous action spaces and very large and sparse states spaces, and long-time credit assignment challenges. Impressive results are already being achieved. Leibo et al. [411] have written a manifesto for further research into curriculum learning in multi-agent games.

Vinyals et el. have success in StarCraft II with their program AlphaStar [725] which uses multi-agent reinforcement learning in combination with supervised learning for subparts of the game. The notion of self-play is extended to a group of agents, the league. Using population-based methods agents try to improve the strategies of others in their own league, so that the collective becomes stronger.

Jaderberg et al. [331, 332] describe an impressive result of a multi-level learning system. Their system uses a variant of reinforcement learning that learns a population of agents, in a multiplayer real-time strategy capture-the-flag game, Quake III. The computational demands of their approach are mitigated by not using an MCTS search and using relatively simple and fast RNNs (see also Sect. 8.2.1).

OpenAI is performing research on cooperation with OpenAI Five in DOTA 2, again demonstrating that self-play reinforcement learing can achieve super-human performance in complex environments [70].

8.2.2 Negotiation and Collaboration

Non-zero-sum games are close to everyday life situations. Many real-world situations include negotiation and collaboration and offer win/win situations. AI has studied negotiation and collaboration extensively.

Negotiation and collaboration also occur in card games. Poker and Bridge have large action spaces and a large state space. Poker has been researched for some time, and for simpler (two-player) versions of the game successful programs have been written [92, 470, 103, 376]. Recently, success has also been reported in multi-player Poker. Cooperation and negotiation are central elements of Bridge, and research is continuing [636, 11]. Negotiation has also been studied for some time [338, 383, 339], including negotiation in games such as Diplomacy [505, 13, 167, 170, 169, 168, 384, 550].

Let us now have a closer look at two games, Poker and StarCraft.

8.2.3 Poker

Poker is an excellent game to show what progress has been made in imperfect-information games.

Poker has been studied for some time in artificial intelligence, and computer Poker championships have been conducted regularly [78, 79, 243, 566, 35, 92, 79, 243, 93, 579, 470]. No-limit Texas hold'em is the most popular form of poker. The two-player variant (called Heads Up) prevents opponent collusion. Heads-up no-limit Texas hold'em (HUNL) has been the primary benchmark for imperfect-information game play for several years.

Poker features face-down cards, whose value is unknown to the other players. The face-down cards constitute hidden information. This hidden information creates a large number of possible states, making Poker a game that is far more complex than Chess or Checkers. There are many variants of Poker; the state space of HUNL is reported to be 10^{161}, so simply enumerating the state space to find an optimal policy is infeasible [103]. A further complication is that a player reveals information during the course of play. Therefore, an AI must balance actions, so that the opponent does not find out too much about the cards that the AI has. Players may be misled through bluffing, i.e., deliberately betting a large sum to make the opponent believe that one has stronger cards than one has.

In 2018, one of the top programs, Libratus, defeated top human professionals in HUNL in a 20-day, 120,000-hand competition featuring a $200,000 prize pool. We will now describe this program in more details, based in [103]. Libratus consists of three main modules.

The first module computes a smaller version of the game, and then computes game-theoretic strategies. The algorithm used is a variant of counterfactual regret minimization (CFR). CFR is an algorithm to find Nash equilibrium strategies that is widely used in computer Poker [779]. CFR is based on multi-armed bandit theory. CFR is a recursive algorithm that starts with a random strategy. It then simulates playing games against itself. After every game, it improves its decisions. It repeats this process many times, constantly improving the strategy. As it plays, it comes closer to an optimal strategy, a strategy that can do (on average) no worse than tie against any opponent. CFR generates strategies that minimize exploitability, which means that it plays conservatively. CFR algorithms do not exploit imperfect play from opponents in a way that a human would. From a game-theoretic point of view, a perfect strategy is one that cannot expect to lose to any other player's strategy. A perfect strategy in the presence of suboptimal players who have weaknesses would be one that exploits those weaknesses.

When a later part of the game is reached during play, the second module of Libratus constructs a finer-grained abstraction for that subgame and solves it in real time.

The third module is the self-improver, which enhances the first policy. It fills in missing branches in the first version of the game and computes a game-theoretic policy for those branches. Computing this in advance is infeasible. Libratus uses the opponents' actual moves to suggest where in the game tree this is worthwhile.

In the experiment against human players Libratus analyzed the bet sizes that were most heavily used by its opponents during each day of the competition. On the basis of the frequency of the opponent bet, the program chose some bet sizes for which it would try to calculate a response overnight. Each of those bet sizes was then added to the strategy, together with the newly computed policy following that bet size. In this way, the program was able to narrow its gaps as the competition proceeded.

Interestingly, Libratus was originally based on heuristics, abstraction, and game-theoretical algorithms, and not on deep reinforcement learning. However, later work introduced deep counterfactual regret minimization [102], a form of CFR that approximates CFR equilibria in large games, using a 7 layer neural network. This algorithm is also the basis for Pluribus, the later multi-player program, defeating top players in six-player Poker [104]. Pluribus uses a form of self-play in combination with search.

Another top program, DeepStack, does use randomly generated games to train its deep value function network [470]. In Poker we see two different approaches achieving success.

8.2.4 StarCraft

StarCraft is a multi-player real-time strategy game of even larger complexity [496]. It is a good test bed for AI research, since it features decision making under uncertainty, spatial and temporal reasoning, collaboration and competition, opponent modeling, and real-time planning. The companies DeepMind and Blizzard have released a Python interface to stimulate research in StarCraft [727, 725].

The state space of real-time strategy games is larger than traditional board games such as Chess, Checkers, or Go. The state space has been estimated to be on the order of 10^{1685}, a very large number, even for this book [496]. The number of actions in each state is also large. Standard exact planning methods are not feasible, and need to be augmented with approximate methods to be effective. Planning in real-time strategy games has multiple levels of abstraction (see hierarchical reinforcement learning in Sect. 7.3.5). At a high level of abstraction, long-term planning is needed; at a low level of abstraction, tactical battles must be fought and individual units must be moved.

StarCraft offers opportunities to explore many challenging new methods in reinforcement learning. First, it is an imperfect-information game. The terrain map is partially visible. A local camera must be moved by the player to acquire information. There is a "fog-of-war" that obscures unvisited regions. The map must be explored proactively to determine the opponents' state. Second, StarCraft is a multi-agent game in which several players compete for influence and resources. StarCraft is also multi-agent at another level. Each player controls many units that need to cooperate to achieve the player's goal. Third, the action space is large and diverse. There are around 108 actions for a player, which can be selected with a point-and-click interface. There are many different types of units and buildings, each type with its own local actions.

Furthermore, the legal actions vary during play as it advances through possible technologies. Finally, games are long. They last for thousands of states and actions. Decisions early in the game, such as which units to build, have consequences that will be seen much later in the game when armies meet in battle. There is a long distance in credit assignment, and exploration is important in StarCraft [496].

In a series of test matches held in December 2018, DeepMind's AlphaStar beat two top players in two-player single-map matches, using a different user interface. The neural network was initially trained by supervised learning from anonymized human games, that were then further trained by playing against other AlphaStar agents, using a population-based version of self-play reinforcement learning [725].

8.2.5 General Game Playing

As has already been mentioned a few times, another approach to studying generality in game intelligence is general game playing (GGP). GGP takes a different approach, not using concrete existing games, but using abstract generative games.

GGP started after Deep Blue won from Kasparov, and the field was looking for their new *Drosophila*. One of the criticisms of the field of game playing was that all programs had to be specifically developed for each game anew. Human intelligence, on the other hand, is general, and can just as easily be applied to different tasks.

A general game playing system should be able to play any game for which it is given the rules. It was hoped that the general methods coming out of GGP research would also be able to help in other areas, such as in assisting search and rescue missions [514, 240]. The Logic group at Stanford University currently hosts the General Game Playing project [240, 683] and initiates competitions.

The GGP approach is to create a system and a language in which many games can be expressed. The challenge is then to create a single game player that can play any game that occurs in a tournament. A GGP program must be able to accept any model that can be expressed in the game description language. The game description language is similar to PROLOG. In GGP a parser for the game description must be written, which implements the state/action transition function, and termination rules. The program has to come up with an efficient search procedure, and a good evaluation function. It is hard to preprogram heuristics when the domain is unknown. It was hoped that GGP would stimulate the creation of general problem solving methods. It is therefore curious to note that a method developed in Go, the other *Drosophila*, has been successful in GGP. Monte Carlo Tree Search is a general search procedure that does not need domain-specific heuristics, and turned out to be well suited for GGP.

Arguably GGP is a less spectacular *Drosophila*, since there is no human world champion to beat, and there is no active human gaming community. In another sense GGP is more spectacular since it tries to find solutions that work for all games.

GGP has yielded a range of interesting advances towards more general AI. Much research in GGP is being performed [516, 681, 598, 682, 683, 604, 447, 605, 216,

83, 633, 634, 740, 736]. It will be interesting to see if more techniques from the two fields (i.e., general and special game playing) will cross over.

There are other general game playing systems, which use their own languages for defining the game rules. In 1992, Pell introduced Meta-Game Playing, one of the earliest programs to use automated game generation. Pell's Metagamer was able to play Chess-like games, given game rules definition in a language called the Game Description Language [514, 515, 240]. Following the GGP idea a General Video Game Playing competition has been started [518, 517, 391].[2]

Both AlphaZero and GGP show how general game play can be achieved. The AlphaZero approach to general game playing is less general, requiring hand-designed input and output layers, where GGP programs generate these automatically from a description of the rules. The game complexity of Go, Chess, and Shogi is much larger than that of typical GGP challenges.

8.3 A Computer's Look at Human Intelligence

Now that we have discussed the reinforcement learning methods, and discussed future challenges in reinforcement learning in games, it is time to compare the artificial approach to intelligence with the other approach, the human kind.

8.3.1 Human Intelligence

As we already mentioned in Chap. 2, human intelligence is a complex, multifaceted concept. Many different definitions of intelligence have been proposed. Intelligence involves recognition, reasoning, memory, learning, problem solving, and creativity. Human intelligence is usually also assumed to include understanding, emotion, self-awareness, and purpose (volition). Intelligence is the ability to infer knowledge from information, and to apply that knowledge towards adaptive behavior within a context. See, for example, Legg et al. [410] or Neisser et al. [482].

We will now discuss these elements of intelligence in more detail, and analyze how human and artificial intelligence differ in their approach.

Memory and Recognition

One of the basic elements of intelligence is the ability to recognize objects or features that have been encountered before. This requires sensors, a recognition system, and a functioning memory. All have been studied widely in human perception. In

---

[2] http://www.gvgai.net

Kahneman's terminology, system 1 is the part of our thinking that recognizes objects. Human recognition works fast and associatively.

Computers have always had memories, and over the years the amount of memory of computers has grown greatly. Computers have long struggled with the kind of recognition that humans do so easily. Only after CNNs were introduced (fashioned after an animal visual cortex) and after enough training data became available in MNIST and ImageNet, and after enough computing power in the form of GPUs became available, did computer recognition for images start to achieve impressive results.

Reasoning

Reasoning is another core element of intelligence. In Kahneman's terminology, reasoning is system 2, or thinking slow. Reasoning is considered a positive trait, and many humans and scientists pride themselves on their capacity for elaborate and deep logic reasoning. It is something that children are trained at in school topics such as calculus, mathematics, and history. It is the reason why Chess classes are present at schools.

Indeed, one of the precepts of classical economics is the assumption of rational behavior of the homo economicus. One of the interesting aspects of Kahneman's book is that it stresses the importance of system 1, the fast, intuitive, type of thinking. The non rational part of our thinking is guiding much of our daily behavior. (Why do people buy lottery tickets, if we know that the expected value of a lottery is negative?) Indeed, Kahneman's work on prospect theory, together with many other important insights from psychology, has been instrumental for the field of behavioral economics. Thaler and Sunstein have written a popular book on nudging [680], applying insights from behavioral economics to influence behavior of people.

Computers are good at reasoning, and are typically considered to be faster at reasoning than humans. In artificial intelligence, systems for logic reasoning were one of the first systems built, right up there with Chess and Checkers programs [764, 396, 484]. Some of the many successful results of this research are the programming language PROLOG [147, 94], research into semantic reasoning [17, 301], and negotiation [423].

Learning

One of the central aspects of intelligence is the ability to adapt one's behavior based on information from the environment. The ability to learn is certainly a crucial aspect of intelligence. When children are young, learning and playing are closely related. Johan Huizinga, an eminent Dutch historian, argues in *Homo Ludens* [322] that play may be the primary educational element in human culture. Small children learn through playing, through interaction with their environments. Later, they learn in school, in a less-playful regimented curriculum. Some of our learning is by repeated exposure to examples. In supervised learning we teach ourselves associations and reflexes. Children who have been taught the tables of multiplication can immediately answer the question: "What is six times seven?" using their system 1. Others have to use system 2 to answer this question.

In computers, machine learning also uses memory and recognition capacities to build up associations. If we teach (supervise) ourselves, we use our rational reasoning capacities to do so. Learning was recognized early on as a second central element of artificial intelligence. Computers have become quite good at learning, in image recognition, and now also in Go. Due to curriculum learning AlphaGo Zero learns Go in days, where for humans this takes years of study.

Indeed, since the impressive results with deep learning in image recognition, the term machine learning has become almost synonymous with artificial intelligence, sometimes forgetting about symbolic reasoning altogether (our societal memory is imperfect).

Creativity

Creativity is the process by which something new and valuable is created [529]. Creativity is strongly associated with human intelligence.

There have been quite some studies into artificial creativity. A computational view has emerged, in which creativity emerges out of computational processes [600]. Indeed, in addition to automated theorem proving [764, 430, 76], fields such as artificial painting [148] and artificial music [211, 702] have a long history in AI.[3] A formal theory of creativity has been put forward by Schmidhuber [601]. If we think back to Fan Hui's description of AlphaGo's moves ("speechless") we see words describing beauty and creativity (Sect. 2.3.5).

Understanding

Understanding is a concept that is related to human intelligence. Clearly, humans can lay claim to understanding something. Insofar as computers are not self-aware or have an identity, computers cannot be said to understand something. Computers can be made to analyze a concept and explain the reasoning that supports a certain conclusion, but it would be harder to claim that an explanation is equivalent to understanding [126].

A Chess end-game analysis can produce the exact subtree proving why a certain move is the best move in a position. That does not mean that the computer has an understanding of what it analyzed, even if the explanation is identical to one given by a human.

---

[3] See, for example, the International Computer Music Association at http://www.computermusic.org.

Emotion

A similar reasoning applies to emotion. Emotion is an important aspect that determines much of human thought and behavior. Much of our evolutionary survival skills are encoded in our emotional reactions, and much of our daily behavior is too [347, 424, 99].

In artificial intelligence, the field of affective computing studies the formalization, recognition, and reasoning with emotions [424, 89]. As with understanding, a computer may be able to recognize emotions, it can be made to behave as if it has emotions, but few people would say that it has emotions.

Affective computing, and the models of emotion, will yield better human–computer interactions, and interactions with robots that appear more natural.

Self-Awareness, Purpose

Most people would argue that computers do not possess self-awareness, but humans do. Together with our free will, we believe that it guides much of our intelligent behavior. Intelligent computer behavior is guided by one or more goals that it tries to achieve. Humans decide on their own goal; for computers the goal is externally specified.

Note that the strict behavioral approach of the Turing test could allow a situation where a machine is so good at answering questions concerning self-awareness and introspection that we must conclude that it is indistinguishable from a sentient human. The question of self-aware machines raises many interesting neurological and philosophical question. See, for example, [372, 259].

System 1 and System 2

Kahneman describes two kinds of human thinking: thinking fast and thinking slow [347], also known as system 1 and system 2. In this book, we have seen how artificial intelligence in games is created out of planning and learning. The exact and approximate methods in the search-eval architecture all have parallels to thinking fast and slow (Table 8.1).

In addition to these parallels, there are important differences between human and artificial intelligence. Human intelligence is genera; artificial intelligence is mostly specific to one domain. Human intelligence is self-aware; artificial intelligence is judged by behavior, to pass the Turing test.

Let us first look at thinking fast. Thinking fast is reflex-like recognition. It is not so much like the training of the function approximator, which is off-line, and takes days, as it is the usage of the approximator, which is on-line, and takes milliseconds.

This brings us to revisit a point made earlier. We want to understand Kahneman's scheme of two kinds of thinking, in which system 1 is thinking fast, and system 2 is thinking slow. Now self-play has an analogon in Kahneman's world. Self-play consists

System 1	System 2
fast	slow
recognition	reasoning
reflex	rational
approximate	exact
train	plan
eval	search

Table 8.1 Fast and slow, eval and search

of exact planning methods being used to generate examples to train the function approximator (Fig. 8.2). System 2 (slow) can be used not only to reason and solve complicated problems such as what is the product of 6 and 7, but can also be used to train system 1 by repeatedly exposing system 1 to examples that system 2 generates. In this way we create a mode of thinking that can be called conscious *learning* or *training*. Anyone who has learned words of a different language, or has recited the tables of multiplication at school is familiar with this kind of learning. Practice makes perfect. Learning by self-play exists both in AI and in human intelligence. In the next section we will discuss a consequence of the fact that artificial intelligence is now able to do this kind of training.

Now that we have seen some similarities between human and artificial intelligence, let us have a look at some of the differences.

8.3.2 General Intelligence

We have superficially explored the limits of artificial intelligence; let us also look at its strengths. Some of the aspects of human intelligence can readily be simulated by a computer, such as recognition, memory, reasoning, and learning.

Artificial Intelligence

For a computer to behave artificially intelligent it should behave the same as human intelligence. An intelligent computer must be able to remember, to recognize, to reason, and to learn, in order to pass the Turing test.

As we have seen in this book, there is much research on techniques for recognition, memory, reasoning, and learning. In describing the behavior of Deep Blue and AlphaGo, some Chess and Go players have described it in terms of beauty, divine intervention, and other language usually used for creative works.

In the fields of game playing it can reasonably be argued that genuine artificial intelligence exists. In Backgammon, Checkers, Chess, Atari, and Go, the best games are played by silicon.

Game Intelligence

Exceptional intelligence in a single field is valued highly among humans. Exceptional Soccer intelligence, Tennis intelligence, violin intelligence, novelist intelligence, or Chess intelligence is scarce (and can be monetized through prize money and sponsor deals).

Computers have such specialized intelligence. In fact, that is all they have. Computers can do one thing wel; humans can do many things. Evolution has endowed humans with intelligence that allows them to do many things, in order to survive in the world in which they live. The intelligence of game playing programs has not evolved. Game playing programs have been programmed to (learn to) excel at one game. They have specific intelligence.

When looking carefully at the history of game intelligence, an interesting pattern emerges. The specific game intelligence started with search algorithms that exploit the game structure (two-player zero-sum adversarial games following the minimax rule). Game-specific heuristic search enhancements made the programs even more game specific, and the eval algorithms are based on game-specific heuristics as well. In some cases the evaluation function is tuned with a (general) learning algorithm.

The minimax algorithm itself is general in the sense that it applies to all two-player zero-sum games.

A subsequent search algorithm is MCTS. It is more general than minimax, since it also works for single-agent problems. It also is more general because it works without a domain-specific evaluation function.

To achieve high performance, domain-specific heuristic methods were added, such as pattern-based playouts, and selection rules that can incorporate priors.

Next are even more general learning algorithms, such as supervised and reinforcement learning neural network function approximators. They are more general, in theory, although tuning a network architecture is a long and tedious process in which different network architectures and hyperparameters are tried and tested on the specific game for which it should work.

Self-play takes this a step further, forgoing the games databases of grandmaster games, and learning itself in a curriculum learning fashion to play a game.

The pattern that emerges is that the methods in reinforcement learning in games have progressed from domain specific to general (which is then partly undone by domain-specific performance tuning). The trend is towards more generality in methods, and this generality has now reached the point where it is starting to spill over to general application domains. As we saw in Sect. 8.2, more and more applications emerge where the self-play AI methods work, and a single architecture may even work in a few different games.

General Intelligence

For humans, intelligence is general. The intelligence of humans applies to many different domains. A human being with little general intelligence and high intelligence in one special domain is unusual. However, most individual humans do have certain specialities in which they excel.

Some game playing programs have been designed to exhibit general intelligence. The AlphaZero architecture can teach itself to play three games exceedingly well, provided that the right input and output layer of the neural network are specialized. General game playing programs are designed to be general enough to interpret all games that can be specified by the Game Description Language.

Practicing, or the 10,000 Hour Rule

How does one achieve high levels of intelligence? To reach the top in Tennis, soccer, violin playing, writing, or Chess requires talent and practice. Indeed, it is sometimes argued that "all" it takes to achieve success is a total of 10,000 hours of focused practice [245]. Scientific studies dispute this point of view and the number of 10,000, and argue that the focus on practice is an oversimplification. However, it is clear that, in addition to talent, practice is indeed important in games, music, and sports (see [434]).

To learn new behavior, deliberate attention of system 2 is necessary. During training we perform the actions repeatedly, under the conscious guidance of system 2. At some point, system 1 will have picked up enough to perform the behavior semi-automatically. Less attention of system 2 is needed. After enough practice, the behavior will be performed without any deliberate attention. System 1 has learned to do it unattended. $6 \times 7 = 42$.

8.3.3 Next Steps: Sample Efficiency and Collaboration

Although artificial intelligence achieves impressive results in single domains, and methods are becoming more general, the difference with human intelligence remains large. The steps that will be made on the path to achieve general, human, intelligence will be small.

Two important challenges towards general intelligence are sample efficiency and collaboration. The training time for current AI is still quite long. For each new task a very large number of samples is needed for current reinforcement learning methods.

Collaboration is the second challenge. The essence of zero-sum games is competition. Multi-agent games feature collaboration, and allow modeling of teamwork and forms of man/machine interaction.

Curriculum Learning

Following a suitable curriculum improves training results. A good curriculum speeds up training, and achieves better end results [194]. Human formal teaching (in schools) follows a curriculum, and the same improvements have been found in supervised and reinforcement learning in artificial intelligence.

Self-play in games creates a curriculum-like setting, where training examples are generated from easy to hard. This allows for quick and effective training. Indeed, as was mentioned in Sect. 7.1.4, AlphaZero learns to play at a level beyond that of human world champions in days, where human champions take years of dedicated training to reach that level.

AlphaZero is not only better at playing, but also learns much faster than human champions.

Sample Efficiency for AGI

However, the sample efficiency for each task is still low, since for each new task learning is starting all over, from scratch. Even AlphaZero did not achieve transfer learning, where (a part of) a trained network could be transfered for (pre)training of another task.

The field of transfer learning studies how sample efficiency in new tasks can be increased through the reuse of trained knowledge between related tasks. Transfer learning can thus contribute to more general AI. Knowledge transfer can be achieved in various ways: through network parameters, or through hyperparameters.

Transfer learning is related to pretraining, few-shot learning, and life-long learning [687]. Section 7.3.2 discussed transfer learning. Related to transfer learning is meta-learning. Meta-learning studies mechanisms that learn to learn. It is related to algorithm selection and to transfer learning in the sense that its aim is to adapt to new environments with few training examples. It is a very active area of research [214, 226, 321].

Two other methods that aim at reducing the sample efficiency problem are hierarchical learning and model-based learning. Hierarchical learning aims to model problems hierarchically so that a subproblem can be solved independently, in sequence. Model-based learning aims to learn a model of the problem first, and then use the model with other methods, such as planning [524]. In doing so model-based learning is more sample efficient than model-free learning. The AlphaGo approach is a model-based approach. More recently MuZero is a model-based approach that learns a latent model of the problem end-to-end [607]: AlphaGo Zero needed to be provided with the rules of the game, but MuZero infers the rules from the environment, and then learns to play at a high level.

The promise of life-long learning, transfer learning, and meta-learning is faster learning, by reusing knowledge that was learned in one domain for a new domain. These methods are inspired by human learning, just as the original inspiration of reinforcement learning is in conditioning experiments with humans and animals.

Collaboration

Artificial intelligence has achieved very strong results in specific domains, and the challenge is now to extend these results to more general domains, to different games, and beyond games, to fields such as negotiation and human-robot interaction.

As our computational abilities increase, collaboration is becoming more important in reinforcement learning and games. Recent advances in Poker [104], StarCraft [725], Capture the Flag [332], and DOTA 2 [497] show that reinforcement learning versions of population-based methods are able to achieve a high level of collaboration in leagues consisting of humans and computers.

Researchers are arguing for more research into curriculum learning in multi-agent games [411]. More can be expected in AI for negotiation and team collaboration.

Faster and Together

We have come to the end of this book. We have discussed a wide array of artificial intelligence technologies, and we have seen programs reach amazing achievements. In reinforcement learning agents can train to transcend the level of supervisors or teachers. The search-eval architecture has been the basis for all technological advances that we covered in this book—from planning, sampling, and function approximation to self-play.

This book has shown how game playing programs have progressed from game-specific heuristic methods to general learning methods that teach themselves to play (and beat world champions). In this chapter we have looked at the link between artificial and human intelligence, in general terms of recognition, reasoning, and self-awareness. Although progress has been made, the gap with human intelligence remains large. So far, AI has achieved success in narrow fields. In describing this progress, we have noted parallels between planning and learning, symbolic and connectionst, and thinking fast and slow.

With progress in transfer learning, we can expect AI to become more general in the near future. With self-play, computers fashion their own training curriculums and training progresses faster than before. For the games of Chess, Shogi, and Go, a computer was able to teach itself to play at world champion level and beyond in a matter of days. Humans take years of dedicated study to reach this level of play. In these games, computers not only play better, but also learn faster.

Collaboration and negotiation are becoming increasingly important in AI research. Research in games such as Poker and StarCraft has shown fast and powerful learning in team play. Games research is continuing towards faster learning and towards teams in which computers and humans collaborate.

The future of AI is human.

8.4 Practice

Below are some questions to check your understanding of this chapter. Each question is a closed question where a simple, one sentence answer is possible.

Questions

1. Explain the search-eval architecture briefly.
2. Describe bootstrapping and optimization.
3. Why is diversity important in learning?
4. Explain triple-nested recursive optimization.
5. How does automation lead to generalization?
6. Why are enhancements important?
7. Describe the relation between recursion, optimization, features, generalization, learning, and intelligence.
8. Why is Poker an interesting research topic?
9. What is general game playing?
10. How does AlphaGo Zero join symbolic AI and connectionist AI?
11. Describe system 1, system 2, and self-play learning.
12. Describe general and special intelligence.

At this point, you have become quite proficient at implementing reinforcement learning in games technology. Below are ideas for larger projects, to help you on the path to further research. These are challenging projects, perhaps suitable for a thesis.

Exercises

1. Design a simple imperfect-information game and implement it in A0G. For example: Blackjack. Does it learn? Does self-play work in imperfect information?
2. Write a self-play single-agent player for your single-agent optimization problem of choice. [challenging]
3. Interface A0G with the StarCraft interface, and create a multi-player self-play system. [challenging]
4. Design a a cooperative multi-player game. For example, merging traffic on a highway on-ramp, with or without signalling/negotiation. [challenging]
5. Write a negotiation or Diplomacy game. See [25] for negotiation competitions. [highly challenging]

Summary

In order to look to the future, in this chapter we have looked back at what we have covered in this book. We have looked at the methods that form the search-eval architecture. The search-eval architecture can also be seen as an architecture with several nested levels of optimization, of which self-play is just one. We see how artificial intelligence methods are used to achieve higher levels of intelligence, or more general intelligence.

We have also briefly discussed other application domains, beyond two-player zero-sum perfect information. Multi-agent imperfect-information games approach more aspects of the real world. Our techniques have progressed to the point where creating players for Poker and StarCraft are realistic challenges that are succeeding.

We discussed an alternative *Drosophila*, general game playing (GGP). Where the challenge of Go lies primarily in the size of the state space, in GGP the challenge lies in being able to play a game for which the rules are not known beforehand.

We have compared artificial intelligence with human intelligence. We have looked at Kahneman's two systems, system 1 for thinking fast, and system 2 for thinking slow. Thinking fast resembles a function approximator, and thinking slow resembles planning. Self-play uses planning to generate examples for the function approximator to learn from.

Self-play learns relatively fast, due to curriculum learning. We have noted that AlphaGo Zero needed days to teach itself to play Go, whereas humans need years of dedicated study to learn this level of Go, if they succeed at all.

We have looked at the elements that compose human intelligence, and noted again that artificial intelligence is special. At least in the narrow domain of zero-sum board games, we have the situation that computers play better and learn faster then humans. However, human intelligence is more general.

Future research will try to enlarge the domains in which artificial intelligence works. Sample efficiency and collaboration will be important topics. The techniques covered in this book will contribute to this research.

Appendix A
Deep Reinforcement Learning Environments

Artificial intelligence is an open field of research. Many researchers publish their code, allowing for easy reproduction of experiments, and allowing researchers to build upon each other's progress. This appendix contains pointers to software environments that are meant to help you further in your own research.

We list three types of environments: general programming and learning environments, deep learning environments, and self-learning environments.

We start with general learning environments.

General Learning Environments

Name	Type	URL	Ref.
Python	General-purpose language	https://www.python.org	[562]
Weka	Machine learning env.	https://www.cs.waikato.ac.nz/ml/weka	[762]
Scikit-Learn	Machine learning env.	https://scikit-learn.org	[513]
Caffe	Deep learning env.	http://caffe.berkeleyvision.org	[334]
PyTorch	Deep learning env.	https://pytorch.org	[508]
TensorFlow	Deep learning env.	https://www.tensorflow.org	[2]
Keras	Deep learning library	https://keras.io	[140]

Table A.1 General learning environments

General-purpose programming languages such as Python allow us to program the experiments that we wish to perform. One step further are machine learning environments such as Weka [762, 272] and Scikit-Learn [513].

For deep learning, well-known environments are Caffe [334], Facebook's PyTorch [508], Theano [64] which has been subsumed by Google's TensorFlow [1, 2], and its user friendly add-on Keras [139]. Keras is perhaps the easiest way to start with deep learning. PyTorch offers great flexibility. TensorFlow may well be the most

A. Plaat, *Learning to Play*, https://doi.org/10.1007/978-3-030-59238-7

popular environment. All environments offer seamless integration with CPU and
GPU backends; no specialized GPU programming knowledge is needed.

Table A.1 summarizes the general learning environments.

Deep Reinforcement Learning Environments

Name	Type	URL	Ref.
ALE	Atari Games	`https://github.com/mgbellemare/Arcade-` `Learning-Environment`	[53]
Gym	RL environments	`https://gym.openai.com`	[98]
Stable Baselines	RL algorithms	`https://stable-baselines.readthedocs.io`	[291]
Dopamine	Deep RL env.	`https://github.com/google/dopamine`	[123]
RLlib	Distributed RL	`https://docs.ray.io/en/latest/rllib.html`	[417]
Bsuite	RL environments	`https://github.com/deepmind/bsuite`	[498]
OpenSpiel	RL in games env.	`https://github.com/deepmind/open_spiel`	[399]
Meta World	Meta-learning	`https://meta-world.github.io`	[773]

Table A.2 Deep reinforcement learning environments

Reinforcement learning has seen much interest from researchers. The availability
of environments has stimulated this research greatly. Bellemare et al. introduced
the Atari Learning Environment [53] that has subsequently been incorporated into
OpenAI Gym. The Gym Github page can be found here.[1] OpenAI Gym has, in
addition to ALE, classic reinforcement learning examples such as Cartpole and
Mountain Car. OpenAI also provides baseline implementations of reinforcement
learning algorithms [173]. A great introduction on their use is at Spinning up:
OpenAIs Spinning Up, and the code repo, which is here.[2]

Subsequently, refactored versions of baselines are presented as the Stable Baselines.
Note: Stable Baselines supports TensorFlow versions from 1.8.0 to 1.14.0, and may
not yet work on TensorFlow versions 2.0.0 and above. Support for TensorFlow 2 API
is planned.

The Baseline Zoo contains trained models for the stable baselines.

Dopamine [123] is a framework by DeepMind for deep reinforcement learning.

RLlib [417] provides abstractions for distributing reinforcement learning on
large-scale clusters of machines.

Bsuite [498] is a behavior suite for reinforcement learning.

OpenSpiel [399] is a framework for reinforcement learning in games, implementing
many of the algorithms that are discussed in this book.

---

[1] `https://github.com/openai/gym`

[2] `https://github.com/openai/spinningup`

Meta World [773] is a benchmark and evaluation suite for multi-task and meta reinforcement learning.

Table A.2 summarizes the deep reinforcement learning environments.

Open Reimplementations of AlphaZero Self-Play

Name	Type	URL	Ref.
AlphaZero General	AlphaZero in Python	https://github.com/suragnair/alpha-zero-general	[679]
ELF	Game framework	https://github.com/pytorch/ELF	[689]
Leela	AlphaZero for Chess, Go	https://github.com/LeelaChessZero/lczero	[507]
PhoenixGo	AlphaZero-based Go prog.	https://github.com/Tencent/PhoenixGo	[775]
PolyGames	Env. for Zero learning	https://github.com/facebookincubator/Polygames	[124]

Table A.3 Self-learning environments

The publication of the AlphaGo papers created great interest in the research community in self-learning self-play approaches. The DeepMind team has not yet published their code, but the publications [623, 624] (and especially [626]) provide enough detail for researchers to create their own versions, some of which are open sourced on GitHub. We will describe some of them.

A0G: AlphaZero General

Thakoor et al. [679] created a self-play system as part of a course project. The system is called AlphaZero General (A0G), and is on GitHub. It is implemented in Python and TensorFlow, Keras, and PyTorch, and suitably scaled down for smaller computational resources. It has implementations for 6×6 Othello, Tic Tac Toe, Gobang, and Connect4, all small games of significantly less complexity than Go. Its main network architecture is a four layer CNN followed by two fully connected layers. The code is easy to understand in an afternoon of study, and is well suited for educational purposes. The course project write-up provides some documentation [679].

Facebook ELF

ELF stands for Extensible Lightweight Framework. It is a framework for game research in C++ and Python [689]. Originally developed for real-time strategy games by Facebook, it includes the Arcade Learning Environment and the Darkforest[3] Go program [691]. ELF can be found at GitHub ELF. ELF also contains the self-play program OpenGo [690], a reimplementation of AlphaGo Zero (in C++).

Leela

Another reimplementation of AlphaZero is Leela. Both a Chess and a Go version of Leela exist. The Chess version is based on Chess engine Sjeng. The Go[4] version is based on Go engine Leela. Leela does not come with trained weights of the network. Part of Leela is a community effort to compute these weights.

PhoenixGo

PhoenixGo is a strong self-play Go program by Tencent [775]. It is based on the AlphaGo Zero architecture. It can be found at Github PhoenixGo. A trained network is available as well.

PolyGames

PolyGames [124] is an environment for Zero-based learning (MCTS with deep reinforcement learning) inspired by AlphaGo Zero. Relevant learning methods are implemented, and bots for Hex, Othello, and Havannah have been implemented. PolyGames can be found at PolyGames.

Table A.3 summarizes the self-learning environments.

---

[3] https://github.com/facebookresearch/darkforestGo
[4] https://github.com/gcp/leela-zero

Appendix B
*AlphaGo Technical Details

This appendix contains more technical details for the AlphaGo, AlphaGo Zero, and AlphaZero programs, that were too technical to fit in the main text of Chap. 7, but are important to truly understand how things work. All information in this appendix is from the three papers by Silver et al. [623, 626, 625].

B.1 AlphaGo

We start with AlphaGo. The AlphaGo program is a complicated program. All details are described in Silver et al. [623]. In this appendix we summarize some of the more technical details from this publication.

Search Algorithm

The search algorithm of AlphaGo is MCTS (see also Sect. 5.2 and [108]). The four MCTS operations are implemented as follows.

Selection For selection, a variant of P-UCT [561, 440] is used, which allows integration of prior information into the UCT selection formula. This is especially important for new, unexplored children, to be able to use the information of the policy net. With the policy net, AlphaGo does not employ the all-moves-as-first or rapid action value estimation heuristics used in most other programs, since the policy net provides priors of better quality (Sect. 5.3.2). In addition AlphaGo does not use progressive widening [132], dynamic komi [39], or an opening book, which most other Go programs do.

The constant C_p determines the exploration/exploitation trade-off. A high value means more exploration. AlphaGo uses $C_p = 5$. This is high compared with most Go programs, where values of $C_p < 0.75$ or even $C_p \approx 0$ were used for programs that use RAVE [239, 129]. AlphaGo favors a considerable amount of exploration compared with earlier Go programs. Section 5.3.1 discusses the performance sensitivity of C_p.

© Springer Nature Switzerland AG 2020
A. Plaat, *Learning to Play*, https://doi.org/10.1007/978-3-030-59238-7

Expansion Children of leaves of the MCTS tree are expanded when the visit count exceeds a threshold. New children get prior probabilities from the policy network, and are put in the queue for evaluation by the GPU with both the policy and the value network. The threshold is determined by the length of the work queue for the GPU.

Rollout Leaves in AlphaGo are evaluated both by the value network (GPU queue) and rollouts with the fast rollout network. Results are combined with a parameter $\lambda = 0.5$ (half rollout, half value network).

Backup The rollout statistics are updated as usual in MCTS (visit count and win count). AlphaGo is a tree parallel program [131], which means that multiple processes can update the MCTS tree concurrently. AlphaGo uses standard techniques for ensuring efficient parallel selection (virtual loss [614, 453]) and correctness of the tree (lock free updates [200, 455]).

Network Architecture

For the fast rollout policy network, the function approximator is based on a hash table. The fast rollout policy is based on small (3×3) patterns that are also found in other Go programs [239, 236]. It is based on a hash table of the *last good reply* heuristic [29].

The function approximator for the selection policy is based on a 13-layer convolutional neural network. It has 12 convolutional hidden layers (plus one input layer and one fully connected output layer). The first convolutional layers uses a kernel size of 5×5; the other hidden layers use 3×3. A ReLU unit is applied at each layer.

The network for the value network has one convolutional layer more than the policy network, for a total of 14 layers.

Input/Output Features

The input layer is $19 \times 19 \times 48$ with 48 feature planes. The inputs to the AlphaGo nets are more than just the stones on the board. The features of each point include stone color, how many times ago a turn was played, the number of liberties, how many opponent stones would be captured, how many own stones would be captured, the number of liberties after the move is played, ladder status, ladder escape, if a point fills an own eye, and color to play.

The output layer is a fully connected layer with a soft-max function for the policy network and a single tanh unit for the value network.

Performance of the Three Networks

We will now discuss the three networks in more detail.

Fast Rollout Policy Network The fast rollout policy network is based on 3×3 patterns. Its function is to replace (or enhance) the random rollouts of MCTS. It achieves only 24% accuracy on a test set, but it replies with an answer in $2\mu s$, which is 1500 times faster than the slow policy network, on the hardware used by the AlphaGo team.

Selection Policy Network The network trained by supervised learning is trained on 29 million positions for classification of expert moves on a dataset of internet games (split into a test set of one million positions, and a training set of 28 million positions). This policy network achieves 57% accuracy of correct actions after training. Its time to compute an answer is 3 ms. It is trained by asynchronous stochastic gradient descent. The supervised training took three weeks; 340 million training steps were performed.

The policy network is further refined by reinforcement learning with self-play positions. It was trained for one full day of self-play of 10,000 mini-batches of 128 games, randomized to prevent correlations using positions from a pool of opponents. The training algorithm is policy gradient descent, with the REINFORCE algorithm [659]. This network performs quite well. Without any search at all, it won 85% of games against Pachi, a strong open-source MCTS program.[1] The reinforcement learning is important, since a no-search network based on supervised learning won only 11% against Pachi. Curiously, it is the weaker supervised net that was used in MCTS selection in AlphaGo. The paper speculates that this is because of greater variation in the supervised network, it chooses from a wider repertoire of "best" moves, whereas the reinforcement network chooses always the single best move [623]. Still, it is surprising that a weaker network is used in favor of a stronger network, and more work is needed to fully understand the reasons.

Value Network The value network is trained as a regression of the policy network. The value represents the probability of winning. For the value network 30 million training positions were used from self-play games. To avoid overfitting the training positions were created so as not to be correlated, using a small self-play search based on the positions that were used for the supervised selection policy network. The training algorithm is stochastic gradient descent as in the supervised training phase, based on the mean squared error between the predicted values and the observed rewards. This training phase took 50 GPUs one week.

Many more details of the various training methods can be found in the original publication [623].

Compute Hardware

Training the networks occurs off-line, before a match is played, and large amounts of computation power and time are available. During a match the time to compute is limited. Function approximation does not come cheap. Position evaluation requires evaluating multiple networks, which costs orders of magnitude more computation than traditional heuristic programs. Combining MCTS with deep neural networks has required quite some software engineering. AlphaGo uses an asynchronous multi-

---

[1] Pachi code is at http://pachi.or.cz

threaded search that executes simulations on CPUs, and computes policy and value networks in parallel on GPUs. AlphaGo used 40 search threads, 48 CPU cores, and 8 GPUs. A distributed version was also developed, to make use of a cluster of machines. It has been run on 1202 CPUs and 176 GPUs.

Google developed a special kind of GPU optimized for tensor computations in TensorFlow, named TPU, for tensor processing unit. DeepMind started using TPUs for AlphaGo in 2016. TPUs are designed for high-throughput low-precision computations (as low as 8-bit precision) whereas GPUs are typically optimized for 32- or 64-bit precision operations, and memory throughput is often a bottleneck [341].

B.2 AlphaGo Zero

A year later, AlphaGo Zero was introduced. The paper by Silver et al. [626] contains all the details. We highlight some here.

Detailed Self-Play Training

Let us look at how self-play is implemented. The neural network is trained as follows. A self-play reinforcement learning algorithm uses MCTS to play each move. First, the neural network is initialized to random weights θ_0. At each subsequent iteration i, games of self-play, or episodes, are generated, consisting of a sequence of moves. For each move of each episode t, an MCTS search π_t is performed using the previous neural network θ_{i-1} and a move is played sampled from π_t. The game t terminates when both players pass at step T at which point the game is scored $z = \{-1, +1\}$. The data are stored in a state-policy-distribution-reward triple (s_t, π_t, z_t) as examples in the example buffer for training the network parameters θ_i. The network $(p, v) = f_{\theta_i}(s)$ is trained by sampling uniformly over the example triples of all time steps (episodes) of the last iterations of self-play. A loss function is chosen to minimize the error between predicted value v and self-play outcome z, and to maximize the similarity of predicted move probabilities p and search probabilities π. Policy and value were used as a combined loss function that sums over the mean squared value error and cross entropy policy losses: $l = (z - v)^2 - \pi^T \log p + c\|\theta\|^2$, where c is the controlling parameter for L2 weight regularization to prevent overfitting [250, 626].

Network Architecture

The new function approximation architecture is simpler than in AlphaGo. It consists of one residual network (Sect. 6.2.1) instead of a value net, a slow selection policy net, and a fast rollout policy net. The ResNet has one input and two outputs: a policy head and a value head. The ResNet is trained by self-play; the databases of positions

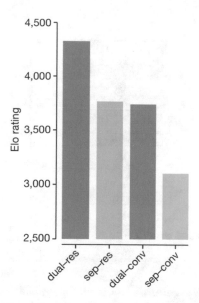

Fig. B.1 Comparison of dual-headed and separate, and of convolutional and residual networks [626]

for supervised and reinforcement learning have disappeared. MCTS no longer does rollouts, so the fast rollout net has gone as well.

It is reported that combining policy and value into a single network slightly reduces move prediction accuracy, but also reduces the value error. It improved playing performance in AlphaGo Zero by 600 Elo points, in part because the dual objective regularizes the network better.

Figure B.1 shows the difference in performance between the combined dual policy/value network and the separate networks, and the convolutional and residual networks [626].

The ResNet consists of blocks of convolutions [281] with batch normalization [328] and ReLU units. Interestingly, after experimenting with 40 block ResNets against 20 block ResNets, the team decided to use the 20 block net in the tournament version of the player. The added complexity of 40 block nets did not increase performance enough to outweigh computational cost.

As before, neural network parameters are optimized by stochastic gradient descent with momentum and learning rate annealing. In a comparison against AlphaGo the ResNet was more accurate, achieved lower errors and improved performance in AlphaGo by over 600 Elo [626].

The input to the neural network is a $19 \times 19 \times 17$ image stack comprising 17 binary feature planes. The 17 feature planes contain the current board and a history of the 8 previous moves, both for black and for white, and the color to play. The input features are processed by a residual network tower. The tower consists of a single convolutional block followed by either 19 or 39 residual blocks, one of which is shown in Fig. B.2. The total network depth, in the 20 or 40 block network, is thus 39

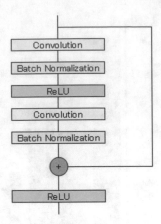

Fig. B.2 AlphaGo Zero residual block [626]

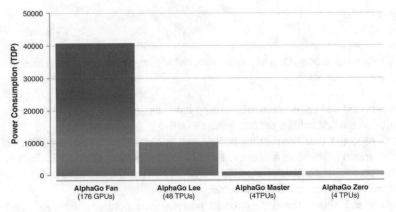

Fig. B.3 Comparison of power consumption for training [582]

or 79 parameterized layers (since a ResNet block has 2 convolutional layers) plus 2 layers for the policy head and 3 layers for the value head, consisting of a block ending in a fully connected layer. See the paper for details [626].

Compute Hardware

Originally, each neural network was trained with TensorFlow, with 64 GPU workers and 19 CPU parameter servers. Later, TPUs were used. Figure B.3 shows the difference in total dissipated power consumption between the different versions of AlphaGo.

Search Algorithm

The search algorithm of AlphaGo Zero is MCTS. For selection, the same P-UCT [561] variant was used, which incorporates priors from the policy head, and not RAVE. This MCTS did not use rollouts at the leaves of the MCTS tree, but value head lookups. In the self-play, a total of 25,000 games were played in each self-play iteration. MCTS performs 1600 simulations for each move. MCTS hyperparameters were selected by Gaussian process optimization [617].

Input/Output Features

The input planes of AlphaGo Zero are simpler than in AlphaGo. Only the board information is used; no additional information such as ko, or liberties, is used. Even the basic heuristic of not playing moves that would fill the player's own eyes is excluded. AlphaGo Zero learns from scratch. No heuristic information is given to the program.

B.3 AlphaZero

Again a year later Silver et al. [625] published their AlphaZero paper, showing how the simpler architecture of AlphaGo Zero was also a more general architecture. This appendix describes some of the more technical elements.

Input/Output Features

The input and output layers are different for each game. For Go, the same $19 \times 19 \times 17$ planes as in AlphaGo Zero were used in AlphaZero, where 8 moves of history is encoded in addition to the stones on the board (Table 7.2). Move encoding in Go is simply a coordinate of a stone.

For Chess, a similar encoding scheme is used, although more elaborate using many more planes. The scheme encodes all possible moves from a position in different binary planes. In Chess there is a greater variety of possible moves, and the encoding scheme therefore uses more planes than in Go, $8 \times 8 \times 73$.[2]

Shogi has an even greater variety of moves, leading to a stack of $9 \times 9 \times 139$ planes as input. The paper mentions that experiments with different coding schemes worked as well, although training efficiency was affected somewhat.

---

[2] Silver et al. [625] contains the details of their elaborate encoding. The encoding scheme is quite complex, although it is noted that simpler encoding schemes also work.

Compute Hardware

Both Stockfish (Chess) and Elmo (Shogi) ran with 44 threads on 44 cores (2 Intel Xeon Broadwell CPUs with 22 cores) with 32 GB transposition tables and 3 hour per match time controls with 15 seconds per move extra. AlphaZero ran on a single machine with 44 CPU cores, and 4 first-generation TPUs.

Appendix C
Matches of Fan Hui, Lee Sedol, and Ke Jie

This appendix contains the games of the matches played by AlphaGo against Fan Hui, Lee Sedol, and Ke Jie.

Note that games can be played online at DeepMind.[1] You can also find match commmentary at this site. SGF files of the games are easily found online, allowing interactive replay with an SGF viewer. The match diagrams below are based on [623, 626].

Fan Hui

In October 2015 European Champion Fan Hui 2p played the following games against AlphaGo in London. AlphaGo won 5-0. See the games in Figs. C.1–C.5.

Lee Sedol

In March 2016 Lee Sedol 9p played the following games against AlphaGo in Seoul. AlphaGo won 4-1. See Figs. C.6–C.10.

Ke Jie

In May 2017 Ke Jie 9p played the following games against AlphaGo in Wuzhen. AlphaGo won 3-0. See Figs. C.11–C.13. AlphaGo played white in game 1 and black in game 2 and 3.

---

[1]   https://deepmind.com/research/alphago/match-archive/alphago-games-english/

© Springer Nature Switzerland AG 2020
A. Plaat, *Learning to Play*, https://doi.org/10.1007/978-3-030-59238-7

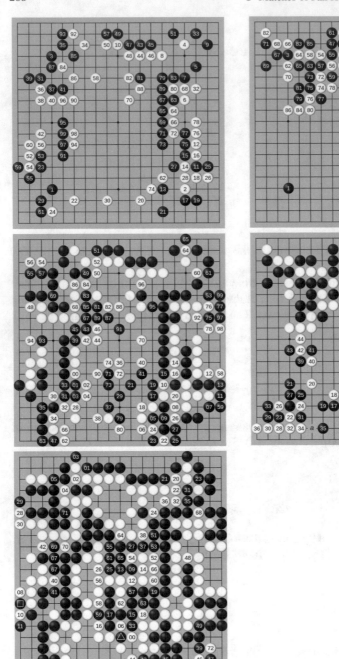

Fig. C.1 Game 1 Fan Hui (black) vs. AlphaGo (white): move 1–99, move 100–199, and move 200–272. Move 234 is played at triangle, move 250 at square. AlphaGo won by 2.5 points.

Fig. C.2 Game 2 AlphaGo (black) vs. Fan Hui (white): move 1–99, and move 100–183 (move 182 at 169). AlphaGo did not play 135 at "a," but played a safer move to win. AlphaGo won by resignation.

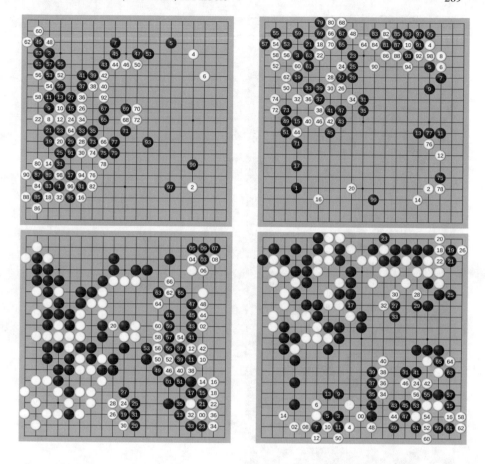

Fig. C.3 Game 3 Fan Hui (black) vs. AlphaGo (white): move 1–99, and move 100–166. AlphaGo won by resignation.

Fig. C.4 Game 4 AlphaGo (black) vs. Fan Hui (white): move 1–99 (move 96 at 10), and move 100–165. AlphaGo won by resignation.

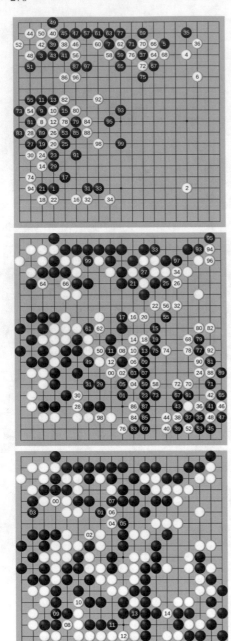

Fig. C.5 Game 5 Fan Hui (black) vs. AlphaGo
(white): move 1–99, move 100–199 (moves
151/157/163 at 141, 154/160 at 148), and move
200–214. AlphaGo won by resignation.

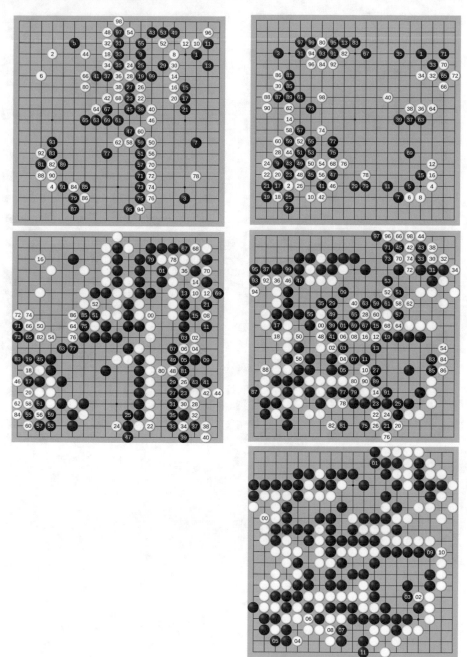

Fig. C.6 Game 1 Lee Sedol (black) vs. AlphaGo (white): move 1–99, and move 100–186. AlphaGo won by resignation.

Fig. C.7 Game 2 AlphaGo (black) vs. Lee Sedol (white): move 1–99, move 100–199, and move 200–211. Move 37 is a famous move by AlphaGo. AlphaGo won by resignation.

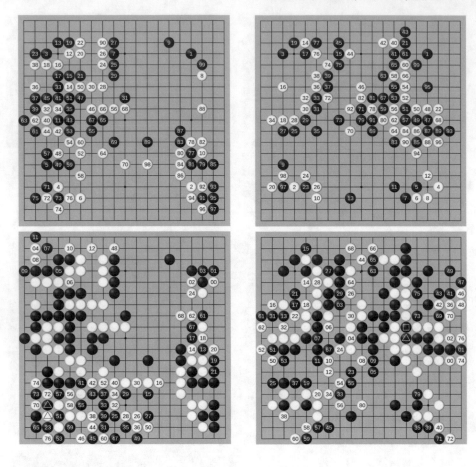

Fig. C.8 Game 3 Lee Sedol (black) vs. AlphaGo (white): move 1–99, and move 100–176 (move 122 at 113, 154 at white triangle, 163 at 145, 164 at 151, 166 and 171 at 160, 169 at 145, 175 at black triangle). AlphaGo won by resignation.

Fig. C.9 Game 4 AlphaGo (black) vs. Lee Sedol (white): move 1–99, and move 100–180 (move 177 at square, 178 at triangle). Move 78 by Lee Sedol is considered a brilliant move. Lee Sedol won by resignation.

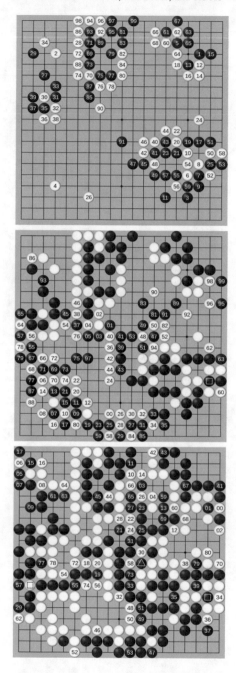

Fig. C.10 Game 5 Lee Sedol (black) vs. AlphaGo (white): move 1-99, move 100-199 (118 at 107, 161 at square), and move 200-280 (240 at 200, 271 at black square, 275 at white square, 276 at black triangle). AlphaGo won by resignation.

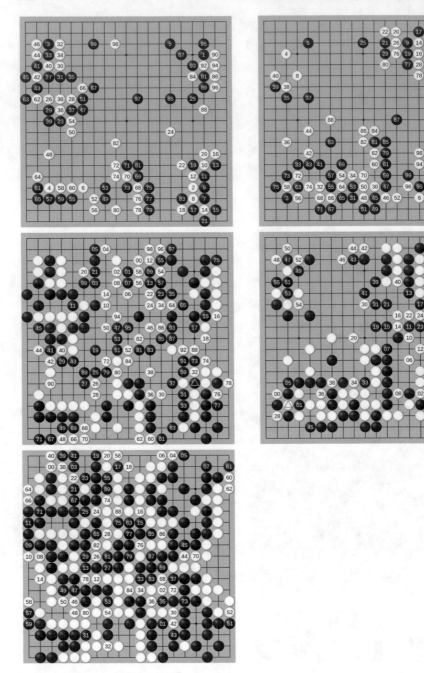

Fig. C.11 Game 1 Ke Jie (black) vs. AlphaGo (white): move 1-99, move 100-199 (139 at triangle), and move 200-289. AlphaGo won by resignation.

Fig. C.12 Game 2 AlphaGo (black) vs. Ke Jie (white): move 1-99, and move 100-155 (104/132/137 at triangle, 129/135 at 101). AlphaGo won by resignation.

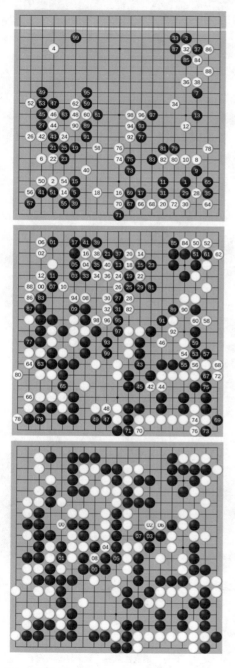

Fig. C.13 Game 3 AlphaGo (black) vs. Ke Jie (white): move 1-99, move 100-199, and move 200-209. AlphaGo won by resignation.

Appendix D
Learning to Play and Program Go and Chess

Go and Chess are challenging games. They challenge computers as well as humans, and they provide endless fun and enjoyment. If you would like to learn to play Go or Chess, then this appendix provides links to help you get started in the world of game playing. If you would like to learn to program these games, then you will find pointers here as well.

D.1 Learning to Play

D.1.1 Go

The best and most fun way to learn to play Go is by playing against people. Find a local club and go. Go is played by millions of people, and there are many clubs around the world. Your school may have a Go club. Search for "Go Club" on the internet and you will find nearby clubs where you will find people to play Go with, and you will start to learn this fascinating game. Once you make progress, you may even want to join one of the national Go associations. All addresses can be found easily online.

There are also many online possibilities to play Go. Table D.1 lists a few of the better known online Go servers. Just click on the link, maybe download a client, follow some games, and start playing. There are also tutorials and books on learning to play online (Table D.2), and in your library and book store.

D.1.2 Chess

Chess is a different game, with more types of pieces than Go, and a more tactical kind of play. Like Go, it is a game requiring a high level of intelligence to play well (and to program well). Chess has a long and distinguished history of well-known

© Springer Nature Switzerland AG 2020
A. Plaat, *Learning to Play*, https://doi.org/10.1007/978-3-030-59238-7

Server	Name	Link
OGS	Online Go Server	`https://online-go.com`
KGS	Kiseido Go Server	`http://www.gokgs.com`
IGS	Pandanet Internet Go Server	`http://www.pandanet-igs.com`
Tygem	Tygem Baduk	`http://www.tygembaduk.com`
Fox	Fox Weiqi (Chinese)	`https://www.foxwq.com`
Dragon	Dragon Go Server for correspondence	`https://www.dragongoserver.net`

Table D.1 Internet Go Servers

Tutorial	Link
Kiseido	`https://www.kiseido.com/ff.htm`
Nordic	`https://www.nordicgodojo.eu/post/212/a-simple-beginners-guide-to-go`
Online Go	`https://online-go.com/learn-to-play-go`
Wikipedia	`https://en.wikipedia.org/wiki/Go_(game)`

Table D.2 Go Tutorials

players and champions. Chances are that your school has a Chess club. Many books have been written, for beginners and for advanced players.

There are many servers on the Internet where you can play online Chess. Table D.3 lists a few of the better known online Chess servers. They also provide tutorial material on how to learn to play.

Server	Link
Chess.com	`https://chess.com`
Internet Chess Club	`http://chessclub.com`
Chessbase	`https://en.chessbase.com`
Chess24	`https://chess24.com/en/play/chess`
Lichess	`https://lichess.org`
Wikipedia	`https://en.wikipedia.org/wiki/Chess`

Table D.3 Internet Chess Resources

D.2 Learning to Program

Software for Go and Chess is widely available. On your computer or phone you can probably find a program or app for playing Go or Chess.

There are also many resources avaliable if you want to learn how to program.

D.2.1 Go

For Go, there are three basic approaches: heuristic planning, MCTS, and self-play. Software for hand-held devices is typically of the first two categories, because of the computational demands of self-play. At Senseis.net[1] many articles can be found on computer Go for all three approaches. The Computer Go Server[2] allows Go programs to play against each other over the internet using the Go Text Protocol.[3] A mailing list for computer Go can be found here.[4]

Self-play environments were listed in a previous appendix in Table A.3. The environments are open-source, so you can learn from the code and experiment with your own improvements. A book devoted to building your own Alpha(Go) Zero clone is [537].

D.2.2 Chess

For Chess, there are also many open-source programs available. Most programs follow the classic and highly successful heuristic planning approach, see Table D.4. A valuable resource with a wealth of information is the Chess Programming Wiki.[5] Many of the concepts and programming tricks that are used in the programs are explained in the wiki.

Engine	Link
Stockfish	https://stockfishchess.org
Komodo	http://komodochess.com
Houdini	http://www.cruxis.com/chess/houdini.htm
Critter	http://www.vlasak.biz/critter/
Ethereal	https://github.com/AndyGrant/Ethereal
Gull	https://sourceforge.net/projects/gullchess/
Leela Chess Zero	https://github.com/LeelaChessZero/lc0

Table D.4 Open-source Chess Programs

---

[1] https://senseis.xmp.net/?ComputerGoProgramming

[2] http://www.yss-aya.com/cgos/19x19/standings.html

[3] http://www.lysator.liu.se/~gunnar/gtp/

[4] http://computer-go.org

[5] https://www.chessprogramming.org/Main_Page

D.3 Scientific Journals and Conferences

From an AI perspective the question whether a program can play games for which humans need intelligence, is a highly relevant question. Many of the papers on computer game programming have been published in AI journals (Table D.5 lists a few relevant journals). Games papers are often published at AI conferences (Table D.6 lists a few relevant conferences). Your library and the internet should have the issues and proceedings.

Most authors make their work available as preprint at the arXiv preprint server for early access before a paper is accepted for publication.[6] The latest news can be found at this server, unfiltered.

Abbreviation	Journal
PAMI	IEEE Transactions on Pattern Analysis and Machine Intelligence
AIJ	Artificial Intelligence Journal
JAIR	Journal of AI Research
ToG	IEEE Transactions on Games
ICGAJ	ICCA/ICGA Journal
Science	Science
Nature	Nature

Table D.5 Journals

Abbreviation	Conference
IJCAI	International Joint Conference on AI
AAAI	Association for the Advancement of AI
ECAI	European Conference on AI
FDG	Foundations of Digital Games
CoG	Conference on Games
NeurIPS	Neural Information Processing Systems
ICML	International Conference on Machine Learning
ICLR	International Conference on Learning Representations
ACC/ACG	Advances in Computer Chess/Games
CG	Conference on Computers and Games

Table D.6 Conferences

---

[6] https://arxiv.org/list/cs.AI/recent

Appendix E
Running Python

Python is a modern programming language that is quite popular in AI. Many machine learning packages have Python interfaces, such as TensorFlow and Keras. This appendix shows how to start working with Python. Python was developed by Guido van Rossum while he was a researcher at the national research center for mathematics and computer science CWI in Amsterdam [432].

Before you install Python you should check if it is already available on your computer. Start a terminal, or a command prompt, and, at the prompt $, type python. Now one of two things will have happened. If you see an error message then Python is not installed correctly on your computer. If you see a response of the form

```
Python 3.6.0 (v3.6.0:41df79263a11, Dec 22 2016, 17:23:13)
[GCC 4.2.1 (Apple Inc. build 5666) (dot 3)] on darwin
Type "help", "copyright", "credits" or "license" for more
                                               information.
>>>
```

then Python is working already on your computer. You can get out of Python by typing Ctrl-D or quit(). Interactive help is available by typing help(). You can skip the rest of this appendix, and start playing around with the examples and exercises. How to install TensorFlow and Keras is discussed in the chapters (Sect. 6.5).

To install Python, go to the python.org website.[1] Go to Downloads, click on it, and you should see the latest version of Python being offered for your current operating system (Linux, macOS, or Windows). Click the button to start the download, and when the download is finished after a few minutes, launch the installer. While you are waiting, browse around on the website to the Documentation section. There are great reference works and tutorials on learning Python. Please consult your library or bookstore or the Internet. Try Google or Stackoverflow.

One of the advantages of Python is the wealth of high-quality software packages that are available, especially for data science and artificial intelligence. Among them are popular packages such as scikit-learn, numpy, matplotlib, TensorFlow, PyTorch,

---

[1] https://www.python.org

© Springer Nature Switzerland AG 2020

A. Plaat, *Learning to Play*, https://doi.org/10.1007/978-3-030-59238-7

and Gym. These packages can be installed easily by typing `pip install numpy` for installing the numpy numerical package.

Python 2 and Python 3

There are two version of Python that you may encounter, version 2 and version 3. There are small but critical differences in the language. For example, the `print` statement in Python 2 does not use parentheses, but in Python 3 it follows the ordinary function call convention and it does.

We use Python 3 in this book, and I suggest you do the same. So if you start up `python` on your machine you may want to check for the version number that it prints. And perhaps install Python 3.

You may also want to consider using an integrated development environment of graphical editor, interpreter, and debugger to ease your development. PyCharm, Netbeans, Spyder, and Visual Studio are popular choices, but feel free to look around. Most are free or have free student editions.

Python is a highly popular programming language, because it is powerful and elegant, but also because it is easy and fun to learn to program in Python. Please go ahead and enjoy programming in Python!

References

1. Martín Abadi, Ashish Agarwal, Paul Barham, Eugene Brevdo, Zhifeng Chen, Craig Citro, Greg S. Corrado, Andy Davis, Jeffrey Dean, Matthieu Devin, Sanjay Ghemawat, Ian Goodfellow, Andrew Harp, Geoffrey Irving, Michael Isard, Yangqing Jia, Rafal Jozefowicz, Lukasz Kaiser, Manjunath Kudlur, Josh Levenberg, Dandelion Mané, Rajat Monga, Sherry Moore, Derek Murray, Chris Olah, Mike Schuster, Jonathon Shlens, Benoit Steiner, Ilya Sutskever, Kunal Talwar, Paul Tucker, Vincent Vanhoucke, Vijay Vasudevan, Fernanda Viégas, Oriol Vinyals, Pete Warden, Martin Wattenberg, Martin Wicke, Yuan Yu, and Xiaoqiang Zheng. TensorFlow: Large-scale machine learning on heterogeneous systems, 2015. Software available from tensorflow.org. 155, 255
2. Martín Abadi, Paul Barham, Jianmin Chen, Zhifeng Chen, Andy Davis, Jeffrey Dean, Matthieu Devin, Sanjay Ghemawat, Geoffrey Irving, Michael Isard, et al. Tensorflow: A system for large-scale machine learning. In *12th USENIX Symposium on Operating Systems Design and Implementation (OSDI 16)*, pages 265–283, 2016. 155, 255
3. Pieter Abbeel, Adam Coates, Morgan Quigley, and Andrew Y Ng. An application of reinforcement learning to aerobatic helicopter flight. In *Advances in Neural Information Processing Systems*, pages 1–8, 2007. 225, 232
4. Harold Abelson, Gerald Jay Sussman, and Julie Sussman. *Structure and interpretation of computer programs*. MIT Press, 1996. 164
5. Bruce Abramson. Expected-outcome: A general model of static evaluation. *IEEE Transactions on Pattern Analysis and Machine Intelligence*, 12(2):182–193, 1990. 115
6. L Victor Allis. *Searching for solutions in games and artificial intelligence*. PhD thesis, Maastricht University, 1994. 74, 75, 100
7. L Victor Allis, Maarten van der Meulen, and H Jaap Van Den Herik. Proof-number search. *Artificial Intelligence*, 66(1):91–124, 1994. 100
8. Ethem Alpaydin. *Introduction to machine learning*. MIT press, 2009. 51, 325
9. Ingo Althöfer. Root evaluation errors: How they arise and propagate. *ICGA Journal*, 11(2-3):55–63, 1988. 102
10. Thomas Anantharaman, Murray S Campbell, and Feng-hsiung Hsu. Singular extensions: Adding selectivity to brute-force searching. *Artificial Intelligence*, 43(1):99–109, 1990. 101
11. Takahisa Ando, Noriyuki Kobayashi, and Takao Uehara. Cooperation and competition of agents in the auction of computer bridge. *Electronics and Communications in Japan (Part III: Fundamental Electronic Science)*, 86(12):76–86, 2003. 240
12. Anonymous. Go AI strength vs. time. *Reddit post*, 2017. 211, 321
13. Thomas Anthony, Tom Eccles, Andrea Tacchetti, János Kramár, Ian Gemp, Thomas C Hudson, Nicolas Porcel, Marc Lanctot, Julien Pérolat, Richard Everett, et al. Learning to play no-press diplomacy with best response policy iteration. *arXiv preprint arXiv:2006.04635*, 2020. 240

© Springer Nature Switzerland AG 2020

A. Plaat, *Learning to Play*, https://doi.org/10.1007/978-3-030-59238-7

14. Thomas Anthony, Robert Nishihara, Philipp Moritz, Tim Salimans, and John Schulman. Policy gradient search: Online planning and expert iteration without search trees. *arXiv preprint arXiv:1904.03646*, 2019. 226

15. Thomas Anthony, Zheng Tian, and David Barber. Thinking fast and slow with deep learning and tree search. In *Advances in Neural Information Processing Systems*, pages 5360–5370, 2017. 184, 186

16. Antreas Antoniou, Harrison Edwards, and Amos Storkey. How to train your MAML. *arXiv preprint arXiv:1810.09502*, 2018. 221

17. Grigoris Antoniou and Frank Van Harmelen. *A semantic web primer*. 2004. 11, 245

18. Oleg Arenz. Monte Carlo Chess. Master's thesis, Universität Darmstadt, 2012. 232

19. Andreas Argyriou, Theodoros Evgeniou, and Massimiliano Pontil. Multi-task feature learning. In *Advances in Neural Information Processing Systems*, pages 41–48, 2007. 220

20. Broderick Arneson, Ryan B Hayward, and Philip Henderson. Monte Carlo Tree Search in Hex. *IEEE Transactions on Computational Intelligence and AI in Games*, 2(4):251–258, 2010. 133

21. John Asmuth, Lihong Li, Michael L Littman, Ali Nouri, and David Wingate. A Bayesian sampling approach to exploration in reinforcement learning. In *Proceedings of the Twenty-Fifth Conference on Uncertainty in Artificial Intelligence*, pages 19–26. AUAI Press, 2009. 227

22. Peter Auer. Using confidence bounds for exploitation-exploration trade-offs. *Journal of Machine Learning Research*, 3(Nov):397–422, 2002. 53, 122, 133

23. Peter Auer, Nicolo Cesa-Bianchi, and Paul Fischer. Finite-time analysis of the multiarmed bandit problem. *Machine Learning*, 47(2-3):235–256, 2002. 115, 122

24. Peter Auer and Ronald Ortner. UCB revisited: Improved regret bounds for the stochastic multi-armed bandit problem. *Periodica Mathematica Hungarica*, 61(1-2):55–65, 2010. 122

25. Tim Baarslag, Katsuhide Fujita, Enrico H Gerding, Koen Hindriks, Takayuki Ito, Nicholas R Jennings, Catholijn Jonker, Sarit Kraus, Raz Lin, Valentin Robu, et al. Evaluating practical negotiating agents: Results and analysis of the 2011 international competition. *Artificial Intelligence*, 198:73–103, 2013. 232, 253

26. Thomas Bäck. *Evolutionary algorithms in theory and practice: evolutionary strategies, evolutionary programming, genetic algorithms*. Oxford University Press, 1996. 222

27. Thomas Bäck and Hans-Paul Schwefel. An overview of evolutionary algorithms for parameter optimization. *Evolutionary Computation*, 1(1):1–23, 1993. 11, 222, 232

28. Adrià Puigdomènech Badia, Bilal Piot, Steven Kapturowski, Pablo Sprechmann, Alex Vitvitskyi, Daniel Guo, and Charles Blundell. Agent57: Outperforming the Atari human benchmark. *arXiv preprint arXiv:2003.13350*, 2020. 172, 190

29. Hendrik Baier and Peter D Drake. The power of forgetting: Improving the last-good-reply policy in Monte Carlo Go. *IEEE Transactions on Computational Intelligence and AI in Games*, 2(4):303–309, 2010. 260

30. Bowen Baker, Otkrist Gupta, Nikhil Naik, and Ramesh Raskar. Designing neural network architectures using reinforcement learning. *arXiv preprint arXiv:1611.02167*, 2016. 222

31. Bram Bakker and Jürgen Schmidhuber. Hierarchical reinforcement learning based on subgoal discovery and subpolicy specialization. In *Proc. of the 8-th Conf. on Intelligent Autonomous Systems*, pages 438–445, 2004. 232

32. Pierre Baldi, Peter Sadowski, and Daniel Whiteson. Searching for exotic particles in high-energy physics with deep learning. *Nature Communications*, 5:4308, 2014. 232

33. Bruce W Ballard. The *-minimax search procedure for trees containing chance nodes. *Artificial Intelligence*, 21(3):327–350, 1983. 100

34. Trapit Bansal, Jakub Pachocki, Szymon Sidor, Ilya Sutskever, and Igor Mordatch. Emergent complexity via multi-agent competition. *arXiv preprint arXiv:1710.03748*, 2017. 240

35. Nolan Bard, John Hawkin, Jonathan Rubin, and Martin Zinkevich. The annual computer poker competition. *AI Magazine*, 34(2):112, 2013. 241

36. Andrew G Barto and Sridhar Mahadevan. Recent advances in hierarchical reinforcement learning. *Discrete Event Dynamic Systems*, 13(1-2):41–77, 2003. 232

37. Thomas Bartz-Beielstein, Marco Chiarandini, Luís Paquete, and Mike Preuss. *Experimental methods for the analysis of optimization algorithms*. Springer, 2010. 67, 110

38. OpenAI Baselines. `https://openai.com/blog/openai-baselines-dqn/`, 2017. 174, 177

39. Petr Baudiš. Balancing MCTS by dynamically adjusting the komi value. *ICGA Journal*, 34(3):131–139, 2011. 259

40. Petr Baudiš and Jean-loup Gailly. Pachi: State of the art open source Go program. In *Advances in Computer Games*, pages 24–38. Springer, 2011. 116

41. Seth Baum. A survey of artificial general intelligence projects for ethics, risk, and policy. 2017. 17

42. Jonathan Baxter, Andrew Tridgell, and Lex Weaver. Knightcap: a chess program that learns by combining TD (λ) with game-tree search. *arXiv preprint cs/9901002*, 1999. 104, 231

43. Jonathan Baxter, Andrew Tridgell, and Lex Weaver. Learning to play chess using temporal differences. *Machine Learning*, 40(3):243–263, 2000. 231

44. Don Beal. Recent progress in understanding minimax search. In *Proceedings of the 1983 Annual Conference on Computers: Extending the Human Resource*, pages 164–169. ACM, 1983. 80, 92, 112

45. Don Beal. Experiments with the null move. *Advances in Computer Chess*, 5:65–79, 1989. 102

46. Don Beal. A generalised quiescence search algorithm. *Artificial Intelligence*, 43(1):85–98, 1990. 102, 106

47. Don Beal and Martin C Smith. Learning piece-square values using temporal differences. *ICGA Journal*, 22(4):223–235, 1999. 104

48. Don Beal and Martin C. Smith. Temporal difference learning for heuristic search and game playing. *Information Sciences*, 122(1):3–21, 2000. 231

49. Mark F Bear, Barry W Connors, and Michael A Paradiso. *Neuroscience*, volume 2. Lippincott Williams & Wilkins, 2007. 139

50. Harkirat Singh Behl, Atılım Güneş Baydin, and Philip HS Torr. Alpha MAML: Adaptive Model-Agnostic Meta-Learning. *arXiv preprint arXiv:1905.07435*, 2019. 221

51. Marc Bellemare, Joel Veness, and Michael Bowling. Bayesian learning of recursively factored environments. In *International Conference on Machine Learning*, pages 1211–1219, 2013. 227

52. Marc G Bellemare, Will Dabney, and Rémi Munos. A distributional perspective on reinforcement learning. *arXiv preprint arXiv:1707.06887*, 2017. 178, 180, 223

53. Marc G Bellemare, Yavar Naddaf, Joel Veness, and Michael Bowling. The Arcade Learning Environment: An evaluation platform for general agents. *Journal of Artificial Intelligence Research*, 47:253–279, 2013. 63, 171, 172, 173, 186, 213, 256

54. Richard Bellman. *Dynamic programming*. Courier Corporation, 1957, 2013. 49

55. Richard Bellman. On the application of dynamic programing to the determination of optimal play in chess and checkers. *Proceedings of the National Academy of Sciences*, 53(2):244–247, 1965. 105

56. Irwan Bello, Hieu Pham, Quoc V Le, Mohammad Norouzi, and Samy Bengio. Neural combinatorial optimization with reinforcement learning. *arXiv preprint arXiv:1611.09940*, 2016. 224

57. Yoshua Bengio. *Learning Deep Architectures for AI*. Now Publishers Inc, 2009. 141

58. Yoshua Bengio. Practical recommendations for gradient-based training of deep architectures. In *Neural networks: Tricks of the trade*, pages 437–478. Springer, 2012. 205

59. Yoshua Bengio, Samy Bengio, and Jocelyn Cloutier. Learning a synaptic learning rule. Technical report, Montreal, 1990. 220

60. Yoshua Bengio, Aaron Courville, and Pascal Vincent. Representation learning: A review and new perspectives. *IEEE Transactions on Pattern Analysis and Machine Intelligence*, 35(8):1798–1828, 2013. 142, 157, 232

61. Yoshua Bengio, Pascal Lamblin, Dan Popovici, and Hugo Larochelle. Greedy layer-wise training of deep networks. In *Advances in Neural Information Processing Systems*, pages 153–160, 2007. 142, 144

62. Yoshua Bengio, Jérôme Louradour, Ronan Collobert, and Jason Weston. Curriculum learning. In *Proceedings of the 26th Annual International Conference on Machine Learning*, pages 41–48, 2009. 142, 144, 205, 232

63. David B Benson. Life in the game of Go. *Information Sciences*, 10(1):17–29, 1976. 231

64. James Bergstra, Frédéric Bastien, Olivier Breuleux, Pascal Lamblin, Razvan Pascanu, Olivier Delalleau, Guillaume Desjardins, David Warde-Farley, Ian Goodfellow, Arnaud Bergeron, et al. Theano: Deep learning on GPUs with Python. In *NIPS 2011, BigLearning Workshop, Granada, Spain*, volume 3, pages 1–48. Citeseer, 2011. 155, 255

65. James Bergstra and Yoshua Bengio. Random search for hyper-parameter optimization. *Journal of Machine Learning Research*, 13(Feb):281–305, 2012. 221

66. James S Bergstra, Rémi Bardenet, Yoshua Bengio, and Balázs Kégl. Algorithms for hyper-parameter optimization. In *Advances in Neural Information Processing Systems*, pages 2546–2554, 2011. 222, 232

67. Elwyn Berlekamp and David Wolfe. *Mathematical Go: Chilling gets the last point*. AK Peters/CRC Press, 1994. 231

68. Hans J Berliner. Experiences in evaluation with BKG—a program that plays backgammon. In *IJCAI*, pages 428–433, 1977. 27

69. Hans J Berliner. Backgammon computer program beats world champion. *Artificial Intelligence*, 14(2):205–220, 1980. 27

70. Christopher Berner, Greg Brockman, Brooke Chan, Vicki Cheung, Przemysław Debiak, Christy Dennison, David Farhi, Quirin Fischer, Shariq Hashme, Chris Hesse, et al. Dota 2 with large scale deep reinforcement learning. *arXiv preprint arXiv:1912.06680*, 2019. 240

71. Tim Berners-Lee, James Hendler, Ora Lassila, et al. The semantic web. *Scientific American*, 284(5):28–37, 2001. 11

72. R Bertolami, H Bunke, S Fernandez, A Graves, M Liwicki, and J Schmidhuber. A novel connectionist system for improved unconstrained handwriting recognition. *IEEE Transactions on Pattern Analysis and Machine Intelligence*, 31(5), 2009. 162

73. Dimitri P Bertsekas. Rollout algorithms for discrete optimization: A survey. In *Handbook of combinatorial optimization*, pages 2989–3013. Springer, 2013. 130

74. Dimitri P Bertsekas and John Tsitsiklis. *Neuro-dynamic programming*. MIT Press Cambridge, 1996. 69

75. Shalabh Bhatnagar, Doina Precup, David Silver, Richard S Sutton, Hamid R Maei, and Csaba Szepesvári. Convergent temporal-difference learning with arbitrary smooth function approximation. In *Advances in Neural Information Processing Systems*, pages 1204–1212, 2009. 194

76. Wolfgang Bibel. *Automated theorem proving*. Springer Science & Business Media, 1987. 246

77. Darse Billings, Neil Burch, Aaron Davidson, Robert Holte, Jonathan Schaeffer, Terence Schauenberg, and Duane Szafron. Approximating game-theoretic optimal strategies for full-scale poker. In *IJCAI*, volume 3, page 661, 2003. 27

78. Darse Billings, Aaron Davidson, Jonathan Schaeffer, and Duane Szafron. The challenge of poker. *Artificial Intelligence*, 134(1-2):201–240, 2002. 241

79. Darse Billings, Aaron Davidson, Terence Schauenberg, Neil Burch, Michael Bowling, Robert Holte, Jonathan Schaeffer, and Duane Szafron. Game-tree search with adaptation in stochastic imperfect-information games. In *International Conference on Computers and Games*, pages 21–34. Springer, 2004. 241

80. Darse Billings, Denis Papp, Jonathan Schaeffer, and Duane Szafron. Opponent modeling in poker. *AAAI/IAAI*, 493:499, 1998. 105

81. Christopher M Bishop. *Pattern recognition and machine learning*. Information science and statistics. Springer Verlag, Heidelberg, 2006. 18, 60, 136, 137, 151, 194

82. Christopher M Bishop et al. *Neural networks for pattern recognition*. Oxford University Press, 1995. 141

83. Yngvi Bjornsson and Hilmar Finnsson. Cadiaplayer: A simulation-based general game player. *IEEE Transactions on Computational Intelligence and AI in Games*, 1(1):4–15, 2009. 244

84. Yngvi Björnsson and Tony A Marsland. Multi-cut $\alpha\beta$-pruning in game-tree search. *Theoretical Computer Science*, 252(1-2):177–196, 2001. 102

85. Eric Bonabeau, Marco Dorigo, Guy Theraulaz, et al. *Swarm intelligence: from natural to artificial systems*. Number 1. Oxford University Press, 1999. 11

86. Édouard Bonnet, Florian Jamain, and Abdallah Saffidine. On the complexity of trick-taking card games. In *IJCAI*, pages 482–488, 2013. 74

87. Mark Boon. Overzicht van de ontwikkeling van een Go spelend programma. 1991. 114

88. Bernhard E Boser, Isabelle M Guyon, and Vladimir N Vapnik. A training algorithm for optimal margin classifiers. In *Proceedings of the Fifth Annual Workshop on Computational learning theory*, pages 144–152. ACM, 1992. 193

89. Tibor Bosse, Catholijn M Jonker, and Jan Treur. Formalisation of Damasio's theory of emotion, feeling and core consciousness. *Consciousness and Cognition*, 17(1):94–113, 2008. 247

90. Bruno Bouzy and Bernard Helmstetter. Monte Carlo Go developments. In *Advances in Computer Games*, pages 159–174. Springer, 2004. 115, 119

91. Bruno Bouzy, Marc Métivier, and Damien Pellier. MCTS experiments on the Voronoi game. In *Advances in Computer Games*, pages 96–107. Springer, 2011. 125

92. Michael Bowling, Neil Burch, Michael Johanson, and Oskari Tammelin. Heads-up limit hold'em poker is solved. *Science*, 347(6218):145–149, 2015. 40, 232, 240, 241

93. Michael Bowling, Nicholas Abou Risk, Nolan Bard, Darse Billings, Neil Burch, Joshua Davidson, John Hawkin, Robert Holte, Michael Johanson, Morgan Kan, et al. A demonstration of the polaris poker system. In *Proceedings of The 8th International Conference on Autonomous Agents and Multiagent Systems-Volume 2*, pages 1391–1392. International Foundation for Autonomous Agents and Multiagent Systems, 2009. 40, 241

94. Ivan Bratko. *Prolog programming for artificial intelligence*. Pearson Education, 2001. 245

95. Pavel Brazdil, Christophe Giraud Carrier, Carlos Soares, and Ricardo Vilalta. *Metalearning: Applications to data mining*. Springer Science & Business Media, 2008. 220

96. Eric Brochu, Vlad M Cora, and Nando De Freitas. A tutorial on Bayesian optimization of expensive cost functions, with application to active user modeling and hierarchical reinforcement learning. *arXiv preprint arXiv:1012.2599*, 2010. 227

97. Mark G Brockington. Keyano unplugged—the construction of an Othello program. Technical report, Technical Report TR 97-05, Department of Computing Science, University of Alberta, 1997. 103

98. Greg Brockman, Vicki Cheung, Ludwig Pettersson, Jonas Schneider, John Schulman, Jie Tang, and Wojciech Zaremba. OpenAI Gym. *arXiv preprint arXiv:1606.01540*, 2016. 186, 213, 256

99. Joost Broekens. Emotion and reinforcement: affective facial expressions facilitate robot learning. In *Artifical Intelligence for Human Computing*, pages 113–132. Springer, 2007. 247

100. Joost Broekens, Marcel Heerink, Henk Rosendal, et al. Assistive social robots in elderly care: a review. *Gerontechnology*, 8(2):94–103, 2009. 232

101. Rodney A Brooks. Intelligence without representation. *Artificial Intelligence*, 47(1-3):139–159, 1991. 11

102. Noam Brown, Adam Lerer, Sam Gross, and Tuomas Sandholm. Deep counterfactual regret minimization. *arXiv preprint arXiv:1811.00164*, 2018. 242

103. Noam Brown and Tuomas Sandholm. Superhuman AI for heads-up no-limit poker: Libratus beats top professionals. *Science*, 359(6374):418–424, 2018. 27, 40, 240, 241

104. Noam Brown and Tuomas Sandholm. Superhuman AI for multiplayer poker. *Science*, 365(6456):885–890, 2019. 28, 40, 242, 252

105. Noam Brown, Tuomas Sandholm, and Brandon Amos. Depth-limited solving for imperfect-information games. *arXiv preprint arXiv:1805.08195*, 2018. 40

106. Cameron Browne. Hex strategy. *AK Peters, Wellesley MA*, 2000. 132

107. Cameron Browne, Dennis JNJ Soemers, and Eric Piette. Strategic features for general games. In *KEG@ AAAI*, pages 70–75, 2019. 227

108. Cameron B Browne, Edward Powley, Daniel Whitehouse, Simon M Lucas, Peter I Cowling, Philipp Rohlfshagen, Stephen Tavener, Diego Perez, Spyridon Samothrakis, and Simon Colton. A survey of Monte Carlo Tree Search methods. *IEEE Transactions on Computational Intelligence and AI in Games*, 4(1):1–43, 2012. 113, 116, 117, 118, 119, 120, 126, 128, 132, 133, 202, 259, 320, 321, 325

109. Bernd Brügmann. Monte Carlo Go. Technical report, Syracuse University, 1993. 115, 119, 128

110. Bruno Buchberger, George E Collins, Rüdiger Loos, and Rudolph Albrecht. Computer algebra symbolic and algebraic computation. *ACM SIGSAM Bulletin*, 16(4):5–5, 1982. 11

111. Cristian Buciluă, Rich Caruana, and Alexandru Niculescu-Mizil. Model compression. In *Proceedings of the 12th ACM SIGKDD International Conference on Knowledge Discovery and Data Mining*, pages 535–541, 2006. 227

112. Edmund K Burke, Michel Gendreau, Matthew Hyde, Graham Kendall, Gabriela Ochoa, Ender Özcan, and Rong Qu. Hyper-heuristics: A survey of the state of the art. *Journal of the Operational Research Society*, 64(12):1695–1724, 2013. 222

113. Michael Buro. Logistello: A strong learning Othello program. In *19th Annual Conference Gesellschaft für Klassifikation eV*, volume 2. Citeseer, 1995. 26, 36, 184, 231

114. Michael Buro. Statistical feature combination for the evaluation of game positions. *Journal of Artificial Intelligence Research*, 3:373–382, 1995. 81

115. Michael Buro. Experiments with Multi-ProbCut and a new high-quality evaluation function for Othello. *Games in AI Research*, pages 77–96, 1997. 98, 102, 103, 112, 231

116. Michael Buro. The Othello match of the year: Takeshi Murakami vs. Logistello. *ICGA Journal*, 20(3):189–193, 1997. 36

117. Michael Buro. The evolution of strong Othello programs. In *Entertainment Computing*, pages 81–88. Springer, 2003. 36

118. Lucian Busoniu, Robert Babuska, and Bart De Schutter. A comprehensive survey of multiagent reinforcement learning. *IEEE Transactions on Systems, Man, And Cybernetics-Part C: Applications and Reviews, 38 (2), 2008*, 2008. 224

119. Murray Campbell, A Joseph Hoane Jr, and Feng-hsiung Hsu. Deep Blue. *Artificial Intelligence*, 134(1-2):57–83, 2002. 35, 104, 185

120. Rich Caruana. Multitask learning. *Machine Learning*, 28(1):41–75, 1997. 220

121. Rich Caruana, Steve Lawrence, and C Lee Giles. Overfitting in neural nets: Backpropagation, conjugate gradient, and early stopping. In *Advances in Neural Information Processing Systems*, pages 402–408, 2001. 151

122. Cristiano Castelfranchi, Frank Dignum, Catholijn M Jonker, and Jan Treur. Deliberative normative agents: Principles and architecture. In *International Workshop on Agent Theories, Architectures, and Languages*, pages 364–378. Springer, 1999. 232

123. Pablo Samuel Castro, Subhodeep Moitra, Carles Gelada, Saurabh Kumar, and Marc G Bellemare. Dopamine: A research framework for deep reinforcement learning. *arXiv preprint arXiv:1812.06110*, 2018. 256

124. Tristan Cazenave, Yen-Chi Chen, Guan-Wei Chen, Shi-Yu Chen, Xian-Dong Chiu, Julien Dehos, Maria Elsa, Qucheng Gong, Hengyuan Hu, Vasil Khalidov, et al. Polygames: Improved zero learning. *arXiv preprint arXiv:2001.09832*, 2020. 257, 258

125. Tristan Cazenave and Bernard Helmstetter. Combining tactical search and Monte-Carlo in the game of Go. *CIG*, 5:171–175, 2005. 115

126. Gregory Chaitin. The limits of reason. *Scientific American*, 294(3):74–81, 2006. 246

127. Hyeong Soo Chang, Michael C Fu, Jiaqiao Hu, and Steven I Marcus. An adaptive sampling algorithm for solving Markov decision processes. *Operations Research*, 53(1):126–139, 2005. 115, 122

128. Henry Charlesworth. Application of self-play reinforcement learning to a four-player game of imperfect information. *arXiv preprint arXiv:1808.10442*, 2018. 224

129. Guillaume Chaslot. *Monte-Carlo tree search*. PhD thesis, Maastricht University, 2010. 116, 119, 128, 133, 259

130. Guillaume Chaslot, Sander Bakkes, Istvan Szita, and Pieter Spronck. Monte-Carlo tree search: A new framework for game AI. In *AIIDE*, 2008. 116, 125, 133

131. Guillaume Chaslot, Mark HM Winands, and H Jaap van den Herik. Parallel Monte-Carlo tree search. In *International Conference on Computers and Games*, pages 60–71. Springer, 2008. 129, 134, 260

132. Guillaume MJB Chaslot, Mark HM Winands, H Jaap van den Herik, Jos WHM Uiterwijk, and Bruno Bouzy. Progressive strategies for Monte-Carlo tree search. *New Mathematics and Natural Computation*, 4(03):343–357, 2008. 259

133. Kumar Chellapilla and David B Fogel. Evolving neural networks to play checkers without relying on expert knowledge. *IEEE Transactions on Neural Networks*, 10(6):1382–1391, 1999. 171, 193, 231

134. Ken Chen and Zhixing Chen. Static analysis of life and death in the game of Go. *Information Sciences*, 121(1-2):113–134, 1999. 114

135. Xinlei Chen, Hao Fang, Tsung-Yi Lin, Ramakrishna Vedantam, Saurabh Gupta, Piotr Dollár, and C Lawrence Zitnick. Microsoft COCO captions: Data collection and evaluation server. *arXiv preprint arXiv:1504.00325*, 2015. 163, 320

136. Yu Cheng, Duo Wang, Pan Zhou, and Tao Zhang. A survey of model compression and acceleration for deep neural networks. *arXiv preprint arXiv:1710.09282*, 2017. 227

137. Ping-Chung Chi and Dana S Nau. Comparison of the minimax and product back-up rules in a variety of games. In *Search in artificial intelligence*, pages 450–471. Springer, 1988. 100

138. Jaeyoung Choi, Jack J Dongarra, and David W Walker. PB-BLAS: a set of parallel block basic linear algebra subprograms. *Concurrency: Practice and Experience*, 8(7):517–535, 1996. 155

139. Francois Chollet. *Deep learning with Python*. Manning Publications Co., 2017. 155, 255

140. François Chollet et al. Keras. https://keras.io, 2015. 255

141. Patryk Chrabaszcz, Ilya Loshchilov, and Frank Hutter. Back to basics: Benchmarking canonical evolution strategies for playing Atari. *arXiv preprint arXiv:1802.08842*, 2018. 223

142. Dan Cireşan, Ueli Meier, and Jürgen Schmidhuber. Multi-column deep neural networks for image classification. *arXiv preprint arXiv:1202.2745*, 2012. 147

143. Dan Claudiu Cireşan, Ueli Meier, Luca Maria Gambardella, and Jürgen Schmidhuber. Deep, big, simple neural nets for handwritten digit recognition. *Neural Computation*, 22(12):3207–3220, 2010. 155

144. Christopher Clark and Amos Storkey. Teaching deep convolutional neural networks to play Go. arxiv preprint. *arXiv preprint arXiv:1412.3409*, 1, 2014. 171, 193, 231

145. Christopher Clark and Amos Storkey. Training deep convolutional neural networks to play Go. In *International Conference on Machine Learning*, pages 1766–1774, 2015. 184, 193, 231

146. Caroline Claus and Craig Boutilier. The dynamics of reinforcement learning in cooperative multiagent systems. *AAAI/IAAI*, 1998:746–752, 1998. 224

147. William F Clocksin and Christopher S Mellish. *Programming in Prolog: Using the ISO standard*. Springer Science & Business Media, 1981. 11, 245

148. Simon Colton. The painting fool: Stories from building an automated painter. In *Computers and creativity*, pages 3–38. Springer, 2012. 246

149. Kevin Coplan. A special-purpose machine for an improved search algorithm for deep chess combinations. In *Advances in Computer Chess*, pages 25–43. Elsevier, 1982. 98

150. Rémi Coulom. Go ratings. https://www.goratings.org/en/history/. 39

151. Rémi Coulom. Efficient selectivity and backup operators in Monte-Carlo Tree Search. In *International Conference on Computers and Games*, pages 72–83. Springer, 2006. 113, 115, 133

152. Rémi Coulom. Monte-Carlo tree search in Crazy Stone. In *Proc. Game Prog. Workshop, Tokyo, Japan*, pages 74–75, 2007. 115, 116, 119

153. Rémi Coulom. The Monte-Carlo revolution in Go. In *The Japanese-French Frontiers of Science Symposium (JFFoS 2008), Roscoff, France*, 2009. 115

154. Joseph C Culberson and Jonathan Schaeffer. Pattern databases. *Computational Intelligence*, 14(3):318–334, 1998. 105, 119

155. Ken Currie and Austin Tate. O-plan: the open planning architecture. *Artificial Intelligence*, 52(1):49–86, 1991. 226

156. George Cybenko. Approximations by superpositions of a sigmoidal function. *Mathematics of Control, Signals and Systems*, 2:183–192, 1989. 141

157. Kamil Czarnogórski. Monte Carlo Tree Search beginners guide https://int8.io/monte-carlo-tree-search-beginners-guide/, 2018. 118, 120, 325

158. Will Dabney, Zeb Kurth-Nelson, Naoshige Uchida, Clara Kwon Starkweather, Demis Hassabis, Rémi Munos, and Matthew Botvinick. A distributional code for value in dopamine-based reinforcement learning. *Nature*, pages 1–5, 2020. 180

159. Shubhomoy Das, Weng-Keen Wong, Thomas Dietterich, Alan Fern, and Andrew Emmott. Incorporating expert feedback into active anomaly discovery. In *2016 IEEE 16th International Conference on Data Mining (ICDM)*, pages 853–858. IEEE, 2016. 206

160. Omid E David, Nathan S Netanyahu, and Lior Wolf. Deepchess: End-to-end deep neural network for automatic learning in chess. In *International Conference on Artificial Neural Networks*, pages 88–96. Springer, 2016. 104, 184, 193, 231

161. Omid E David, H Jaap van den Herik, Moshe Koppel, and Nathan S Netanyahu. Genetic algorithms for evolving computer chess programs. *IEEE Transactions on Evolutionary Computation*, 18(5):779–789, 2014. 81

162. Omid David-Tabibi, Moshe Koppel, and Nathan S Netanyahu. Genetic algorithms for mentor-assisted evaluation function optimization. In *Proceedings of the 10th Annual Conference on Genetic and Evolutionary Computation*, pages 1469–1476. ACM, 2008. 104

163. Morton D Davis. *Game theory: a nontechnical introduction*. Courier Corporation, 2012. 21

164. Arie De Bruin, Wim Pijls, and Aske Plaat. Solution trees as a basis for game-tree search. *ICCA Journal*, 17(4):207–219, 1994. 83

165. Luis M De Campos, Juan M Fernandez-Luna, José A Gámez, and José M Puerta. Ant colony optimization for learning Bayesian networks. *International Journal of Approximate Reasoning*, 31(3):291–311, 2002. 227

166. Jeffrey De Fauw, Joseph R Ledsam, Bernardino Romera-Paredes, Stanislav Nikolov, Nenad Tomasev, Sam Blackwell, Harry Askham, Xavier Glorot, Brendan O'Donoghue, Daniel Visentin, et al. Clinically applicable deep learning for diagnosis and referral in retinal disease. *Nature Medicine*, 24(9):1342, 2018. 232

167. Dave De Jonge. *Negotiations over large agreement spaces*. PhD thesis, Universitat Autònoma de Barcelona, 2015. 240

168. Dave De Jonge, Tim Baarslag, Reyhan Aydoğan, Catholijn Jonker, Katsuhide Fujita, and Takayuki Ito. The challenge of negotiation in the game of diplomacy. In *International Conference on Agreement Technologies*, pages 100–114. Springer, 2018. 21, 240

169. Dave De Jonge and Carles Sierra. D-brane: a Diplomacy playing agent for automated negotiations research. *Applied Intelligence*, 47(1):158–177, 2017. 240

170. Dave De Jonge and Dongmo Zhang. Automated negotiations for general game playing. In *Proceedings of the 16th Conference on Autonomous Agents and MultiAgent Systems*, pages 371–379. International Foundation for Autonomous Agents and Multiagent Systems, 2017. 240

171. Rina Dechter. *Learning while searching in constraint-satisfaction problems*. University of California, Computer Science Department, 1986. 153

172. Jia Deng, Wei Dong, Richard Socher, Li-Jia Li, Kai Li, and Li Fei-Fei. Imagenet: A large-scale hierarchical image database. In *2009 IEEE Conference on Computer Vision and Pattern Recognition*, pages 248–255. Ieee, 2009. 152, 156

173. Prafulla Dhariwal, Christopher Hesse, Oleg Klimov, Alex Nichol, Matthias Plappert, Alec Radford, John Schulman, Szymon Sidor, Yuhuai Wu, and Peter Zhokhov. OpenAI baselines. https://github.com/openai/baselines, 2017. 189, 190, 256, 325

174. Philip K Dick. Do androids dream of electric sheep? 1968. *New York: Del Rey*, 1996. 194

175. Dirk Dickmanns, Jürgen Schmidhuber, and Andreas Winklhofer. Der genetische Algorithmus: Eine Implementierung in Prolog. *Fortgeschrittenenpraktikum, Institut für Informatik, Lehrstuhl Prof. Radig, Technische Universit at München*, 1987. 220

176. Thomas G Dietterich. Hierarchical reinforcement learning with the MAXQ value function decomposition. *Journal of Artificial Intelligence Research*, 13:227–303, 2000. 63

177. Thang Doan, Joao Monteiro, Isabela Albuquerque, Bogdan Mazoure, Audrey Durand, Joelle Pineau, and R Devon Hjelm. On-line adaptative curriculum learning for GANs. In *Proceedings of the AAAI Conference on Artificial Intelligence*, volume 33, pages 3470–3477, 2019. 206

178. Samuel Dodge and Lina Karam. A study and comparison of human and deep learning recognition performance under visual distortions. In *Computer Communication and Networks (ICCCN), 2017 26th International Conference on*, pages 1–7. IEEE, 2017. 159

179. Jeffrey Donahue, Lisa Anne Hendricks, Sergio Guadarrama, Marcus Rohrbach, Subhashini Venugopalan, Kate Saenko, and Trevor Darrell. Long-term recurrent convolutional networks for visual recognition and description. In *Proceedings of the IEEE Conference on Computer Vision and Pattern Recognition*, pages 2625–2634, 2015. 165

180. Jack J Dongarra, Jeremy Du Croz, Sven Hammarling, and Richard J Hanson. An extended set of FORTRAN basic linear algebra subprograms. *ACM Transactions on Mathematical Software (TOMS)*, 14(1):1–17, 1988. 155

181. Christian Donninger. Null move and deep search. *ICGA Journal*, 16(3):137–143, 1993. 98, 103, 112

182. Derek Doran, Sarah Schulz, and Tarek R Besold. What does explainable AI really mean? a new conceptualization of perspectives. *arXiv preprint arXiv:1710.00794*, 2017. 227

183. Marco Dorigo and Luca Maria Gambardella. Ant colony system: a cooperative learning approach to the traveling salesman problem. *IEEE Transactions on Evolutionary Computation*, 1(1):53–66, 1997. 11

184. Kenji Doya. Reinforcement learning in continuous time and space. *Neural Computation*, 12(1):219–245, 2000. 225

185. Anders Drachen, Matthew Yancey, John Maguire, Derrek Chu, Iris Yuhui Wang, Tobias Mahlmann, Matthias Schubert, and Diego Klabjan. Skill-based differences in spatio-temporal team behaviour in Defence of the Ancients 2 (DOTA 2). In *2014 IEEE Games Media Entertainment*, pages 1–8. IEEE, 2014. 240

186. Sacha Droste and Johannes Fürnkranz. Learning of piece values for chess variants. Technical report, Tech. Rep. TUD–KE–2008-07, Knowledge Engineering Group, TU Darmstadt, 2008. 104

187. Yan Duan, Xi Chen, Rein Houthooft, John Schulman, and Pieter Abbeel. Benchmarking deep reinforcement learning for continuous control. In *International Conference on Machine Learning*, pages 1329–1338, 2016. 182

188. Yan Duan, John Schulman, Xi Chen, Peter L Bartlett, Ilya Sutskever, and Pieter Abbeel. RL^2: Fast reinforcement learning via slow reinforcement learning. *arXiv preprint arXiv:1611.02779*, 2016. 221

189. John Duchi, Elad Hazan, and Yoram Singer. Adaptive subgradient methods for online learning and stochastic optimization. *Journal of Machine Learning Research*, 12(Jul):2121–2159, 2011. 141

190. Richard D Duke and Jac Geurts. *Policy games for strategic management*. Rozenberg Publishers, 2004. 21

191. Gabriel Dulac-Arnold, Richard Evans, Hado van Hasselt, Peter Sunehag, Timothy Lillicrap, Jonathan Hunt, Timothy Mann, Theophane Weber, Thomas Degris, and Ben Coppin. Deep reinforcement learning in large discrete action spaces. *arXiv preprint arXiv:1512.07679*, 2015. 225

192. Adrien Ecoffet, Joost Huizinga, Joel Lehman, Kenneth O Stanley, and Jeff Clune. Go-explore: a new approach for hard-exploration problems. *arXiv preprint arXiv:1901.10995*, 2019. 225

193. Daniel James Edwards and TP Hart. The alpha-beta heuristic. Technical Report AI Memo 030, MIT, 1961. 103

194. Jeffrey L Elman. Learning and development in neural networks: The importance of starting small. *Cognition*, 48(1):71–99, 1993. 207, 250

195. Ahmed A Elnaggar, Mahmoud Gadallah, Mostafa Abdel Aziem, and Hesham El-Deeb. A comparative study of game tree searching methods. *International Journal of Advanced Computer Science and Applications*, 5(5):68–77, 2014. 77, 320

196. Arpad E Elo. *The rating of chessplayers, past and present*. Arco Pub., 1978. 18

197. Thomas Elsken, Jan Hendrik Metzen, and Frank Hutter. Neural architecture search: A survey. *arXiv preprint arXiv:1808.05377*, 2018. 222

198. Herbert D Enderton. The Golem Go program. Technical report, Carnegie Mellon University, 1991. 185

199. Markus Enzenberger. The integration of a priori knowledge into a Go playing neural network. 1996. 184, 185, 193, 194

200. Markus Enzenberger and Martin Müller. A lock-free multithreaded Monte-Carlo tree search algorithm. In *Advances in Computer Games*, pages 14–20. Springer, 2009. 260

201. Markus Enzenberger, Martin Muller, Broderick Arneson, and Richard Segal. Fuego—an open-source framework for board games and Go engine based on Monte Carlo tree search. *IEEE Transactions on Computational Intelligence and AI in Games*, 2(4):259–270, 2010. 116

202. Dumitru Erhan, Yoshua Bengio, Aaron Courville, Pierre-Antoine Manzagol, Pascal Vincent, and Samy Bengio. Why does unsupervised pre-training help deep learning? *Journal of Machine Learning Research*, 11(Feb):625–660, 2010. 205

203. Damien Ernst, Pierre Geurts, and Louis Wehenkel. Tree-based batch mode reinforcement learning. *Journal of Machine Learning Research*, 6(Apr):503–556, 2005. 194

204. Theodoros Evgeniou and Massimiliano Pontil. Regularized multi-task learning. In *Proceedings of the tenth ACM SIGKDD International Conference on Knowledge Discovery and Data Mining*, pages 109–117. ACM, 2004. 220

205. Haw-ren Fang, Tsan-sheng Hsu, and Shun-chin Hsu. Construction of Chinese chess endgame databases by retrograde analysis. In *International Conference on Computers and Games*, pages 96–114. Springer, 2000. 105

206. Gregory Farquhar, Tim Rocktäschel, Maximilian Igl, and SA Whiteson. TreeQN and ATreeC: Differentiable tree planning for deep reinforcement learning. International Conference on Learning Representations, 2018. 232

207. Li Fei-Fei, Jia Deng, and Kai Li. Imagenet: Constructing a large-scale image database. *Journal of Vision*, 9(8):1037–1037, 2009. 152

208. Alan Fern and Paul Lewis. Ensemble Monte-Carlo planning: An empirical study. In *ICAPS*, 2011. 129, 134

209. Santiago Fernández, Alex Graves, and Jürgen Schmidhuber. An application of recurrent neural networks to discriminative keyword spotting. In *International Conference on Artificial Neural Networks*, pages 220–229. Springer, 2007. 162

210. Matthias Feurer, Aaron Klein, Katharina Eggensperger, Jost Springenberg, Manuel Blum, and Frank Hutter. Efficient and robust automated machine learning. In *Advances in Neural Information Processing Systems*, pages 2962–2970, 2015. 222

211. Rebecca Anne Fiebrink. *Real-time human interaction with supervised learning algorithms for music composition and performance*. Citeseer, 2011. 246

212. Richard E Fikes, Peter E Hart, and Nils J Nilsson. Learning and executing generalized robot plans. *Artificial Intelligence*, 3:251–288, 1972. 226

213. Richard E Fikes and Nils J Nilsson. STRIPS: A new approach to the application of theorem proving to problem solving. *Artificial Intelligence*, 2(3-4):189–208, 1971. 11

214. Chelsea Finn, Pieter Abbeel, and Sergey Levine. Model-Agnostic Meta-Learning for fast adaptation of deep networks. *arXiv preprint arXiv:1703.03400*, 2017. 221, 251

215. Chelsea Finn, Kelvin Xu, and Sergey Levine. Probabilistic Model-Agnostic Meta-Learning. In *Advances in Neural Information Processing Systems*, pages 9516–9527, 2018. 221

216. Hilmar Finnsson and Yngvi Björnsson. Learning simulation control in general game-playing agents. In *AAAI*, volume 10, pages 954–959, 2010. 244

217. John P Fishburn. Analysis of speedup in distributed algorithms. 1982. 86, 95

218. Yannis Flet-Berliac. The promise of hierarchical reinforcement learning. `https://thegradient.pub/the-promise-of-hierarchical-reinforcement-learning/`, March 2019. 226

219. Jakob Foerster, Nantas Nardelli, Gregory Farquhar, Triantafyllos Afouras, Philip HS Torr, Pushmeet Kohli, and Shimon Whiteson. Stabilising experience replay for deep multi-agent reinforcement learning. *arXiv preprint arXiv:1702.08887*, 2017. 214

220. David B Fogel. An introduction to simulated evolutionary optimization. *IEEE Transactions on Neural Networks*, 5(1):3–14, 1994. 11

221. David B Fogel. *Blondie24: Playing at the Edge of AI*. Elsevier, 2001. 184, 193, 231

222. David B Fogel, Timothy J Hays, Sarah L Hahn, and James Quon. Further evolution of a self-learning chess program. In *CIG*, 2005. 104

223. David B Fogel, Timothy J Hays, Sarah L Hahn, and James Quon. The Blondie25 chess program competes against Fritz 8.0 and a human chess master. In *IEEE Symposium on Computational Intelligence and Games*, pages 230–235. Citeseer, 2006. 104

224. Meire Fortunato, Mohammad Gheshlaghi Azar, Bilal Piot, Jacob Menick, Ian Osband, Alex Graves, Vlad Mnih, Remi Munos, Demis Hassabis, Olivier Pietquin, et al. Noisy networks for exploration. *arXiv preprint arXiv:1706.10295*, 2017. 177, 181

225. Aviezri S Fraenkel and David Lichtenstein. Computing a perfect strategy for $n \times n$ chess requires time exponential in n. In *International Colloquium on Automata, Languages, and Programming*, pages 278–293. Springer, 1981. 74

226. Kevin Frans, Jonathan Ho, Xi Chen, Pieter Abbeel, and John Schulman. Meta learning shared hierarchies. *arXiv preprint arXiv:1710.09767*, 2017. 232, 251

227. Jerome Friedman, Trevor Hastie, and Robert Tibshirani. *The elements of statistical learning*, volume 1. Springer series in statistics New York, NY, USA:, 2001. 136

228. Andrea Frome, Greg S Corrado, Jon Shlens, Samy Bengio, Jeff Dean, Marc'Aurelio Ranzato, and Tomas Mikolov. Devise: A deep visual-semantic embedding model. In *Advances in Neural Information Processing Systems*, pages 2121–2129, 2013. 221

229. Nicholas Frosst and Geoffrey Hinton. Distilling a neural network into a soft decision tree. *arXiv preprint arXiv:1711.09784*, 2017. 227

230. Johannes Fürnkranz. Machine learning in computer chess: The next generation. *ICGA Journal*, 19(3):147–161, 1996. 104

231. Luca M Gambardella and Marco Dorigo. Ant-Q: A reinforcement learning approach to the traveling salesman problem. In *Machine Learning Proceedings 1995*, pages 252–260. Elsevier, 1995. 224

232. Sam Ganzfried and Tuomas Sandholm. Game theory-based opponent modeling in large imperfect-information games. In *The 10th International Conference on Autonomous Agents and Multiagent Systems-Volume 2*, pages 533–540. International Foundation for Autonomous Agents and Multiagent Systems, 2011. 105

233. Artur d'Avila Garcez, Tarek R Besold, Luc De Raedt, Peter Földiak, Pascal Hitzler, Thomas Icard, Kai-Uwe Kühnberger, Luis C Lamb, Risto Miikkulainen, and Daniel L Silver. Neural-symbolic learning and reasoning: contributions and challenges. In *2015 AAAI Spring Symposium Series*, 2015. 19

234. Ralph Gasser. Solving nine men's morris. *Computational Intelligence*, 12(1):24–41, 1996. 105

235. Sylvain Gelly, Levente Kocsis, Marc Schoenauer, Michele Sebag, David Silver, Csaba Szepesvári, and Olivier Teytaud. The grand challenge of computer Go: Monte Carlo tree search and extensions. *Communications of the ACM*, 55(3):106–113, 2012. 116, 124, 133, 185, 320

236. Sylvain Gelly and David Silver. Combining online and offline knowledge in UCT. In *Proceedings of the 24th International Conference on Machine learning*, pages 273–280. ACM, 2007. 128, 133, 185, 260

237. Sylvain Gelly and David Silver. Achieving master level play in 9×9 computer Go. In *AAAI*, volume 8, pages 1537–1540, 2008. 128, 185, 231

238. Sylvain Gelly and David Silver. Monte-Carlo tree search and rapid action value estimation in computer go. *Artificial Intelligence*, 175(11):1856–1875, 2011. 128, 133

239. Sylvain Gelly, Yizao Wang, and Olivier Teytaud. Modification of UCT with patterns in Monte-Carlo Go. Technical Report RR-6062, INRIA, 2006. 115, 119, 128, 133, 184, 231, 259, 260

240. Michael Genesereth, Nathaniel Love, and Barney Pell. General game playing: Overview of the AAAI competition. *AI magazine*, 26(2):62, 2005. 243, 244

241. Aurélien Géron. *Hands-on machine learning with Scikit-Learn and TensorFlow: concepts, tools, and techniques to build intelligent systems*. O'Reilly Media, Inc., 2019. 164, 188, 193, 194

242. Felix A Gers, Jürgen Schmidhuber, and Fred Cummins. Learning to forget: Continual prediction with LSTM. In *1999 Ninth International Conference on Artificial Neural Networks ICANN 99. (Conf. Publ. No. 470)*. IET, 1999. 165

243. Andrew Gilpin and Tuomas Sandholm. A competitive Texas Hold'em poker player via automated abstraction and real-time equilibrium computation. In *Proceedings of the National Conference on Artificial Intelligence*, volume 21, page 1007. Menlo Park, CA; Cambridge, MA; London; AAAI Press; MIT Press; 1999, 2006. 241

244. Alexios Giotis, Michael Emmerich, Boris Naujoks, Kyriakos Giannakoglou, and Thomas Bäck. Low-cost stochastic optimization for engineering applications. 232

245. Malcolm Gladwell. *Outliers: The story of success*. Hachette UK, 2008. 250

246. Adam Gleave, Michael Dennis, Neel Kant, Cody Wild, Sergey Levine, and Stuart Russell. Adversarial policies: Attacking deep reinforcement learning. *arXiv preprint arXiv:1905.10615*, 2019. 206

247. Peter W Glynn and Donald L Iglehart. Importance sampling for stochastic simulations. *Management Science*, 35(11):1367–1392, 1989. 60

248. Gordon Goetsch and Murray S Campbell. Experiments with the null-move heuristic. In *Computers, Chess, and Cognition*, pages 159–168. Springer, 1990. 103

249. Irving John Good. A five-year plan for automatic chess. *Machine Intelligence 2*, pages 89–118, 1968. 103

250. Ian Goodfellow, Yoshua Bengio, and Aaron Courville. *Deep learning*. MIT Press, Cambridge, 2016. 136, 141, 145, 147, 151, 152, 194, 262, 320

251. Ian Goodfellow, Jean Pouget-Abadie, Mehdi Mirza, Bing Xu, David Warde-Farley, Sherjil Ozair, Aaron Courville, and Yoshua Bengio. Generative adversarial nets. In *Advances in Neural Information Processing Systems*, pages 2672–2680, 2014. 160, 191, 194

252. Geoffrey J Gordon. Stable function approximation in dynamic programming. In *Machine Learning Proceedings 1995*, pages 261–268. Elsevier, 1995. 194

253. Tobias Graf and Marco Platzner. Adaptive playouts in Monte-Carlo tree search with policy-gradient reinforcement learning. In *Advances in Computer Games*, pages 1–11. Springer, 2015. 231

254. Alex Graves. Supervised sequence labelling. In *Supervised sequence labelling with recurrent neural networks*, pages 5–13. Springer, 2012. 194

255. Alex Graves, Marc G Bellemare, Jacob Menick, Remi Munos, and Koray Kavukcuoglu. Automated curriculum learning for neural networks. *arXiv preprint arXiv:1704.03003*, 2017. 207

256. Alex Graves, Santiago Fernández, and Jürgen Schmidhuber. Bidirectional LSTM networks for improved phoneme classification and recognition. In *International Conference on Artificial Neural Networks*, pages 799–804. Springer, 2005. 165, 194

257. Alex Graves and Navdeep Jaitly. Towards end-to-end speech recognition with recurrent neural networks. In *International Conference on Machine Learning*, pages 1764–1772, 2014. 165

258. Alex Graves, Greg Wayne, and Ivo Danihelka. Neural Turing machines. *arXiv preprint arXiv:1410.5401*, 2014. 220

259. Michael SA Graziano and Sabine Kastner. Human consciousness and its relationship to social neuroscience: a novel hypothesis. *Cognitive Neuroscience*, 2(2):98–113, 2011. 247

260. Richard D Greenblatt, Donald E Eastlake III, and Stephen D Crocker. The Greenblatt chess program. In *Proceedings of the November 14-16, 1967, Fall Joint Computer Conference*, pages 801–810, 1967. 102

261. Klaus Greff, Rupesh K Srivastava, Jan Koutník, Bas R Steunebrink, and Jürgen Schmidhuber. LSTM: A search space odyssey. *IEEE Transactions on Neural Networks and Learning Systems*, 28(10):2222–2232, 2017. 165, 194

262. Ivo Grondman, Lucian Busoniu, Gabriel AD Lopes, and Robert Babuska. A survey of actor-critic reinforcement learning: Standard and natural policy gradients. *IEEE Transactions on Systems, Man, and Cybernetics, Part C (Applications and Reviews)*, 42(6):1291–1307, 2012. 55, 180, 182

263. Audrunas Gruslys, Will Dabney, Mohammad Gheshlaghi Azar, Bilal Piot, Marc Bellemare, and Remi Munos. The reactor: A fast and sample-efficient actor-critic agent for reinforcement learning. *arXiv preprint arXiv:1704.04651*, 2017. 181

264. Arthur Guez, Mehdi Mirza, Karol Gregor, Rishabh Kabra, Sébastien Racanière, Théophane Weber, David Raposo, Adam Santoro, Laurent Orseau, Tom Eccles, et al. An investigation of model-free planning. *arXiv preprint arXiv:1901.03559*, 2019. 227

265. Arthur Guez, Théophane Weber, Ioannis Antonoglou, Karen Simonyan, Oriol Vinyals, Daan Wierstra, Rémi Munos, and David Silver. Learning to search with MCTSnets. *arXiv preprint arXiv:1802.04697*, 2018. 227

266. David Gunning. Explainable artificial intelligence (XAI). *Defense Advanced Research Projects Agency (DARPA), nd Web*, 2, 2017. 227

267. Xiaoxiao Guo, Satinder Singh, Honglak Lee, Richard L Lewis, and Xiaoshi Wang. Deep learning for real-time Atari game play using offline Monte-Carlo tree search planning. In *Advances in Neural Information Processing Systems*, pages 3338–3346, 2014. 232

268. Yanming Guo, Yu Liu, Ard Oerlemans, Songyang Lao, Song Wu, and Michael S Lew. Deep learning for visual understanding: A review. *Neurocomputing*, 187:27–48, 2016. 156, 159

269. Abhishek Gupta, Benjamin Eysenbach, Chelsea Finn, and Sergey Levine. Unsupervised meta-learning for reinforcement learning. *arXiv preprint arXiv:1806.04640*, 2018. 232

270. Abhishek Gupta, Russell Mendonca, YuXuan Liu, Pieter Abbeel, and Sergey Levine. Meta-reinforcement learning of structured exploration strategies. *arXiv preprint arXiv:1802.07245*, 2018. 232

271. Danijar Hafner, Timothy Lillicrap, Ian Fischer, Ruben Villegas, David Ha, Honglak Lee, and James Davidson. Learning latent dynamics for planning from pixels. *arXiv preprint arXiv:1811.04551*, 2018. 227, 232

272. Mark Hall, Eibe Frank, Geoffrey Holmes, Bernhard Pfahringer, Peter Reutemann, and Ian H Witten. The WEKA data mining software: an update. *ACM SIGKDD Explorations Newsletter*, 11(1):10–18, 2009. 136, 255

273. Eric A Hansen and Rong Zhou. Anytime heuristic search. *Journal of Artificial Intelligence Research*, 28:267–297, 2007. 90

274. Mark Harman. The current state and future of search based software engineering. In *2007 Future of Software Engineering*, pages 342–357. IEEE Computer Society, 2007. 221

275. Hado V Hasselt. Double Q-learning. In *Advances in Neural Information Processing Systems*, pages 2613–2621, 2010. 179

276. Johan Håstad and Mikael Goldmann. On the power of small-depth threshold circuits. *Computational Complexity*, 1(2):113–129, 1991. 142, 144

277. Thomas Hauk, Michael Buro, and Jonathan Schaeffer. Rediscovering *-minimax search. In *International Conference on Computers and Games*, pages 35–50. Springer, 2004. 100

278. Simon Haykin. *Neural networks: a comprehensive foundation*. Prentice Hall PTR, 1994. 11

279. Simon S Haykin et al. *Neural networks and learning machines/Simon Haykin*. New York: Prentice Hall, 2009. 141

280. Ryan B Hayward and Bjarne Toft. *Hex: The Full Story*. CRC Press, 2019. 132

281. Kaiming He, Xiangyu Zhang, Shaoqing Ren, and Jian Sun. Deep residual learning for image recognition. In *Proceedings of the IEEE Conference on Computer Vision and Pattern Recognition*, pages 770–778, 2016. 158, 159, 263, 320

282. David Heckerman, Dan Geiger, and David M Chickering. Learning Bayesian networks: The combination of knowledge and statistical data. *Machine Learning*, 20(3):197–243, 1995. 227

283. Nicolas Heess, David Silver, and Yee Whye Teh. Actor-critic reinforcement learning with energy-based policies. In *EWRL*, pages 43–58, 2012. 171

284. Nicolas Heess, Dhruva TB, Srinivasan Sriram, Jay Lemmon, Josh Merel, Greg Wayne, Yuval Tassa, Tom Erez, Ziyu Wang, SM Eslami, et al. Emergence of locomotion behaviours in rich environments. *arXiv preprint arXiv:1707.02286*, 2017. 183

285. Johannes Heinrich and David Silver. Deep reinforcement learning from self-play in imperfect-information games. *arXiv preprint arXiv:1603.01121*, 2016. 214, 224

286. Ernst A Heinz. Adaptive null-move pruning. *ICGA Journal*, 22(3):123–132, 1999. 103

287. Ernst A Heinz. New self-play results in computer chess. In *International Conference on Computers and Games*, pages 262–276. Springer, 2000. 232

288. David P Helmbold and Aleatha Parker-Wood. All-Moves-As-First heuristics in Monte-Carlo Go. In *IC-AI*, pages 605–610, 2009. 128

289. Peter Henderson, Riashat Islam, Philip Bachman, Joelle Pineau, Doina Precup, and David Meger. Deep reinforcement learning that matters. In *Thirty-Second AAAI-Conference on Artificial Intelligence*, 2018. 213, 230

290. Matteo Hessel, Joseph Modayil, Hado Van Hasselt, Tom Schaul, Georg Ostrovski, Will Dabney, Dan Horgan, Bilal Piot, Mohammad Azar, and David Silver. Rainbow: Combining improvements in deep reinforcement learning. *arXiv preprint arXiv:1710.02298*, 2017. 178, 179, 180, 191, 321

291. Ashley Hill, Antonin Raffin, Maximilian Ernestus, Adam Gleave, Anssi Kanervisto, Rene Traore, Prafulla Dhariwal, Christopher Hesse, Oleg Klimov, Alex Nichol, Matthias Plappert, Alec Radford, John Schulman, Szymon Sidor, and Yuhuai Wu. Stable baselines. `https://github.com/hill-a/stable-baselines`, 2018. 256

292. Geoffrey Hinton, Oriol Vinyals, and Jeff Dean. Distilling the knowledge in a neural network. *arXiv preprint arXiv:1503.02531*, 2015. 227

293. Geoffrey E Hinton, Simon Osindero, and Yee-Whye Teh. A fast learning algorithm for deep belief nets. *Neural Computation*, 18(7):1527–1554, 2006. 138, 149

294. Geoffrey E Hinton and Ruslan R Salakhutdinov. Reducing the dimensionality of data with neural networks. *Science*, 313(5786):504–507, 2006. 141, 205

295. Geoffrey E Hinton, Nitish Srivastava, Alex Krizhevsky, Ilya Sutskever, and Ruslan R Salakhutdinov. Improving neural networks by preventing co-adaptation of feature detectors. *arXiv preprint arXiv:1207.0580*, 2012. 152

296. Sepp Hochreiter. Untersuchungen zu dynamischen neuronalen Netzen. *Diploma, Technische Universität München*, 91(1), 1991. 149

297. Sepp Hochreiter, Yoshua Bengio, Paolo Frasconi, and Jürgen Schmidhuber. Gradient flow in recurrent nets: the difficulty of learning long-term dependencies. In *A Field Guide to Dynamical Recurrent Neural Networks*. IEEE Press, 2001. 149

298. Sepp Hochreiter and Jürgen Schmidhuber. Long short-term memory. *Neural Computation*, 9(8):1735–1780, 1997. 162, 165, 194

299. John Holland. Adaptation in natural and artificial systems: an introductory analysis with application to biology. *Control and Artificial Intelligence*, 1975. 53

300. John H Holland. Genetic algorithms. *Scientific American*, 267(1):66–73, 1992. 11

301. Alec Holt, Isabelle Bichindaritz, Rainer Schmidt, and Petra Perner. Medical applications in case-based reasoning. *The Knowledge Engineering Review*, 20(3):289–292, 2005. 245

302. Holger H Hoos and Thomas Stützle. *Stochastic local search: Foundations and applications*. Elsevier, 2004. 221

303. John J Hopfield. Neural networks and physical systems with emergent collective computational abilities. *Proceedings of the National Academy of Sciences*, 79(8):2554–2558, 1982. 162

304. Edward Hordern. *Sliding piece puzzles*. Number 4. Oxford University Press, USA, 1986. 20, 319

305. Timothy Hospedales, Antreas Antoniou, Paul Micaelli, and Amos Storkey. Meta-learning in neural networks: A survey. *arXiv preprint arXiv:2004.05439*, 2020. 220, 221

306. Ronald A Howard. *Dynamic programming and Markov processes*. New York: John Wiley, 1964. 44

307. Meng Hsuen Hsieh, Meng Ju Hsieh, Chin-Ming Chen, Chia-Chang Hsieh, Chien-Ming Chao, and Chih-Cheng Lai. Comparison of machine learning models for the prediction of mortality of patients with unplanned extubation in intensive care units. *Scientific Reports*, 8(1):17116, 2018. 232

308. Ming Yu Hsieh and Shi-Chun Tsai. On the fairness and complexity of generalized k-in-a-row games. *Theoretical Computer Science*, 385(1-3):88–100, 2007. 74

309. Feng-Hsiung Hsu. *Behind Deep Blue: Building the computer that defeated the world chess champion*. Princeton University Press, 2004. 35, 42, 81, 101

310. Feng-hsiung Hsu, Thomas Anantharaman, Murray Campbell, and Andreas Nowatzyk. A grandmaster chess machine. *Scientific American*, 263(4):44–51, 1990. 35, 184

311. Bojun Huang. Pruning game tree by rollouts. In *AAAI*, pages 1165–1173, 2015. 130, 131, 133, 325

312. Gao Huang, Zhuang Liu, Laurens Van Der Maaten, and Kilian Q Weinberger. Densely connected convolutional networks. In *Proceedings of the IEEE Conference on Computer Vision and Pattern Recognition*, pages 4700–4708, 2017. 159

313. Sandy Huang, Nicolas Papernot, Ian Goodfellow, Yan Duan, and Pieter Abbeel. Adversarial attacks on neural network policies. *arXiv preprint arXiv:1702.02284*, 2017. 194, 206

314. Shih-Chieh Huang, Broderick Arneson, Ryan B Hayward, Martin Müller, and Jakub Pawlewicz. Mohex 2.0: a pattern-based MCTS Hex player. In *International Conference on Computers and Games*, pages 60–71. Springer, 2013. 132

315. Timothy Huang, Graeme Connell, and Bryan McQuade. Learning opening strategy in the game of Go. In *FLAIRS Conference*, pages 434–438, 2003. 185

316. David H Hubel and TN Wiesel. Shape and arrangement of columns in cat's striate cortex. *The Journal of Physiology*, 165(3):559–568, 1963. 145

317. David H Hubel and Torsten N Wiesel. Receptive fields and functional architecture of monkey striate cortex. *The Journal of Physiology*, 195(1):215–243, 1968. 145

318. Barbara J (Liskov) Huberman. A program to play chess end games. Technical report, Stanford University Department of Computer Science, 1968. 99, 112

319. Fan Hui. Fan Hui commentary game 2 move 37 Lee Sedol. https://deepmind.com/research/alphago/match-archive/alphago-games-english/, 2018. 39

320. Jonathan Hui. RL—DQN Deep Q-network https://medium.com/@jonathan_hui/rl-dqn-deep-q-network-e207751f7ae4. Medium post. 174, 321

321. Mike Huisman, Jan van Rijn, and Aske Plaat. In: Pavel Brazdil et al. *Metalearning for deep neural networks*. Springer, 2021. 220, 232, 251

322. Johan Huizinga. *Homo ludens: proeve eener bepaling van het spel-element der cultuur. English: Homo Ludens: A Study of the Play-Element in Culture*. Amsterdam University Press, London: Routledge & Kegan Paul, 1938, 2008. 245

323. Matthew Hutson. Artificial Intelligence faces reproducibility crisis, 2018. 213

324. Frank Hutter, Holger H Hoos, and Kevin Leyton-Brown. Sequential model-based optimization for general algorithm configuration. In *International Conference on Learning and Intelligent Optimization*, pages 507–523. Springer, 2011. 222, 232

325. Robert M Hyatt and Monty Newborn. Crafty goes deep. *ICGA Journal*, 20(2):79–86, 1997. 112

326. Hiroyuki Iida, Makoto Sakuta, and Jeff Rollason. Computer shogi. *Artificial Intelligence*, 134(1-2):121–144, 2002. 74

327. Queensland Brain Institute. History of artificial intelligence https://qbi.uq.edu.au/brain/intelligent-machines/history-artificial-intelligence, 2018. 13, 319

328. Sergey Ioffe. Batch renormalization: Towards reducing minibatch dependence in batch-normalized models. In *Advances in Neural Information Processing Systems*, pages 1945–1953, 2017. 150, 152, 193, 263

329. Riashat Islam, Peter Henderson, Maziar Gomrokchi, and Doina Precup. Reproducibility of benchmarked deep reinforcement learning tasks for continuous control. *arXiv preprint arXiv:1708.04133*, 2017. 213

330. Shigeki Iwata and Takumi Kasai. The othello game on an $n \times n$ board is PSPACE-complete. *Theoretical Computer Science*, 123(2):329–340, 1994. 74

331. Max Jaderberg, Wojciech M Czarnecki, Iain Dunning, Luke Marris, Guy Lever, Antonio Garcia Castaneda, Charles Beattie, Neil C Rabinowitz, Ari S Morcos, Avraham Ruderman, et al. Human-level performance in first-person multiplayer games with population-based deep reinforcement learning. *arXiv preprint arXiv:1807.01281*, 2018. 240

332. Max Jaderberg, Wojciech M Czarnecki, Iain Dunning, Luke Marris, Guy Lever, Antonio Garcia Castaneda, Charles Beattie, Neil C Rabinowitz, Ari S Morcos, Avraham Ruderman, et al. Human-level performance in 3D multiplayer games with population-based reinforcement learning. *Science*, 364(6443).859–865, 2019. 240, 252

333. Max Jaderberg, Valentin Dalibard, Simon Osindero, Wojciech M Czarnecki, Jeff Donahue, Ali Razavi, Oriol Vinyals, Tim Green, Iain Dunning, Karen Simonyan, et al. Population based training of neural networks. *arXiv preprint arXiv:1711.09846*, 2017. 222

334. Yangqing Jia, Evan Shelhamer, Jeff Donahue, Sergey Karayev, Jonathan Long, Ross Girshick, Sergio Guadarrama, and Trevor Darrell. Caffe: Convolutional architecture for fast feature embedding. In *Proceedings of the 22nd ACM International Conference on Multimedia*, pages 675–678. ACM, 2014. 155, 255

335. Nanlin Jin, Peter Flach, Tom Wilcox, Royston Sellman, Joshua Thumim, and Arno Knobbe. Subgroup discovery in smart electricity meter data. *IEEE Transactions on Industrial Informatics*, 10(2):1327–1336, 2014. 232

336. Michael Johanson. Measuring the size of large no-limit poker games. *arXiv preprint arXiv:1302.7008*, 2013. 27

337. Matthew Johnson, Jeffrey M Bradshaw, Paul J Feltovich, Robert R Hoffman, Catholijn Jonker, Birna van Riemsdijk, and Maarten Sierhuis. Beyond cooperative robotics: The central role of interdependence in coactive design. *IEEE Intelligent Systems*, 26(3):81–88, 2011. 232

338. Catholijn M Jonker, Reyhan Aydogan, Tim Baarslag, Katsuhide Fujita, Takayuki Ito, and Koen V Hindriks. Automated negotiating agents competition (ANAC). In *AAAI*, pages 5070–5072, 2017. 240

339. Catholijn M Jonker, Valentin Robu, and Jan Treur. An agent architecture for multi-attribute negotiation using incomplete preference information. *Autonomous Agents and Multi-Agent Systems*, 15(2):221–252, 2007. 240

340. Michael Irwin Jordan. *Learning in graphical models*, volume 89. Springer Science & Business Media, 1998. 227

341. Norman P Jouppi, Cliff Young, Nishant Patil, David Patterson, Gaurav Agrawal, Raminder Bajwa, Sarah Bates, Suresh Bhatia, Nan Boden, Al Borchers, et al. In-datacenter performance analysis of a tensor processing unit. In *Computer Architecture (ISCA), 2017 ACM/IEEE 44th Annual International Symposium on*, pages 1–12. IEEE, 2017. 262

342. Andreas Junghanns and Jonathan Schaeffer. Search versus knowledge in game-playing programs revisited. In *IJCAI (1)*, pages 692–697, 1997. 112

343. Leslie Pack Kaelbling. Hierarchical learning in stochastic domains: Preliminary results. In *Proceedings of the tenth International Conference on Machine Learning*, volume 951, pages 167–173, 1993. 232

344. Leslie Pack Kaelbling, Michael L Littman, and Anthony R Cassandra. Planning and acting in partially observable stochastic domains. *Artificial Intelligence*, 101(1-2):99–134, 1998. 240

345. Leslie Pack Kaelbling, Michael L Littman, and Andrew W Moore. Reinforcement learning: A survey. *Journal of Artificial Intelligence Research*, 4:237–285, 1996. 56, 69

346. Leslie Pack Kaelbling and Tomás Lozano-Pérez. Hierarchical planning in the now. In *Workshops at the Twenty-Fourth AAAI Conference on Artificial Intelligence*, 2010. 232

347. Daniel Kahneman. *Thinking, fast and slow*. Farrar, Straus and Giroux, 2011. 12, 21, 42, 110, 247

348. H Kaindl. Dynamic control of the quiescence search in computer chess. *Cybernetics and Systems Research*, pages 973–977, 1982. 102

349. Hermann Kaindl. Minimaxing: Theory and practice. *AI Magazine*, 9(3):69, 1988. 102

350. Lukasz Kaiser, Mohammad Babaeizadeh, Piotr Milos, Blazej Osinski, Roy H Campbell, Konrad Czechowski, Dumitru Erhan, Chelsea Finn, Piotr Kozakowski, Sergey Levine, et al. Model-based reinforcement learning for Atari. *arXiv preprint arXiv:1903.00374*, 2019. 227, 232

351. Satwik Kansal and Brendan Martin. Learn data science webpage., 2018. 64, 65, 66, 67, 320, 325

352. Steven Kapturowski, Georg Ostrovski, John Quan, Remi Munos, and Will Dabney. Recurrent experience replay in distributed reinforcement learning. In *International conference on learning representations*, 2018. 181

353. Sergey Karakovskiy and Julian Togelius. The Mario AI benchmark and competitions. *IEEE Transactions on Computational Intelligence and AI in Games*, 4(1):55–67, 2012. 213

354. Andrej Karpathy. The unreasonable effectiveness of recurrent neural networks. http://karpathy.github.io/2015/05/21/rnn-effectiveness/, 2015. 163, 164, 165, 194, 320

355. Andrej Karpathy. Deep reinforcement learning: Pong from pixels http://karpathy.github.io/2016/05/31/rl/. Andrej Karpathy Blog, 2016. 177

356. Tero Karras, Timo Aila, Samuli Laine, and Jaakko Lehtinen. Progressive growing of GANs for improved quality, stability, and variation. *arXiv preprint arXiv:1710.10196*, 2017. 161, 191, 320

357. Michael N Katehakis and Arthur F Veinott Jr. The multi-armed bandit problem: decomposition and computation. *Mathematics of Operations Research*, 12(2):262–268, 1987. 122

358. John D Kelleher, Brian Mac Namee, and Aoife D'Arcy. *Fundamentals of machine learning for predictive data analytics: algorithms, worked examples, and case studies*. MIT Press, 2015. 194

359. Stephen Kelly and Malcolm I Heywood. Multi-task learning in atari video games with emergent tangled program graphs. In *Proceedings of the Genetic and Evolutionary Computation Conference*, pages 195–202. ACM, 2017. 220

360. Stephen Kelly and Malcolm I Heywood. Emergent tangled program graphs in multi-task learning. In *IJCAI*, pages 5294–5298, 2018. 220

361. James Kennedy. Swarm intelligence. In *Handbook of nature-inspired and innovative computing*, pages 187–219. Springer, 2006. 11

362. Pascal Kerschke, Holger H Hoos, Frank Neumann, and Heike Trautmann. Automated algorithm selection: Survey and perspectives. *Evolutionary Computation*, 27(1):3–45, 2019. 220

363. Anders Kierulf, Ken Chen, and Jurg Nievergelt. Smart game board and Go explorer: a study in software and knowledge engineering. *Communications of the ACM*, 33(2):152–166, 1990. 114

364. Hajime Kimura, Shigenobu Kobayashi, et al. An analysis of actor-critic algorithms using eligibility traces: reinforcement learning with imperfect value functions. *Journal of Japanese Society for Artificial Intelligence*, 15(2):267–275, 2000. 55

365. D Kinga and J Ba. Adam: method for stochastic optimization. In *International Conference on Learning Representations (ICLR)*, volume 5, 2015. 141

366. Hiroaki Kitano. Designing neural networks using genetic algorithms with graph generation system. *Complex Systems*, 4(4):461–476, 1990. 222

367. Julien Kloetzer. Monte-Carlo opening books for amazons. In *International Conference on Computers and Games*, pages 124–135. Springer, 2010. 125

368. Craig A Knoblock. Learning abstraction hierarchies for problem solving. In *AAAI*, pages 923–928, 1990. 226

369. Donald E Knuth and Ronald W Moore. An analysis of alpha-beta pruning. *Artificial Intelligence*, 6(4):293–326, 1975. 84, 95, 112

370. Donald Ervin Knuth. *The art of computer programming: sorting and searching*, volume 3. Pearson Education, 1997. 98

371. Jens Kober, J Andrew Bagnell, and Jan Peters. Reinforcement learning in robotics: A survey. *The International Journal of Robotics Research*, 32(11):1238–1274, 2013. 56, 69, 225

372. Christof Koch. *The quest for consciousness: A neurobiological approach*. Roberts and Company Englewood, CO, 2004. 247

373. Levente Kocsis and Csaba Szepesvári. Bandit based Monte-Carlo planning. In *European Conference on Machine Learning*, pages 282–293. Springer, 2006. 119, 120, 133, 203

374. Vincent J Koeman, Harm J Griffioen, Danny C Plenge, and Koen V Hindriks. Starcraft as a testbed for engineering complex distributed systems using cognitive agent technology. In *Proceedings of the 17th International Conference on Autonomous Agents and MultiAgent Systems*, pages 1983–1985. International Foundation for Autonomous Agents and Multiagent Systems, 2018. 213

375. Teun Koetsier. On the prehistory of programmable machines: musical automata, looms, calculators. *Mechanism and Machine Theory*, 36(5):589–603, 2001. 12

376. Daphne Koller and Avi Pfeffer. Representations and solutions for game-theoretic problems. *Artificial Intelligence*, 94(1-2):167–215, 1997. 240

377. Vijay R Konda and John N Tsitsiklis. Actor–critic algorithms. In *Advances in Neural Information Processing Systems*, pages 1008–1014, 2000. 55

378. Vijaymohan R Konda and Vivek S Borkar. Actor–Critic-type learning algorithms for Markov Decision Processes. *SIAM Journal on Control and Optimization*, 38(1):94–123, 1999. 55

379. Wouter Kool, Herke Van Hoof, and Max Welling. Attention, learn to solve routing problems! *arXiv preprint arXiv:1803.08475*, 2018. 224

380. Richard E Korf. Recent progress in the design and analysis of admissible heuristic functions. In *International Symposium on Abstraction, Reformulation, and Approximation*, pages 45–55. Springer, 2000. 105

381. Richard E Korf and Larry A Taylor. Finding optimal solutions to the twenty-four puzzle. In *Proceedings of the national conference on Artificial Intelligence*, pages 1202–1207, 1996. 20

382. Lars Kotthoff, Chris Thornton, Holger H Hoos, Frank Hutter, and Kevin Leyton-Brown. Auto-WEKA 2.0: Automatic model selection and hyperparameter optimization in WEKA. *The Journal of Machine Learning Research*, 18(1):826–830, 2017. 222

383. Sarit Kraus, Eithan Ephrati, and Daniel Lehmann. Negotiation in a non-cooperative environment. *Journal of Experimental & Theoretical Artificial Intelligence*, 3(4):255–281, 1994. 21, 240

384. Sarit Kraus and Daniel Lehmann. Diplomat, an agent in a multi agent environment: An overview. In *Computers and Communications, 1988. Conference Proceedings., Seventh Annual International Phoenix Conference on*, pages 434–438. IEEE, 1988. 240

385. Alex Krizhevsky and Geoffrey Hinton. Learning multiple layers of features from tiny images. Technical report, Citeseer, 2009. 152

386. Alex Krizhevsky, Ilya Sutskever, and Geoffrey E Hinton. Imagenet classification with deep convolutional neural networks. In *Advances in Neural Information Processing Systems*, pages 1097–1105, 2012. 149, 153, 177, 186

387. Kai A Krueger and Peter Dayan. Flexible shaping: How learning in small steps helps. *Cognition*, 110(3):380–394, 2009. 207

388. Jan Kuipers, Aske Plaat, JAM Vermaseren, and H Jaap van den Herik. Improving multivariate Horner schemes with Monte Carlo tree search. *Computer Physics Communications*, 184(11):2391–2395, 2013. 125, 126, 127, 133, 320

389. Tejas D Kulkarni, Karthik Narasimhan, Ardavan Saeedi, and Josh Tenenbaum. Hierarchical deep reinforcement learning: Integrating temporal abstraction and intrinsic motivation. In *Advances in Neural Information Processing Systems*, pages 3675–3683, 2016. 232

390. Vipin Kumar, Dana S Nau, and Laveen N Kanal. A general branch-and-bound formulation for and/or graph and game tree search. In *Search in Artificial Intelligence*, pages 91–130. Springer, 1988. 112

391. Kamolwan Kunanusont, Simon M Lucas, and Diego Pérez-Liébana. General video game AI: learning from screen capture. In *Evolutionary Computation (CEC), 2017 IEEE Congress on*, pages 2078–2085. IEEE, 2017. 244

392. Michail G Lagoudakis and Ronald Parr. Least-squares policy iteration. *Journal of Machine Learning Research*, 4(Dec):1107–1149, 2003. 194

393. Matthew Lai. Giraffe: Using deep reinforcement learning to play chess. *arXiv preprint arXiv:1509.01549*, 2015. 104, 184, 185, 194

394. Tze Leung Lai and Herbert Robbins. Asymptotically efficient adaptive allocation rules. *Advances in Applied Mathematics*, 6(1):4–22, 1985. 53, 122, 123

395. Tze-Leung Lai and Sidney Yakowitz. Machine learning and nonparametric bandit theory. *IEEE Transactions on Automatic Control*, 40(7):1199–1209, 1995. 122

396. John E Laird, Allen Newell, and Paul S Rosenbloom. Soar: An architecture for general intelligence. *Artificial Intelligence*, 33(1):1–64, 1987. 245

397. Brenden M Lake, Ruslan Salakhutdinov, and Joshua B Tenenbaum. Human-level concept learning through probabilistic program induction. *Science*, 350(6266):1332–1338, 2015. 220

398. Robert Lake, Jonathan Schaeffer, and Paul Lu. *Solving large retrograde analysis problems using a network of workstations*. Department of Computing Science, University of Alberta, 1993. 105

399. Marc Lanctot, Edward Lockhart, Jean-Baptiste Lespiau, Vinicius Zambaldi, Satyaki Upadhyay, Julien Pérolat, Sriram Srinivasan, Finbarr Timbers, Karl Tuyls, Shayegan Omidshafiei, et al. Openspiel: A framework for reinforcement learning in games. *arXiv preprint arXiv:1908.09453*, 2019. 42, 256

400. Marc Lanctot, Abdallah Saffidine, Joel Veness, Christopher Archibald, and Mark HM Winands. Monte Carlo*-minimax search. In *IJCAI*, pages 580–586, 2013. 100

401. Evgenii Mikhailovich Landis and Isaak Moiseevich Yaglom. About Aleksandr Semenovich Kronrod. *Russian Mathematical Surveys*, 56(5):993–1007, 2001. 17

402. Raúl Lara-Cabrera, Carlos Cotta, and Antonio J Fernández-Leiva. A review of computational intelligence in RTS games. In *2013 IEEE Symposium on Foundations of Computational Intelligence (FOCI)*, pages 114–121. IEEE, 2013. 240

403. Alexandre Laterre, Yunguan Fu, Mohamed Khalil Jabri, Alain-Sam Cohen, David Kas, Karl Hajjar, Torbjorn S Dahl, Amine Kerkeni, and Karim Beguir. Ranked reward: Enabling self-play reinforcement learning for combinatorial optimization. *arXiv preprint arXiv:1807.01672*, 2018. 229

404. Steffen L Lauritzen. *Graphical models*, volume 17. Clarendon Press, 1996. 227

405. Yann LeCun, Yoshua Bengio, and Geoffrey Hinton. Deep learning. *Nature*, 521(7553):436, 2015. 11, 138, 141, 142, 157, 158, 193, 232

406. Yann LeCun, Bernhard Boser, John S Denker, Donnie Henderson, Richard E Howard, Wayne Hubbard, and Lawrence D Jackel. Backpropagation applied to handwritten zip code recognition. *Neural Computation*, 1(4):541–551, 1989. 146

407. Yann LeCun, Léon Bottou, Yoshua Bengio, and Patrick Haffner. Gradient-based learning applied to document recognition. *Proceedings of the IEEE*, 86(11):2278–2324, 1998. 153, 154, 325

408. Chang-Shing Lee, Martin Müller, and Olivier Teytaud. Special issue on Monte Carlo techniques and computer Go. *IEEE Transactions on Computational Intelligence and AI in Games*, (4):225–228, 2010. 116

409. Honglak Lee, Roger Grosse, Rajesh Ranganath, and Andrew Y Ng. Convolutional deep belief networks for scalable unsupervised learning of hierarchical representations. In *Proceedings of the 26th Annual International Conference on Machine Learning*, pages 609–616. ACM, 2009. 142, 320

410. Shane Legg, Marcus Hutter, et al. A collection of definitions of intelligence. *Frontiers in Artificial Intelligence and Applications*, 157:17, 2007. 244

411. Joel Z Leibo, Edward Hughes, Marc Lanctot, and Thore Graepel. Autocurricula and the emergence of innovation from social interaction: A manifesto for multi-agent intelligence research. *arXiv preprint arXiv:1903.00742*, 2019. 231, 240, 252

412. Charles Leiserson and Aske Plaat. Programming parallel applications in Cilk. *SINEWS: SIAM News*, 31(4):6–7, 1998. 112

413. Fabien Letouzey. Fruit chess program. http://www.fruitchess.com/about.htm. 112

414. Sergey Levine and Vladlen Koltun. Guided policy search. In *International Conference on Machine Learning*, pages 1–9, 2013. 186

415. Andrew Levy, Robert Platt, and Kate Saenko. Hierarchical reinforcement learning with hindsight. *arXiv preprint arXiv:1805.08180*, 2018. 232

416. David Levy and Monty Newborn. *How computers play chess*, volume 8. Computer Science Press, New York, 1991. 35, 42, 87

417. Eric Liang, Richard Liaw, Philipp Moritz, Robert Nishihara, Roy Fox, Ken Goldberg, Joseph E Gonzalez, Michael I Jordan, and Ion Stoica. RLlib: abstractions for distributed reinforcement learning. *arXiv preprint arXiv:1712.09381*, 2017. 256

418. Timothy P Lillicrap, Jonathan J Hunt, Alexander Pritzel, Nicolas Heess, Tom Erez, Yuval Tassa, David Silver, and Daan Wierstra. Continuous control with deep reinforcement learning. *arXiv preprint arXiv:1509.02971*, 2015. 225

419. Milton Lim. History of AI Winters. https://www.actuaries.digital/2018/09/05/history-of-ai-winters/, 2018. 13, 14, 319

420. Long-Ji Lin. Self-improving reactive agents based on reinforcement learning, planning and teaching. *Machine Learning*, 8(3–4):293–321, 1992. 175, 194

421. Long-Ji Lin. Reinforcement learning for robots using neural networks. Technical report, Carnegie-Mellon Univ Pittsburgh PA School of Computer Science, 1993. 175

422. Raz Lin and Sarit Kraus. Can automated agents proficiently negotiate with humans? *Communications of the ACM*, 53(1):78–88, 2010. 232

423. Raz Lin, Sarit Kraus, Tim Baarslag, Dmytro Tykhonov, Koen Hindriks, and Catholijn M Jonker. Genius: An integrated environment for supporting the design of generic automated negotiators. *Computational Intelligence*, 30(1):48–70, 2014. 245

424. Christine L Lisetti. *Affective computing*. Springer, 1998. 247

425. Michael L Littman. Markov games as a framework for multi-agent reinforcement learning. In *Machine Learning Proceedings 1994*, pages 157–163. Elsevier, 1994. 224

426. Hui Liu, Song Yu, Zhangxin Chen, Ben Hsieh, and Lei Shao. Sparse matrix-vector multiplication on NVIDIA GPU. *International Journal of Numerical Analysis & Modeling, Series B*, 3(2):185–191, 2012. 155

427. Manuel López-Ibáñez, Jérémie Dubois-Lacoste, Leslie Pérez Cáceres, Mauro Birattari, and Thomas Stützle. The irace package: Iterated racing for automatic algorithm configuration. *Operations Research Perspectives*, 3:43–58, 2016. 222

428. Richard J Lorentz. Experiments with Monte-Carlo tree search in the game of Havannah. *ICGA Journal*, 34(3):140–149, 2011. 125

429. Richard J Lorentz. An MCTS program to play EinStein würfelt nicht! In *Advances in Computer Games*, pages 52–59. Springer, 2011. 125

430. Donald W Loveland. *Automated Theorem Proving: a logical basis*. Elsevier, 2016. 246

431. Ryan Lowe, Yi Wu, Aviv Tamar, Jean Harb, Pieter Abbeel, and Igor Mordatch. Multi-agent Actor–Critic for mixed cooperative-competitive environments. In *Advances in Neural Information Processing Systems*, pages 6379–6390, 2017. 224

432. Mark Lutz. *Programming Python*, volume 8. O'Reilly, 1996. 281

433. Laurens van der Maaten and Geoffrey Hinton. Visualizing data using t-SNE. *Journal of Machine Learning Research*, 9(Nov):2579–2605, 2008. 138, 221

434. Brooke N Macnamara, David Z Hambrick, and Frederick L Oswald. Deliberate practice and performance in music, games, sports, education, and professions: A meta-analysis. *Psychological Science*, 25(8):1608–1618, 2014. 250

435. Chris J Maddison, Aja Huang, Ilya Sutskever, and David Silver. Move evaluation in Go using deep convolutional neural networks. *arXiv preprint arXiv:1412.6564*, 2014. 185, 193

436. A Madrigal. How checkers was solved, the story of a duel between two men, one who dies, and the nature of the quest to build artificial intelligence (2017). *The Atlantic*, July 2017. 33

437. Rajbala Makar, Sridhar Mahadevan, and Mohammad Ghavamzadeh. Hierarchical multi-agent reinforcement learning. In *Proceedings of the Fifth International Conference on Autonomous Agents*, pages 246–253. ACM, 2001. 232

438. Tambet Matiisen, Avital Oliver, Taco Cohen, and John Schulman. Teacher-student curriculum learning. *arXiv preprint arXiv:1707.00183*, 2017. 205, 224, 232

439. Masakazu Matsugu, Katsuhiko Mori, Yusuke Mitari, and Yuji Kaneda. Subject independent facial expression recognition with robust face detection using a convolutional neural network. *Neural Networks*, 16(5-6):555–559, 2003. 145

440. Kiminori Matsuzaki. Empirical analysis of puct algorithm with evaluation functions of different quality. In *2018 Conference on Technologies and Applications of Artificial Intelligence (TAAI)*, pages 142–147. IEEE, 2018. 122, 203, 259

441. David Allen McAllester. Conspiracy numbers for min-max search. *Artificial Intelligence*, 35(3):287–310, 1988. 100

442. James L McClelland, Bruce L McNaughton, and Randall C O'Reilly. Why there are complementary learning systems in the hippocampus and neocortex: insights from the successes and failures of connectionist models of learning and memory. *Psychological Review*, 102(3):419, 1995. 175

443. Pamela McCorduck. *Machines who think: A personal inquiry into the history and prospects of artificial intelligence*. AK Peters/CRC Press, 2009. 10, 12

444. Warren S McCulloch and Walter Pitts. A logical calculus of the ideas immanent in nervous activity. *The Bulletin of Mathematical Biophysics*, 5(4):115–133, 1943. 139

445. Donald Michie. Game-playing and game-learning automata. In *Advances in programming and non-numerical computation*, pages 183–200. Elsevier, 1966. 100

446. Donald Michie. Machine learning in the next five years. In *Proceedings of the 3rd European Conference on European Working Session on Learning*, pages 107–122. Pitman Publishing, Inc., 1988. 213

447. Daniel Michulke and Michael Thielscher. Neural networks for state evaluation in general game playing. In *Joint European Conference on Machine Learning and Knowledge Discovery in Databases*, pages 95–110. Springer, 2009. 244

448. Risto Miikkulainen, Jason Liang, Elliot Meyerson, Aditya Rawal, Daniel Fink, Olivier Francon, Bala Raju, Hormoz Shahrzad, Arshak Navruzyan, Nigel Duffy, et al. Evolving deep neural networks. In *Artificial Intelligence in the Age of Neural Networks and Brain Computing*, pages 293–312. Elsevier, 2019. 222

449. Tomáš Mikolov. Statistical language models based on neural networks. *Presentation at Google, Mountain View, 2nd April*, 80, 2012. 194

450. Jonathan K Millen. Programming the game of Go. *Byte Magazine*, 1981. 36

451. S Ali Mirsoleimani, Aske Plaat, Jaap van den Herik, and Jos Vermaseren. Ensemble UCT needs high exploitation. In *ICAART2016, 8th International Conference on Agents and Artificial Intelligence*, 2016. 129

452. S Ali Mirsoleimani, Aske Plaat, Jaap van den Herik, and Jos Vermaseren. Structured parallel programming for Monte Carlo tree search. Technical report, arXiv preprint arXiv:1704.00325, 2017. 129

453. S Ali Mirsoleimani, Aske Plaat, H Jaap van den Herik, and Jos Vermaseren. An analysis of virtual loss in parallel MCTS. In *ICAART (2)*, pages 648–652, 2017. 260

454. S Ali Mirsoleimani, Aske Plaat, Jaap Van Den Herik, and Jos Vermaseren. Scaling Monte Carlo tree search on Intel Xeon Phi. In *Parallel and Distributed Systems (ICPADS), 2015 IEEE 21st International Conference on*, pages 666–673. IEEE, 2015. 129

455. S Ali Mirsoleimani, Jaap van den Herik, Aske Plaat, and Jos Vermaseren. A lock-free algorithm for parallel MCTS. In *ICAART (2)*, pages 589–598, 2018. 260

456. S Ali Mirsoleimani, Jaap van den Herik, Aske Plaat, and Jos Vermaseren. Pipeline pattern for parallel MCTS. In *ICAART (2)*, pages 614–621, 2018. 129, 134

457. Tom M Mitchell. *The need for biases in learning generalizations*. Department of Computer Science, Carnegie Mellon University, 1980. 207

458. Tom M Mitchell. *The discipline of machine learning*, volume 9. Carnegie Mellon University, School of Computer Science, Machine Learning, 2006. 207

459. Volodymyr Mnih, Adria Puigdomenech Badia, Mehdi Mirza, Alex Graves, Timothy Lillicrap, Tim Harley, David Silver, and Koray Kavukcuoglu. Asynchronous methods for deep reinforcement learning. In *International Conference on Machine Learning*, pages 1928–1937, 2016. 177, 182

460. Volodymyr Mnih, Nicolas Heess, Alex Graves, et al. Recurrent models of visual attention. In *Advances in Neural Information Processing Systems*, pages 2204–2212, 2014. 165

461. Volodymyr Mnih, Koray Kavukcuoglu, David Silver, Alex Graves, Ioannis Antonoglou, Daan Wierstra, and Martin Riedmiller. Playing Atari with deep reinforcement learning. *arXiv preprint arXiv:1312.5602*, 2013. 32, 63, 135, 169, 170, 171, 172, 173, 178, 184, 186, 194

462. Volodymyr Mnih, Koray Kavukcuoglu, David Silver, Andrei A Rusu, Joel Veness, Marc G Bellemare, Alex Graves, Martin Riedmiller, Andreas K Fidjeland, Georg Ostrovski, et al. Human-level control through deep reinforcement learning. *Nature*, 518(7540):529, 2015. 172, 173, 175, 178, 186, 188, 192

463. Thomas M Moerland, Joost Broekens, and Catholijn M Jonker. Efficient exploration with double uncertain value networks. *arXiv preprint arXiv:1711.10789*, 2017. 180, 223

464. Thomas M Moerland, Joost Broekens, and Catholijn M Jonker. The potential of the return distribution for exploration in RL. *arXiv preprint arXiv:1806.04242*, 2018. 180, 223

465. Thomas M Moerland, Joost Broekens, and Catholijn M Jonker. Model-based reinforcement learning. A survey. *arXiv preprint arXiv:2006.16712*, 2020. 59

466. Thomas M Moerland, Joost Broekens, Aske Plaat, and Catholijn M Jonker. A0c: Alpha zero in continuous action space. *arXiv preprint arXiv:1805.09613*, 2018. 133, 203, 224, 225

467. Thomas M Moerland, Joost Broekens, Aske Plaat, and Catholijn M Jonker. Monte Carlo tree search for asymmetric trees. *arXiv preprint arXiv:1805.09218*, 2018. 133

468. Grégoire Montavon, Wojciech Samek, and Klaus-Robert Müller. Methods for interpreting and understanding deep neural networks. *Digital Signal Processing*, 73:1–15, 2018. 158, 221

469. James Moor. The Dartmouth College artificial intelligence conference: The next fifty years. *AI Magazine*, 27(4):87, 2006. 12

470. Matej Moravčík, Martin Schmid, Neil Burch, Viliam Lisỳ, Dustin Morrill, Nolan Bard, Trevor Davis, Kevin Waugh, Michael Johanson, and Michael Bowling. Deepstack: Expert-level artificial intelligence in heads-up no-limit poker. *Science*, 356(6337):508–513, 2017. 40, 232, 240, 241, 242

471. Andreas C Müller, Sarah Guido, et al. *Introduction to machine learning with Python: a guide for data scientists*. O'Reilly Media, Inc., 2016. 194

472. Martin Müller. Computer Go. *Artificial Intelligence*, 134(1-2):145–179, 2002. 114

473. Martin Müller. Fuego at the Computer Olympiad in Pamplona 2009: A tournament report. *University of Alberta, TR*, pages 09–09, 2009. 116

474. Rémi Munos, Tom Stepleton, Anna Harutyunyan, and Marc Bellemare. Safe and efficient off-policy reinforcement learning. In *Advances in Neural Information Processing Systems*, pages 1054–1062, 2016. 60

475. Ofir Nachum, Mohammad Norouzi, Kelvin Xu, and Dale Schuurmans. Bridging the gap between value and policy based reinforcement learning. In *Advances in Neural Information Processing Systems*, pages 2775–2785, 2017. 58

476. Prabhat Nagarajan, Garrett Warnell, and Peter Stone. Deterministic implementations for reproducibility in deep reinforcement learning. *arXiv preprint arXiv:1809.05676*, 2018. 213

477. Sanmit Narvekar, Bei Peng, Matteo Leonetti, Jivko Sinapov, Matthew E Taylor, and Peter Stone. Curriculum learning for reinforcement learning domains: A framework and survey. *arXiv preprint arXiv:2003.04960*, 2020. 205, 207

478. Dana Nau, Paul Purdom, and Chun-Hung Tzeng. Experiments on alternatives to minimax. *International Journal of Parallel Programming*, 15(2):163–183, 1986. 100

479. Dana S Nau. Pathology on game trees: A summary of results. In *AAAI*, pages 102–104, 1980. 80, 92, 112

480. Richard E Neapolitan et al. *Learning Bayesian networks*, volume 38. Pearson Prentice Hall, Upper Saddle River, NJ, 2004. 227

481. Joseph Needham. Science and civilisation in china, vol. 4: Physics and physical technology. part iii. *Civil Engineering and Nautics (d) Building Technology, Cambridge University Press*, pages 60–66, 1965. 12

482. Ulric Neisser, Gwyneth Boodoo, Thomas J Bouchard Jr, A Wade Boykin, Nathan Brody, Stephen J Ceci, Diane F Halpern, John C Loehlin, Robert Perloff, Robert J Sternberg, et al. Intelligence: Knowns and unknowns. *American Psychologist*, 51(2):77, 1996. 244

483. Monty Newborn. *Deep Blue: an artificial intelligence milestone*. Springer Science & Business Media, 2013. 35

484. Allen Newell, John Calman Shaw, and Herbert A Simon. Elements of a theory of human problem solving. *Psychological Review*, 65(3):151, 1958. 245

485. Allen Newell and Herbert Simon. Computer science as empirical enquiry: Symbols and search. *CACM*, 1976. 112

486. Alexander E Nezhinsky and Fons J Verbeek. Pattern recognition for high throughput zebrafish imaging using genetic algorithm optimization. In *IAPR International Conference on Pattern Recognition in Bioinformatics*, pages 301–312. Springer, 2010. 232

487. Andrew Y Ng. Feature selection, L 1 vs. L 2 regularization, and rotational invariance. In *Proceedings of the Twenty-first International Conference on Machine Learning*, page 78. ACM, 2004. 151

488. Nils J Nilsson. *The quest for artificial intelligence*. Cambridge University Press, 2009. 11

489. T Nitsche. A learning chess program. In *Advances in Computer Chess*, pages 113–120. Elsevier, 1982. 104

490. Ruth Nussinov, Chung-Jung Tsai, Amarda Shehu, and Hyunbum Jang. Computational structural biology: Successes, future directions, and challenges. *Molecules*, 24(3):637, 2019. 196

491. Brendan O'Donoghue, Remi Munos, Koray Kavukcuoglu, and Volodymyr Mnih. Combining policy gradient and Q-learning. *arXiv preprint arXiv:1611.01626*, 2016. 55

492. Junhyuk Oh, Matteo Hessel, Wojciech M Czarnecki, Zhongwen Xu, Hado van Hasselt, Satinder Singh, and David Silver. Discovering reinforcement learning algorithms. *arXiv preprint arXiv:2007.08794*, 2020. 221

493. Kyoung-Su Oh and Keechul Jung. GPU implementation of neural networks. *Pattern Recognition*, 37(6):1311–1314, 2004. 155

494. Chris Olah. Understanding LSTM networks. http://colah.github.io/posts/2015-08-Understanding-LSTMs/, 2015. 162, 320

495. Joseph O'Neill, Barty Pleydell-Bouverie, David Dupret, and Jozsef Csicsvari. Play it again: reactivation of waking experience and memory. *Trends in Neurosciences*, 33(5):220–229, 2010. 175

496. Santiago Ontanón, Gabriel Synnaeve, Alberto Uriarte, Florian Richoux, David Churchill, and Mike Preuss. A survey of real-time strategy game AI research and competition in StarCraft. *IEEE Transactions on Computational Intelligence and AI in Games*, 5(4):293–311, 2013. 29, 40, 242, 243

497. OpenAI. OpenAI five. https://blog.openai.com/openai-five/, 2018. 240, 252

498. Ian Osband, Yotam Doron, Matteo Hessel, John Aslanides, Eren Sezener, Andre Saraiva, Katrina McKinney, Tor Lattimore, Csaba Szepezvari, Satinder Singh, et al. Behaviour suite for reinforcement learning. *arXiv preprint arXiv:1908.03568*, 2019. 256

499. Christopher Painter-Wakefield and Ronald Parr. Greedy algorithms for sparse reinforcement learning. *arXiv preprint arXiv:1206.6485*, 2012. 225

500. Sinno Jialin Pan, Qiang Yang, et al. A survey on transfer learning. *IEEE Transactions on Knowledge and Data Engineering*, 22(10):1345–1359, 2010. 220

501. Liviu Panait and Sean Luke. Cooperative multi-agent learning: The state of the art. *Autonomous Agents and Multi-Agent Systems*, 11(3):387–434, 2005. 224

502. Zhen-Jia Pang, Ruo-Ze Liu, Zhou-Yu Meng, Yi Zhang, Yang Yu, and Tong Lu. On reinforcement learning for full-length game of StarCraft. In *Proceedings of the AAAI Conference on Artificial Intelligence*, volume 33, pages 4691–4698, 2019. 226

503. Giuseppe Davide Paparo, Vedran Dunjko, Adi Makmal, Miguel Angel Martin-Delgado, and Hans J Briegel. Quantum speedup for active learning agents. *Physical Review X*, 4(3):031002, 2014. 232

504. Gisele L Pappa, Gabriela Ochoa, Matthew R Hyde, Alex A Freitas, John Woodward, and Jerry Swan. Contrasting meta-learning and hyper-heuristic research: the role of evolutionary algorithms. *Genetic Programming and Evolvable Machines*, 15(1):3–35, 2014. 222

505. Philip Paquette, Yuchen Lu, Steven Bocco, Max Smith, O-G Satya, Jonathan K Kummerfeld, Joelle Pineau, Satinder Singh, and Aaron C Courville. No-press diplomacy: Modeling multi-agent gameplay. In *Advances in Neural Information Processing Systems*, pages 4476–4487, 2019. 240

506. Razvan Pascanu, Yujia Li, Oriol Vinyals, Nicolas Heess, Lars Buesing, Sebastien Racanière, David Reichert, Théophane Weber, Daan Wierstra, and Peter Battaglia. Learning model-based planning from scratch. *arXiv preprint arXiv:1707.06170*, 2017. 186

507. Gian-Carlo Pascutto. Leela zero. https://github.com/leela-zero/leela-zero, 2017. 257

508. Adam Paszke, Sam Gross, Francisco Massa, Adam Lerer, James Bradbury, Gregory Chanan, Trevor Killeen, Zeming Lin, Natalia Gimelshein, Luca Antiga, et al. Pytorch: An imperative style, high-performance deep learning library. In *Advances in Neural Information Processing Systems*, pages 8024–8035, 2019. 155, 255

509. Judea Pearl. Scout: A simple game-searching algorithm with proven optimal properties. In *AAAI*, pages 143–145, 1980. 95, 96, 325

510. Judea Pearl. On the nature of pathology in game searching. *Artificial Intelligence*, 20(4):427–453, 1983. 80, 92, 112

511. Judea Pearl. *Heuristics: Intelligent Search Strategies for Computer Problem Solving*. Addison-Wesley, Reading, MA, 1984. 79, 112, 235

512. Judea Pearl and Dana Mackenzie. *The book of why: the new science of cause and effect*. Basic Books, 2018. 112

513. Fabian Pedregosa, Gaël Varoquaux, Alexandre Gramfort, Vincent Michel, Bertrand Thirion, Olivier Grisel, Mathieu Blondel, Peter Prettenhofer, Ron Weiss, Vincent Dubourg, et al. Scikit-learn: Machine learning in Python. *Journal of Machine Learning Research*, 12(Oct):2825–2830, 2011. 222, 255

514. Barney Pell. Metagame: A new challenge for games and learning. In *Heuristic Programming in Artificial Intelligence 3 – The Third Computer Olympiad*. Ellis Horwood, 1992. 243, 244

515. Barney Pell. Logic programming for general game-playing. Technical report, University of Cambridge, Computer Laboratory, 1993. 244

516. Barney Pell. A strategic metagame player for general chess-like games. *Computational Intelligence*, 12(1):177–198, 1996. 244

517. Diego Perez Liebana, Jens Dieskau, Martin Hunermund, Sanaz Mostaghim, and Simon Lucas. Open loop search for general video game playing. In *Proceedings of the 2015 Annual Conference on Genetic and Evolutionary Computation*, pages 337–344. ACM, 2015. 244

518. Diego Perez-Liebana, Spyridon Samothrakis, Julian Togelius, Tom Schaul, Simon M Lucas, Adrien Couëtoux, Jerry Lee, Chong-U Lim, and Tommy Thompson. The 2014 general video game playing competition. *IEEE Transactions on Computational Intelligence and AI in Games*, 8(3):229–243, 2016. 244

519. Theodore J Perkins, Doina Precup, et al. Using options for knowledge transfer in reinforcement learning. *University of Massachusetts, Amherst, MA, USA, Tech. Rep*, 1999. 232

520. Nicola Pezzotti, Thomas Höllt, Jan Van Gemert, Boudewijn PF Lelieveldt, Elmar Eisemann, and Anna Vilanova. Deepeyes: Progressive visual analytics for designing deep neural networks. *IEEE Transactions on Visualization and Computer Graphics*, 24(1):98–108, 2017. 158, 221

521. Hieu Pham, Melody Y Guan, Barret Zoph, Quoc V Le, and Jeff Dean. Efficient neural architecture search via parameter sharing. *arXiv preprint arXiv:1802.03268*, 2018. 222

522. Wim Pijls and Arie de Bruin. Another view on the SSS* algorithm. In *Algorithms*, pages 211–220. Springer, 1990. 83, 112

523. Aske Plaat. *Research re: search and re-search*. PhD thesis, Erasmus University Rotterdam, 1996. 97, 112

524. Aske Plaat, Walter Kosters, and Mike Preuss. Model-based deep reinforcement learning for high-dimensional problems: A survey. Technical report, preprint arXiv:2008.05598, 2020. 56, 59, 227, 232, 251

525. Aske Plaat, Jonathan Schaeffer, Wim Pijls, and Arie De Bruin. A new paradigm for minimax search. Technical Report arXiv 1404.1515, University of Alberta, 1994. 95

526. Aske Plaat, Jonathan Schaeffer, Wim Pijls, and Arie De Bruin. Best-first fixed-depth minimax algorithms. *Artificial Intelligence*, 87(1-2):255–293, 1996. 95, 97, 98, 112, 325

527. Aske Plaat, Jonathan Schaeffer, Wim Pijls, and Arie De Bruin. Exploiting graph properties of game trees. In *AAAI/IAAI, Vol. 1*, pages 234–239, 1996. 75

528. Matthias Plappert. Keras-RL. https://github.com/keras-rl/keras-rl, 2016. 188

529. Jonathan A Plucker and Joseph S Renzulli. Psychometric approaches to the study of human creativity. *Handbook of creativity*, pages 35–61, 1999. 246

530. Jordan B Pollack and Alan D Blair. Why did TD-gammon work? In *Advances in Neural Information Processing Systems*, pages 10–16, 1997. 171

531. Aditya Prasad. Lessons from implementing alphazero https://medium.com/oracledevs/lessons-from-implementing-alphazero-7e36e9054191, 2018. 204

532. Lorien Y Pratt. Discriminability-based transfer between neural networks. In *Advances in Neural Information Processing Systems*, pages 204–211, 1993. 220, 232

533. Lutz Prechelt. Automatic early stopping using cross validation: quantifying the criteria. *Neural Networks*, 11(4):761–767, 1998. 151

534. Lutz Prechelt. Early stopping-but when? In *Neural Networks: Tricks of the trade*, pages 55–69. Springer, 1998. 151

535. Mike Preuss, Nicola Beume, Holger Danielsiek, Tobias Hein, Boris Naujoks, Nico Piatkowski, Raphael Stuer, Andreas Thom, and Simon Wessing. Towards intelligent team composition and maneuvering in real-time strategy games. *IEEE Transactions on Computational Intelligence and AI in Games*, 2(2):82–98, 2010. 240

536. Adrià Puigdomènech Badia, Bilal Piot, Steven Kapturowski, Pablo Sprechmann, Alex Vitvitskyi, Daniel Guo, and Charles Blundell. Agent57: Outperforming the Atari human benchmark. *arXiv*, pages arXiv–2003, 2020. 181

537. Max Pumperla and Kevin Ferguson. *Deep Learning and the Game of Go*. Manning, 2019. 231, 279

538. Zhiwei Qin, Weichang Li, and Firdaus Janoos. Sparse reinforcement learning via convex optimization. In *International Conference on Machine Learning*, pages 424–432, 2014. 225

539. J Ross Quinlan. Learning efficient classification procedures and their application to chess end games. In *Machine Learning*, pages 463–482. Springer, 1983. 104

540. J. Ross Quinlan. Induction of decision trees. *Machine Learning*, 1(1):81–106, 1986. 227

541. Jacob Rafati and David C Noelle. Learning representations in model-free hierarchical reinforcement learning. *arXiv preprint arXiv:1810.10096*, 2018. 226

542. Rajat Raina, Alexis Battle, Honglak Lee, Benjamin Packer, and Andrew Y Ng. Self-taught learning: transfer learning from unlabeled data. In *Proceedings of the 24th International Conference on Machine learning*, pages 759–766. ACM, 2007. 232

543. Kate Rakelly, Aurick Zhou, Deirdre Quillen, Chelsea Finn, and Sergey Levine. Efficient off-policy meta-reinforcement learning via probabilistic context variables. *arXiv preprint arXiv:1903.08254*, 2019. 221

544. Raghuram Ramanujan, Ashish Sabharwal, and Bart Selman. On adversarial search spaces and sampling-based planning. In *ICAPS*, volume 10, pages 242–245, 2010. 216

545. J. Rapin and O. Teytaud. Nevergrad - A gradient-free optimization platform. `https://GitHub.com/FacebookResearch/Nevergrad`, 2018. 222

546. Sachin Ravi and Hugo Larochelle. Optimization as a model for few-shot learning. In *International Conference on Learning Representations (ICLR)*, 2017. 221

547. Andrew L Reibman and Bruce W Ballard. Non-minimax search strategies for use against fallible opponents. In *AAAI*, pages 338–342, 1983. 100

548. Alexander Reinefeld. *Spielbaum-Suchverfahren*, volume 200. Springer-Verlag, 1989. 95, 96, 325

549. Danilo Jimenez Rezende, Shakir Mohamed, Ivo Danihelka, Karol Gregor, and Daan Wierstra. One-shot generalization in deep generative models. *preprint arXiv:1603.05106*, 2016. 221

550. Joao Ribeiro, Pedro Mariano, and Luís Seabra Lopes. Darkblade: A program that plays Diplomacy. In *Portuguese Conference on Artificial Intelligence*, pages 485–496. Springer, 2009. 240

551. John R. Rice. The algorithm selection problem. *Advances in Computers*, 15(65-118):5, 1976. 220

552. Martin Riedmiller. Neural fitted q iteration–first experiences with a data efficient neural reinforcement learning method. In *European Conference on Machine Learning*, pages 317–328. Springer, 2005. 194

553. Arpad Rimmel, Olivier Teytaud, Chang-Shing Lee, Shi-Jim Yen, Mei-Hui Wang, and Shang-Rong Tsai. Current frontiers in computer Go. *IEEE Transactions on Computational Intelligence and AI in Games*, 2(4):229–238, 2010. 116

554. Sebastian Risi and Mike Preuss. From Chess and Atari to StarCraft and Beyond: How Game AI is Driving the World of AI. *KI-Künstliche Intelligenz*, pages 1–11, 2020. 17

555. Ronald L Rivest. Game tree searching by min/max approximation. *Artificial Intelligence*, 34(1):77–96, 1987. 130

556. Kamil Rocki and Reiji Suda. Large-scale parallel Monte Carlo Tree Search on GPU. In *2011 IEEE International Symposium on Parallel and Distributed Processing Workshops and Phd Forum*, pages 2034–2037. IEEE, 2011. 129

557. John W Romein and Henri E Bal. Solving awari with parallel retrograde analysis. *Computer*, 36(10):26–33, 2003. 100, 105

558. Bernardino Romera-Paredes and Philip Torr. An embarrassingly simple approach to zero-shot learning. In *International Conference on Machine Learning*, pages 2152–2161, 2015. 221

559. Tord Romstad, Marco Costalba, and Joona Kiiski. `https://stockfishchess.org` Source code at `https://github.com/official-stockfish/Stockfish`. Stockfish open source chess program. 80, 217

560. Frank Rosenblatt. The perceptron: a probabilistic model for information storage and organization in the brain. *Psychological Review*, 65(6):386, 1958. 193

561. Christopher D Rosin. Multi-armed bandits with episode context. *Annals of Mathematics and Artificial Intelligence*, 61(3):203–230, 2011. 122, 203, 259, 265

562. Guido Rossum. Python reference manual. 1995. 255

563. Burkhard Rost and Chris Sander. Prediction of protein secondary structure at better than 70% accuracy. *Journal of Molecular Biology*, 232(2):584–599, 1993. 193

564. Sam T Roweis and Lawrence K Saul. Nonlinear dimensionality reduction by locally linear embedding. *Science*, 290(5500):2323–2326, 2000. 138

565. Neil Rubens, Mehdi Elahi, Masashi Sugiyama, and Dain Kaplan. Active learning in recommender systems. In *Recommender systems handbook*, pages 809–846. Springer, 2015. 206

566. Jonathan Rubin and Ian Watson. Computer poker: A review. *Artificial intelligence*, 175(5-6):958–987, 2011. 241

567. Ben Ruijl. Games and loop integrals. *Journal of Physics: Conference Series*, 1085:022007, Sep 2018. 129

568. Ben Ruijl, Jos Vermaseren, Aske Plaat, and Jaap van den Herik. Combining simulated annealing and Monte Carlo tree search for expression simplification. *arXiv preprint arXiv:1312.0841*, 2013. 129

569. Ben Ruijl, Jos Vermaseren, Aske Plaat, and Jaap van den Herik. Hepgame and the simplification of expressions. *arXiv preprint arXiv:1405.6369*, 2014. 129, 224, 232

570. David E Rumelhart, James L McClelland, PDP Research Group, et al. *Parallel distributed processing*, volume 1. MIT Press, Cambridge, MA, 1987. 193

571. Olga Russakovsky, Jia Deng, Hao Su, Jonathan Krause, Sanjeev Satheesh, Sean Ma, Zhiheng Huang, Andrej Karpathy, Aditya Khosla, Michael Bernstein, et al. Imagenet large scale visual recognition challenge. *International journal of computer vision*, 115(3):211–252, 2015. 156

572. Stuart J Russell and Peter Norvig. *Artificial intelligence: a modern approach*. Pearson Education Limited, Malaysia, 2016. 10, 11, 41, 60, 112, 136, 224, 234

573. Aleksander Sadikov, Ivan Bratko, and Igor Kononenko. Bias and pathology in minimax search. *Theoretical Computer Science*, 349(2):268–281, 2005. 80, 92, 112

574. Sumit Saha. A comprehensive guide to convolutional neural networks — the eli5 way. *Towards Data Science*, (https://towardsdatascience.com/a-comprehensive-guide-to-convolutional-neural-networks-the-eli5-way-3bd2b1164a53), 2018. 143, 148, 320

575. Tim Salimans, Jonathan Ho, Xi Chen, Szymon Sidor, and Ilya Sutskever. Evolution strategies as a scalable alternative to reinforcement learning. *preprint arXiv:1703.03864*, 2017. 223

576. Brian Sallans and Geoffrey E Hinton. Reinforcement learning with factored states and actions. *Journal of Machine Learning Research*, 5(Aug):1063–1088, 2004. 171

577. Arthur L Samuel. Some studies in machine learning using the game of checkers. *IBM Journal of Research and Development*, 3(3):210–229, 1959. 31, 81, 104, 183, 184

578. Jason Sanders and Edward Kandrot. *CUDA by example: an introduction to general-purpose GPU programming*. Addison-Wesley Professional, 2010. 155

579. Tuomas Sandholm. The state of solving large incomplete-information games, and application to poker. *AI Magazine*, 31(4):13–32, 2010. 40, 241

580. Juan C Santamaría, Richard S Sutton, and Ashwin Ram. Experiments with reinforcement learning in problems with continuous state and action spaces. *Adaptive Behavior*, 6(2):163–217, 1997. 225

581. Adam Santoro, Sergey Bartunov, Matthew Botvinick, Daan Wierstra, and Timothy Lillicrap. Meta-learning with memory-augmented neural networks. In *International Conference on Machine Learning*, pages 1842–1850, 2016. 221

582. Kaz Sato, Cliff Young, and David Patterson. An in-depth look at Google's first Tensor Processing Unit (TPU) https://cloud.google.com/blog/products/gcp/an-in-depth-look-at-googles-first-tensor-processing-unit-tpu, 2017. 264, 321

583. Maarten Schadd and Mark Winands. Quiescence search for stratego. In *Proceedings of the 21st Benelux Conference on Artificial Intelligence. Eindhoven, the Netherlands*, 2009. 102

584. Maarten PD Schadd, Mark HM Winands, H Jaap Van Den Herik, Guillaume MJ-B Chaslot, and Jos WHM Uiterwijk. Single-player Monte Carlo tree search. In *International Conference on Computers and Games*, pages 1–12. Springer, 2008. 125

585. Steve Schaefer. Mathematical recreations. http://www.mathrec.org/old/2002jan/solutions.html, 2002. 75

586. Jonathan Schaeffer. *Experiments in search and knowledge.* PhD thesis, Department of Computing Science, University of Alberta, 1986. 87, 99

587. Jonathan Schaeffer. The history heuristic and alpha-beta search enhancements in practice. *IEEE Trans. on Pattern Analysis and Machine Intelligence*, 11(11):1203–1212, 1989. 99, 112

588. Jonathan Schaeffer. *One jump ahead: computer perfection at checkers.* Springer Science & Business Media, 2008. 31, 33, 42

589. Jonathan Schaeffer, Neil Burch, Yngvi Björnsson, Akihiro Kishimoto, Martin Müller, Robert Lake, Paul Lu, and Steve Sutphen. Checkers is solved. *Science*, 317(5844):1518–1522, 2007. 24, 33, 74, 100, 105

590. Jonathan Schaeffer, Joseph Culberson, Norman Treloar, Brent Knight, Paul Lu, and Duane Szafron. A world championship caliber checkers program. *Artificial Intelligence*, 53(2-3):273–289, 1992. 33, 102, 184

591. Jonathan Schaeffer, Robert Lake, Paul Lu, and Martin Bryant. Chinook, the world man-machine checkers champion. *AI Magazine*, 17(1):21, 1996. 33, 105, 185

592. Jonathan Schaeffer and Aske Plaat. New advances in alpha-beta searching. In *Proceedings of the 1996 ACM 24th Annual Conference on Computer science*, pages 124–130. ACM, 1996. 92

593. Jonathan Schaeffer and Aske Plaat. Kasparov versus Deep Blue: The rematch. *ICGA Journal*, 20(2):95–101, 1997. 35

594. Jonathan Schaeffer, Aske Plaat, and Andreas Junghanns. Unifying single-agent and two-player search. *Information Sciences*, 135(3-4):151–175, 2001. 112, 178, 239

595. Tom Schaul, Daniel Horgan, Karol Gregor, and David Silver. Universal value function approximators. In *International Conf. on Machine Learning*, pages 1312–1320, 2015. 226

596. Tom Schaul, John Quan, Ioannis Antonoglou, and David Silver. Prioritized experience replay. *arXiv preprint arXiv:1511.05952*, 2015. 177, 179

597. Tom Schaul and Jürgen Schmidhuber. Metalearning. *Scholarpedia*, 5(6):4650, 2010. 220

598. Stephan Schiffel and Michael Thielscher. Fluxplayer: A successful general game player. In *AAAI*, volume 7, pages 1191–1196, 2007. 244

599. Jürgen Schmidhuber. Learning complex, extended sequences using the principle of history compression. *Neural Computation*, 4(2):234–242, 1992. 149, 193

600. Jürgen Schmidhuber. Developmental robotics, optimal artificial curiosity, creativity, music, and the fine arts. *Connection Science*, 18(2):173–187, 2006. 246

601. Jürgen Schmidhuber. Formal theory of creativity, fun, and intrinsic motivation (1990–2010). *IEEE Transactions on Autonomous Mental Development*, 2(3):230–247, 2010. 246

602. Jürgen Schmidhuber. Deep learning in neural networks: An overview. *Neural Networks*, 61:85–117, 2015. 142, 193

603. Jürgen Schmidhuber, F Gers, and Douglas Eck. Learning nonregular languages: A comparison of simple recurrent networks and LSTM. *Neural Computation*, 14(9):2039–2041, 2002. 165

604. Michael John Schofield, Timothy Joseph Cerexhe, and Michael Thielscher. Hyperplay: A solution to general game playing with imperfect information. In *AAAI*, 2012. 244

605. Michael John Schofield and Michael Thielscher. Lifting model sampling for general game playing to incomplete-information models. In *AAAI*, volume 15, pages 3585–3591, 2015. 244

606. Nicol N Schraudolph, Peter Dayan, and Terrence J Sejnowski. Temporal difference learning of position evaluation in the game of Go. In *Advances in Neural Information Processing Systems*, pages 817–824, 1994. 171, 184, 185

607. Julian Schrittwieser, Ioannis Antonoglou, Thomas Hubert, Karen Simonyan, Laurent Sifre, Simon Schmitt, Arthur Guez, Edward Lockhart, Demis Hassabis, Thore Graepel, et al. Mastering Atari, Go, chess and shogi by planning with a learned model. *arXiv preprint arXiv:1911.08265*, 2019. 227, 251

608. Günther Schrüfer. Presence and absence of pathology on game trees. In *Advances in Computer Chess*, pages 101–112. Pergamon Press, Inc., 1986. 102

609. John Schulman, Sergey Levine, Pieter Abbeel, Michael Jordan, and Philipp Moritz. Trust region policy optimization. In *International Conference on Machine Learning*, pages 1889–1897, 2015. 181, 182

610. John Schulman, Filip Wolski, Prafulla Dhariwal, Alec Radford, and Oleg Klimov. Proximal policy optimization algorithms. *arXiv preprint arXiv:1707.06347*, 2017. 177, 182

611. Nicolas Schweighofer and Kenji Doya. Meta-learning in reinforcement learning. *Neural Networks*, 16(1):5–9, 2003. 232

612. Marco Scutari et al. Learning Bayesian networks with the bnlearn R package. *Journal of Statistical Software*, 35(i03), 2010. 227

613. John R Searle. *Mind, language and society: Philosophy in the real world*. Basic Books, 2008. 17

614. Richard B Segal. On the scalability of parallel UCT. In *International Conference on Computers and Games*, pages 36–47. Springer, 2010. 129, 260

615. Marwin HS Segler, Mike Preuss, and Mark P Waller. Planning chemical syntheses with deep neural networks and symbolic AI. *Nature*, 555(7698):604, 2018. 232

616. Burr Settles. Active learning literature survey. Technical report, University of Wisconsin-Madison Department of Computer Sciences, 2009. 206

617. Bobak Shahriari, Kevin Swersky, Ziyu Wang, Ryan P Adams, and Nando De Freitas. Taking the human out of the loop: A review of Bayesian optimization. *Proceedings of the IEEE*, 104(1):148–175, 2016. 265

618. Claude E Shannon. Programming a computer for playing chess. In *Computer chess compendium*, pages 2–13. Springer, 1988. 29, 73, 74, 75, 106

619. Stuart C Shapiro. The Turing Test and the economist. *ACM SIGART Bulletin*, 3(4):10–11, 1992. 16

620. Rishi Sharma, Shane Barratt, Stefano Ermon, and Vijay Pande. Improved training with curriculum GANs. *arXiv preprint arXiv:1807.09295*, 2018. 206

621. Daniel L Silver, Qiang Yang, and Lianghao Li. Lifelong machine learning systems: Beyond learning algorithms. In *2013 AAAI Spring Symposium Series*, 2013. 220

622. David Silver. *Reinforcement learning and simulation based search in the game of Go*. PhD thesis, University of Alberta, 2009. 119, 185

623. David Silver, Aja Huang, Chris J. Maddison, Arthur Guez, Laurent Sifre, George van den Driessche, Julian Schrittwieser, Ioannis Antonoglou, Veda Panneershelvam, Marc Lanctot, Sander Dieleman, Dominik Grewe, John Nham, Nal Kalchbrenner, Ilya Sutskever, Timothy Lillicrap, Madeleine Leach, Koray Kavukcuoglu, Thore Graepel, and Demis Hassabis. Mastering the game of Go with deep neural networks and tree search. *Nature*, 529(7587):484, 2016. 32, 56, 81, 184, 196, 208, 210, 216, 231, 257, 259, 261, 267, 321

624. David Silver, Thomas Hubert, Julian Schrittwieser, Ioannis Antonoglou, Matthew Lai, Arthur Guez, Marc Lanctot, Laurent Sifre, Dharshan Kumaran, Thore Graepel, et al. Mastering chess and shogi by self-play with a general reinforcement learning algorithm. *arXiv preprint arXiv:1712.01815*, 2017. 215, 257

625. David Silver, Thomas Hubert, Julian Schrittwieser, Ioannis Antonoglou, Matthew Lai, Arthur Guez, Marc Lanctot, Laurent Sifre, Dharshan Kumaran, Thore Graepel, Timothy Lillicrap, Karen Simonyan, and Demis Hassabis. A general reinforcement learning algorithm that masters chess, shogi, and Go through self-play. *Science*, 362(6419):1140–1144, 2018. 81, 184, 196, 215, 216, 217, 231, 259, 265, 321

626. David Silver, Julian Schrittwieser, Karen Simonyan, Ioannis Antonoglou, Aja Huang, Arthur Guez, Thomas Hubert, Lucas Baker, Matthew Lai, Adrian Bolton, Yutian Chen, Timothy Lillicrap, Fan Hui, Laurent Sifre, George van den Driessche, Thore Graepel, and Demis Hassabis. Mastering the game of Go without human knowledge. *Nature*, 550(7676):354, 2017. 32, 39, 81, 104, 184, 196, 203, 204, 205, 213, 214, 215, 216, 222, 231, 257, 259, 262, 263, 264, 267, 321, 323

627. David Silver, Richard S Sutton, and Martin Müller. Reinforcement learning of local shape in the game of Go. In *IJCAI*, volume 7, pages 1053–1058, 2007. 185, 231

628. David Silver, Richard S Sutton, and Martin Müller. Temporal-difference search in computer Go. *Machine Learning*, 87(2):183–219, 2012. 185, 194

629. David Silver, Hado van Hasselt, Matteo Hessel, Tom Schaul, Arthur Guez, Tim Harley, Gabriel Dulac-Arnold, David Reichert, Neil Rabinowitz, Andre Barreto, et al. The predictron: End-to-end learning and planning. In *Proceedings of the 34th International Conference on Machine Learning*, pages 3191–3199, 2017. 165, 232

630. David Silver and Joel Veness. Monte-Carlo planning in large POMDPs. In *Advances in Neural Information Processing Systems*, pages 2164–2172, 2010. 133

631. Karen Simonyan and Andrew Zisserman. Very deep convolutional networks for large-scale image recognition. *arXiv preprint arXiv:1409.1556*, 2014. 158

632. Satinder P Singh. Reinforcement learning with a hierarchy of abstract models. In *Proceedings of the National Conference on Artificial Intelligence*, number 10, page 202. John Wiley & Sons, 1992. 232

633. Chiara F Sironi and Mark HM Winands. Comparison of rapid action value estimation variants for general game playing. In *Computational Intelligence and Games (CIG), 2016 IEEE Conference on*, pages 1–8. IEEE, 2016. 244

634. Chiara F Sironi and Mark HM Winands. On-line parameter tuning for Monte-Carlo tree search in General Game Playing. In *Workshop on Computer Games*, pages 75–95. Springer, 2017. 244

635. Kate A Smith. Neural networks for combinatorial optimization: a review of more than a decade of research. *INFORMS Journal on Computing*, 11(1):15–34, 1999. 224

636. Stephen J Smith, Dana Nau, and Tom Throop. Computer bridge: A big win for AI planning. *AI Magazine*, 19(2):93, 1998. 240

637. Alex J Smola and Bernhard Schölkopf. *Learning with kernels*, volume 4. Citeseer, 1998. 193

638. Jasper Snoek, Hugo Larochelle, and Ryan P Adams. Practical Bayesian optimization of machine learning algorithms. In *Advances in Neural Information Processing Systems*, pages 2951–2959, 2012. 222

639. Deepak Soekhoe, Peter Van Der Putten, and Aske Plaat. On the impact of data set size in transfer learning using deep neural networks. In *International Symposium on Intelligent Data Analysis*, pages 50–60. Springer, 2016. 232

640. Edward J Sondik. The optimal control of partially observable Markov processes over the infinite horizon: Discounted costs. *Operations Research*, 26(2):282–304, 1978. 240

641. Fengguang Song and Jack Dongarra. Scaling up matrix computations on shared-memory manycore systems with 1000 CPU cores. In *Proceedings of the 28th ACM International Conference on Supercomputing*, pages 333–342. ACM, 2014. 155

642. Mei Song, A Montanari, and P Nguyen. A mean field view of the landscape of two-layers neural networks. In *Proceedings of the National Academy of Sciences*, volume 115, pages E7665–E7671, 2018. 141

643. Nitish Srivastava, Geoffrey Hinton, Alex Krizhevsky, Ilya Sutskever, and Ruslan Salakhutdinov. Dropout: a simple way to prevent neural networks from overfitting. *The Journal of Machine Learning Research*, 15(1):1929–1958, 2014. 152

644. David Stern, Ralf Herbrich, and Thore Graepel. Bayesian pattern ranking for move prediction in the game of Go. In *Proceedings of the 23rd International Conference on Machine Learning*, pages 873–880. ACM, 2006. 231

645. George C Stockman. A minimax algorithm better than alpha-beta? *Artificial Intelligence*, 12(2):179–196, 1979. 112

646. Lise Stork, Katherine Wolstencroft, Andreas Weber, Fons Verbeek, and Aske Plaat. Priming digitisation: Learning the textual structure in field books. In *ICT. OPEN 2018: The Conference for ICT-Research in the Netherlands*, 2018. 232

647. David Stoutamire. Machine learning applied to Go. *MS thesis*, 1991. 185

648. Christopher S Strachey. Logical or non-mathematical programmes. In *Proceedings of the 1952 ACM National Meeting (Toronto)*, pages 46–49. ACM, 1952. 31

649. Darin Straus. Alphazero implementation and tutorial https://towardsdatascience.com/alphazero-implementation-and-tutorial-f4324d65fdfc, 2018. 204

650. Freek Stulp and Stefan Schaal. Hierarchical reinforcement learning with movement primitives. In *Humanoid Robots (Humanoids), 2011 11th IEEE-RAS International Conference on*, pages 231–238. IEEE, 2011. 232

651. Jiawei Su, Danilo Vasconcellos Vargas, and Kouichi Sakurai. One pixel attack for fooling deep neural networks. *IEEE Transactions on Evolutionary Computation*, 2019. 160

652. Sainbayar Sukhbaatar, Emily Denton, Arthur Szlam, and Rob Fergus. Learning goal embeddings via self-play for hierarchical reinforcement learning. *arXiv preprint arXiv:1811.09083*, 2018. 232

653. Ilya Sutskever. *Training recurrent neural networks*. PhD thesis, 2013. 194

654. Ilya Sutskever, James Martens, and Geoffrey E Hinton. Generating text with recurrent neural networks. In *Proceedings of the 28th International Conference on Machine Learning (ICML-11)*, pages 1017–1024, 2011. 165

655. Ilya Sutskever and Vinod Nair. Mimicking Go experts with convolutional neural networks. In *International Conf. on Artificial Neural Networks*, pages 101–110. Springer, 2008. 171, 193

656. Ilya Sutskever, Oriol Vinyals, and Quoc V Le. Sequence to sequence learning with neural networks. In *Adv. in Neural Information Processing Systems*, pages 3104–3112, 2014. 165

657. Richard S Sutton. *Temporal credit assignment in reinforcement learning*. PhD thesis, Univ Mass Amherst, 1984. 55

658. Richard S Sutton. Learning to predict by the methods of temporal differences. *Machine Learning*, 3(1):9–44, 1988. 53, 182

659. Richard S Sutton and Andrew G Barto. *Reinforcement learning, An Introduction, Second Edition*. MIT Press, 2018. 19, 44, 45, 47, 50, 51, 55, 56, 66, 69, 122, 168, 170, 182, 189, 226, 261, 319, 320, 321

660. Richard S Sutton, David A McAllester, Satinder P Singh, and Yishay Mansour. Policy gradient methods for reinforcement learning with function approximation. In *Advances in Neural Information Processing Systems*, pages 1057–1063, 2000. 55

661. Richard S Sutton, Doina Precup, and Satinder Singh. Between MDPs and semi-MDPs: a framework for temporal abstraction in reinforcement learning. *Artificial intelligence*, 112(1-2):181–211, 1999. 226

662. Vivienne Sze, Yu-Hsin Chen, Tien-Ju Yang, and Joel S Emer. Efficient processing of deep neural networks: A tutorial and survey. *Proceedings of the IEEE*, 105(12):2295–2329, 2017. 155

663. Christian Szegedy, Wei Liu, Yangqing Jia, Pierre Sermanet, Scott Reed, Dragomir Anguelov, Dumitru Erhan, Vincent Vanhoucke, and Andrew Rabinovich. Going deeper with convolutions. In *Proceedings of the IEEE Conference on Computer Vision and Pattern Recognition*, pages 1–9, 2015. 158

664. Christian Szegedy, Vincent Vanhoucke, Sergey Ioffe, Jon Shlens, and Zbigniew Wojna. Rethinking the inception architecture for computer vision. In *Proceedings of the IEEE Conference on Computer Vision and Pattern Recognition*, pages 2818–2826, 2016. 158

665. Christian Szegedy, Wojciech Zaremba, Ilya Sutskever, Joan Bruna, Dumitru Erhan, Ian Goodfellow, and Rob Fergus. Intriguing properties of neural networks. *arXiv preprint arXiv:1312.6199*, 2013. 160

666. István Szita, Guillaume Chaslot, and Pieter Spronck. Monte-Carlo tree search in Settlers of Catan. In *Advances in Computer Games*, pages 21–32. Springer, 2009. 125

667. Aviv Tamar, Yi Wu, Garrett Thomas, Sergey Levine, and Pieter Abbeel. Value iteration networks. In *Adv. in Neural Information Processing Systems*, pages 2154–2162, 2016. 232

668. Ming Tan. Multi-agent reinforcement learning: Independent vs. cooperative agents. In *Proceedings of the Tenth Intl. Conf. on Machine Learning*, pages 330–337, 1993. 224

669. Ryutaro Tanno, Kai Arulkumaran, Daniel C Alexander, Antonio Criminisi, and Aditya Nori. Adaptive neural trees. *arXiv preprint arXiv:1807.06699*, 2018. 227

670. Matthew E Taylor and Peter Stone. Transfer learning for reinforcement learning domains: A survey. *Journal of Machine Learning Research*, 10(Jul):1633–1685, 2009. 220

671. Shoshannah Tekofsky, Pieter Spronck, Martijn Goudbeek, Aske Plaat, and Jaap van den Herik. Past our prime: A study of age and play style development in Battlefield 3. *IEEE Transactions on Computational Intelligence and AI in Games*, 7(3):292–303, 2015. 240

672. Joshua B Tenenbaum, Vin De Silva, and John C Langford. A global geometric framework for nonlinear dimensionality reduction. *Science*, 290(5500):2319–2323, 2000. 138

673. Gerald Tesauro. Neurogammon wins Computer Olympiad. *Neural Computation*, 1(3):321–323, 1989. 32, 81, 184

674. Gerald Tesauro. Neurogammon: A neural-network backgammon program. In *1990 IJCNN Intl. Joint Conference on Neural Networks*, pages 33–39. IEEE, 1990. 185, 193, 194

675. Gerald Tesauro. TD-gammon: A self-teaching backgammon program. In *Applications of Neural Networks*, pages 267–285. Springer, 1995. 27, 104, 171, 184, 193

676. Gerald Tesauro. Temporal difference learning and TD-Gammon. *Communications of the ACM*, 38(3):58–68, 1995. 32, 53, 185, 193

677. Gerald Tesauro. Programming backgammon using self-teaching neural nets. *Artificial Intelligence*, 134(1-2):181–199, 2002. 32, 185

678. Marc Teyssier and Daphne Koller. Ordering-based search: A simple and effective algorithm for learning Bayesian networks. *arXiv preprint arXiv:1207.1429*, 2012. 227

679. Shantanu Thakoor, Surag Nair, and Megha Jhunjhunwala. Learning to play othello without human knowledge. Stanford University CS238 Final Project Report, 2017. 204, 257

680. Richard H Thaler and Cass R Sunstein. *Nudge: Improving decisions about health, wealth, and happiness*. Penguin, 2009. 21, 245

681. Michael Thielscher. Answer set programming for single-player games in general game playing. In *International Conference on Logic Programming*, pages 327–341. Springer, 2009. 244

682. Michael Thielscher. A general game description language for incomplete information games. In *AAAI*, volume 10, pages 994–999, 2010. 244

683. Michael Thielscher. The general game playing description language is universal. In *IJCAI Proceedings-International Joint Conference on Artificial Intelligence*, volume 22, page 1107, 2011. 243, 244

684. Ken Thompson. Retrograde analysis of certain endgames. *ICCA Journal*, 9(3):131–139, 1986. 105

685. Chris Thornton, Frank Hutter, Holger H Hoos, and Kevin Leyton-Brown. Auto-WEKA: combined selection and hyperparameter optimization of classification algorithms. In *Proceedings of the 19th ACM SIGKDD International Conference on Knowledge Discovery and Data Mining*, pages 847–855. ACM, 2013. 222

686. Sebastian Thrun. Learning to play the game of chess. In *Advances in Neural Information Processing Systems*, pages 1069–1076, 1995. 104, 184, 185

687. Sebastian Thrun. *Explanation-based neural network learning: A lifelong learning approach*, volume 357. Springer Science & Business Media, 2012. 220, 251

688. Sebastian Thrun and Lorien Pratt. *Learning to learn*. Springer Science & Business Media, 2012. 220, 232

689. Yuandong Tian, Qucheng Gong, Wenling Shang, Yuxin Wu, and C Lawrence Zitnick. Elf: An extensive, lightweight and flexible research platform for real-time strategy games. In *Advances in Neural Information Processing Systems*, pages 2659–2669, 2017. 204, 257

690. Yuandong Tian, Jerry Ma, Qucheng Gong, Shubho Sengupta, Zhuoyuan Chen, and C. Lawrence Zitnick. ELF OpenGo. https://github.com/pytorch/ELF, 2018. 213, 258

691. Yuandong Tian and Yan Zhu. Better computer Go player with neural network and long-term prediction. *arXiv preprint arXiv:1511.06410*, 2015. 184, 185, 258

692. Julian Togelius, Mike Preuss, Nicola Beume, Simon Wessing, Johan Hagelbäck, and Georgios N Yannakakis. Multiobjective exploration of the starcraft map space. In *Proceedings of the 2010 IEEE Conf. on Computational Intelligence and Games*, pages 265–272. IEEE, 2010. 40, 240

693. Julian Togelius, Georgios N Yannakakis, Kenneth O Stanley, and Cameron Browne. Search-based procedural content generation. In *European Conference on the Applications of Evolutionary Computation*, pages 141–150. Springer, 2010. 42

694. Armon Toubman, Jan Joris Roessingh, Pieter Spronck, Aske Plaat, and Jaap van den Herik. Transfer learning of air combat behavior. In *2015 IEEE 14th International Conference on Machine Learning and Applications (ICMLA)*, pages 226–231. IEEE, 2015. 232

695. Luan Tran, Xi Yin, and Xiaoming Liu. Disentangled representation learning GAN for pose-invariant face recognition. In *CVPR*, volume 3, page 7, 2017. 191

696. Eleni Triantafillou, Tyler Zhu, Vincent Dumoulin, Pascal Lamblin, Utku Evci, Kelvin Xu, Ross Goroshin, Carles Gelada, Kevin Swersky, Pierre-Antoine Manzagol, et al. Meta-dataset: A dataset of datasets for learning to learn from few examples. *arXiv preprint arXiv:1903.03096*, 2019. 221

697. John Tromp. Number of legal Go states, 2016. 75

698. John Tromp and Gunnar Farnebäck. Combinatorics of Go. In *International Conference on Computers and Games*, pages 84–99, https://tromp.github.io/go/gostate.pdf, 2006. Springer. 74, 75

699. John N Tsitsiklis and Benjamin Van Roy. Analysis of temporal-diffference learning with function approximation. In *Advances in Neural Information Processing Systems*, pages 1075–1081, 1997. 170

700. Alan M Turing. Computing machinery and intelligence. In *Parsing the Turing Test*, pages 23–65. Springer, 1950, 2009. 15, 319

701. Alan M Turing. Digital computers applied to games. *Faster than thought*, 1953. 31, 73, 106

702. George Tzanetakis and Perry Cook. Musical genre classification of audio signals. *IEEE Transactions on Speech and Audio Processing*, 10(5):293–302, 2002. 246

703. Alberto Uriarte and Santiago Ontanón. A benchmark for starcraft intelligent agents. In *11th Artificial Intelligence and Interactive Digital Entertainment Conference*, 2015. 213, 240

704. Computer Shogi Association. http://www2.computer-shogi.org/index_e.html. Website. 217

705. Leslie G Valiant. Knowledge infusion: In pursuit of robustness in artificial intelligence. In *IARCS Annual Conference on Foundations of Software Technology and Theoretical Computer Science*. Schloss Dagstuhl-Leibniz-Zentrum für Informatik, 2008. 19

706. Kyriakos G Vamvoudakis and Frank L Lewis. Online Actor–Critic algorithm to solve the continuous-time infinite horizon optimal control problem. *Automatica*, 46(5):878–888, 2010. 55

707. Michiel Van Der Ree and Marco Wiering. Reinforcement learning in the game of othello: learning against a fixed opponent and learning from self-play. In *2013 IEEE Symposium on Adaptive Dynamic Programming and Reinforcement Learning (ADPRL)*, pages 108–115. IEEE, 2013. 231

708. Erik Van Der Werf. *AI techniques for the game of Go*. PhD thesis, Maastricht University, 2004. 185

709. Erik Van Der Werf, Jos WHM Uiterwijk, Eric Postma, and Jaap Van Den Herik. Local move prediction in Go. In *International Conference on Computers and Games*, pages 393–412. Springer, 2002. 185

710. Hado Van Hasselt, Yotam Doron, Florian Strub, Matteo Hessel, Nicolas Sonnerat, and Joseph Modayil. Deep reinforcement learning and the deadly triad. *preprint arXiv:1812.02648*, 2018. 171, 176

711. Hado Van Hasselt, Arthur Guez, and David Silver. Deep reinforcement learning with Double Q-Learning. In *AAAI*, volume 2, page 5. Phoenix, AZ, 2016. 177, 179

712. Matthijs Van Leeuwen and Arno Knobbe. Non-redundant subgroup discovery in large and complex data. In *Joint European Conference on Machine Learning and Knowledge Discovery in Databases*, pages 459–474. Springer, 2011. 232

713. Peter Van-Roy, Seif Haridi, et al. *Concepts, techniques, and models of computer programming*. MIT Press, 2004. 164

714. Bas van Stein, Hao Wang, and Thomas Bäck. Automatic configuration of deep neural networks with ego. *arXiv preprint arXiv:1810.05526*, 2018. 222

715. Bas van Stein, Hao Wang, Wojtek Kowalczyk, Thomas Bäck, and Michael Emmerich. Optimally weighted cluster kriging for big data regression. In *International Symposium on Intelligent Data Analysis*, pages 310–321. Springer, 2015. 222

716. Gerard JP Van Westen, Jörg K Wegner, Peggy Geluykens, Leen Kwanten, Inge Vereycken, Anik Peeters, Adriaan P IJzerman, Herman WT van Vlijmen, and Andreas Bender. Which compound to select in lead optimization? prospectively validated proteochemometric models guide preclinical development. *PloS One*, 6(11):e27518, 2011. 232

717. Joaquin Vanschoren. Meta-learning: A survey. *arXiv preprint arXiv:1810.03548*, 2018. 220

718. Francisco Varela, Evan Thompson, and Eleanor Rosch. *The embodied mind: cognitive science and human experience.* MIT Press, Cambridge, 1991. 10

719. Joel Veness, David Silver, Alan Blair, and William Uther. Bootstrapping from game tree search. In *Advances in Neural Information Processing Systems*, pages 1937–1945, 2009. 231

720. Subhashini Venugopalan, Marcus Rohrbach, Jeffrey Donahue, Raymond Mooney, Trevor Darrell, and Kate Saenko. Sequence to sequence-video to text. In *Proceedings of the IEEE International Conference on Computer Vision*, pages 4534–4542, 2015. 163

721. Jos AM Vermaseren. New features of form. *arXiv preprint math-ph/0010025*, 2000. 125

722. Jos AM Vermaseren, Aske Plaat, Jan Kuiper, and Jaap van den Herik. Investigations with Monte Carlo tree search for finding better multivariate Horner schemes. In *Agents and Artificial Intelligence: 5th International Conference, ICAART 2013, Barcelona, Spain, February 15-18, 2013. Revised Selected Papers*, volume 449, page 3. Springer, 2014. 125, 126, 127

723. Alexander Vezhnevets, Volodymyr Mnih, Simon Osindero, Alex Graves, Oriol Vinyals, John Agapiou, et al. Strategic attentive writer for learning macro-actions. In *Advances in Neural Information Processing Systems*, pages 3486–3494, 2016. 232

724. Ricardo Vilalta and Youssef Drissi. A perspective view and survey of meta-learning. *Artificial Intelligence Review*, 18(2):77–95, 2002. 232

725. Oriol Vinyals, Igor Babuschkin, Wojciech M Czarnecki, Michaël Mathieu, Andrew Dudzik, Junyoung Chung, David H Choi, Richard Powell, Timo Ewalds, Petko Georgiev, et al. Grandmaster level in StarCraft II using multi-agent reinforcement learning. *Nature*, 575(7782):350–354, 2019. 28, 40, 196, 240, 242, 243, 252, 319

726. Oriol Vinyals, Charles Blundell, Timothy Lillicrap, Daan Wierstra, et al. Matching networks for one shot learning. In *Advances in Neural Information Processing Systems*, pages 3630–3638, 2016. 221

727. Oriol Vinyals, Timo Ewalds, Sergey Bartunov, Petko Georgiev, Alexander Sasha Vezhnevets, Michelle Yeo, Alireza Makhzani, Heinrich Küttler, John Agapiou, Julian Schrittwieser, et al. Starcraft II: A new challenge for reinforcement learning. *arXiv preprint arXiv:1708.04782*, 2017. 40, 213, 240, 242

728. Oriol Vinyals, Meire Fortunato, and Navdeep Jaitly. Pointer networks. In *Advances in Neural Information Processing Systems*, pages 2692–2700, 2015. 224

729. Oriol Vinyals, Alexander Toshev, Samy Bengio, and Dumitru Erhan. Show and tell: A neural image caption generator. In *Proceedings of the IEEE Conference on Computer Vision and Pattern Recognition*, pages 3156–3164, 2015. 163

730. John Von Neumann and Oskar Morgenstern. *Theory of games and economic behavior.* Princeton University Press, 1944. 21

731. John Von Neumann, Oskar Morgenstern, and Harold William Kuhn. *Theory of games and economic behavior (commemorative edition).* Princeton University Press, 2007. 21

732. Loc Vu-Quoc. Neuron and myelinated axon, 2018. 139, 320

733. Niklas Wahlström, Thomas B Schön, and Marc Peter Deisenroth. From pixels to torques: Policy learning with deep dynamical models. *arXiv preprint arXiv:1502.02251*, 2015. 186

734. Matthieu Walraet and John Tromp. A googolplex of Go games. In *International Conference on Computers and Games*, pages 191–201. Springer, 2016. 75

735. Hao Wang, Thomas Bäck, Aske Plaat, Michael Emmerich, and Mike Preuss. On the potential of evolutionary algorithms for replacing backpropagation for network weight optimization. In *GECCO*, 2019. 222

736. Hui Wang, Michael Emmerich, and Aske Plaat. Assessing the potential of Classical Q-learning in General Game Playing. *arXiv preprint arXiv:1810.06078*, 2018. 244

737. Hui Wang, Michael Emmerich, Mike Preuss, and Aske Plaat. Alternative loss functions in AlphaZero-like self-play. In *2019 IEEE Symposium Series on Computational Intelligence (SSCI)*, pages 155–162, 2019. 232

738. Hui Wang, Michael Emmerich, Mike Preuss, and Aske Plaat. Hyper-parameter sweep on AlphaZero General. arxiv, arXiv:1903.08129, 2019. 222

739. Hui Wang, Michael Emmerich, Mike Preuss, and Aske Plaat. Analysis of hyper-parameters for small games: Iterations or epochs in self-play? *arXiv preprint arXiv:2003.05988*, 2020. 222

740. Hui Wang, Yanni Tang, Jiamou Liu, and Wu Chen. A search optimization method for rule learning in board games. In Xin Geng and Byeong-Ho Kang, editors, *PRICAI 2018: Trends in Artificial Intelligence*, pages 174–181, Cham, 2018. Springer International Publishing. 244

741. Jane X Wang, Zeb Kurth-Nelson, Dhruva Tirumala, Hubert Soyer, Joel Z Leibo, Remi Munos, Charles Blundell, Dharshan Kumaran, and Matt Botvinick. Learning to reinforcement learn. *arXiv preprint arXiv:1611.05763*, 2016. 221

742. Panqu Wang and Garrison W Cottrell. Basic level categorization facilitates visual object recognition. *arXiv preprint arXiv:1511.04103*, 2015. 207

743. Tingwu Wang, Xuchan Bao, Ignasi Clavera, Jerrick Hoang, Yeming Wen, Eric Langlois, Shunshi Zhang, Guodong Zhang, Pieter Abbeel, and Jimmy Ba. Benchmarking model-based reinforcement learning. *preprint arXiv:1907.02057*, 2019. 56, 59, 227

744. Zijie J Wang, Robert Turko, Omar Shaikh, Haekyu Park, Nilaksh Das, Fred Hohman, Minsuk Kahng, and Duen Horng Chau. Cnn explainer: Learning convolutional neural networks with interactive visualization. *arXiv preprint arXiv:2004.15004*, 2020. 158

745. Ziyu Wang, Frank Hutter, Masrour Zoghi, David Matheson, and Nando de Feitas. Bayesian optimization in a billion dimensions via random embeddings. *Journal of Artificial Intelligence Research*, 55:361–387, 2016. 221

746. Ziyu Wang, Tom Schaul, Matteo Hessel, Hado Hasselt, Marc Lanctot, and Nando Freitas. Dueling network architectures for deep reinforcement learning. In *International conference on machine learning*, pages 1995–2003, 2016. 181

747. Ziyu Wang, Tom Schaul, Matteo Hessel, Hado Van Hasselt, Marc Lanctot, and Nando De Freitas. Dueling network architectures for deep reinforcement learning. *arXiv preprint arXiv:1511.06581*, 2015. 60, 177, 180

748. Christopher JCH Watkins. *Learning from delayed rewards*. PhD thesis, King's College, Cambridge, 1989. 58, 69

749. Manuel Watter, Jost Springenberg, Joschka Boedecker, and Martin Riedmiller. Embed to control: A locally linear latent dynamics model for control from raw images. In *Advances in Neural Information Processing Systems*, pages 2746–2754, 2015. 186

750. Théophane Weber, Sébastien Racanière, David Reichert, Lars Buesing, Arthur Guez, Danilo Jimenez Rezende, Adria Puigdomenech Badia, Oriol Vinyals, Nicolas Heess, Yujia Li, et al. Imagination-augmented agents for deep reinforcement learning. In *Advances in Neural Information Processing Systems*, pages 5690–5701, 2017. 186, 232

751. Eddie Weill. LeNet in Keras on Github. `https://github.com/eweill/keras-deepcv/tree/master/models/classification`. 154, 325

752. Jean-Christophe Weill. The NegaC* search. *ICGA Journal*, 15(1):3–7, 1992. 98

753. Daphna Weinshall, Gad Cohen, and Dan Amir. Curriculum learning by transfer learning: Theory and experiments with deep networks. *preprint arXiv:1802.03796*, 2018. 205, 207

754. Joseph Weizenbaum et al. Eliza—a computer program for the study of natural language communication between man and machine. *Comm. of the ACM*, 9(1):36–45, 1966. 16

755. Lilian Weng. Curriculum for reinforcement learning `https://lilianweng.github.io/lil-log/2020/01/29/curriculum-for-reinforcement-learning.html`. Lil'Log, January 2020. 206, 207, 232

756. Paul Werbos. Beyond regression: New tools for prediction and analysis in the behavioral sciences. *Ph. D. dissertation, Harvard University*, 1974. 139, 193

757. Marco A Wiering. Self-play and using an expert to learn to play backgammon with temporal difference learning. *JILSA*, 2(2):57–68, 2010. 231

758. Daan Wierstra, Tom Schaul, Jan Peters, and Jürgen Schmidhuber. Natural evolution strategies. In *Evolutionary Computation, 2008. CEC 2008.(IEEE World Congress on Computational Intelligence). IEEE Congress on*, pages 3381–3387. IEEE, 2008. 223

759. Ronald J Williams. Simple statistical gradient-following algorithms for connectionist reinforcement learning. *Machine Learning*, 8(3-4):229–256, 1992. 54

760. Brandon Wilson, Austin Parker, and DS Nau. Error minimizing minimax: Avoiding search pathology in game trees. In *Proceedings of International Symposium on Combinatorial Search (SoCS-09)*, 2009. 80, 92, 112

761. Ian H Witten. The apparent conflict between estimation and control—a survey of the two-armed bandit problem. *Journal of the Franklin Institute*, 301(1-2):161–189, 1976. 53

762. Ian H Witten, Eibe Frank, Mark A Hall, and Christopher J Pal. *Data Mining: Practical machine learning tools and techniques*. Morgan Kaufmann, 2016. 255

763. Anson Wong. Solving the multi-armed bandit problem. *Towards Data Science*, 2017 https://towardsdatascience.com/solving-the-multi-armed-bandit-problem-b72de40db97c. 122, 320

764. Larry Wos, Ross Overbeck, Ewing Lusk, and Jim Boyle. *Automated reasoning: introduction and applications*. Prentice Hall Inc., Old Tappan, NJ, 1984. 245, 246

765. David J Wu. Accelerating self-play learning in Go. *preprint arXiv:1902.10565*, 2019. 213

766. Dominik Wujastyk. *The roots of ayurveda: Selections from Sanskrit medical writings*. Penguin, 2003. 12

767. Yongqin Xian, Bernt Schiele, and Zeynep Akata. Zero-shot learning—the good, the bad and the ugly. In *Proceedings of the IEEE Conference on Computer Vision and Pattern Recognition*, pages 4582–4591, 2017. 220, 221

768. Ruiyang Xu and Karl Lieberherr. Learning self-game-play agents for combinatorial optimization problems. *arXiv preprint arXiv:1903.03674*, 2019. 224, 229

769. Xin Yang, Yuezun Li, and Siwei Lyu. Exposing deep fakes using inconsistent head poses. In *ICASSP 2019-2019 IEEE International Conference on Acoustics, Speech and Signal Processing*, pages 8261–8265. IEEE, 2019. 160, 161, 320

770. Georgios N Yannakakis and Julian Togelius. *Artificial intelligence and games*. Springer, 2018. 42

771. Xin Yao. Evolving artificial neural networks. *Proceedings of the IEEE*, 87(9):1423–1447, 1999. 222

772. Nozomu Yoshinari, Kento Uchida, Shota Saito, Shinichi Shirakawa, and Youhei Akimoto. Probabilistic model-based dynamic architecture search. In *International Conference on Learning Representations (ICLR)*, 2019. 222

773. Tianhe Yu, Deirdre Quillen, Zhanpeng He, Ryan Julian, Karol Hausman, Chelsea Finn, and Sergey Levine. Meta-world: A benchmark and evaluation for multi-task and meta reinforcement learning. *arXiv preprint arXiv:1910.10897*, 2019. 221, 256, 257

774. Matthew D Zeiler and Rob Fergus. Visualizing and understanding convolutional networks. In *European Conference on Computer Vision*, pages 818–833. Springer, 2014. 157, 232, 320

775. Qinsong Zeng, Jianchang Zhang, Zhanpeng Zeng, Yongsheng Li, Ming Chen, and Sifan Liu. PhoenixGo. https://github.com/Tencent/PhoenixGo, 2018. 204, 257, 258

776. Ruixiang Zhang, Tong Che, Zoubin Ghahramani, Yoshua Bengio, and Yangqiu Song. Meta-GAN: An adversarial approach to Few-Shot learning. In *Advances in Neural Information Processing Systems*, pages 2365–2374, 2018. 221

777. Shangtong Zhang and Richard S Sutton. A deeper look at experience replay. *arXiv preprint arXiv:1712.01275*, 2017. 175

778. Yuan Zhou. *Rethinking Opening Strategy: AlphaGo's Impact on Pro Play*. CreateSpace, 2018. 1, 36, 212

779. Martin Zinkevich, Michael Johanson, Michael Bowling, and Carmelo Piccione. Regret minimization in games with incomplete information. In *Advances in Neural Information Processing Systems*, pages 1729–1736, 2008. 28, 241

780. Albert L Zobrist. A new hashing method with application for game playing by. Technical report, University of Wisconsin, Madison, 1970. 91

781. Barret Zoph and Quoc V Le. Neural architecture search with reinforcement learning. *arXiv preprint arXiv:1611.01578*, 2016. 222

List of Figures

© Springer Nature Switzerland AG 2020
A. Plaat, *Learning to Play*, https://doi.org/10.1007/978-3-030-59238-7

List of Tables

© Springer Nature Switzerland AG 2020
A. Plaat, *Learning to Play*, https://doi.org/10.1007/978-3-030-59238-7

List of Algorithms

© Springer Nature Switzerland AG 2020
A. Plaat, *Learning to Play*, https://doi.org/10.1007/978-3-030-59238-7

Index

Printed in the United States
by Baker & Taylor Publisher Services